PRAISE FOR
EMILY BAZELON
AND CHARGED

"Bazelon tells the tales of Noura and Kevin in rich, novelistic prose, which at its best puts one in mind of Adrian Nicole LeBlanc's book *Random Family*. . . . This combination of powerful reporting with painstaking research yields a comprehensive examination of the modern American criminal justice system that appeals to both the head and the heart."   —*The New York Times Book Review*

"Emily Bazelon's new book about the American judicial system reads like two books. Both are crucial to understanding the wretchedness of the American criminal legal process, and both offer something missing from most other books about mass incarceration: hope. The first book in *Charged* grabs for the heart: It is a riveting page-turner about two criminal defendants and their prosecutors. The second one goes for the reader's mind: It's a lucid synthesis of the most important research on mass incarceration and an insightful analysis of the politics of law and order in the era of President Trump and Black Lives Matter."   —*The Washington Post*

"[*Charged*] achieves what in-depth first-person reporting should: it humanizes the statistics, makes us aware that every courtroom involves the bureaucratic regimentation of an individual's life."   —*The New Yorker*

"Ms. Bazelon practices collaboration as capably as she advises it. . . . If legal discussions have at times struck you as overly hypothetical, rest assured that Emily Bazelon is obsessed with real people, both those trapped within the criminal justice system and those seeking to reform it."

—*Pittsburgh Post-Gazette*

"Bazelon adeptly explains the culture that drives traditional district attorneys and the philosophies of reform-minded district attorneys, then briefly delves into the difficulty of preventing prosecutorial misconduct, the inequities of a bail system that effectively criminalizes poverty, systemic racial disparities, the sociological arguments for diversion, and how severe mandatory sentences distort the criminal justice system. Then, with modest optimism, she presents a road map for the emerging reform movement. This is a powerful indictment of the traditional prosecution model."—*Publisher's Weekly* (starred review)

"Bazelon unravels these two stories [of Kevin and Noura] suspensefully over the course of this excellently paced book. In the process, she exposes a lack of oversight and a trail of cases in which prosecutors either misplaced or intentionally hid evidence, forcing readers to question whether justice is really being served. She presents hope in the form of a new way forward, offering insights into reform-minded campaigns from a new generation of lawyers and scholars who prize transparency and fairness in sentencing." —*Booklist* (starred review)

"As Bazelon makes abundantly clear through her cogent, credible arguments, a sensible, compassionate system never would have arrested or prosecuted Kevin. Throughout the two narratives, the author demonstrates occasional optimism due to the election of reform-minded prosecutors in a few cities. A vitally important new entry in the continued heated debates about criminal justice."

—*Kirkus Review* (starred review)

"For those whose day-to-day lives are not directly affected by the criminal legal system, there is nothing in this book that should seem normal, and there is an obligation on us all to avoid becoming numb. Bazelon's call to action is not subtle. Its urgency grips the author and jumps off the page, from the opening reflection . . . to the closing thoughts . . . [*Charged*] is a book written to destroy your complacency, and it succeeds."

—*Harvard Law Book Review*

"This is a vivid, disturbing primer on American criminal justice, and readers will come away better informed and motivated for change. And if the book spreads the word about progressive prosecution—prompting people to turn out and vote for reform candidates—it will have served a larger purpose." —*The American Prospect*

"*Charged* is a very interesting and eye-opening book about the power of prosecutors and their role in the US criminal justice system."   —*Arab News*

"*Charged* does as good a job as any book in recent memory of weaving together individual stories, timely reporting, and the latest criminal justice research. . . . By anchoring her analysis in deeply-researched case studies, she fosters refreshingly precise thinking—as opposed to slogans— about what we should expect from prosecutors. Bazelon also provides a helpful explanation for reformers' prosecutorial focus."   —*SSRN*

"For years, Emily Bazelon has been exposing the incessant horror of the American criminal justice system with excruciating clarity. Now, in *Charged,* she walks the reader through the steps of a criminal case, untangling our impenetrable and complex system and providing crucial context for understanding the depths of the problem. Touching, unnerving, and at times infuriating, *Charged* is for novices and experts alike—a book for anyone concerned about those suffering from injustice, and outraged by those perpetuating it."

—JOSIE DUFFY RICE, co-host of the *Justice in America* podcast and senior strategist at The Justice Collaborative

"This book made me feel better. Hopeful, even! Because Emily Bazelon, cogent and clear-eyed as ever, lays out a welcome double-barreled argument: A prosecutorial shift toward mercy and fairness is crucial to healing our busted criminal justice system, and it's already happening. What's that, you say? You want step-by-step instructions for how to reform your local prosecutor's office? No sweat: *Charged* has that, too. Just skip to the end."

—SARAH KOENIG, host of *Serial*

"In this deeply researched, elegantly told book, Emily Bazelon reveals how unchecked prosecutorial power has damaged the American justice system. *Charged* shows that our courts are not level playing fields. Rather, accused citizens, defense attorneys, and even judges are at the mercy of prosecutors who have used their influence to drive the prison boom. This harrowing, often enraging book is a hopeful one, as well, profiling innovative new approaches and the frontline advocates who champion them. This is a necessary read for those who care about inequality, the law, and the future of American justice."

—MATTHEW DESMOND, author of *Evicted*

"An insightful, highly readable examination of local prosecutors—who they are, what they do, and how they do it . . . At a moment when electing progressive prosecutors has become a cornerstone of the movement against mass incarceration, this book offers reasons for both caution and hope."

—JAMES FORMAN, JR., Pulitzer Prize–winning author of *Locking Up Our Own*

BY EMILY BAZELON

*Sticks and Stones: Defeating the Culture of Bullying and
Rediscovering the Power of Character and Empathy*

*Charged: The New Movement to Transform American
Prosecution and End Mass Incarceration*

CHARGED

CHARGED

THE NEW MOVEMENT TO TRANSFORM AMERICAN PROSECUTION AND END MASS INCARCERATION

EMILY BAZELON

RANDOM HOUSE NEW YORK

2020 Random House Trade Paperback Edition

Published in the United States by Random House, an imprint and
division of Penguin Random House LLC, New York.

RANDOM HOUSE and the HOUSE colophon are registered
trademarks of Penguin Random House LLC.

Originally published in hardcover by Random House, an imprint and
division of Penguin Random House LLC, in 2019.

Grateful acknowledgment is made to Graywolf Press for permission to reprint
an excerpt from "Rally" from *Crave Radiance: New and Selected Poems 1990–2010*
by Elizabeth Alexander, copyright © 2010 by Elizabeth Alexander.
Reprinted with the permission of The Permissions Company, Inc.,
on behalf of Graywolf Press, Minneapolis, Minnesota,
www.graywolfpress.org.

LIBRARY OF CONGRESS CATALOGING-IN-PUBLICATION DATA
Names: Bazelon, Emily, author.
Title: Charged: the new movement to transform American prosecution
and end mass incarceration / Emily Bazelon.
Description: New York: Random House, 2019. | Includes index.
Identifiers: LCCN 2018045826 | ISBN 9780399590030 (trade paperback) |
ISBN 9780399590023 (ebook)
Subjects: LCSH: Prosecution—United States—Decision making. |
Prosecutorial misconduct—United States. | Public prosecutors—United States. |
Sentences (Criminal procedure)—United States. | Imprisonment—United States. |
Criminal justice, Administration of—Corrupt practices—United States. | BISAC: LAW /
Criminal Law / Sentencing. | POLITICAL SCIENCE / Public Policy / General.
Classification: LCC KF9640 .B39 2019 | DDC 345.73/05042—dc23
LC record available at https://lccn.loc.gov/2018045826

Printed in the United States of America on acid-free paper

randomhousebooks.com

2 4 6 8 9 7 5 3 1

Book design by Jo Anne Metsch

For my parents, Rick and Eileen,
and my sisters, Lara, Jill, and Dana,
for their strong moral compass

Then the crowd made noise that gathered and grew
until it was loud and was loud as the sea.

What it meant or would mean was not yet fixed
nor could be, though human beings ever tilt toward *we*.

—ELIZABETH ALEXANDER

CONTENTS

PART II: THE QUALITY OF MERCY

INTRODUCTION

THE GUN WAS AN OFFERING.

Kevin heard about it around midnight on a May evening. He'd gone to the corner store to buy a single cigarette and was heading back to his high-rise in a housing project in Brownsville, a neighborhood in the middle of Brooklyn. The people he'd grown up with were often out at night, and he saw a knot of them, young men around his age, twenty, hanging out by a pair of green benches in a grassy spot near his building. As they swapped greetings, Kevin's friend Mason flicked his eyes at a plastic shopping bag on the ground, lying there like a piece of trash.

We got the jawn, he said.

Jawn could stand for a lot of things—a pair of shoes, a person—but Kevin knew exactly what Mason meant: there was a gun in that bag.

I know things are crazy for y'all here, Mason said, *so I got this for you.*

The police were a frequent presence around the projects, so no one picked up the bag or asked to see the gun. Kevin said his good-byes and started walking away in the alert and fluid way he had, shoulders back and arms swinging, tall and lean and young, his hair pulled back in a ponytail and his gray hoodie sweatshirt zipped, always aware of where he was but trying not to look over his shoulder. It was important not to look skittish, not around his friends and not if the police were watching, but Kevin also didn't want to hang around with a weapon lying at his feet. He didn't want the trouble a gun brought.

Kevin's housing project, a cluster of brick buildings, was one of eighteen in Brownsville, making the neighborhood one of the densest concentrations of public housing in the country, with more than sixty thousand people packed into 1.2 square miles. The project could feel like a small town, in an old-fashioned way. It had its own recreation center and known personalities and raffish identity. Kevin got a laugh out of the nicknames for the loudmouths or tough guys: Koolaid and Lil Head and OgLoc. He'd lived there his whole life, with his older sister and her two-year-old daughter, his younger brother, and his mother, who'd raised her kids mostly on her own, working retail jobs and caring for the elderly and disabled. The average rent in the Brownsville projects was $430 a month. Families tended to stay for years once they got off the waiting list for an apartment. "We stick together," Kevin said. "We went to school together. Your apartment might be on top of mine. Your mom might have babysat me."

On a good day, the project's residents would come outside to play music and catch up. You knew it was spring when older people brought small towels to sit on and raised their faces to the sun. "That kind of day, I'm going to be where everyone is, the girls, the mamas, the babies," Kevin said, thinking on it. "That kind of day, it's perfect."

But Brownsville was also one of New York's most disadvantaged communities, measured by health as well as economic insecurity, and one of its most dangerous. The year Kevin was twelve, more than a hundred people were shot in and around Brownsville and another thirty were killed, about half the number in all of Manhattan. Guns were a fact of life. "I could find someone with a gun before I could find someone with a diploma," Kevin told me. Over the years, he'd lost people he knew, including close friends. The beefing wasn't mainly between the gangs with well-known names, like the Bloods or the Crips. They existed, but their presence in the neighborhood was fading. More trouble came from menacing rivalries that pitted groups in the projects against their peers in other projects. The conflicts and alliances shifted, but there was one other project in particular that was the main foe of Kevin and his friends.

Kevin's father lived in the rival development. He'd moved back in with Kevin's grandmother when he and Kevin's mother split up, back when their children were young. Kevin's dad paid child support regularly, and they talked once in a while, but Kevin hadn't gone over to see him in years. One day, standing on the street outside his building, he gestured toward the windows of his grandmother's apartment, visible a couple of blocks away, above the trees. "I can't remember what the inside of my nana's crib looks like," he said.

The battle lines between the projects were drawn when Kevin's father was growing up, when established gangs fought over territory so they could sell drugs. Kevin didn't know why—and it didn't really matter how the trouble started back in the day. Fresh insults piled on top of old grudges. The reason for a fight or even a shooting could be minor—disrespecting someone on social media, or flirting with his girlfriend. Kevin found it disturbing. Most people he knew did. But that wasn't the same as knowing how to end it. There was too much bad blood. He'd learned you could defend a place, and your people in it, yet at the same time wish you were anywhere else.

When Kevin was thirteen, he went to the store for his mother and got jumped. All he knew was that the people who beat him up and took his money were from another project, and that now he and his friends would have a problem with them. Months later, one of his eighth-grade classmates was killed in a shooting. Kevin didn't know why that happened, either.

At fifteen, he got jumped again and was slashed in the face with a razor blade. Conflict built until trauma begot trauma in Brownsville. In a focus group of young men of color coming home from Rikers Island, nine out of ten said they'd been robbed, jumped, or "seriously hurt in a fight they didn't start," though none of them identified as victims of crime. Writing up the results, the Vera Institute of Justice pointed out that if they don't sufficiently recover, people who are victimized, especially when they're young, are more likely to gravitate toward peers they think can protect them and to commit retaliatory violence themselves. After Kevin was jumped, he couldn't afford to look like an easy target. He and some of his friends found one of the boys who had assaulted him and beat him up.

Kevin got arrested for the first time just after he turned sixteen, when a friend who'd already graduated from his high school came to campus with a car. Kevin asked to drive it. "At the time, I didn't think it was a serious thing to drive without a license. He hands me the keys, and I'm like, 'Lemme put my book bag in your car.' I snuck out at lunch, ran to the car quick, opened the door to the backseat, and put my book bag inside, and as soon as I closed the door, officers are swarming me, guns out." The car was stolen. Kevin didn't tell the police about his friend and he was charged with possession of stolen property. He got five hundred hours of community service, which he worked off by cleaning the piers near the Brooklyn Bridge.

Kevin's father tried to step in after he was arrested. "He tried to come play the father figure. I told him, 'These words don't mean nothing.' I made an example to him like this: 'If something happens to me right now, who you think I'm gonna go get, you or my mans?'" Kevin meant an older friend who had his back in the beefing. "My pops is looking at me with a dumb face. I'm like, 'It's not supposed to be like that. You supposed to be protecting me.' We had a fight. He swung at me and I swung at him. 'Look, all you do is give my mom money. You weren't here. You don't know me. My mom takes care of me. She sees me every day. She has the right to put her hands on me but she don't. You, I speak to you on the phone and you pop up once in a blue.'"

Kevin went to Rikers Island for the first time two years later, spending a couple of nights in the jail after another fight between the projects. He didn't start it but he didn't back away, either. He and his friend pummeled two boys, and they ran off, their iPhones falling to the ground in the melee. Kevin picked the phones up. He considered them trophies for a fight that had remained in-bounds, with no one seriously injured.

But the parents of one of the kids he'd fought went to the police, and Kevin and a couple of his friends were charged with robbery. In exchange for pleading guilty, Kevin got a break that benefits a lot of teenagers in the state of New York: he qualified for a one-time get-out-of-jail-free card called youthful offender eligibility. The judge sent him to a year-long program offered by CASES (the Center for Alternative Sentencing and Employment Services), with group sessions and volunteer assignments at his local recreation center. Kevin liked the work, which was a mix of playing with younger kids and cleaning up. He got to go on a trip to Ohio. He met a girl in the program who became his long-term, on-again/off-again girlfriend.

Over the next few years, Kevin lived on the edge of trouble. He had friends at the center: "I sometimes chilled with people who did wild shit," he said. When they got into fights, he tried to set limits without leaving anyone in the lurch or risking his status. He had a personal code: he fought with his fists, not with weapons. Kevin knew people who were doing twenty-five to life. He wanted no part of that.

Guns were for protection, which wasn't the same as self-defense, as researchers have explored. In the early 2000s, when he was a twenty-five-year-old graduate student, Victor Rios did fieldwork in the streets of Oakland, where he'd once been in a gang himself. Shadowing forty teenage boys, Rios regularly came across knives and guns; they sent a signal about how you carried yourself on the street, about how you belonged, precisely because they were dangerous. And yet "although many of the boys had easy access to weapons, they rarely used them," wrote Rios, who became a sociologist at the University of California at Santa Barbara. They didn't want to risk retaliation or prison. They didn't want to take a life.

But sometimes they did. The guns could no more be controlled, in the end, than the damage they did could be contained.

Mason, the friend who'd brought the gun to Kevin's group, didn't live in Brownsville anymore. His family had moved to a safer part of Brooklyn when he was in middle school, and his mother was focused on keeping him out of the projects. But he kept up with Kevin and the rest of their crew, texting and visiting. Through posts on Facebook and homemade videos on YouTube, often narrated by whoever was holding out his phone as a camera, Mason could track the sparring along with the rest of them.

When Mason brought the gun, a silver semiautomatic pistol with scratch marks where the serial number was supposed to be, he didn't say how he'd gotten it and Kevin didn't ask. Bringing it to the group showed Mason stood with them, and it was also a way to seem hard without much likelihood that he'd suffer violence, since he could go back to his safer neighborhood when he wanted. But the next day, the gun showed up in a flashy video that another friend, Chris, posted of himself on Facebook. There was Chris onscreen, the camera jumping around as he showed off the gun to a couple of girls he was with and whoever tuned in to his feed.

The video wasn't online for long, and Kevin missed it. He spent that day inside his family's apartment with his girlfriend, staying off the internet because his phone, which was old, was only half working. It was evening again when he walked her outside to catch the subway to her night job in Manhattan, wearing his gray hoodie and white sneakers, with a durag in the pocket of his sweatpants. After dropping off his girlfriend, he texted Chris, who lived on another floor of his building. Chris was home with Mason and another guy whom Kevin didn't know well. He told Kevin to come on up. It was a few minutes before 11:00 p.m.

Kevin didn't think about the gun until he saw it sitting on a side table near the door. This time, he didn't walk away. Someone rolled him a blunt. He poured a little liquor into a glass and took a few sips. He was settling in when one of Chris's friends decided to leave. As the one sitting closest to the door, Kevin got up to lock it behind him.

When Chris's friend turned the knob and opened the door to leave, Kevin was standing just behind, ready to close the door after him. Over the friend's shoulder he saw two men standing at the threshold, as if they were about to knock. One was white and one was black. They weren't in uniform, but Kevin recognized them from the neighborhood: they were in plainclothes, but he knew them as police officers. Chris had been arrested for assault and harassment five months earlier, and the police thought he was involved with a gang, so they'd been watching his social media accounts, it turned out. They'd seen the gun in the Facebook video and come looking for him.

Standing there behind Chris's friend, with the cops in the doorway, Kevin felt a jolt of adrenaline. What would the cops do if they saw the gun? Chris, with his record, would definitely go to prison if the police pinned the gun on him, and he was the obvious suspect, since it was his apartment. Or what if Mason got arrested? He'd gotten jumped once and just handed over his phone to the attackers. He wasn't a fighter. Later, describing what was going through his mind in this moment, Kevin brought up the story of Kalief Browder, a touchstone in his world; Jay-Z had called him a prophet and made a documentary about him. Kalief, who was from the Bronx, wasn't a fighter, either. Accused of stealing a backpack, he spent three years at Rikers Island, enduring solitary confinement and beatings, and afterward, at the age of twenty-two, he killed himself.

Did Kevin remember Kalief in the moment? Probably not. "What were you thinking?" his mother would ask him later. He didn't have a good answer. In that instant, he had some wild notion of getting rid of the pistol by dashing down the hallway and flushing the gun down the toilet. It was a *crazy* idea, he could see later, full of risk—of leaving the apartment in handcuffs or even getting shot by a nervous cop. But young people do rash and impulsive things, especially when they're under pressure. They tend to believe nothing truly terrible will ever befall them, and even though Kevin had a rap sheet, he didn't think of himself as someone who would get into serious trouble with the law. He thought he could draw a line and stay on the safe side of it.

Kevin also wanted to be the kind of person who would come through for his friends, the man in the room who could handle himself. At that moment, those feelings were paramount.

With the police at the door, he picked up the gun.

Seven months later, on a chilly day in December, Kevin sat waiting on a wood bench, in a seat next to the aisle, in an empty courtroom on the nineteenth floor of Brooklyn's towering courthouse, located downtown at 320 Jay Street. He was jittery, jiggling one leg and moving the zipper up and down on his black sweatshirt. It was his ninth court appearance since his arrest in Chris's apartment on that May night for gun possession. It had all happened so fast: the officers burst in through the open door, and by that point there was no way to get rid of the gun. The police asked whose it was.

Kevin had a choice in the moment. Though he'd picked up the gun, he could have tried to duck the blame for it. But he felt bound by loyalty and a kind of honor. "A lot of people don't do what I did," he said later. "But it's protocol. 'You knew what it was when you signed up for it'—that's a saying with us. Like if somebody comes up and says, 'Yo, let's go smoke weed in the park,'" and you're like 'All right,' then you know what you're getting into if the cops come. You don't say, 'Oh, it's his weed and he told me to come smoke with him.' No. Same thing with a gun. I had the gun on me, so it was only right to say it was mine." Maybe the logic wasn't airtight, but this was his self-justification and his code.

This was the first time Kevin's case was scheduled for a full-blown hearing with testimony rather than a momentary appearance before the judge. He wasn't sure what to expect. He was thinking about his girlfriend. She'd gotten pregnant over the summer, and at first they both wanted to have the baby. But with the criminal charges dangling over his head, everything felt too uncertain. *We've got to better ourselves first*, they decided, and she made an appointment at an abortion clinic in Long Island to end the pregnancy. Kevin went with her. In case he had to go straight from court to jail, he'd worn a pair of old sneakers and sweatpants so he wouldn't have to hand over a nice set of clothes when he changed into a jumpsuit. He'd put out a call to his friends, asking them to come to court "in case someone needs to hold my stuff." But while they'd wished him luck, they hadn't shown up.

Kevin was also worried about a job interview he had at UPS, scheduled for the next day. The company was staffing for the holiday rush, and the position paid better, with more hours, than the part-time work he had cleaning office buildings. But he wasn't sure he'd make it to the interview or be able to take the job if he got it. "I just want this whole thing to be over so bad," he said to his lawyer, Debora Silberman of Brooklyn Defender Services, who'd come into the courtroom to find out when the hearing would begin and check on Kevin.

"Hey, nothing is changing today," Silberman answered, her tone upbeat. "You're going home. Remember that."

The door in the back of the courtroom opened, and a woman with long blond hair and a serious expression walked in, wearing a flowing black pantsuit and ballet flats. Silberman, a thirty-two-year-old who'd grown up in Houston and wore makeup and high heels to court to look formidable, walked over to her. Kevin turned around to watch them talk. He could see their lips moving but he couldn't hear what they were saying. He knew the blond woman was from the Brooklyn district attorney's office. She was the one who would determine the course his case would take—and his life along with it.

Caryn Teitelman became a prosecutor in Brooklyn straight out of law school: two decades later, she still couldn't imagine doing anything else. The daughter of public school teachers, Teitelman grew up on Staten Island, New York City's most conservative borough. Her father spent his thirty-year career at a tough, low-income school in Bushwick, Brooklyn. He often said he stuck it out through the worst years, when crack and violence riddled the neighborhood, because he loved the kids. Teitelman felt that her job, like her father's, was about helping people and making Brooklyn safer. In 2002, she tried a man who forced his way into an apartment by pretending to be delivering flowers. With an accomplice, he bound a seven-year-old girl and her parents with duct tape and robbed the place. Afterward he escaped capture for years before getting caught on another violent felony charge with a victim. Teitelman won a conviction, and the man was sentenced to twenty-three years to life. A result like that felt pure to Teitelman. "A person like that should not be walking around," she said. "He's dangerous. Think about the scars that child will have for the rest of her life."

Teitelman called that robbery her most serious case. She wrestled, though, with cases like Kevin's.

Teitelman's thinking was pivotal because she was now the lead prosecutor in a specialized gun court, established in 2016, and it was her job to decide which charges to pursue. There was no sign at the entrance to the gun court, but on most weekday mornings, it occupied two well-lit rooms with blond wood paneling and "In God We Trust" mounted in large letters above the judge's chair.

Lawyers and social workers toting large manila folders sat on the first row of benches once they knew their cases would be called. Their clients waited in the rows behind them.

The proceedings in the gun court were civil and orderly—and if you knew how to look for it, they offered a display of enormous prosecutorial power. The law that governed here gave the D.A.'s office an array of options, each choice marked in the charging sheet with its own acronym. On the high end, Teitelman could prosecute someone like Kevin, accused of simple possession of an unlicensed loaded gun, with a serious violent felony in New York—without proving he intended to use the weapon, and even if he had no criminal record. This maximum charge was called criminal possession of a weapon in the second degree, or CPW2, and it carried a mandatory minimum sentence of three and a half years in prison with a high of fifteen, plus parole. Alternatively, Teitelman could choose criminal possession of a weapon in the third degree. Some provisions of that count almost always came with a mandatory minimum sentence as well—two years in prison, plus parole—and a maximum of seven years. In other words, if Kevin was found guilty of one of these two felonies, a judge would have to send him to prison, whether or not she thought that was just. But the prosecutor also had the discretion to go down to a misdemeanor charge (criminal possession of a weapon in the fourth degree, or CPW4), with no prison or jail time at all.

How dangerous was Kevin? What punishment did he deserve, and what consequence for him would serve the community's interests? Teitelman knew the police found it frustrating to catch someone with a gun and then see him returned to the neighborhood, but she felt that the gun court "shouldn't be a one-way ticket to jail." Her job was to "get it right" by looking at each case individually. Most of the gun-court defendants who went to prison would come back to Brooklyn, and she knew that incarceration often had the opposite effect of what she intended. It might well increase the chance that they'd commit more crimes on release.

In the moments before Kevin's hearing, Silberman tried to nudge Teitelman and her assistants toward mercy by giving them a fresh copy of a report about him and his future. Written by the social worker at Brooklyn Defender Services who was working with Kevin, the report described him as standing at his own fork in the road. "We foresee two distinct paths," the social worker wrote. One led to prison and the loss of his public housing upon release. ("How will he get a job with a conviction?" asked the report. "Where will he live?") The other began with diversion—a program that would offer Kevin services instead of prison. If Kevin could get in, his lawyer and social worker imagined an alternative path for him: a job, the chance to save some money, enrollment in community college, an apartment with his girlfriend.

The diversion program was run by the D.A.'s office, so the decision about whom to admit lay in the prosecutors' hands. As Teitelman weighed it, the choice between prison and freedom was hers to make. She hated to think about her job like that, but it was the reality of the gun court. Another reality: in about nine of ten cases, prosecutors gave themselves maximum leverage at the outset by charging CPW2. When Kevin was arrested, he was actually charged with the lesser felony of CPW3 and the misdemeanor CPW4. But a few weeks later, when his case was transferred to the gun court, the D.A.'s office loaded on CPW2, the most serious possible charge.

As a result, Kevin was facing a mandatory sentence of at least three and a half years. All, as he saw it, for picking up a pistol that wasn't his in a friend's apartment. He felt like he was in a slow-motion tailspin, with the years, his plans, and his life as he'd known it whirling away from him.

Caught up in the process of the gun court, Kevin felt subject to whims and judgment calls and unwritten rules. It seemed like anything could happen and he would never really know why. As he sensed, what happened next wasn't really up to the judge or what anyone said in open court. His fate lay in the behind-the-scenes decisions of Teitelman and the Brooklyn D.A.'s office. The prosecutors held power in the Brooklyn gun court, and Kevin had entered the system at a moment in which that was more true, in courts across the country, than ever before.

This book will show that American prosecutors have breathtaking power, leading to disastrous results for millions of people churning through the criminal justice system. Over the last forty years, prosecutors have amassed more power than our system was designed for. And they have mostly used it to put more people in prison, contributing to the scourge of mass incarceration, which continues to rip apart poor communities, especially if they are mostly black or brown, and long ago passed the level required for public safety.

The unfettered power of prosecutors is the missing piece for explaining how the number of people incarcerated in the United States has *quintupled* since the 1980s, to a total of almost 2.2 million. Our level of imprisonment is five to ten times higher than that of other liberal democracies—nine times Germany's and seven times France's. There's more: when the system misfires in the worst way possible, by convicting an innocent person, a prosecutor's errors (or, less frequently, willful misconduct) often account for the breakdown, at least in part. And when black defendants are punished more severely than white defendants for similar crimes, the choices of prosecutors are largely to blame. Though they're not the only ones at fault, their decisions are the ones that matter most of all.

Jail and prison have a role to play in our society. Some people commit truly serious crimes—not that many, relatively speaking, but some—and a subset cause unconscionable harm. In the United States, however, the criminal justice net has expanded to envelope immense numbers of people who don't fit into those categories. The overuse of incarceration isn't necessary, or even a sound strategy, for keeping the public safe. The crime rate has dropped in parts of the United States where incarceration is also falling and also in countries where imprisonment has remained low. The American focus on prison also drains resources from other means of preventing crime that can strengthen communities and improve people's lives. There's nothing pragmatic about the status quo. Lifetime consequences, government overreach, racial disparity—these are sources of suffering and also American disasters, adding up to one of the most pressing problems of our time. They have not been fixed, not by any means. In many places in the country, they haven't even been addressed. Our justice system regularly operates as a system of *injustice*, grinding out unwarranted and counterproductive levels of punishment. This is, in large part, because of the outsize role prosecutors now play. "The power imbalance blew my mind, frankly: I couldn't figure out for the life of me how prosecutors had so much power with so little accountability," says Angela J. Davis, a law professor who was formerly the director of the Public Defender Service in Washington, D.C., and the author of a 2007 book about prosecutors. "They were allowed to do things, some unconstitutional, some perfectly legal but with horrific results that most human beings would think were unfair. I thought, how can this be?"

We often think of prosecutors and defense lawyers as points of a triangle on the same plane, with the judge poised above them: equal contest, level playing field, neutral arbiter, et cetera. That image is entirely out of date. It's not how the system works anymore. Much of the time, prosecutors, more than judges, control the outcome. They answer to no one else and make most of the key decisions in a case, from choosing the charge to making the bail demand to determining the plea bargain. The officer in uniform and the judge in robes are our indelible images of criminal justice. No one needs to explain the power they wield. Yet it is Caryn Teitelman, in her pantsuit and ballet flats, who today embodies the might and majesty of the state. "It's all about discretion," says Eric Gonzalez, the district attorney of Brooklyn and Teitelman's boss. "Do you authorize the arrest, request bail, argue to keep them in jail or let them out, go all out on the charges or take a plea bargain? Prosecutors decide, especially, who gets a second chance."

Here's the thing: prosecutors also hold the key to change. They can protect against convicting the innocent. They can guard against racial bias. They can curtail mass incarceration.

Change who occupies the prosecutor's office, and you can make the system begin to operate differently. The power of the D.A.* makes him or her the actor—the only actor—who can start to fix what's broken without changing a single law.

A movement of organizers and activists and local leaders and defense lawyers and professors and students and donors is fighting for that change. This movement is working to elect a new type of D.A. in city after city and county after county. The movement is a groundswell. It's growing. And it's causing the first major shift in the politics and incentives of American prosecution in decades.

The candidates for D.A. the movement embraces see ensuring fairness as integral to public safety. They know that people who have faith in the criminal justice system are more likely to help the police solve crimes and to testify as witnesses in court. In a democracy, people tend to uphold the law when they believe it is fair. It's an understanding that's fundamental to the legitimacy of state power.

The movement to transform American prosecution is bipartisan. It has roots in civil rights history, the Black Lives Matter campaign against violence and racism, libertarian skepticism of government overreach, and conservative concerns about waste and spending. So far, the newly elected D.A.s represent a small fraction of the more than twenty-four hundred prosecutors who hold elected office nationwide. But they include Democrats and Republicans, in

---

* District attorneys, also called state or county attorneys, are the chief prosecutors in the state court system and are elected in almost every state. The lawyers who work for them are called assistant district attorneys or line prosecutors. U.S. attorneys, the chief prosecutors in ninety-three federal offices around the country under the umbrella of the Justice Department, are appointed by the president and confirmed by the Senate. The lawyers who work for them are called assistant U.S. attorneys.

red states as well as purple and blue ones, and they hold the reins of law enforcement in an increasing number of major cities as well as scattered rural areas.

Because campaigns to reform D.A.'s offices are local, they show how urban strongholds can control their destinies without waiting for state legislatures to get on board. And as the movement spreads, it's beyond the control of Washington and the Trump administration to stop. Local prosecutors handle more than 95 percent of the nation's criminal docket, and by reinventing how they do their jobs, they can stand up to Trump, on issues surrounding punishment but also on immigration, drug policy, and civil rights.

We, the people, elect state prosecutors, and that means their power is our power. At this moment in twenty-first-century America, we have an opportunity. Most of us are safer from crime than we have been for generations. The murder rate remains close to a fifty-year low. State legislatures are rethinking the wisdom of spending more than $43 billion a year on prisons and jails, at a cost of $15,000 to $70,000 annually per prisoner. Falling crime and mounting costs are opening a window for deep reform.

At the same time, the shape of mass incarceration has begun to shift since the scarring war on drugs of the 1990s. In New York and some other states, sentences for drug offenses have already plummeted, and more than half of state prisoners nationwide are now behind bars for crimes that are designated as violent. Nationally, cutting the prison population by 50 percent or more requires going much further than leniency for people who are low-level or first-time defendants. Ending mass incarceration means narrowing the current conception of who counts as a violent felon and doing far more to ensure that the jailhouse gate isn't a revolving door. It means dismantling the barriers that regularly freeze people out of housing and employment after they're released. It means giving former felons the vote. It means treating them not like ex-cons, forever trailed by the worst thing they did, but as returning citizens, defined by who they may become. It means betting, far more often, on the future of people like Kevin.

It's not clear yet whether the movement to transform American prosecution will be equal to the challenge—whether it will spread beyond a few dozen D.A.'s offices, and thus impact incarceration on a national scale. In much of the country, prosecutors still lean hard toward punitive outcomes and toward retribution. Reform-minded prosecutors venture down a new path, while their old-school counterparts stick with the practices of the last forty years. This book uses a wide lens to explore the history of the American way of prosecution and the macro forces that could reshape it. To tell the full story, I focus on two very different elected D.A.s, Eric Gonzalez in Brooklyn and Amy Weirich in Memphis, and two young people caught up in the system: Kevin, who picked up his friend's gun as the cops burst in, and Noura Jackson, a teenage girl whom Weirich charged with murder.

Kevin's case is about the ordinary and perfectly legal exercise of a prosecutor's power, beginning with the decision about how to charge a crime. Noura's case is different: it shades into the abuse of power, showing just how much can go wrong when a prosecutor breaks the legal and ethical rules that are supposed to protect all of us from being squeezed in the state's vise. I'll follow each case through the criminal process, from arrest and charging to bail, plea bargaining or trial, and sentencing. These two stories illustrate the damage prosecutors can do and also the precious second chances they can extend that allow people to make things right in their own lives. You'll see how criminal prosecutions can go wrong *and why they don't have to*. I'll also explore how new D.A.s elected in cities around the country, including Philadelphia, Chicago, Jacksonville, St. Louis, Denver, and Houston, are coming together to lobby nationally for more rational and merciful law enforcement. At the end of the book, I'll share a blueprint for twenty-first-century prosecution.

On TV serials and in the press, prosecutors tend to be portrayed as calculating politicians, white-hat heroes, or rote functionaries. These are not fair or full portraits. Prosecutors have always been obligated to pursue a dual mission: seek convictions and act as ministers of justice. The roles are "obviously unharmonious," Supreme Court Justice Thurgood Marshall once wrote, a phrase that captures the difficulty inherent in playing both at once. But mastering that duality is fundamental to a prosecutor's professional and ethical calling. Good prosecutors know it and live it and teach it. The prosecutor "is in a peculiar and very definite sense the servant of the law, the twofold aim of which is that guilt shall not escape or innocence suffer," Supreme Court Justice George Sutherland wrote in 1935. "The citizen's safety lies in the prosecutor who tempers zeal with human kindness," Justice Robert Jackson added five years later. In other words, the prosecutor's job is *not* to exact the greatest possible punishment. It is not to win at all costs. It's to offer mercy in equal measure to justice.

Prosecutors are not solely responsible for the state of the criminal justice system, of course. They respond to the cues of judges, to legislators and other elected officials, and to the priorities of the police, who are their closest partners. The quality of defense lawyers, especially those who represent the poor, matters a great deal for the quality of justice, and adequate funding for public defenders is an absolute necessity. When prosecutors make decisions about which defendants to charge to the max and which to spare, those charged with crimes need good defense attorneys with the time, resources, and heart to tell the stories of their clients and make the case for mercy. Judges still have some ability to keep prosecutors within certain bounds. The Supreme Court matters, too, perhaps most of all for what it hasn't done. The Court has not reined in the power of prosecutors at plea bargaining or enforced any limits of proportionality on punishment. Perhaps most damagingly of all, the justices have bestowed upon prosecutors absolute immunity from lawsuits, making them even harder to sue than the police.

It's still important to persuade legislators to change the laws, elevate judges who care about fairness, and create the conditions for first-rate defense work. But we can stop caging people needlessly *right now* if we choose prosecutors who will open the locks. While it would be nice if lawmakers and the courts threw themselves into fixing the criminal justice system, in the meantime, elections for prosecutors represent a shortcut to addressing a lot of dysfunction. Cities and counties can model change that can spread statewide and nationally. This movement deserves your attention. There's good reason to think the United States could safely reduce the number of people in prison and jail by half or even more. In time, the country's embrace of mass incarceration, in its vast cruelty, may come to seem nearly as shameful as slavery does now.

PART ONE

THE
POWER
OF
THE
CHARGE

1

CHARGE

THE BLOOD WAS everywhere. Spattered on the floor of the hallway, on the doorframe of the bedroom, and on the bedposts. Soaked into the sheets and pillows, and covering the body splayed on the floor at the foot of the bed. Jennifer Jackson was naked. Her face was covered by a wastepaper basket. Her chest and torso and hands were slashed, the pale skin torn by the blade of a knife. She'd been stabbed a total of fifty times.

Noura Jackson, Jennifer's eighteen-year-old daughter, called 911 at 5:00 a.m. on Sunday, June 5, 2005. "Please, I need, I need an ambulance, I need an ambulance right now!" Noura cried. "Someone broke into my house. My mom—my mom is bleeding." She waited a few long seconds for the operator to transfer her. "She's not breathing," Noura said, sounding desperate, when an emergency dispatcher came on the line. "She's not breathing. She's not breathing. Please help me."

The medics arrived at the Jackson home, in a well-kept Memphis neighborhood, and pronounced her dead at 5:18 a.m. Jennifer was a thirty-nine-year-old investment banker. A few months earlier, she'd brought her daughter to a celebratory dinner where she received an award for her professional success. The award was shaped like a gold bat to show that the winner had hit a home run in the market. Jennifer lived alone with Noura, her only child, born in the first year of her marriage to Nazmi Hassanieh, a former Lebanese army captain, whom she met while she was waiting tables to pay her way through college. Noura's parents divorced when she was a baby; Jennifer thought Nazmi was too controlling, a problem she had later with other men. At the time of her death, she had an on-again/off-again boyfriend who called her around midnight on the night she was killed. Questioned by the police, he said that he hung up before she answered and then went to sleep at his home, more than an hour from her home in Memphis.

The police also questioned Noura. She told them she'd found her mother's body when she came home after being out all night. She had gone to a couple of parties with friends and then drove around by herself in a way that made it seem like she could have been stoned, stopping at Taco Bell, then realizing she didn't have her wallet, going back to a friend's house to find it, and buying some gas. She said she had no idea who would want to kill her mother.

The police checked the doors to the Jackson house and found them locked. No neighbor had seen an intruder. But there was broken glass on the kitchen floor, from a windowpane in the door that led from the kitchen to the garage. The window seemed to have been broken from the inside (the hole in the glass lined up with a door lock that could be seen only from the kitchen). It was a confusing crime scene, with no clear leads.

The brutality of Jennifer's killing, on a quiet block, made local headlines and roiled the middle-class parts of the city. Days passed, then weeks. The longer the investigation continued without a break, the more anxiety seemed to grow. Murder was all too common in the poor and black communities of Memphis, but not among its white and affluent residents. Would Jennifer's assailant strike again?

"Mystery Stabbing: Death Unsolved After Two Months," the local ABC affiliate reported that August.

In the prosecutor's office, the Jackson case went to Amy Weirich, a rising star in the Memphis courthouse. A forty-year-old long-distance runner with sandy blond hair cut in a feathered bob, Weirich was a churchgoing Catholic, the mother of four children, and a former chief of the gang-and-narcotics unit in her office. Among her coworkers, opinion about her was split. Some of her peers saw her as highly skilled and admirable. One former colleague called Weirich "kind and humble." Watching her try cases, "she was my hero," this prosecutor said.

Other coworkers, however, saw Weirich as a bully who wasn't trustworthy. "She's the kind of person who would stab you in the back to advance her own cause," a former prosecutor who worked with her for years told me. "Amy thinks she can do no wrong," another colleague said. "She never admits mistakes. Never apologizes." If her attitude irked some of her peers, it also helped Weirich move up the ranks to become the first woman to be named deputy district attorney in Shelby County, an office of more than one hundred prosecutors. She was a Republican, like her boss, District Attorney Bill Gibbons, in a state where her party was dominant. As she rose, she cultivated connections beyond her office as well as inside it.

Jennifer Jackson's murder presented Weirich with the biggest spotlight of her career. The attention was an opportunity. But as the police struggled to crack the case, it was also a problem. Following the ABC television report, homicide investigators told the local press that they had no obvious leads. They said they were waiting for DNA testing. They hoped the results would lead to an arrest.

In the meantime, a subplot emerged, with tantalizing possible links to Jackson's stabbing. Noura's father, Nazmi Hassanieh, had been shot to death in the Memphis convenience store he owned sixteen months before his ex-wife was killed. He was running a limousine service that ferried clients to and from a strip club next to his store. Surveillance video footage showed a male assailant ransacking the store, as if he was looking for something without finding it, after he shot Hassanieh. Rumors swirled that Hassanieh was renting out limos to a prostitution ring and had compromising videotapes of clients who had ridden in his cars.

When Noura was about eight, her mother broke off contact with Hassanieh; she told Noura later that she thought he was irresponsible. For years, Noura thought he'd left Memphis and deserted her. When she was sixteen, though, she walked into a convenience store across town and a man came out of an office at the back. Noura thought she recognized him. She asked the woman behind the register what his name was. Nazmi, the woman said. Noura spotted an old photograph, taped to the register; it showed him holding a baby girl. She rushed out the door and confronted her father. "I hurled questions at him: Where had he been for all those years? Why hadn't he come to find me? I didn't think I missed him, but it all just came out." Hassanieh told Noura he'd been waiting to get back in touch with her until he got his green card, but later he confessed to her that he just didn't know how to reenter her life. He'd named his convenience store Noura's Kwik Shop, though he'd never told her.

Once Hassanieh and Noura found each other, he started texting and calling her often. Sometimes she felt he was overbearing—he didn't want her to hang out with boys—but she also appreciated his interest and the care he showed her. When he was killed, Noura felt that they hadn't found their footing and she was still just getting to know him.

Noura was Hassanieh's heir, so Jennifer went to his store and collected his belongings for their daughter. She and Noura also took possession of the car he drove, a black 1990s Mercedes, which Jennifer started driving and parking in her driveway. If whoever killed Hassanieh felt he had to look again for whatever he'd searched for fruitlessly in Hassanieh's store, Jennifer and Noura's home was the logical first stop. And the house was ransacked the night of Jennifer's murder, according to the police.

The possible link between the murders of Noura's parents contributed to the sensation surrounding Jennifer's death. It offered an avenue for the police to explore. But there was a problem: Hassanieh's murder was unsolved. From the point of view of the police and prosecutors, the open case on Hassanieh was a giant question mark—but without a new break, it was a dead end for solving Jackson's murder. Over the summer, with the DNA from Jennifer Jackson's bedroom awaiting testing at the Tennessee crime lab, the investigation veered away from Hassanieh's unknown killer and toward other parts of Jennifer's life—and Noura's.

By all accounts, Jennifer Jackson was a warm and loving mother. When Noura was in preschool, Jennifer got engaged to an older man, Bill Shelton. They never married, but in the three and a half years they spent together, Shelton saw Jennifer's affection for her daughter as he became attached to Noura himself. "Jennifer would read stories to her every night, simple stories and fables," Shelton told me. "Noura would look at the pictures and at her mother's face. I remember once when we were driving, Jennifer laughed in this characteristic way she had, with her voice and her whole body, and when I looked in the rearview mirror, Noura was laughing in exactly the same way." Jennifer's playful streak ran deep and wide. Friends told me about Jennifer dressing up as Captain Hook to Noura's Peter Pan at Noura's eighth-birthday party. "Keds were really big then," Noura remembered. "When my mom called everybody to invite them, she asked them to RSVP with the size of their tennis shoe, and for the party, she got that puff paint, and everybody decorated a pair of shoes."

Jennifer and Shelton broke up when Noura was five, and she married another man a couple of years later. But her second marriage turned abusive. Noura said she saw her stepfather throw Jennifer against a wall during a fight. He brought a gun to the divorce negotiations, according to Noura's uncle Eric (her mother's half brother, who was nine years older than his niece and came to live with Jennifer and Noura when he was in high school). Jackson divorced her second husband after three years.

When Noura became a teenager, Jennifer sometimes acted more like an older sister than a parent. Once when Noura refused to take antibiotics for an infection, Jennifer called Ansley Larsson, the mother of Noura's middle-school boyfriend, for help. "She said, 'Noura won't listen to me, will you talk to her?'" Larsson remembers. Jennifer and Noura had similar taste in movies—they loved *Steel Magnolias* and *Terms of Endearment*—and shopped for clothes together. Noura got decent grades and played soccer and basketball. Jennifer came to her games, and other parents teased her for cheering louder than anyone else.

In tenth grade, Noura switched from a Catholic girls' school to public high school. Before long, she started going out and experimenting with drinking beer and smoking pot. Once she tried cocaine. She was also taking the opioid Lortab, prescribed to her for pain caused by endometriosis, a chronic disorder of the uterine tissue.

When Noura was sixteen, a series of traumatic events made her life feel unsteady. First, her maternal grandmother died. Noura was close to her and keenly felt the loss. Then her father was murdered—a second blow—and, ten months later, her best friend from childhood, Anna, died in a car accident. Noura tattooed Anna's name on her right foot. The cascade of deaths affected her deeply. She started having trouble concentrating in school and stopped going to classes instead of completing eleventh grade. She promised to finish her coursework at home but left most of it unfinished.

Though Jennifer could see that her daughter was struggling and talked to friends about how to help, it wasn't easy for her. Setting boundaries and imposing discipline had never been her way. Instead,

Jennifer cooked for the friends Noura brought over and joked with one of them when she caught him smoking pot in the backyard. Noura was too old for her mother to dress up like Captain Hook, but Jennifer still had a bag of tricks for snapping her daughter out of her funk. For Noura's seventeenth birthday, Jennifer spent two weeks taking classes for a specialized license so she could drive a limo. As a surprise, she appeared at the front door one afternoon dressed in a tuxedo, like a chauffeur, and whisked Noura off to Florida for a spa weekend at the beach.

That was a high, but there were also lows, usually associated with men. When Jennifer felt badly treated, Noura comforted her, but they also argued. Noura thought the men her mother dated didn't treat her well, and when Jennifer got back together with her boyfriend that year—the one she was seeing at the time of her death—Noura urged her mother to break up with him once and for all.

Noura didn't drop out of school, but she also didn't progress to senior year. She spent the year she was supposed to finish high school completing her courses at home, swinging between periods of depression and relative normalcy, putting off her schoolwork, eating dinner and watching movies with her mom as usual, and going out to party. In May of what would have been her senior year, as Noura's friends got ready to graduate, Jennifer grew increasingly worried and frustrated. She set a curfew for Noura and told her to stop smoking pot. Over Memorial Day weekend, several days before Jennifer's death, mother and daughter drove to Florida, along with Jennifer's half brother Eric, to visit Jennifer's younger sisters— Cindy, whose home they stayed in, and Grace, who came from Atlanta.

Jennifer's sisters were married to well-off men and didn't work. Noura felt judged by her aunts, as she had since childhood. They had disapproved of Hassanieh and wanted nothing to do with him or the daughter who looked like him. Noura had her father's dark hair and eyes and an olive complexion, and her aunts made her feel like an interloper. She remembered them shaving her arms, to her shame. She wished she could be fair-skinned and blond, like her mother. She wished that her name was spelled in the normal way. Her mom told her she chose it because it was special, but to Noura, who as soon as she was old enough streaked her hair to lighten it, it seemed like one more mark of foreignness.

In Florida at Cindy's house, late on Saturday night, Jennifer got a call from the police: they'd received a complaint from the neighbors and found Noura's high school boyfriend, Perry, throwing a party at her house. Jennifer got angry at Perry, and at Noura for failing to stop him. With Grace and Cindy urging her to rein in Noura, she floated the idea of boarding school or even military school. Noura didn't want to go, but she didn't argue or yell. She just left the room.

Later, Weirich would make a big deal of Noura's heightened emotions and her friction with her mother on the Florida trip. Yet Eric told investigators that Noura and Jennifer made up on the long drive home, stopping at a mall to shop for shoes together. "They did not have a bad, stormy relationship," Dana Fredrick, the mother of one of Noura's friends, told the local press a few months later. "Noura would drop whatever plans she had to spend the evening with her mom—go to the movies, out to dinner, whatever they wanted to do," Ansley Larsson, her middle-school boyfriend's mother, told me. "Even when she fought with Jennifer, like teenagers do, it was clear how much she loved her mother."

In the hours after her mother's death, Noura was distraught to the point of unraveling, according to two of her neighbors. "What am I going to do?" she asked. "I just lost my dad. Why is this happening to me?" A paramedic saw her standing on the curb, crying. At around 8:00 a.m., three hours after Noura called 911, a police officer took her to the station, where another officer took a statement from her. TV crews and onlookers were gathered outside her house when she returned, at about noon. She said she felt uncomfortable, and a friend of the family, Regina Hunt, took her out for lunch and then to Hunt's home. On the way, they stopped at the cemetery where her friend Anna was buried. Noura sobbed at her grave.

Grace flew to Memphis the next day. Cindy, who was in Portugal on vacation, arrived a day later. Noura's aunts checked into a hotel while she stayed with friends, moving from house to house. They soon starting fighting over the plans for her mother's funeral. Noura wanted the service to include "My Heart Will Go On," Céline Dion's song from the film *Titanic*. "That was a song my mom loved," she told me. "It was my recital piece when I was younger, and every time I played it, she would cry. I always thought it was because I played so beautifully. When I turned eighteen, she told me the real reason—it reminded her of a guy. It was funny. It was our inside joke. But Grace and Cindy said the song was corny. I was like, 'But Mom was corny! This is not y'all's funeral. This is Mom's funeral.' They left me there, in the lobby of the hotel." Noura called a friend to take her to the crematorium, where she picked out her mother's urn by herself.

Regina Hunt was concerned and took Noura to see a child psychologist, who suggested a stay at Lakeside Behavioral Health System, a residential mental health treatment center nearby. Her aunts urged her to go as well. "They said, 'We just want to make sure you're OK, and you won't miss your mom's funeral,'" Noura said. "I didn't realize I was checking myself in."

Grace and Cindy were late to pick Noura up for her mother's funeral. After an hour, she started to panic about missing it and was given a sedative. When she returned to Lakeside after the ceremony, still dazed, two detectives were waiting for her. They handed her a piece of paper. It was a warrant to search her body for cuts, bruises, or contusions. They took Noura into an office and asked her to take off her clothes so they could photograph her from head to toe. "It was one of the most horrible moments in my life," she remembered. "I was on suicide watch for seventy-two hours after they left."

Noura stayed at Lakeside for thirty days, getting grief counseling and going to group therapy meetings with other teenagers. When her insurance coverage ran out, Grace and Cindy paid for her to move into an apartment complex where Eric and his girlfriend lived. Her aunts paid the rent but didn't visit. Noura didn't mourn her mother in the way people around her expected. Feeling lost, she tried to draw her friends close, and that turned into gatherings in her apartment. Neighbors complained about the noise from loud nighttime parties. Noura brought her cat to the apartment although it was against the rules. She and her boyfriend, Perry, broke up. He started dating another girl in their circle, but he and Noura also kept seeing each other.

In August, about a month after moving to the apartment, Noura got evicted and spent the next month crashing on friends' couches. On the afternoon of September 29, she was finishing up a babysitting job for a couple who'd just come home when she heard someone say, "Put the baby down." Noura was standing at the changing table. She turned around and saw three plainclothes police officers. One had his gun drawn. They asked her name, and when she told them, they put her in handcuffs, though they wouldn't tell her why. Two more officers waited outside by a car. They drove Noura to the local jail, where her clothes were taken, including her underwire bra, and she was given an orange prison shirt and blue pants and assigned to a top bunk in a small room with painted cement walls, a desk with a stool attached, and a toilet and sink. Noura was able to sneak in one thing: a white Abercrombie & Fitch T-shirt Perry had given her. It was her only physical tie to her old life.

It's extremely rare for daughters to kill their mothers, especially without a history of abuse. Noura had no record of violence. But in the months since Jackson's death, before the DNA results came back, Weirich and the police had been exploring the theory that Noura killed Jackson in an act of rage and rebellion. Bridling under her mother's rules, Weirich argued, Noura committed the brutal stabbing to get her mother's money and use it to party with her friends. (Jennifer's estate, including her life insurance policy, was valued at $1.5 million.) Weirich also said that Noura and her mother were arguing over whether to sell her father's cars—the black Mercedes and another one he was thought to own, though in the end he didn't have title to it.

To fill in the narrative and to make the case against Noura stick, the police interviewed her aunts and uncle, a wide circle of her friends, and their parents. The investigators heard about the tumult of the late spring and summer. Noura's friends told them about smoking pot in the Jacksons' backyard and then, after Jennifer's death, about drinking beer and smoking pot in Noura's apartment. Perry reported on a night when Noura called him from outside his house, climbed in through his bedroom window, and had sex with him. Weirich would later present all of this as evidence of Noura's wild streak and guilt, not loneliness or vulnerability. She also homed in on gaps and inconsistencies in the account Noura had initially given the police of the night of her mother's death. The early part of the evening checked out. Friends confirmed that Noura went to the Italian Festival, an annual outdoor event in Memphis, then to a party at a friend's house, and then to Perry's. During the same period, Jennifer went to a wedding downtown and from there to a bar. Noura told the police that her mom had called her shortly after midnight, from their house. She was going to bed and, according to Noura, reminded her that church would start late the next morning, in case they decided to go together. Noura said she was spending the night out, and they left their plans for the next day open-ended. Phone records showed the call and also corroborated Noura's account of some calls and texts she later made to friends from her cellphone.

Jennifer died sometime between her call to Noura at 12:20 a.m. and 5:00 a.m. When Noura told the police where she went during those hours—to a friend's house, a gas station, and Taco Bell—she left out a stop she made at Walgreens around 4:00 a.m. The police collected grainy video footage from the store, which showed her buying bandages and skin-care products. She also took a length of toilet paper from the clerk for a small cut on her left hand, between her thumb and forefinger. The next morning, when she went to the police station, the cut was covered with adhesive tape, which the police officer who took pictures of her that morning, including close-ups of her hands, didn't take off. At that point, they treated the cut as insignificant. But the police grew suspicious when they asked Noura's friends and relatives about it, and heard she'd given different accounts of how and when she got it.

After she was arrested, Noura tried to explain. She said she didn't tell the police about the stop at Walgreens because she didn't think it was important. She was vague about other details because she didn't want to get herself or her friends in trouble for smoking pot and drinking. She'd cut her hand on a broken beer bottle while she was out the Friday night before her mother died—she didn't remember telling anyone anything different. One of her friends backed up this story by telling investigators that Noura asked for a bandage at the party on Saturday night, in the hours before her mother was killed. The police also found a shopping list in the Jacksons' kitchen; it included "Band-aids," jotted down in Jennifer's handwriting.

Then there was Noura's manicure. She showed it off to her friends on Saturday night: her nails were shiny and perfect, with white tips. Someone took a picture, which was later admitted into evidence. The manicure was still in perfect condition the next morning, the photos taken at the precinct showed. The medical examiner was certain that Jennifer fought back hard against her attacker. If Noura had had to subdue her mother to kill her, would her manicure have emerged intact? And if she cut her hand in the act of murder, why wasn't blood from her cut found in the bedroom?

If Weirich asked herself those questions, there is no record of it. For her, Noura's fraying relationship with her aunts, not the physical evidence, loomed large. When she was taken to jail, Noura called Cindy, and the police taped the call. Cindy asked where she was the night her mother was murdered. "I don't know," Noura answered. "I don't know." Cindy and Grace took her answer as evidence of guilt; neither aunt ever spoke to her again. When they heard that Bill Shelton, Jennifer's former fiancé, went to see Noura in jail, the aunts called him and told him not to help their niece. "Basically, they said it was a family situation and I shouldn't get involved." One by one, most of Jennifer's friends turned against Noura. "Her aunts started a social campaign against her," Shelton told me. "They wanted to isolate her from any possible support."

At her first court appearance, Noura stood silent, in an orange jumpsuit, as reporters crowded into the courtroom. "I was shaking," she remembered. "Sergeant Nichols, she was the bailiff in that courtroom. She came over and patted my hand. She said, 'You'll be OK.'" Noura tried to focus on that comfort as Amy Weirich rose to address the judge assigned to the case. His name was Chris Craft. He'd been on the Memphis bench for a decade, after spending twelve years as a Shelby County prosecutor.

Weirich announced the charge for Noura—first-degree murder. She asked for a life sentence.

"How do you plead?" Judge Craft asked Noura.

"Not guilty," she said.

The evidence against Noura was entirely circumstantial. No physical evidence linked her to the crime—no fingerprints or hair, not a piece of clothing. None ever emerged.

To the contrary, three months after Noura was charged, the Tennessee crime lab identified two DNA profiles, from two different people, in the blood in Jennifer's bedroom. Neither was a match for Noura, nor anyone else known to the police. A third partial profile also came up as "unknown." Long blond hairs were found in Jennifer's hand, but they were not tested for DNA. Neither was a condom wrapper with a fingerprint on it, found on the floor.

When DNA evidence points away from a suspect, it can change

the course of an investigation or prosecution. But that didn't happen in Noura's case. When her lawyers saw the DNA results, they asked for the state's full report from the crime lab. They argued that the DNA in Jennifer's bedroom indicated the involvement of someone other than Noura in the murder. It seemed like an obvious interpretation. Weirich did not agree. "This is simply incorrect," she wrote in response. "Nothing that has been provided (to the defense) indicates the 'involvement' of anyone else."

When I spoke to Weirich about the case a dozen years later, she said she remained absolutely certain of Noura's guilt. I asked what she thought when she found out that the DNA results pointed to an unknown suspect rather than to Noura.

"They didn't point to anything," Weirich said. "DNA often doesn't. Sometimes the DNA is very helpful in eliminating suspects. Sometimes the DNA is very helpful in identifying suspects. But we had a mountain of circumstantial evidence that put the defendant in that home, killing her mother at the time, and lying about it every chance she got afterward."

"So, when you got that DNA and it was not Noura, that didn't make you hesitate?" I asked.

"No," Weirich said.

Prosecutors, like other professionals who have to make difficult judgment calls, must be on guard against tunnel vision. It's a natural human tendency, and it often affects people as they sort through disparate and contradictory bits of information. Psychologists have identified a variety of cognitive distortions that contribute to tunnel vision. One is confirmation bias: the tendency to seek out and interpret evidence that supports a preexisting belief or expectation. Another is hindsight bias: the tendency to see the outcome you seek as a foregone conclusion, to overestimate the degree to which you knew it (or thought you knew it) all along, and to see the judgment you made as the right one.

Tunnel vision is often to blame when doctors make the wrong diagnosis. Attending only to the symptoms that fit their initial hypothesis, they can miss others that lead down a different path. Errors like this are not the product of malice. Physicians don't set out to treat the wrong illness, and prosecutors, unless they have truly lost their way, don't deliberately put the wrong person in prison. And yet the risk of tunnel vision persists as institutional pressures come to bear. Caution and delay are often less valued than confidence and speed. Admitting error is hard for most of us in the first place and harder still once we've committed to a course of action.

In 2002, an Illinois commission found that the tunnel vision of prosecutors contributed to the convictions of thirteen men who were subsequently exonerated and released from death row. The governor, who had already declared a moratorium on executions, commuted more than 160 death sentences the following year. In 2004, a government report in Canada (which has a justice system that resembles the one in the United States in important ways) identified tunnel vision as a common factor in wrongful convictions.

Keith Findley, a law professor at the University of Wisconsin, became alert to the problem of tunnel vision when he helped found the Wisconsin Innocence Project two decades ago. He and his colleagues focused on cases in which they uncovered new evidence—like DNA, or the recantation of a witness—that recast facts that previously supported a conviction. The old chain of connections would break and a new one would assemble itself. Some prosecutors quickly grasped the implications of this and even joined forces with the innocence lawyers. But more often, Findley watched prosecutors hold fast to the old conclusions, dismissing facts he brought to their attention or coming up with new theories and straining to incorporate the new facts so that the conviction could remain intact. "You have to believe in your case in order to prosecute it, and then cognitive dissonance sets in if someone confronts you with the evidence that you were wrong," Findley said. "I saw it happen over and over again. Prosecutors say to themselves, 'I'm a good person. I wouldn't prosecute someone innocent. Therefore, this person must be guilty.' You sweep away the reasons for doubt."

In a 2006 article for the *Wisconsin Law Review* (coauthored with Michael Scott), Findley argued that prosecutors, even more than police officers or judges, are susceptible to tunnel vision because the public sees their job narrowly. Conviction rates are the statistic many D.A.s cite in seeking reelection. And when a case draws headlines—especially the kind that makes middle-class people wonder whether they're safe in their own homes—locking someone up for it becomes a driving imperative. There's a murderer on the loose, and you were the person elected to keep the public safe! In addition, the family members of victims are often looking to you for justice. The pressure to act, for the sake of your career and self-image, is heavy and real. And if you have to nail someone, tunnel vision is a natural response once you pick the culprit.

Movies and TV reinforce the dynamic. *Law and Order* episodes turn on guilty verdicts, not dismissals. The obligation to act as a minister of justice is abstract. And while the presumption of innocence remains an ideal, it's not always easy for prosecutors to keep front and center. After all, to press charges in the first place, a prosecutor "must be convinced of the righteousness of his position," Findley and Scott observed. They went on to quote another law professor: " 'The honorable prosecutor simply cannot believe that he is prosecuting the blameless.' " The perseverance of that belief is strong. When a prosecutor refuses to drop the charges against a rape suspect after DNA testing shows that a different man is almost certainly the culprit, defense lawyers sarcastically refer to the new claim that both men committed the rape as the theory of the "unindicted co-ejaculator." In other words, a prosecutor has come up with a reason to keep the original defendant in prison even when there's no proof he contributed any DNA.

In 1975, the constitutional law professor George Felkenes coined the phrase "conviction psychology" to describe the mindset of a prosecutor who "reasons that an innocent person would not be introduced into the system." Felkenes believed that prosecutors become more prone to see every defendant as guilty the longer they stay in the job. That can happen, but it's far from inevitable. Recent research suggests that the culture of a district attorney's office, more than longevity in the job, shapes whether conviction psychology takes hold. In a study based on more than 250 interviews with prosecutors in eight offices across the Southeast and Southwest, the law professors Ronald Wright and Kay Levine talked to assistant district attorneys, many of whom described themselves as white knights battling evil. As one even put it, "I want to give the death penalty when somebody steals a bag of potato chips!" Over time, however, some of the prosecutors learn to think in shades of gray. Training, supervision, and reward structures geared toward restraint can instill an ethos of balance and mitigate against a rush to judgment.

But an office culture that prizes aggression and trial victories can reinforce the drive to win at all costs. And rewarding guilty verdicts can narrow tunnel vision to a pinhole. When Amy Weirich learned to try cases in Shelby County in the 1990s, the office had a tradition called the Hammer Award: a commendation with a picture of a hammer, which supervisors or section chiefs typically taped on the office door of trial prosecutors who won big convictions or long sentences. "Reward structures can have a corrosive effect on character," Stanford law professor Deborah Rhode points out, writing about prosecutorial culture. I spoke to several former Shelby County prosecutors who told me that the Hammer Award fostered the outlook that "everyone is guilty all the time." One of them put it this way: "The measure of your worth came down to the number of cases you tried and the outcomes." Lawyers who cut ethical corners or played hardball—for example, by withholding evidence until the last minute before trial—could still be promoted.

Weirich denied that she placed winning above other values. "Our job is to do justice," she told me, "and sometimes that justice is going to trial and presenting the best case you can, and putting it in the hands of the jury. Oftentimes that justice is dismissing charges, or giving a first-time offender an opportunity to get on the right path." But one of the former prosecutors from Weirich's office told me he got the opposite message when he dismissed the charges in multiple murder cases one year. "The evidence just didn't support a conviction," he said. "But no, I didn't get credit from leadership. In fact, it hurt me. Doing your prosecutorial duty in that office is not considered helpful."

To protect against the danger of tunnel vision, Professor Findley suggested that district attorneys require trial prosecutors to talk through contrary evidence and arguments with a skilled veteran who plays the role of "devil's advocate" in the office. Weirich had a colleague who tried to step in and play that role in Noura's case. In 2005, Lee Coffee, now a judge in Memphis, was a supervising prosecutor in one part of the courthouse, while Weirich oversaw another part. Noura's prosecution could have been assigned to Coffee's division, so he asked to see the case file on Jennifer Jackson's murder before Noura was indicted. He remembers receiving a thin manila folder. "Based on what was in that file, I would not have presented that case for an indictment," Coffee told me. "I did not feel comfortable at all that there was enough evidence that a jury would find her guilty of murder." He called Weirich and told her so. "I said, 'Amy, are you keeping this file? Because I don't see enough reason to do this case.'"

Coffee paused. "I would not have charged it," he said finally. "But prosecutors at that level have wide discretion and latitude."

"Was it in Weirich's power to let Noura go?" I asked.

"One hundred percent. She made the call."

2

THE HEARING

"NUMBER ONE ON the calendar," the clerk in the Brooklyn gun court said, calling Kevin's case. This was the moment he'd been waiting for. It was just before noon on December 8, 2016. Kevin was making his ninth court appearance, but this was the first time the evidence against him would be tested. Based on this pretrial hearing, Judge Cassandra Mullen would determine which facts would be admitted against him if his case later went before a jury. Kevin rose before Judge Mullen, and stood with his hands clasped behind him, as if he were wearing handcuffs. It wasn't a supplicating gesture exactly, but it was nonthreatening.

"Brooklyn Defender Services by Debbie Silberman," his lawyer said in rat-a-tat fashion, standing next to him. "Good morning."

"Good morning, Your Honor," said the assistant district attorney, Edwin Pieters. He was one of the prosecutors supervised by Caryn Teitelman. She watched from the back of the courtroom.

"People ready and defense ready, right?" Judge Mullen asked.

Silberman and Pieters said yes. Kevin sat down. He had no role to play in this hearing, but he knew a lot was riding on the outcome.

In the months that Kevin had been going back and forth to court, Teitelman and her assistants made him the offer that was standard in gun court: plead guilty and go to prison for two years followed by two years of parole. In exchange for the plea, the prosecutors would lower the top charge he faced to attempted criminal possession of a weapon in the second degree—still a violent felony, but with the sentence of two years rather than three and a half to fifteen.

None of this was what Kevin was expecting. When he'd picked up the gun that night in Chris's apartment, he didn't know about the gun court or the prison terms prosecutors were demanding there. Now he wondered if he'd made a mistake by picking up the gun. Maybe that seems obvious, but to him it wasn't necessarily. He could still say he'd had his friends' backs in the moment just like he did when he got caught with the keys to the stolen car in high school and didn't tell the cop his friend took it.

His mother had a different perspective. "If that boy told you to jump out the window, would you do it?" she'd asked more than once. "Would he do it for you?" Kevin's gun charge had frustrated her hope of getting a bigger apartment. They had a two-bedroom unit, which was full to overflowing with Kevin, his brother, his sister, and his sister's three-year-old daughter. They'd been on the waiting list for a three-bedroom apartment. Anytime now, his mother had been told in the months before his arrest. A conviction for a violent felony would disqualify Kevin from living in New York City public housing. His mother was told that while he was facing charges, her application for the larger apartment would be frozen.

"Call your first witness," Judge Mullen said.

"The people call Police Officer Joseph," Pieters announced.

Joseph approached the witness box wearing black pants and an oxford shirt, his usual attire as a plainclothes officer. Kevin had seen him since the arrest. Joseph would stop his car if he saw Kevin and his friends outside, and ask, "Are you good?" He wasn't one of the cops who jacked people up for no reason. While Kevin listened, head bent, Joseph described how he'd gone with another police officer to Chris's building to look for the silver pistol at around eleven o'clock on that May evening, eight months earlier.

"Why were you at this specific location?" Pieters asked.

"Because the defendant who we believed had a firearm lived in one of the apartments in the building," Joseph said, referring to Chris. Joseph explained how he and his partner entered the high-rise through an unlocked outer door and took the elevator to Chris's floor. A detective waited outside, watching the apartment's windows.

"As I was about to knock on the door, the door opens, and four individuals are getting ready to exit the location," Joseph said. Pieters asked if he saw one of them in the courtroom. Joseph pointed to Kevin, calling him the "young gentleman with the black sweatshirt."

"I observed that defendant with a silver firearm try to stick it down his pants," Joseph said. Kevin's head jerked up; later, talking to his lawyer, this was the part of Joseph's story he would contest. In Kevin's version, after he picked up the gun, he ran toward the bathroom with his fanciful idea of flushing it down the toilet. When he realized that would never work, he leaned down to put the gun inside the cuff of his sweatpants, against his sock. His story wasn't all that different from Joseph's, but it was more dignified, and that mattered to him.

Joseph said that as Kevin tried to stick the gun down his pants, "the magazine popped out and fell to the floor."

"What happened next?" Pieters asked.

Joseph said that Chris picked up the magazine, ran into a bedroom with Joseph chasing behind, and threw the ammunition out the window. Joseph placed Chris under arrest. The detective waiting outside retrieved the magazine.

The officer who'd entered the apartment with Joseph was the

one who stayed with Kevin. Telling the story from his partner's perspective, Joseph said that his partner "recovered the firearm from
his pant leg at the bottom," meaning Kevin's pants leg.

"What happened to the defendant and the suspect and the other
two individuals?" Pieters asked.

"They were all arrested," Joseph said. He brought Chris back to
the front of the apartment in handcuffs, and then he and his partner
handcuffed the three others: Chris's friend, Mason, and Kevin.

"What, if anything, did he say at this time?" Pieters asked, referring to Kevin.

"He made a statement regarding why I was arresting the other
individuals that were in the apartment," Joseph said. On this point,
his and Kevin's accounts converged. Kevin said he would "take the
gun," Joseph said, meaning he would take the charge for possessing
the weapon. "Like, he was going to be a man about it."

At this point, Pieters said he had no further questions. Now it
was Silberman's turn. She asked Joseph if he'd gone to Chris's
apartment looking for Kevin. "I've seen him in the streets, but no,"
Joseph said. When Kevin saw the police at the door, "he got the,
you know, deer-in-headlights look."

"And his immediate reaction was to make a gun visible?" Silberman asked incredulously. She wanted the judge to think twice about
this part of the story: why would Kevin show a gun to the police as
they burst into the apartment?

Joseph kept going, saying he'd seen the gun after Kevin picked it
up. "He had the gun at some point getting ready to put into his
pants, and that's when the gun was visible, yes," Joseph said.

"And he didn't run away?" Silberman asked.

"That's correct."

"And it was at that point he was placed in handcuffs in the apartment?" Silberman asked.

Joseph said yes.

"After he was in handcuffs, he wasn't free to leave, correct?"
Joseph said yes again.

"He was in custody, for all intents and purposes?"

"That's correct."

Silberman asked Joseph if he'd told Kevin the police knew the gun belonged to Chris.

"That's not correct," Joseph answered. "What I did say was, 'Whose gun is this?'"

Silberman paused. Judge Mullen leaned forward slightly.

"You asked him whose it is?" Silberman repeated.

"But there were four individuals there," Joseph said, turning toward the judge. "I said, 'Whose gun is this?'" Obviously, Joseph explained, he was speaking to all of them. It was Kevin who answered. "And that's when he said, 'Why are you taking the three other people?'"—meaning, *Why are you arresting my friends as well as me?* "'I have the gun on me.'"

"And prior to asking him about whose gun it was, you never read him his Miranda rights, correct?" Silberman asked.

"I asked the four individuals the question," Joseph said. "Did I read them their rights while I was asking whose gun, the original firearm, this was? No, I did not."

Silberman paused to let the words sink in and then circled back. Was Kevin "one of those four individuals whom you asked, 'Whose gun is this?'"

"I did not ask the defendant that question, 'Whose gun is this?'" Joseph said.

Judge Mullen interjected. "That's not what she asked. Was he one of the four people that you asked the general question to?"

"Yes, Your Honor," Joseph said. "Yes, he was."

Silberman asked Judge Mullen to rule that Kevin's statements taking responsibility for the pistol—"I have the gun on me" and "I'll be a man about it"—should not be admitted as evidence against him. When Joseph asked to whom the gun belonged, Kevin wasn't free to walk away. Effectively, he was in custody, and that meant Joseph was obligated to give him a Miranda warning ("Anything you say can and will be used against you"). Since Joseph hadn't done that, Kevin's admission of responsibility shouldn't be held against him. The gun, too, should be excluded from evidence in the event of a trial, she argued.

Pieters asked Judge Mullen to deny Silberman's request. "It was the defendant that volunteered and who gave a statement in regards to, 'Oh man, why you arresting everyone else?'"

"It's not a matter of whether it was voluntary," Silberman responded. "The question is whether Miranda should have been read the minute that officer was asking questions that were being used for incriminatory purposes."

"OK," Judge Mullen said. "So, decision is reserved."

She wanted time to think and to look at the case law—the relevant decisions other judges had made over time about similar facts, starting with the Supreme Court.

As a general rule, judges in the United States once excluded evidence from the courtroom if they established that it came from an unconstitutional search or seizure. In the foundational 1961 case *Mapp v. Ohio*, the Supreme Court threw out the conviction of a woman who was charged with obscenity, based on a search of her belongings the police conducted after breaking into her house and searching it without a warrant. (The cops also roughed her up, which didn't help the government's case.) The justices rejected the critique that "the criminal is to go free because the constable has blundered," as Judge Benjamin Cardozo, then on the New York Court of Appeals and later a Supreme Court justice, had put it decades earlier.

Writing for the majority in *Mapp*, Justice Tom Clark responded to Cardozo by quoting a previous Court decision: "'There is another consideration—the imperative of judicial integrity.' The criminal goes free, if he must, but it is the law that sets him free. Nothing can destroy a government more quickly than its failure to observe its own laws." In *Miranda v. Arizona*, decided five years later, the Court continued to check the power of law enforcement, ruling that prosecutors could not use confessions at trial if the police elicited them from suspects who were in custody without informing them of their rights.

That was the height of the Supreme Court's jurisprudence on criminal law in the 1960s, when it was led by Chief Justice Earl Warren and took on corrupt or lawbreaking cops as well as prosecutors and judges who look the other way. Since then, however, the Court has maintained the rule for excluding evidence in *Mapp* while weakening it by carving out significant exceptions. In 1984, the Court ruled that the state gets a pass when the police act in good faith on a warrant that turns out to be unsupported by solid evidence (for example, if it's based on the tale of an informant who isn't credible). In 2009, the Court held that evidence from a search is admissible if the police made a mistake (by failing to update their records) because of "isolated negligence" rather than "systematic error or disregard of constitutional requirements." (The case, *Herring v. United States*, was decided by a vote of five to four, conservative justices versus liberals.) Courts increasingly do a cost-benefit test before applying the exclusionary rule. "We're pretty far down the gaping hole of good-faith exceptions," said New York University law professor Erin Murphy, "and a significant number of justices think all exclusion should be done on the basis of the good-faith-versus-bad-faith test, rather than the unconstitutionality of the seizure."

This is dangerous. As the exceptions swallow the rule, we lose one of the only major deterrents to police misconduct. "We don't have strong citizen oversight of police, it is highly politicized work, and civil remedies have been totally neutered," Murphy explained. The rule that excludes evidence from court if it's illegally obtained "is one of the main ways in which police behavior is shaped by outside influence. If law enforcement is left to draw their own boundaries for what is considered a reasonable or unreasonable search under the Fourth Amendment, then it's highly likely that those boundaries will be drawn to give police, not the public, the maximum amount of protection and latitude."

In the United States, the protections stemming from *Miranda v. Arizona* have proved more durable. In 2000, the Supreme Court acknowledged that guilty people may sometimes go free because the police blunder with Miranda warnings, but it retained the rule by a vote of seven to two, pointing out that "the warnings have become part of our national culture." The Court has since, however, allowed the police to proceed when they implied that a suspect waived his right to remain silent though he hadn't said so explicitly.

Many commentators, if they had their way, would return to and expand on the approach of the Warren Court. Its rules of criminal procedure were rooted in the recognition that a police officer who breaks the law can ruin someone's life. The Warren Court's checks on government power usually remain the best tools the defense has for challenging the prosecution. Without them, it's hard to see how our criminal justice system would ensure fairness to any degree.

But an influential, unorthodox Harvard law professor named William Stuntz imagined an alternative legal universe. Stuntz wasn't a dyed-in-the-wool conservative, but before his death in 2011, he argued that the decisions of the Warren Court were a series of wrong turns. He said decisions like *Mapp* and *Miranda* freed too many guilty people and did too little to protect the innocent. He blamed these rulings and others for burdening the courts with time-consuming hearings and other proceedings, and thus decreasing the number of trials over the following decades. Stuntz also thought the Warren Court played into the hands of tough-on-crime politicians, from Richard Nixon to Ronald Reagan. These presidents succeeded, he argued, in attacking the justices for focusing on technicalities, which could be used to free the guilty, rather than on the substance of justice. In Stuntz's preferred world, the Supreme Court would attend to safeguarding innocence, setting limits to make punishment proportionate to the offense, and ensuring equal application of the law across race and class.

But that's not the world we live in. The Court never did what Stuntz wanted, so if lower-court judges want to curb government power, they must use the tools they have. All over the country, the police still barge into homes without warrants and ask people incriminating questions without advising them of their rights. The best way to stop them—the most powerful disincentive—is to strip the state of the capacity to build a prosecution on a rotten foundation.

In the Brooklyn gun court, judges didn't often stop prosecutors from using evidence obtained by the police. Often it's hard to tell whether the police conducted a search legally; it comes down to who you believe, the cop or the suspect (one reason for police officers to wear body cams). Not surprisingly, many judges tend to give the police the benefit of the doubt. But Debora Silberman had won one such ruling in another case of gun possession like Kevin's, so she felt hopeful about Judge Mullen's impending decision as she walked out of the courtroom.

Judge Mullen didn't have the power to order Teitelman and Pieters to reduce the charges against Kevin; she couldn't refuse to impose a mandatory prison sentence if he was convicted. But if she told the D.A.'s office that it couldn't use Kevin's statement at trial, she would weaken their case, increasing Silberman's leverage. And if the judge refused to admit the gun itself, the D.A.'s office would have no choice but to dismiss the case entirely. In the gun court and elsewhere, the ability to suppress evidence was perhaps the greatest power judges had over prosecutors.

In a small conference room off the hallway, Kevin sat down to talk with Silberman and Rebecca Kinsella, his social worker from Brooklyn Defender Services. In a lot of places, this meeting wouldn't have happened: Kevin would have had a lawyer with hundreds of clients, no time, and no social worker. Brooklyn Defender Services, however, was in the vanguard of offering holistic representation, with dedicated teams of a lawyer and a social worker. In 2018, a large-scale study in the Bronx compared holistic defense with the traditional lawyer-only model and made the rare finding of a causal effect—the lawyer–social worker teams reduced the likelihood of a jail or prison sentence by 16 percent and the length of a sentence by 24 percent. The lesson is that the type and quality of defense you get greatly affects your life.

Silberman and Kinsella listened as Kevin told them what he'd wanted to say in court: the gun hadn't slipped down his pants, he insisted. Silberman nodded and then explained that what mattered more, legally speaking, was Officer Joseph's statement that he'd asked Kevin and the others about the gun without a Miranda warning when they were effectively in custody.

"The most important thing is that the judge reserved making her decision" about whether to suppress the evidence, Silberman told him. "When there's a legal issue they think is clear-cut, they just decide on the spot. She didn't do that. That's good for us."

Silberman hoped the hearing, and its outcome, would make the prosecutors receptive to the pleas for mercy she'd been making since Kevin's charging. For all the harshness of the gun court, an escape hatch remained. The Brooklyn D.A.'s office now offered something few cities have been willing to try—diversion for young people charged with crimes the state viewed as violent felonies. Defendants in the gun court between the ages of sixteen and twenty-three could apply for a year-long program called Youth and Congregations in Partnership, or YCP. The rules were strict: nightly curfews, unannounced home visits by the police, random drug testing, and weekly trips to see social workers at the D.A.'s office. But if participants could abide by YCP's rules to the satisfaction of the prosecutors and the judge, they earned the complete dismissal of their convictions, which would then be sealed. Kevin could go to prison for years and come out with a violent felony record, or he could get a second chance. But YCP screened only a small fraction of the gun court defendants and rejected more than half of the young people who were referred to it. In her efforts to persuade Teitelman and her assistants to consider Kevin for the program, Silberman had gotten nowhere so far.

From the prosecutors' point of view, every YCP participant represented a risk. While diversion had become fairly standard for young adults charged with misdemeanors like shoplifting, violent felony charges—whether or not they were based on evidence of actual violence—were an entirely different matter. The New York Police Department urged zero tolerance for gun offenders and wanted to shut YCP down. In the D.A.'s office, the danger that something would go wrong with the program had a name: Tyrone Howard. In 2009, Howard was suspected of participating in a shoot-out with a rival drug dealer on a crowded basketball court in East Harlem, in which two bystanders were injured, but he went unprosecuted when witnesses couldn't say for certain that he'd fired a gun. A few years later, the police caught him on the streets smoking PCP, with two dozen bags of crack in his pockets; not long after that, Howard sold crack to an undercover officer. His record also included an armed robbery conviction. In spite of it all, he received outpatient drug treatment, a form of diversion, instead of prison. "I'm putting some trust in you," said the judge, who didn't know about the shoot-out. "Please don't disappoint me." Months later, Howard shot a New York City police officer in the head. The *New York Post* blamed the prosecutor as well as the judge in a story with the blaring headline "How Accused Cop Killer Dodged Prison for Freedom Before Fatal Shooting."

Tyrone Howard's shadow fell over everyone in the D.A.'s office, all the way up to Eric Gonzalez, Brooklyn's new district attorney. A career prosecutor raised in the poor neighborhoods of East New York and Williamsburg in the 1970s and 1980s, when crack vials littered the streets and violence tormented the neighborhood, Gonzalez grew up close to people who were killed and with friends who were sent to prison—and came back the worse for it. He wanted to be a reformer, but he was feeling his way, sensitive to what the next

Tyrone Howard would mean. "I read every day nationally in the paper about how much time people get, and it seems excessive to me," Gonzalez told me. "But if I do something different, then eventually someone will get out and do something horrible, and that's when I'll need advocates."

Teitelman knew how precarious the politics of diversion could be. Would she gamble on Kevin by putting him into a diversion program? And if she did, would he make it through? Diversion for violent felonies was a gamble. Kevin's fate, along with many other people's, was bound up in the success or failure of the experiment.

In an effort to prove himself worthy, Kevin had been taking GED classes and meeting regularly with his social worker at Brooklyn Defender Services. He still needed to prove to the D.A.'s office that he could handle the program's rules.

"Keep going to school!" Silberman urged. "This is a team effort. You're holding up your end of the bargain. Keep it up."

From kindergarten through eighth grade, Kevin attended a public school where less than 10 percent of the students received a passing score on New York's assessment tests for language arts and math, compared with an average of more than 30 percent in the city's schools at large. From there, he went to four different high schools, bouncing from one to the next when he got in trouble for fighting. "I always liked school, actually," he told Silberman, "but I had problems. I got kicked out of class, but when I was going to class I was paying attention."

At the last high school Kevin attended, in his final semester, he got into another fight and was expelled. That was the end of the road for his education. His failure to graduate weighed on him. "I had thirty-nine credits," he lamented more than once on Facebook. "Passed all my Regents and was gone graduate in January . . . I could have been in college Right Now." When he took the test for placing into his GED class after his arrest, he posted about it with optimism. "Aced that shit with flying colors they putting me inna top class I should be getting my GED quicker than I expected."

It was a tug-of-war in his head always, though, between achieving in the outside world and maintaining his cred among the young men he knew in Brownsville. He wanted to give people a reason to see him as more than his spotty school record and his rap sheet, but he also had to act hard, which meant upholding the protocol of the street rather than questioning it. Anything else was too dangerous. "Don't talk behind my back & pull up on me," he warned on Facebook in the week before his hearing. "Stop playing with me." On another day, he sounded grim and fatalistic: "Getting tired of this shit sometimes. Fuck it though. These the consequences behind the life we choose to live."

One of those consequences was taking the gun charge for Chris, and while Silberman was trying to wipe out his admission of responsibility, Kevin had gotten a lot of respect for what he had done. "People said, 'You held it down,'" he told me later. "They took me out to eat, took me to a club, gave me money. They're like, 'You your own man.'"

Kevin took some pride in this while recognizing it as a kind of trap. "To keep someone out of jail, I messed up my own life," he said. The only clear way to avoid falling down the hole, though, was to steer clear of it in the first place. Kevin's younger brother was doing just that. "To get to my house from the train, you don't have to go through the projects. So my brother will come home and go straight to the house. He's more inside than me. If he comes out, 110 percent he's in the rec center playing basketball."

Kevin had also played a lot of basketball when he was younger. But the rec center court had opened just a few years earlier, so it hadn't been available when he was younger. Kevin thought this could explain the difference between his life and his brother's. Maybe if he'd grown up with a safe place to play, where he didn't have to worry about protecting himself from rivals in the other projects, he wouldn't have been outside getting jumped and arrested for fighting back. His brother often walked around with a basketball under his arm, and Kevin tried to protect him from getting pulled into fights or the beefing between the projects. "I always told him to just keep walking" if someone bothers him. "Don't feel you have to do nothing. That's not for you."

On that December day in court, Kevin talked to Kinsella and Silberman about extracting himself from Brownsville's grip. Maybe he could go to college, too. It wasn't too late. "All the games is done," he said. "It shoulda been done by now. I gotta finish school." A wishful look flitted across his face. "I'm eager to be better."

Kinsella told Kevin she believed in him. Silberman told him once again to follow through on school and reminded him that Judge Mullen had promised an answer about the prosecution's evidence in time for his next court date. That was six weeks away.

3

BAIL

NOURA SPENT HER first days in jail without a bra or warm clothes. She lay in her top bunk, freezing, with a cellmate who had been accused of stabbing her boyfriend. It was hard to think clearly. "I couldn't wrap my mind around what was happening to me," she said. She didn't have money for the commissary, so she washed her hair with soap and brushed her teeth with prison-issue toothpaste, a clear gel that some people used as glue to fix their shoes. The women around her seemed more competent and adult: she didn't even know her own social security number. After a few days, someone gave her a thermal underwear top, and she ventured into the tiny rec yard with two women who seemed friendly. They read her passages from the Bible.

On the single television in the unit, updates on Noura's arrest played on the news. Watching, she saw herself through the eyes of a viewer: a wild child, accused of stabbing her mother fifty times. It was unreal and horrifying and maddening. "When my best friend, Anna, died," she said, "my mother gave me a way of thinking about grief: S-A-R-A-H. First you go through sadness, then anger, resentment, acceptance, and healing. In jail, at the beginning, the anger was what drove me."

One morning in those early weeks, a guard came to Noura's cell and told her she had a visitor: a local attorney named Valerie Corder. Noura had never heard Corder's name before, but she needed a lawyer. She felt a rush of relief as Corder introduced herself and they sat down to talk in a small meeting room.

Valerie Corder opened her own law practice in 1988, when her children were in pre-kindergarten and elementary school. She soon became one of the most sought-after divorce lawyers in Memphis and also handled other kinds of civil suits. Corder relished a court battle, and she took on a limited number of criminal cases. A copy of the Bill of Rights hung in her laundry room. "It's easier for me to wield the sword than sheathe it," she liked to say.

Corder lived in an affluent part of East Memphis, not far from the middle-class neighborhood where the Jackson home sat, on a street of brick and clapboard homes with lawns near a botanic garden. She knew the schools Noura attended and the church Jennifer belonged to. Since the murder, she'd followed news of the investigation. She told Noura that when she heard the TV report of Noura's arrest, it didn't sound right. Why were the police making an arrest without waiting for the DNA results? "She said I needed help and she was the person to help me," Noura said. Corder put it to me this way: "Everyone was so willing to believe the worst of Noura. She had no one to stand up for her."

Noura decided she wanted Corder to represent her. She had a pressing question at that first meeting: could Corder get her out of jail? After an arrest, a defendant is entitled to a hearing about whether he or she may go free before trial. At this point, everyone is presumed innocent, and years can elapse between an arrest and a trial. Noura's bail hearing before a judge had yet to be scheduled. In most states, judges are supposed to weigh whether an accused person poses a danger if she's released, and whether she can be trusted to return to court. In the United States, these questions of liberty are often converted into a calculation about money: should the court set bail, and if so, how high?

The answers to those questions—who has to pay bail, and how much—usually determine who stays in jail and who gets out. Bail is the first domino in a series of decisions affecting guilty pleas and penalties, so it's not an exaggeration to say that whether it's afford-able or not can shape the outcome of a criminal case—and even the rest of a defendant's life. Yet the decision is often made in a few minutes or less, based on the scant information presented early on at an arraignment hearing. Prosecutors speak first, one more advan-tage for them. They draw on the facts in the arrest warrant and rap sheet, reducing the defendant to the police account of what he or she did wrong.

Amy Weirich asked Judge Craft to deny Noura bail entirely. Tennessee law required the setting of bail unless the prosecution sought the death penalty, so Weirich's stance was purely symbolic. Weirich was signaling that Noura should be treated as the worst kind of killer—and that if Judge Craft set any amount that Noura could pay, he'd face the headlines on his own. Corder, appearing for Noura, thought she had no chance of winning her client's release. She asked Judge Craft to postpone his decision. From then on, the press ominously described Noura as "held without bond."

In theory, Judge Craft had the power to ignore Weirich and release Noura on bail she could afford. In practice, judges almost never defy the prosecution by setting low bail when a crime involves sex or vio-lence. Judges may release a defendant arrested for a petty offense when a prosecutor requests bail of under $1,000, because the low amount signals that the case isn't important. But when the charges are more serious, the fear of headlines (the specter of Tyrone Howard) looms larger than the presumption of innocence.

This is dismaying. A judge's fear of political backlash shouldn't play a prominent role in the decision to set bail. The job of a judge is to be above politics. But especially when judges have to run for election—as 90 percent of state judges do—political calculations inevitably come into play. "The judge can't help thinking, 'If I let this person out and something bad happens, I'm on the hook for this,'" said Insha Rahman, a former defense attorney who studies bail at the Vera Institute of Justice in New York. A judge who lets out a defendant over the objections of a prosecutor is especially vulnerable. And so judges rarely do so.

In communities like Brownsville, families would go to great lengths to pay bail in order to keep their relatives out of Rikers. At Kevin's arraignment, after he'd spent sixty-nine hours in a holding cell at Brooklyn central booking, prosecutors asked for bail of $20,000. The judge set that amount, giving Kevin's mother a choice. She could pay the full amount at the bail window in the courthouse and get it back at the end of the case (as long as Kevin didn't skip out on the court). Or she could pay a premium of 10 percent, or $2,000, to a bail company, which would guarantee the full amount—without actually putting down any money with the court. The bail company would keep the $2,000 at the end of the case as long as Kevin made his court appearances. The company could ask for additional collateral, like the title to a property or more money, which it was obligated to return at the end, though Kevin knew people who'd never gotten their money back. If Kevin jumped bail by failing to return to court, his mother would be indebted to the bail company for $18,000 more. (Bail agents were supposed to hand over that money to the court, but in 2011, they owed the city $2 million worth of payments people forfeited in 150 cases over the previous decade.)

Kevin's mother asked if she could put the $20,000 on her credit card. The judge said no, as judges do in New York in 97 percent of cases. Kevin's mother thought she could raise all the money in time, but that meant letting her son sit at Rikers Island, a place of unrelenting violence, with thousands of assaults a year and an alarming rate of solitary confinement. Kevin's mother didn't want him to go there, so she called a bail agency, paid the premium, and brought Kevin home.

When judges set bail, the amount a prosecutor requests sets the baseline and often matters more than anything else. The influence of prosecutors was apparent in a study by the New York City Criminal Justice Agency (CJA). It's the job of CJA to make bail decisions more dispassionate. Staff members review a defendant's criminal history and record of court appearances, then recommend release or a level of bail that is based on their assessment of the likelihood that the person will return to court and refrain from committing another offense. Yet judges often set bail higher than CJA recommends, locking up thousands of people even though the evidence shows it would be safe to release them. To find out why, CJA sent observers to two thousand bail hearings in Brooklyn and Manhattan and found that the prosecution's bail request "was the only important factor in the amount of bail set." Tracking cases over time, CJA's recommendations predicted the risk of flight and rearrest more accurately than did prosecutors' recommendations on average—but to the judges, that didn't much matter.

Why do we have money bail in the first place? Bail was not originally designed to lock people up. The U.S. Constitution includes the protection against "excessive bail" also found in the English Bill of Rights of 1689. "Excessive bail shall not be required, nor excessive fines imposed," the first part of the Eighth Amendment reads. (The last bit forbids cruel and unusual punishment.) Interpreting the clause banning excessive bail in 1951, in a case called *Stack v. Boyle*, the Supreme Court said bail may be set only as high as "reasonably calculated" to ensure the reappearance in court of the accused. But the standard was too vague to have much impact. In the years that followed, thousands of people remained in jail after arrest, pending trial in major cities and in federal court.

In August 1964, the attorney general of the United States, Robert F. Kennedy, testified before the Senate Judiciary Committee to urge passage of what became the Bail Reform Act. The "problem, simply stated, is this," Kennedy said. "The rich man and the poor man do not receive equal justice in our courts." Kennedy told the story of a man in Pennsylvania who spent fifty-four days in jail for a traffic offense with a maximum penalty of five days because he couldn't afford $300 in bail, and another man in New York who was arrested for robbery, lost his job and his car for want of bail, and turned out to have been the victim of mistaken identity. Two years after Kennedy testified, Congress passed the Bail Reform Act, which sought to prevent people from being "needlessly" jailed "regardless of their financial status." The number of pretrial detainees dropped significantly—by one-third between 1962 and 1971.

As crime rose in the late 1970s and early 1980s, however, so did public concern about violence committed by people who were out of jail awaiting trial. In 1984, Congress amended the Bail Reform Act, instructing federal judges to consider dangerousness in setting bail. For crimes of violence, as well as some drug crimes, the presumption in federal cases would now be confinement, not release. Many states followed with similar laws. In 1987, in the case *United States v. Salerno*, the Supreme Court found it constitutional to detain someone based on the perception of *future* risk of danger. The majority opinion by Chief Justice William Rehnquist appeared to set crucial limits, however, calling liberty before trial "the norm" and detention "the carefully limited exception."

Yet in practice the reverse has become true. In 2016, nearly 60 percent of federal defendants were detained before trial (excluding immigration cases) with an average stay of 255 days behind bars. Between ten million and thirteen million people now churn through America's state and county jails each year. Of the roughly 740,000 held on any given day, about two-thirds are awaiting trial because they can't afford to post bail. Over the last two decades, all of the growth in the jail population has consisted of people detained pretrial. These are people who have been found guilty of nothing and who are supposed to be presumed innocent. The cost of locking them up is nearly $25 million a day. The annual total is $9 billion.

That's a colossal waste considering one of the most startling facts about the American bail system: the amount of money it takes to bring someone back to court is usually no money at all. What's more, over time, jail before trial is associated with more future risk of crime, not less. The evidence for this conclusion has been mounting. In 1992, Washington, D.C., effectively got rid of money bail. Ever since, the city has deemed a small percentage of people accused of crimes an unacceptable safety risk (based on their record and the crime they're accused of committing) and sent them to jail while releasing the vast majority before trial. Eighty-eight percent of those who are released make every court appearance. In Kentucky, which also largely doesn't use money bail, the rate of return to court is 85 percent.

Other jurisdictions have experimented with promises to come back to court. In Colorado, unpaid bonds performed as well as paid bonds in terms of court appearances and public safety. In New York City, the Bronx Freedom Fund and the Brooklyn Community Bail Fund have paid bail, in amounts up to $2,000, for thousands of people arrested for misdemeanor offenses like turnstile-jumping and marijuana possession. The recipients sign a pledge to return. They receive reminders of future court dates through phone calls and texts—services that the bail funds regard as critical. About 95 percent make every appearance.

As for the risk that people who've been charged with a crime endanger the public if they're released, it's true that while people sit in jail, they're less likely to cause trouble on the outside. But the trouble prevented appears to be surprisingly small. Of the defendants who are released before trial in Washington, D.C., only 1 percent are arrested for a violent felony while their cases are pending, and only 9 percent are rearrested for any offense at all. The numbers have been about the same for Kentucky.

The results of the biggest-ever bail study are even more telling. In 2016, researchers affiliated with the Quattrone Center for the Fair Administration of Justice at the University of Pennsylvania Law School published a study of bail and detention in more than 380,000 misdemeanor cases in Harris County, Texas (Houston and its suburbs). The analysis showed that the misdemeanor defendants in Harris County who were detained pretrial were 30 percent *more* likely to commit a new felony in the eighteen months after a bail hearing than the people who were released. They were also 20 percent more likely to commit a new misdemeanor. The results seem counterintuitive, but other research has found that jail and prison are "criminogenic"—locking people up makes them prone, on average, to reoffending. They can lose their jobs, housing, and sense of stability, leaving them worse off to the point of desperation.

Ending money bail should be the kind of commonsense measure just about everyone can agree on. It appeals to liberals and conservatives who want to cut government spending on incarceration and minimize "government intrusion into the lives of people who are presumed innocent," as Marc Levin, policy director for the Texas-based group Right on Crime, wrote in 2017. The Charles Koch Foundation gave the Quattrone Center $2.2 million after its study of Harris County. The researchers offered an all-too-vivid illustration of the wasteful, and harmful, nature of unaffordable bail and detention. If the forty thousand people in Harris County who couldn't make bail of $500 had been released instead of held, the state could have prevented four thousand new crimes. Instead, it spent $20 million on four hundred thousand counterproductive days of incarceration.

This is a little like realizing that staying in the hospital exposes some patients to infections that make them sicker. Prosecutors don't set bail but they make the demands for it to which judges accede. And they have the most to gain from locking up people who are waiting for resolution of the criminal charges hanging over them.

The central point is this: in the vast majority of cases, bail doesn't make the public safer and it's not necessary to make sure people come back to court. Its true though unstated function is to keep the wheels of the courthouse—and in the D.A.'s office—turning with quick guilty pleas. In Harris County, people who sat in jail because they couldn't make bail were 25 percent more likely to plead guilty than those who committed similar offenses but were released. The effect of pretrial detention on conviction was twice as great for first-time defendants, suggesting that they were particularly eager—or desperate—to cut a deal. In the end, it's not complicated. *Jails serve as plea mills.* When people are faced with the choice of waiting in jail for months or pleading guilty and getting out, it's not surprising that they often take the deal.

Defendants who plead guilty to get out of jail lose the chance of an acquittal—and the even greater chance that the charges against them will be dropped. In many states, up to a quarter of criminal cases end in dismissal. But dismissals usually take time. While they sit in jail before trial, defendants stand to lose an average of $30,000 in earnings and government benefits. The short-term costs make it hard for people, wanting their freedom, to accurately weigh the consequences of a conviction and a criminal record.

Dismissals take time because a busy prosecutor often takes a cursory look at the evidence at the outset, digging deep only when a trial becomes a real possibility. Delay often serves a defendant's interest, and if you're out on bail, it's easier to wait. "If you're not in custody because you have money to pay your bond, you have a lot of power to extend things," a former Memphis prosecutor explained. "You can have your lawyer file motions and keep resetting the date for trial. You can make it difficult for the state to keep witnesses and victims involved. But on the flip side, say you're in jail because you couldn't make your bond. We offer you six months if you plead guilty. It'll take nine months before you can even think about getting to trial. What does it take to sit in jail, even if you don't think we can prove you did anything wrong?"

Pretrial detention, because of bail that people can't pay, is an axe that falls more than it rationally should on people of color. In a 2017 paper for the National Bureau of Economic Research, a group of economists (controlling for other factors) found significant racial bias in the bail decisions of judges in Philadelphia and Miami. The evidence suggested that the judges were "relying on inaccurate stereotypes that exaggerate the relative danger of releasing black defendants." The reason didn't appear to be simple: the bail calculations of black judges were skewed along with those of white judges, with both groups overestimating the risk that black defendants would commit new violent crimes. Interestingly, more experienced bail judges were less susceptible to the stereotyping trap. "Training or on-the-job feedback" could help, the study authors wrote. Without that kind of cure, though, the burden of pretrial detention will continue to fall too often on African Americans.

Kevin's mother paid the bail agency she hired, Affordable Bails, several hundred dollars in fees. She shielded Kevin from the burden of the payments by not talking about it. Kevin agreed that as long as his case lasted, he would call an automated number each week so the company would know he hadn't skipped town. He was also supposed to show up at the office in person after every court date.

It's easy to see why people strive to make bail. And yet the pressure to pay up creates another form of hardship. Bail companies may be allowed to impose fees and interest at the steep rate of payday lenders, straining families to the breaking point. They also introduce a quasi-private character into the criminal justice system, a vigilante whose power, paradoxically, comes from the state: the bail agent.

Bail agents say they play a vital role by keeping watch over defendants and helping to make sure they go back to court. But the evidence doesn't bear that out and it's not how families who deal with them often see it. "After I graduated from law school, I represented low-income tenants in eviction cases," a lawyer named Gina Clayton told me. "Many were black women who had a close relative in prison. One of the first things they talked about, over and over again, was the bail industry. Women were struggling to decide whether to put up their homes or whatever collateral they had to bail someone out. And if not, they would get into predatory relationships with bail bondsmen."

In 2018, the *New York Times* published a story about a man named Ronald Egana whose bail agent arrested him on his way into court. The agent took Egana to his company's office in handcuffs and demanded $1,500 in what he said were overdue payments. If Egana had been able to pay his $26,000 bail in full, he would have gotten the money back when he returned to court. Instead, the bail agent charged a $3,275 unrecoverable fee, and then $10 a day for an ankle bracelet that the judge hadn't ordered. The *Times* catalogued other kinds of gouging, like a $1,000 courier's fee to walk a bail payment a few blocks to the courthouse.

The United States and the Philippines are the only nations in the world that allow for-profit bond companies to operate. "In England, Canada and other countries, agreeing to pay a defendant's bond in exchange for money is a crime akin to witness tampering or bribing a juror—a form of obstruction of justice," the *New York Times* reporter Adam Liptak explained. In other words, the rest of the world has outlawed the American bail system. The reasons are manifold. Handing over bail to private businesses, which charge a nonrefundable fee, usurps a public function and invites price gouging and bounty hunting. It's also a cause of corruption, giving private companies an incentive to collude with prosecutors and judges to make sure that bail is set high.

American bail businesses often portray themselves as mom-and-pop shops, community-based and family-run. But they collect an estimated $2 billion a year in profits, and the bonds they issue are increasingly underwritten by a small number of giant multinational corporations, such as Tokio Marine, Japan's largest property and casualty insurer, which has more than $47 billion in annual global revenue. The bail industry has its own lobbying group, the American Bail Coalition, which has kept it afloat in most states.

And yet, notwithstanding the bail industry's political clout, states can end commercial bail when they have the political will to do so. Prosecutors, along with judges and law enforcement, play a crucial role. In different ways, that's been the story in three states: Wisconsin, California, and New Jersey.

Prosecutors fought to keep for-profit bail out of Wisconsin, which barred it back in 1979. Courts there take bail payments themselves and return the money if defendants make their court appearances. Bail companies have tried to push their way back into Wisconsin for more than a decade, and prosecutors, judges, and law enforcement have banded together to fight the industry. Joined by the state's attorney general, a Republican, the Wisconsin District Attorneys Association opposed the latest effort in 2013 to resurrect commercial bail, a bill drafted with the help of the American Legislative Exchange Council (ALEC), the conservative group known for drafting model legislation for Republican legislators around the country. "I was and continue to be very much opposed to the idea," Christian Gossett, the Republican district attorney for Winnebago County, told me. The for-profit bail bill still passed the legislature, but Governor Scott Walker vetoed it.

The story of bail reform in California is more tangled. At the end of 2016, a pair of Democrats, Assemblyman Rob Bonta and State Senator Bob Hertzberg, introduced a bill that would largely eliminate money bail. The median bail amount in the state was five times the national average, and thousands of people were in jail because they couldn't pay their way out. The bail industry also had a corruption problem: in a sweep the previous year, thirty-one bail agents were arrested, after a state investigation prompted by mounting complaints of abuses, including scams, extortion, kidnapping, and fraud.

California's bail practices undercut its liberal self-image, and bail reform gained momentum. Gina Clayton, the lawyer who represented tenants for whom bail was a terrible burden, formed the Essie Justice Group (named for her grandmother) to mobilize women. In May 2017, Clayton helped lead a Mama's Bail Out Day, as part of a coalition that included Black Lives Matter and Color of Change. The groups raised money to get women out of jail. A Father's Day bailout followed, attracting support from Jay-Z and John Legend. Tech entrepreneurs raised hundreds of thousands for a nonprofit bail fund. Suddenly, bail reform was a cause célèbre.

The bail industry hit back. Duane Chapman, star of the long-running reality TV show *Dog the Bounty Hunter*, appeared at a statehouse press conference in Sacramento to rail against reform. His wife, Beth Chapman, president of the Professional Bail Agents of the United States, issued a "Declaration of War" in the group's August newsletter. Behind the scenes, Tokio Marine hired a well-connected California lobbying group, Aaron Read and Associates, which also represented the Peace Officers Research Association of California (PORAC), the state's largest law-enforcement group, with seventy thousand members, and a major player in state politics.

Tokio Marine paid Aaron Read $75,000 to lobby against the bail reform bill. PORAC added nearly $200,000. Groups representing California's sheriffs and police chiefs joined the campaign, as did the California District Attorneys Association, a lobbying arm for prosecutors, which publicly warned of a "negative impact on public safety."

Bonta got the impression that the D.A.s weren't especially fond of the bail industry. "But when the lobbyists from Read and Associates came in and organized a law-enforcement coalition, they were all speaking with one voice," he said. Bonta and Hertzberg's bill passed the state senate but got stuck in the assembly, where some Democrats joined the Republicans in opposition. Governor Jerry

Brown, a Democrat who has historically been hesitant to embrace criminal justice reform, called for a halt on the legislation. California attorney general Xavier Becerra was noncommittal. An ardent liberal on other issues, Becerra had recently received about $11,000 in donations from bail companies.

In January 2018, a California appeals court heard the case of a man who'd been accused of robbing a neighbor in his senior housing complex of $5 and a bottle of cologne, and sat in San Francisco County Jail for more than 250 days because he couldn't pay $350,000 in bail. Pretrial detention of that length, in those circumstances, seems illegitimate on its face. Yet it happened. The appeals court ordered a new bail hearing. "A defendant may not be imprisoned solely due to poverty," the presiding justice, J. Anthony Kline, wrote for the court. Legislation was "desperately needed." That summer, a bill passed in California—but it was different from the legislation of 2016. The new bill eliminated money bail and released people accused of low-level misdemeanors within twelve hours. These were real gains. But for many others charged with a crime, the legislation reversed the presumption of release, giving prosecutors far more leeway to ask for preventive detention and judges far more leeway to order it. The law won the support of the D.A.s and police chiefs but lost some of the civil-rights groups that had fought for the bill for two years. "When bail reform becomes a political flag to wave, it matters less to the legislature whether it does something substantive and meaningful for the community," said Gina Clayton of the Essie Justice Group. "I'd rather see no bail reform than this regressive policy."

On January 1, 2017, New Jersey also essentially ended money bail with a law signed three years earlier by Governor Chris Christie, a former federal prosecutor. The structure of the state government, perhaps more than any other factor, made it possible to end money bail and revamp the pretrial process. Prosecutors in the state are appointed rather than elected. They answer to the New Jersey attorney general, who sets policy across the state. Judges, too, are appointed, and work in a unified court system rather than one subject to the control of individual counties. The state's chief justice, Stuart Rabner, took the lead on bail reform. "Some judges and prosecutors were skeptical, but they could be told to fall into line, and they weren't running for office," said Alex Staropoli, policy manager for the state's Drug Policy Alliance, which helped launch the campaign by showing that on a single day, more than fifteen hundred people were in jail in New Jersey because they couldn't afford to pay bail of $2,500 or less.

New Jersey's law replaced bail agents with state employees whose job was to gauge the likelihood of flight or rearrest. They use a risk assessment tool, which scores each case on two scales of 1 to 6, one based on age, prior convictions, and pending charges and the other on previous records of court appearances. Both scores consider how likely the defendant is to commit a new violent crime.

In the first year after the reforms, the jail population dropped significantly while crime, including violent offenses, also fell. Judges detained only 6 percent of all people arrested—the same rate as Washington, D.C.—putting bond agents out of business. "It's as big a change as when the dinosaurs left the earth," Dawn Simonetti, the supervising prosecutor for domestic violence cases in Newark, told me while we watched a new kind of arraignment hearing. As images of people who'd been arrested in the previous twenty-four hours were beamed into the courtroom through videoconferencing from a holding room in the local jail, Simonetti and the assistant prosecutors had to decide whether to request preventive detention until trial. Previously, of course, unaffordable bail had the same effect. But if Simonetti and her assistants opted for detention, they had to show the defense their evidence justifying that within three days. Bail reform was front-loading the system, pushing prosecutors to test the strength of their cases earlier. Some of them said that as they delved into the circumstances of more defendants, they were becoming more aware of factors like mental illness. "A guy punched a priest in a church," said Quovella Spruill, the prosecutor in charge of the investigative unit. "At his detention hearing, he started talking about the Antichrist. Before, we wouldn't have known about that, because he wouldn't have had this type of hearing." Another top prosecutor in Newark, Clara Rodriguez, put it this way: "We're seeing more of what the public defenders see" about the lives of their clients. "We knew we had mental illness, but now we're getting a window into it earlier."

Observing domestic violence cases in Newark, I wondered if the prosecutors' greater awareness translated into better outcomes, like faster dismissals of questionable charges, from the point of view of defense lawyers. "Are we seeing the benefits of better results faster? The short answer is yes," Joseph Krakora, New Jersey's chief public defender, told me. (The state public defender system is also centralized.) "Listen, if you told me before January 1, 2017, this is where we'd be a year and a half later, I'd never have believed you. I didn't believe judges could get away from the culture of money bail. But we've seen money bail in only around forty out of tens of thousands of cases." (The exact number in 2017 was forty-four.) "The judges just stopped doing it. Overall, I think it's remarkable. I couldn't be a bigger proponent. I was first hired by this office in 1986. All those years of seeing judges set bail in relatively minor cases. You'd get up and say, 'I've spoken to Mr. Smith and family, they can only post $1,000, and he only has one prior nonviolent conviction,' and the judge would set bail at $2,000, and your client went to jail. The decision felt so unfair, but I never thought of it as a fundamental problem with the system itself. That's what it is, though. Predicating freedom before trial on your wealth is just fundamentally unfair to poor people. I can't see ever going back to that."

As Noura sat in jail, the days ticked away. She moved from the intake unit to a pod for women who had been charged with serious crimes. They were confined to a two-level enclosure, with a catwalk and sixteen cells along the top and sixteen along the bottom. In the middle were metal tables for meals. Along one wall were phones and a door that led to a tiny rec yard. Noura liked her cellmate, who sang and played basketball. She'd been accused of armed robbery.

As winter turned to spring and her nineteenth birthday neared, Noura felt she was losing control of her case and her life. "When I think back to that time, it's almost like talking about myself in the third person," she told me years later. "It was so horrifying." The jailhouse physician prescribed a regimen of antianxiety medication and antidepressants. The drugs made Noura gain weight and dulled her senses. Friends like Ansley Larsson and Bill Shelton came to see her, and put money in her commissary account. No one from her family visited. She read everything she could borrow from the jail's book cart—*Catcher in the Rye*, and Harlequin novels, and another series of romances by Judith McNaught. She hated wearing orange. She wanted to put her long hair into a ponytail or a bun, but for a time there were no ponytail holders in the commissary. "We ripped the top off rubber gloves to use the elastic to put our hair up. We couldn't wear earrings, so we snapped the teeth off small black plastic combs and put them through the holes in our ears to keep them open." For about six months, she succeeded in hiding the Abercrombie & Fitch T-shirt she'd smuggled in. When the guards finally took it from her during a shakedown, she broke down. "That was my last tie to the free world."

The first date for Noura's trial, in early 2008, came and went, with lawyers on both sides requesting delays. During her second winter in jail, Noura got into a fight, lunging across a table one day at a woman who told her she'd wind up as "a dyke in prison" because "you killed your motherfucking mama." She came away with bloody scratches and a patch of her hair ripped out. Her punishment was being placed on "deadlock": for a month she had no access to a phone, visits, a television, or the commissary; for nine months she was held in solitary confinement twenty-three hours a day.

When Noura got back into the general population, she was desperate to interact with people and to get out of the small part of the jail she'd been restricted to for more than two years. "I had to get out of that box," she said. Some people had jobs in the laundry room, in an adjacent wing, or farther afield, in the kitchen, the medical unit, or the intake area. To be cleared for work, you had to have a bond set, according to the jail's rules. Noura begged Corder to ask Judge Craft for a bond hearing. It was finally scheduled for February 2008, two and a half years after her arrest.

Corder warned Noura not to get her hopes up. But Noura couldn't help imagining that maybe, given the time she'd already served, Judge Craft would see his way to letting her go. She was afraid her aunts would arrive in court to speak against her petition. When they didn't show as the hearing began, Noura's hopes rose.

Then she heard Weirich ask Judge Craft, again, to deny bail entirely. The prosecutor remained intent on portraying Noura as a dangerous killer, a threat to public safety who should not be allowed even the faintest possibility of release. Judge Craft nodded. He noted that Noura had no support from her family, and mused that releasing her would be "a big question mark," because "she may be a rebellious, out-of-control teenager." It was a great sound bite for the prosecution, picked up by the press.

When it was Noura's turn to speak, she looked Judge Craft in the eye and tried to assure him that she posed no flight risk. If she could make bail, she would live with Bill Shelton. "The only important people left in my life live here," she told the judge. "I have no one else."

In that moment, looking at Judge Craft, she still had a "little-girl feeling" of hope. The tangle of her life could still be straightened out. It could all come out right.

Judge Craft set Noura's bond at $500,000, the maximum that he could impose while allowing Noura to work in jail. It was far beyond Noura's ability to pay. But she didn't need to do that to get a job in the laundry. She just needed a number on a piece of paper. Looking back, Noura said, "I just felt grateful."

In the middle distance, though, her trial hovered, a gathering cloud.

4

GUN COURT

ON JANUARY 12, 2016, Mayor Bill de Blasio stood at a podium covered in blue velvet and bearing New York City's seal. "We announce today a tremendous step forward in our work to drive down crime in this city," de Blasio declared. Behind him stood a dozen law enforcement officials. They included the city's police commissioner, William Bratton; the district attorney for Manhattan, Cy Vance; and the district attorney for Brooklyn, Ken Thompson. "I want the people in New York City, who get to see these pictures, to realize these are the people who keep you safe every day, all in one room, which is a rarity," de Blasio said.

The mayor's new initiative, called Project Fast Track, was designed to speed up and strengthen the prosecution of gun possession cases in New York. With a consolidated division of two hundred, mostly detectives, the police department would assign an officer to every unlicensed gun they recovered, and that officer would stay on the case from start to finish. Describing the people Project Fast Track would target, de Blasio chose to echo the lock-'em-up rhetoric politicians have used to sow fear since the days of Barry Goldwater and Richard Nixon. These were the city's "remaining evildoers," de Blasio said, "truly bad actors who account for so much of the gun violence." It was the old demonizing language coming from New York's first Democratic mayor in twenty years. He wanted people caught with guns punished more severely. "I believe there are too many situations where someone who belonged in prison didn't get to prison, or someone who didn't belong on the streets remained on the streets."

De Blasio promised to "fast-track" gun cases through the system, in theory a reasonable goal. The initiative would begin in Brooklyn, he announced, with "a new dedicated gun court to handle those cases within six months." The police commissioner spoke next, and the mayor then turned to Ken Thompson, thanking him by name and calling him to the podium.

Thompson was Brooklyn's first African American D.A. He'd won election three years earlier as an outsider—a former federal prosecutor with his own successful private practice. He attacked the incumbent, Joe Hynes, for miring the D.A.'s office in scandal. After more than twenty years in office, Hynes had been forced to order a sweeping review of more than fifty cases handled by a former star detective whose work he had long and fiercely defended. Evidence mounted of the detective's disturbing pattern of fabricating confessions and pressuring witnesses to make false identifications. Defeating Hynes, Thompson swept into office at age forty-seven as the first candidate to take out an incumbent D.A. in Brooklyn in more than a century. Bespectacled and earnest, he garnered praise and media attention by pledging to stop prosecuting most low-level marijuana offenses, forgive old misdemeanor summonses, and build the country's largest unit for reviewing past convictions.

Thompson started out on the wrong foot with the cops, who were leery of his early pronouncements. For all the power prosecutors have, it's a truism that a D.A. antagonizes the police at his or her political peril. Bratton publicly brushed off Thompson's plan to reduce marijuana prosecutions and privately undermined it. In the months leading up to de Blasio's announcement of Project Fast Track, the police went after Thompson on guns, accusing him of lax enforcement of the city's strict laws and embarrassing him by going around his office to route gun cases to federal prosecutors in the U.S. attorney's office.

The police also challenged Thompson by pushing to end the diversion programs—namely, YCP and a second one called Project Redirect—that gave defendants like Kevin the chance to avoid prison. The NYPD's position was that "offering young, gun-toting people any chance at diversion is a failure of the criminal justice system," according to a *New York Times* story that publicized the simmering antagonism. The article featured the photos and stories of Tyrone Howard and of a sixteen-year-old convicted of being an accomplice to the shooting of a rival gang member while he was in Project Redirect. "The message that we want to get out is very clear," said Dermot Shea, then a deputy police commissioner. "If you carry a gun in New York City, we will be relentless in following you."

Diversion for gun offenders predated Thompson, but he wanted to expand the programs, not shut them down. Diversion programs were essential to his plan for considering the cases of young defendants individually and showing some of them mercy in light of their stage of development and the circumstances of their lives. Behind the scenes with the police and in the *Times*, Thompson pushed back. "I believe that it is important to help some of those young men leave those gangs," he said, "because if we don't, they're going to go to prison for a few years at a young age, and they're going to come out and pose more of a problem for us in the community." Thompson acknowledged that some people in the programs would fail. "If we could guarantee 100 percent success in anything we do, obviously that would be ideal. But we're dealing with people. We're dealing with young folks. We invest enormous time and effort in helping these young people in reclaiming their lives. Not because we're soft on crime, but because this is in the best interest of public safety in the long run."

The D.A.'s office had strong results from YCP on its side: none of the fifty-two participants accepted into the program since Thompson took office had been rearrested. The record of the other diversion program, Project Redirect, was mixed: forty-five people had graduated since 2007, and four of them had since picked up additional felony convictions. Another thirty-one people failed to complete Project Redirect and went to prison on their original charges.

Brooklyn had a track record of success with diversion, however, that went beyond these two programs. The borough had a higher rate of screening eligible defendants for drug treatment than Manhattan, and those defendants had a far greater chance of receiving it. In the same hallways as the gun court were two specialized courts with the goal of helping people solve their problems rather than punishing them. One was for people with serious mental health problems and the other was for those in need of drug treatment. In these courtrooms, judges showed forbearance for people who didn't follow their directives.

Another problem-solving court, the Red Hook Community Justice Center, opened in 2000 and included a housing court, where residents could get help negotiating repairs and rent payments, as well as mental health and drug treatment courts. A 2013 study found that people whose cases were handled in Red Hook were far less likely to wind up in jail and had a 10 percent lower rate of reoffending than those whose similar misdemeanor cases were processed downtown. Red Hook defendants were also far less likely to walk away with the quick-and-dirty sentence of time served or a fine. Instead, drug offenders were ordered into treatment and prodded to follow through.

On the day I visited Red Hook, a young man charged with shoplifting and possession of heroin stood up for his 106th court appearance. He was at eye level with the presiding judge, Alex Calabrese, who'd asked to have the height of the bench lowered after he began sitting in Red Hook. Two years earlier, the man had agreed to nearly a year of drug treatment, with the promise of a full dismissal of the charges if he completed it. He'd struggled frequently since then, overdosing twice. But the prosecutor's offer of a dismissal remained in place. At this point, he'd tested clean for eight months and had finished his last two weeks of treatment. The defense lawyer choked up as he described his client's journey. As agreed, the prosecutor dismissed the charges.

The young man thanked Judge Calabrese for "believing in me when I didn't believe in myself."

"We gave you the opportunity and the support," Calabrese said. "You did the work."

This was the Brooklyn advantage—a head start for progressive prosecution. To build on it, Thompson tapped Eric Gonzalez, at the time his number two.

Gonzalez nurtured a small diversion program offered by a group called Common Justice—one of the only efforts in the country to bring together victims and young adults accused of hurting them and facing violent felony charges like aggravated assault and robbery. Brooklyn could point to the program as a model for restorative justice, which treats restitution and taking responsibility for harm as better alternatives than incarceration, with the potential to make the victim whole and change the perpetrator's life.

In 2016, Gonzalez also helped launch a much larger young adult court for sixteen- to twenty-four-year-olds charged with almost any misdemeanor, including assault, shoplifting, trespassing, and turnstile-jumping. The diversion offerings included conflict resolution, job preparation, drug treatment, and a Native American–style peacemaking circle. The programs were provided by the Center for Court Innovation, the group that also headed up diversion in Red Hook and had been working on alternatives to incarceration in New York since the early 1990s. CCI worked with twelve hundred young adults in the court's first year of operation; the number nearly doubled the following year, to two thousand. The D.A.'s office granted it real authority. "If the social worker says this young man would benefit from conflict resolution, then the line prosecutor will ask for three sessions instead of, say, three days in jail," Gonzalez told me. "If the person completes it, we're not criminalizing someone."

But in the view of the police, it was one thing to be patient with people caught jumping turnstiles and another thing entirely to let people caught with guns go home rather than to prison. They wanted to kill the diversion programs for guns, and they wanted Thompson to support Project Fast Track. He agreed to the second and hung on to YCP and Project Redirect. The deal showed the limits of a D.A.'s political power.

At the January press conference, Thompson did his part. He denounced gun violence "from Brownsville to the South Side of Chicago to the parishes of New Orleans," invoking the sweep of African American history in the cadences of the church. He echoed de Blasio's promise to "move gun cases more quickly," and injected some moral urgency, too, by promising that Project Fast Track would rid Brooklyn of "merchants of death"—gun traffickers from other states who sold weapons on the black market.

How the mayor's initiative would stop gun trafficking was not at all clear. Though nobody mentioned it on the podium that day, the new court wasn't for punishing out-of-state gun sellers. It wasn't even for shooters, or people who made threats with a weapon. It was only for cases in which the top charge (the highest charge the prosecution brought) was simply possession of a gun without a license.

The right to carry a firearm is enshrined in the Second Amendment (according to the Supreme Court) and cherished by many Americans, who often share the belief that as long as you don't have a record of violence and a judge hasn't found you to be mentally unstable, you should be able to have a gun with minimal government oversight. In general, possessing a handgun without a license isn't a crime in most states. *Carrying* one without a permit may be, but some states make exceptions if you're in your own home or someone else's with their permission; others treat it as a misdemeanor, often punished with a fine. Twelve states don't even require a permit to carry a gun in public.

In other words, in many parts of the country, Kevin's crime wasn't a crime at all. Most Americans who get caught with guns they're not licensed to carry don't get hauled off in handcuffs, and they don't end up in prison.

New York's stringent gun-possession laws were largely thanks to de Blasio's predecessor as mayor, Michael Bloomberg. As a national leader of the gun control movement, Bloomberg wanted Congress to ban assault rifles and rapid-fire magazine clips. He wanted to close the federal loopholes that allow for gun purchases without background checks. But Congress did none of those things. Instead, from the mid-2000s onward, gun control effectively became a state-level issue. In New York, the movement's most potent legacy was tough mandatory prison sentences for gun possession.

Bloomberg teamed up with Governor George Pataki and successfully lobbied the state legislature to reclassify the simple possession of an illegal loaded gun as criminal possession of a weapon in the second degree, or CPW2. That was the maximum charge for gun possession that Kevin faced, with a mandatory minimum sentence of three and a half years and maximum of fifteen years. The new classification meant that if you were caught with a loaded gun outside your home or place of business in New York City, and you didn't have a license for it from New York State as well as approval from the NYPD, prosecutors could charge CPW2. When prosecutors dropped down a level, to criminal possession of a weapon in the third degree, a conviction still meant a mandatory minimum sentence of two years, with a maximum of seven. In the eyes of the state, these crimes counted as violent felonies, even though the people convicted of them weren't accused of hurting anyone. "New York State is now the toughest place to get caught with an illegal gun," Bloomberg said in July 2007, standing next to a giant poster that read "Guns = Prison."

Ten years later, Ken Thompson was asked to endorse Mayor de Blasio's crackdown on guns and the people who have them. He wasn't the first black prosecutor, or politician, facing that choice.

After the Civil War, black people fought for the right to own guns to defend themselves from white violence and political oppression. When Reconstruction lifted the bans in southern states that prohibited slaves and free black people from having firearms, they armed themselves. "I would say to every colored soldier, 'Bring your gun home,'" a freedman in Louisiana advised. "Remember there are 80,000 black men in the state who can bear Winchester rifles and know how to use them," a petition signed by black citizens of South Carolina declared when whites tried to scare them away from voting in 1876. The civil rights activist Ida B. Wells urged the black community to arm itself in the face of lynchings. In the 1960s, members of the Student Nonviolent Coordinating Committee talked about shotguns and rifles as indispensable for black households in the South.

Malcolm X tapped into this tradition when he called for self-protection "by whatever means necessary." The Black Panthers bought some of their first guns by selling Mao's Little Red Book to college students. In 1967, thirty members of the group protested on the steps of the California statehouse, bearing revolvers, shotguns, and pistols. The day after Reverend Martin Luther King Jr. was assassinated the following year, the black nationalist Stokely Carmichael declared, "Black people know that they have to get guns." Carmichael's group, the Black United Front, opposed all forms of restrictions on gun ownership in Washington, D.C., calling them a tool of white racists.

Yet a few years later, black politicians taking control of a few majority-black cities saw gun restrictions in a very different light, as

Yale law professor James Forman Jr. recounts in *Locking Up Our Own: Crime and Punishment in Black America*. The city leaders were wrestling with problems that at root were economic. With crime continuing to rise in the 1970s, urban areas suffered a simultaneous loss of jobs, as manufacturers moved their factories to places with cheaper labor. Some black residents increasingly feared the threat of violence carried out by the young men of their communities. African American leaders had to decide whether to enforce gun restrictions on their own people.

In the 1970s, black leaders in Washington, Atlanta, and Detroit backed mandatory minimum sentences for gun possession. As Forman points out, they did not see sending gun carriers to prison as the main answer to violence or other urban problems. They lobbied for resources to address poverty and improve the health, job prospects, and education of their citizens. What they got, however, was criminal prosecution of their own people. The national gun market continued to grow but the root causes of violence went inadequately addressed.

In the 1990s, Eric Holder, Barack Obama's future attorney general, became the first African American U.S. attorney for Washington, D.C. As the city's chief prosecutor, Holder's solution to the menace of gun violence was, essentially, stop-and-frisk for drivers. He asked the police to pull people over in high-crime areas, which were predominantly black, whenever they thought a car looked suspicious. The goal was to look for guns. If the police found one, prosecutors asked for jail time. Studies generally showed that for every gun the police recovered in a car stop, twenty to a hundred drivers were stopped unnecessarily. "The people who will be stopped will be young black males, overwhelmingly," Holder acknowledged. He told the police not to doubt the justice of their work. "Young black males are 1 percent of the nation's population but account for 18 percent of the nation's homicides. You all are saving lives, not just getting guns off the street." He was even more pointed at a 1995 birthday celebration for Martin Luther King Jr. held in a hotel ballroom filled with an audience of a thousand people. "Did Martin Luther King successfully fight the likes of Bull Connor so that we could ultimately lose the struggle for civil rights to misguided or malicious members of our own race?" Holder asked.

Time and again, politicians have offered the following trade-off to urban black communities: *To make you safer, we have to stop more of your young men on the streets and put them in prison if they get near a gun.* Meanwhile, the empirical evidence strongly suggests that mandating prison for carrying a gun has not reduced violence. In 1997, for example, federal and state law authorities collaborated on Project Exile in Richmond, Virginia, prosecuting former felons for gun possession under federal law, which set mandatory five-year sentences rather than the lighter state penalties. At first, Project Exile was hailed as a success. But a rigorous evaluation by the economists Steven Raphael and Jens Ludwig later found it did almost nothing to reduce murder or other felonies. Homicides did fall by 40 percent in Richmond between 1997 and 1998, but the decline, according to Steven Levitt, another economist, was "greatly exaggerated because the 1997 rate was itself an aberration—up 30 percent from 1996 even though the trend in Richmond and elsewhere has been persistently downward." In addition, "crime rates were falling everywhere and falling more steeply in high-crime places." Raphael and Ludwig noted that a larger lesson of Project Exile was "the apparent tendency of the public to judge any criminal justice intervention implemented during a period of increasing crime as a failure, while judging those efforts launched during the peak or downside of a crime cycle as a success." Subsequently, other studies of mandatory minimum sentences for gun possession, in Florida, Massachusetts, and Michigan, also found no deterrent effect.

Nevertheless, when more than five hundred people were killed in Chicago in 2012, more than in any other U.S. city that year, Mayor Rahm Emanuel proposed three-year mandatory minimum sentences for guns, like New York's. Chicago's chief prosecutor at the time,

Anita Alvarez, welcomed the bill. African American leaders waged an uphill battle against it. "We spent four years in a row fighting that mandatory minimum gun bill," Mariame Kaba, a co-founder of the Chicago Taskforce on Violence Against Girls and Women who has since become a researcher in residence at Barnard College, told me. "They kept trying to push it through. We organized press conferences and teach-ins, we did social media campaigns, local visits with the alderpeople and legislators, we tried to talk to the NRA—all sorts of different strategies. Mandatory minimums don't work, and they're racist. But still the same failed policies from the past get repeated as though they are brand new."

Most experts agreed. "There is no credible evidence that mandatory sentences lead to crime reduction," argued a report by the Bluhm Legal Clinic at Northwestern Law School before laying out the relevant research. Surprisingly, however, Jens Ludwig, the director of the University of Chicago Crime Lab—and a coauthor of the study that deflated the claims of success for the mandatory gun possession sentences of Project Exile—argued for "increasing the consistency or certainty of sanctions" to "help decrease gun carrying through deterrence." It was an odd claim to make in Chicago, since 75 percent of defendants sentenced for gun possession were already bound for prison. Franklin Zimring, a respected criminologist at the University of California at Berkeley, took apart the weak argument for deterrence in an op-ed in the *Chicago Sun-Times*. "The backgrounds and motives of people who commit gun-carrying offenses—and their danger to the community—are too varied for a mandatory minimum penalty to be fair and reasonable," he wrote. "The mandatory minimum proposal is a temper tantrum masquerading as an act of government."

This time, lawmakers rejected Guns = Prison. Black legislators in Illinois led the way to stopping Emanuel's bill, saying they wanted safe streets but not more incarceration. A small window had opened for recognizing an uncomfortable parallel between the racially disparate enforcement of drug laws and the racially disparate enforcement of gun laws. In her 2010 book *The New Jim Crow*, Michelle Alexander indicted the war on drugs as a tool of racial oppression. Since the 1980s, when arrests and incarceration for drugs skyrocketed, people of color have been arrested and prosecuted for drug crimes more than white people even though their rates of drug use are no higher. The crime of gun possession upholds the same system of racial domination: black people are arrested for it four times as often as white people, even though their reported rate of gun ownership is lower—24 percent compared with 36 percent for whites.

The justification for mandatory prison for gun possession is the same as the justification for the war on drugs: harsh punishment prevents greater harm. The crisis is real. Guns are the leading cause of death for African American men between the ages of fifteen and thirty-four. About half of murder victims and perpetrators are African American. Some sociologists have come to see gun violence as a "social contagion" and a terrible public health problem. One study in Chicago found that 70 percent of gunshot victims had a particular kind of shared network: they'd all been arrested with at least one other person in the group. The overlap was strongest for young black men. The people who get hurt and the people who are in trouble with the law—they don't neatly sort into separate boxes. Violence and victimization overlap.

Mandatory prison sentences for gun possession are a costly answer to all the attendant loss. These sentences fuel "a different kind of violence: the banishment and isolation of large numbers of people, especially people of color and poor people," Maya Schenwar, executive director of the progressive news organization Truthout, argued in the wake of the Chicago debate. James Forman called this the worst of both worlds. "Guns—and gun violence—saturate our inner cities," he wrote, "while the people who go to prison for possessing guns are overwhelmingly black and brown."

Once Mayor Bloomberg left office, with crime down and mass incarceration increasingly of concern to the public, liberals tended to emphasize the tough standards for getting a gun permit rather than the push to send people to prison when they didn't have one. On the other side of the political spectrum, the National Rifle Association didn't spotlight or protest New York's harsh punishments. The NRA preferred to cast gun owners as model citizens, which didn't obviously map onto the people who sat on the benches of the Brooklyn gun court. Regional and racial politics factored in. The NRA's core support is white and rural. In Brooklyn, which is one-third African American, 87 percent of the people prosecuted in the gun court were black.

When de Blasio launched Project Fast Track and the Brooklyn gun court to go after the city's "evildoers," he was searching for an alternative to New York's previous policing strategy: stop-and-frisk. In 2013, a federal judge found the NYPD's practice of questioning anyone an officer deemed suspicious—including for a dubious reason like making "furtive movements"—to be a "policy of indirect racial profiling" that violated the constitutional rights of minority residents. Between 2004 and 2012, millions of searches of people of color were conducted at a higher rate than searches of whites, even though the stops of black and Hispanics were less likely to lead to an arrest. "I also conclude that the city's highest officials have turned a blind eye to the evidence that officers are conducting stops in a racially discriminatory manner," Judge Shira Scheindlin wrote.

As the number of police stops plummeted in response to her ruling, the police, and many experts, expected the corresponding drop in arrests to threaten the remarkable strides New York had made in stamping out crime. They were right about one thing: the city was remarkably safer than it had been. Over the previous two decades, the murder rate fell in New York by an astonishing 82 percent (to fewer than four per hundred thousand). The drop was greater than in any other major American city. Assault, robbery, rape, and property crimes all fell in New York, too. But it turned out that New York's crime drop did not depend on stop-and-frisk or on locking up more people. Instead, for years the incarceration rate had been falling alongside crime, to less than half the level of the 1990s. "This is the most spectacular aspect of the New York City crime debate," Mark A. R. Kleiman, a professor of public policy at New York University who directs the school's crime and justice program, told me. "I don't know anyone who would have bet on crime continuing to go down after the reduction of stop-and-frisk. I'd have said it was worth a small bump in shootings to get rid of most of those stops. But it turned out we didn't even have to pay that price."

It's worth pointing out that the decline in incarceration has not kept pace with the drop in crime. Violent crime and property crime in New York are at 1950s levels, while incarceration is stuck where it was in the mid-1980s. In terms of locking fewer people up, the city has a ways to go.

Still, what explains New York's success in reducing crime and incarceration so far? It's a seriously difficult question. The answer includes several contributing factors, some of which involve law enforcement and some of which don't. "There has always been a healthy argument, in the study of crime, that criminal justice institutions"—police, prosecutors, and courts—"aren't the main explanation for variance in crime, across individuals, cities, or time," said Robert Sampson, a sociologist at Harvard. Going back decades, social factors that could be relevant included increased access to abortion (the idea was that after *Roe v. Wade*, fewer babies were born who grew up at higher risk of becoming criminals). The decrease in childhood exposure to lead (as a result of the shift to unleaded gasoline), which lowers IQ, strongly correlates with the drop in crime. There is evidence that increasing access to treatment for drug addiction and mental illness played a role, too.

Theories like these, however, don't account for the different crime rates among cities. In his 2011 book *The City That Became Safe*, Franklin Zimring tested and discarded several sweeping theories specific to New York. Zimring found that broken-windows policing—the city's crackdown on minor offenses like turnstile-jumping and graffiti beginning in the 1990s—did not deserve most of the credit for the crime drop. He essentially ruled out a change in the racial composition of the city. He found a rise in kids growing up with single parents, and little change in the proportion dropping out of high school. Changing economics affected parts of the city—Manhattan got richer over the twenty years of the big crime drop and Times Square got a makeover—but in the other boroughs, the levels of wealth and social isolation didn't change much and crime still fell.

Incarceration does, of course, take people who have committed crimes off the streets, reducing crime outside prison walls by incapacitating them. And the threat of prison versus no prison separately deters other people. But the debate over deterrence in the United States is mostly about something else—the effects of ratcheting up sentences, from two years to five, say, or from seven to fifteen. In the scheme of America's crime drop, "the incremental deterrent effect of increases in lengthy prison sentences is modest at best," according to a comprehensive review of the academic literature conducted by the National Academy of Sciences in 2014. With a small number of exceptions, as people age, their risk of reoffending declines sharply. Then there's the strong evidence for the "criminogenic" effects of incarceration, showing that people come out more likely to reoffend because of the toll prison takes and the hardening it can cause.

The central point is this: we're long past the point of diminishing returns. Deterrence and public safety don't justify anything like American levels of mass incarceration. The crime rate has been dropping in many countries, like the Netherlands and Germany, which never turned to draconian prison sentences. In the U.S., New York City is one of a number of success stories. California has reduced incarceration without an uptick in violent crime. Nationally, the population of teenagers in detention has dropped by more than

half in roughly the same period that the youth crime rate has plummeted by more than two-thirds.

Focusing on prison takes attention and resources away from
other means of deterrence. "If other policies we are ignoring or not
funding because of prison can achieve the same deterrence at less
financial or social cost, then the 'still some deterrence' argument for
prison becomes weaker," says Fordham law professor John Pfaff.

In New York, law enforcement tactics other than stop-and-frisk
took a bite out of crime. In his book, Zimring eplained how Comp-
Stat, the NYPD's much-copied data system for mapping crime,
helped enable "two proven successes." These were the commonsense shift to concentrating police in crime hot spots rather than
allocating patrol cars by population, and shutting down outdoor
drug markets.

Zimring also praised the city's low rate of gun ownership. This
advantage could largely be the result of civil gun control laws. New
York has one of the most rigorous licensing processes in the country. Less than one-half of 1 percent of the population in New York
City has a license for a handgun, and it's rare for full-carry permits
to be issued to people who are not security guards or retired police
officers. Geography helps, too: you couldn't take a quick trip to a
state with lax rules for gun sales the way you could in Chicago,
where more than 40 percent of the guns seized were purchased in
nearby Indiana, and where the police recovered firearms at a far
higher rate than they did in New York.

Civil-law gun control—tight permitting and purchasing
requirements—is good for health and safety. Gun homicides fell (by
40 percent) in Connecticut after it tightened the background check
for buying a handgun, while in states like Arizona and Missouri,
which loosened permitting requirements, gun-related assaults and
suicides have risen. Strict gun-permit rules offer an alternative to
mandatory prison sentences for gun possession. New York's mandatory sentences can't account for most of its huge crime drop. Eighty

percent of the city's decline in homicides took place before the 2006 mandatory sentences for gun possession went into effect the following year.

It's instructive that Guns = Prison never became the reality in Brooklyn or in the Bronx—primarily because of choices made by prosecutors. In the decade after the mandatory minimum hikes, Manhattan racked up a consistently high rate of convictions and prison sentences, followed closely by Queens and Staten Island. By contrast, in Brooklyn and the Bronx, the boroughs with the highest volume of cases and the most crime and poverty, prosecutors often agreed to plea deals for a lower-level offense like criminal possession of a weapon in the fourth degree, CPW4, which was a misdemeanor. The tacit bargain was this: if you didn't hurt or threaten anyone with your weapon, and you didn't have a long felony record, you would not go to jail or prison for having a gun. Crucially, crime fell significantly in Brooklyn and the Bronx along with the rest of the city.

The differences in punishment among New York City's boroughs showed how the power of prosecutors could surpass the power of lawmakers. As Yale law professor and sociologist Issa Kohler-Hausmann has written, "Laws don't apply themselves."

When I started going to the gun court in 2016 and talking to the people who filled the benches, I heard a common refrain: *I'd rather get caught with a gun than end up dead without one.* Kevin said it. Lots of other young men did, too.

In places of deprivation and segregation, like Brownsville, the impulse to turn to guns for self-protection was understandable even if it was destructive. The odds of being killed there were still up to ten times higher than they were in predominantly white parts of Brooklyn or Manhattan. The heightened danger extended to other violent crimes as well.

One day, I went to talk to Anthony Newerls, who ran another

diversion program for young people called Brownsville In, Violence Out (BIVO). Newerls had a unique niche. Along with his violence prevention work, he served as president of the community council for the 73rd Precinct, which made him the point of contact between residents and the police. He lived near Kevin in one of the projects, Howard Houses, and I was eager to get his perspective: did he think sending more people to prison for gun possession was helpful?

"Every carrier does not use the gun," Newerls explained, sitting in his BIVO office, up a narrow stairway above a KFC. "Not at all. In many cases we see, the carrier is carrying the gun for someone else. What if a shooter knows you, and they know you don't have a record, and they say, 'You walk two blocks behind me and you carry the gun'? If you don't do it, you could get beat up. You think, 'I live in the neighborhood. I don't want problems.' Remember, there's no snitching. So you do it." Other people in Brooklyn talked about the difference between taking a gun out on the street when you knew a fight was brewing and keeping one locked up just in case someone came after you. "Like offense versus defense," one young man put it.

Around the time I talked to Newerls, I went through the files of two hundred defendants in the gun court. (The total number for the court was roughly six hundred for its first year of operation in 2016 and early 2017.) I found that 80 percent had no previous conviction for a violent felony, and 70 percent had no felony conviction of any kind. Two-thirds were in their teens or twenties. In other words, on paper a lot of them looked like Kevin—young people without any proven history of violence. The mayor's office, the D.A.'s office, and the NYPD were also closely watching Project Fast Track. According to their quarterly reports, 75 percent of the gun court defendants were facing firearms charges for the first time, and 25 percent were in court for their first-ever criminal case of any sort.

To be sure, a smaller fraction—20 percent—had ten or more previous charges. Maybe they qualified as de Blasio's "evildoers." But even that seemed like a stretch, since the records I looked at had many more misdemeanors than felonies. (When I asked de Blasio for comment, he declined through his spokesperson.)

Some prosecutors argued that gun possession was a proxy for other criminal behavior that was harder to prove. "You use what you've got," they told me.

In Brownsville, Newerls had a question for the community and the city. "What do we do for those young people?" he asked of the gun carriers. "Do we say they should get the same kind of time as someone who uses a gun?" In his experience, police and prosecutors didn't think much about these questions. "They don't care which you are. They say, 'We have the gun now. We're going to take it off the street.' They always feel like to get rid of the gun, you have to get rid of the person you found with it. But as far as the prosecution goes, you should look at the cases more carefully, do more to find out the character of the person you're charging. You create a vacuum when you take five young men found with a gun and lock them up. They're absent and their family and their community feels that absence." These concerns mattered a great deal in the neighborhood and not at all in the courthouse.

In the spring of 2016, Ken Thompson fell ill with cancer. He died the following October, at the age of fifty. The sudden loss shook Brooklyn's criminal justice community and pushed into the limelight a man who'd never sought it—Eric Gonzalez.

Raised in Brooklyn by a single mother from Puerto Rico, Gonzalez, at forty-seven, had a salt-and-pepper brush cut, broad shoulders, and an untamed Brooklyn accent. In more than twenty years, he'd climbed the ladder of the D.A.'s office, taking the standard path from misdemeanors to screening arrests—interviewing police officers, victims, and witnesses, to decide which complaints to prosecute—and then felonies. He'd done nearly every job in the office, including special victims prosecutor (handling sex crimes), felony and homicide trial prosecutor, and chief of a trial division.

In his early days, when he declined to indict a case, he heard cops grumble, "I knew the Puerto Rican guy wouldn't charge." Over the years, however, he was able to forge close ties within the NYPD. "Having spent two decades here, trying cases as an assistant and then being a supervisor, many of the officers and detectives I got to know are now leading the department. The police commissioner has known me personally for years. I do have those relationships."

But Gonzalez was virtually unknown outside legal circles when Governor Andrew Cuomo put him in charge in Brooklyn, announcing after Thompson's death that Gonzalez would serve as interim district attorney until the election the following November.

Gonzalez didn't know any lawyers growing up. He didn't know anyone who'd gone to college or who went to work in a suit and tie. As a boy, he lived in a small apartment on the border of Williamsburg and Bushwick with his mother, who had come from Puerto Rico before he was born. She worked hard, sewing piecework at a factory at first. Gonzalez knew he had less than some other kids. He ate breakfast at school, where it was free, and a cousin who worked as a police officer brought him and his mother bags of groceries. Sometimes they really had nothing to spare. "Once my mom and I were walking down Graham Avenue—they call it the 'Avenue of Puerto Rico'—a block from my house, and we saw an ice cream truck. I wanted an ice cream cone. I remember saying, 'Can I have twenty-five cents?' She said no. I was a little kid, maybe six. I kept insisting I wanted an ice cream cone, and she really lost it with me, yanked me and maybe slapped me upside my head. I felt embarrassed and I was upset. We got home and she broke down crying. She said, 'I couldn't get you that ice cream cone because I didn't have the twenty-five cents to spend.' She is a tough woman. She hasn't cried a lot in my life."

Gonzalez earned pocket money when he got a little older by helping his mother make *capias*, small party favors people could pin to their shirts or dresses. "I'd make very simple ones, like a flower or a baby bottle, and she'd make fancier kinds, and we'd sell them to the store. We'd stay up late, and I probably slowed her down more than I helped, but it was bonding time, and that way she could let me earn an allowance." Over the next few years, his mother started working as a teacher's aide at his elementary school, where she worked her way up to an administrative position and stayed for thirty years.

When he was around ten, he and his mother moved to her boyfriend's house in East New York, a tough neighborhood east of Brownsville. "I remember walking to school along Pennsylvania Avenue, kicking crack vials down the sidewalk, having to peek around corners to make sure there were no headaches on the next block," Gonzalez said. He was sitting at his desk in the executive suite of the D.A.'s office in downtown Brooklyn, and though he seemed comfortable enough, it didn't look as if he'd made the space his own. Months had passed since Ken Thompson's death, but rows of plaques honoring him still hung in the waiting room.

In high school, Gonzalez got up at 5:00 a.m. for an hour-long subway ride to a deli near Coney Island, where he worked slicing bagels before morning classes began at John Dewey High School. He chose Dewey over schools closer to home because it was more integrated and had an advanced curriculum. A leadership club for Latino and Puerto Rican students, ASPIRA, helped Gonzalez become the first person in his family to go to college.

Some prosecutors get the idea of joining the profession from TV or the movies. If they grew up in the 1990s, they probably watched *Law and Order* and then *CSI* and its spinoffs. Gonzalez's inspiration was something else: Tom Wolfe's biting 1980s fable about New York, *The Bonfire of the Vanities*. "I was an avid reader in high school and I tore through that book when it came out," Gonzalez said. "It was a timepiece of the eighties, all about race and money and politics. That book really meant a lot to me. One character is the Bronx D.A. and another is an assistant D.A. I didn't know anything about prosecutors."

The prosecutors in *Bonfire* weren't good guys, I pointed out.

They were venal and corrupt. And the brand of justice they pursued wasn't a moral ideal; it was transactional, in a naked and cynical way. "Actually, there are no heroes in that book," Gonzalez admitted. What stuck with him, though, was that the Bronx prosecutors determined the fates of other characters, bringing down a high-society Wall Street bond trader ("Master of the Universe," Wolfe called him) as well as ordinary streetwise criminals.

When he graduated from Cornell in 1992, he left New York to attend law school at the University of Michigan. The year before, the number of homicides in Brooklyn ticked up from 800 to 821, more than eight times what it is now. In law school, Gonzalez met and started dating a fellow New Yorker, Dagmar Plaza, who decided to teach at a Brooklyn public school rather than practice law. They got married and bought a house in Williamsburg, raising their three sons while he worked his way up at the Brooklyn D.A.'s office.

Most of Gonzalez's colleagues were white and had more affluent backgrounds than he did. He thought the office needed someone like him. "I never left the D.A.'s office in part because I thought the people making all those decisions sometimes didn't have real skin in the game. They didn't come from the Brooklyn I came from. They didn't know the people I grew up with."

Some of the people Gonzalez grew up with had gone to jail, mostly for short stints related to drugs, which didn't seem to accomplish much. "The convictions I saw didn't punish people at the moment they sold the drugs," he told me. "It was more like an eternal punishment. They couldn't get into college, they struggled with their housing, and we all know most employers are reluctant to hire people with felony records."

Gonzalez had a half brother (the son of his father) who was a year and a half younger than him and struggled with drug addiction from the age of thirteen or fourteen. The family, including Gonzalez and his mother, tried to ease his brother's way into rehab, but it didn't take. In Gonzalez's first year as a prosecutor, when he was twenty-five, his brother was shot in the head in the Bronx and died. For a long time, the family didn't know why. The police had no leads. "It was a terrible thing," Gonzalez said quietly. He'd never talked about the details publicly. "It really destroyed my family."

As far as Gonzalez knew, no one else in the D.A.'s office at the time had lost a close family member to street violence. It made him want to focus the office's resources on serious crime.

The job of Brooklyn D. A. was a political plum. With it came the keys to the third-largest prosecutor's office in the country (less glamorous than Manhattan but a step ahead on lowering the rate of incarceration). If Gonzalez wanted to succeed Thompson as the elected D.A., rather than serving as the interim placeholder for only a year, he'd have to fight off strong challengers who had started to circle soon after Thompson's death. To keep the position he'd been thrust into, he'd have to sell himself as a candidate, something he'd never done or even really imagined. Even his friends and supporters joked about his anti-charisma. If he won, would Gonzalez, with his background as a career prosecutor, disappoint progressives who wanted to remake the system from the bottom up? Or would he help lead the reform movement that was beginning?

5

ELECTIONS

IN FEBRUARY 2016, a thirty-eight-year-old civil rights leader, Rashad Robinson, went to a meeting at the Obama White House with the president, his advisors, and a select group of civil rights leaders. It was in the Roosevelt Room, across from the Oval Office, where a portrait of Theodore Roosevelt on horseback hung above the fireplace. Obama, wearing a dark gray suit and sipping from a cup of coffee, sat in the middle of a long polished wood table between Brittany Packnett, a Black Lives Matter leader, and Representative John Lewis, the longtime Georgia congressman who shed blood on the 1965 march from Selma to Montgomery that helped lead to the passage of the Voting Rights Act.

Robinson's seat was farther from the president, and he was one of the more junior and less famous people in the room. "There are twelve to fifteen of us, and I'm there with the president of the NAACP, and the president of the Urban League, and Al Sharpton, and I don't have the same relationship they do with Obama or Valerie Jarrett or Loretta Lynch." (Jarrett was a senior White House advisor and Lynch was Obama's second attorney general.) Still, Robinson was determined to deliver a message: that it was time to put electing a new kind of D.A. at the top of the civil-rights agenda, though the issue had never been a focus of the movement before.

Robinson wasn't sure how his pitch would go over. As the head of Color of Change, a young and swiftly growing organization founded in the wake of Hurricane Katrina, he had close ties to Black Lives Matter, but his professional background was in gay rights, as a strategist at GLAAD. He was frustrated that the extensive protests about police shootings of the last few years hadn't yielded the same kind of progress toward racial justice in law enforcement as the fight for marriage equality. Michael Brown in Ferguson, Tamir Rice in Cleveland, Eric Garner in Staten Island—their names and those of other unarmed black people killed by the police had become a mantra of sorts for activists and protesters. Color of Change signed up more than 130,000 new members in the eleven days between the decisions not to charge the police officers who killed Brown and Garner, and had more than a million members by 2018. But impunity for the police and mass incarceration for low-income communities of color continued. "Over the last several years, our people kept showing up, making demands, hundreds of thousands signing petitions, asking the local officials to do something, and not really seeing results," Robinson told me. "We were continuing to tell our members that petitions and rallies make change possible, even though in this situation it wasn't actually true. We didn't have the right leverage."

Robinson wanted to help local organizers deliver tangible gains and he hoped to broaden their agenda from police accountability to progressive prosecution. Indicting individual police officers, however important, would not solve mass incarceration. "Really, the biggest problem was that the D.A.s were prosecuting far too many people. We needed to address the outrageous level of overincarceration."

The foremost problem, Robinson argued to the group at the White House, was that 80 percent of incumbent D.A.s ran for reelection unopposed. The D.A.s "weren't listening to us and they didn't think they needed to listen," he said. "I said we have to change America's understanding of what a D.A. is supposed to do and what makes a successful D.A." To Robinson's relief, Obama signaled his agreement as the discussion continued. "The president kept going back to prosecutors. He said they had more power over local criminal justice reform than he did."

It was time for the movement, a coalition that included civil rights, Black Lives Matter, and criminal justice activists, to find D.A. candidates they could get behind. In fact, the field-testing for the idea Robinson pitched at the White House had already begun.

Whitney Tymas had an unusual mix of credentials when she went to work in 2015 for George Soros, the billionaire investor who funds liberal causes. She'd been a public defender in Harlem and the Bronx, and then a prosecutor in Virginia, where she worked for seven years in Richmond for one of the state's first black commonwealth attorneys. She'd also headed a project on community prosecution for the National District Attorneys Association and worked at the Vera Institute of Justice addressing the role of prosecutors in perpetuating racial disparity. She'd become convinced that prosecutors were "the missing piece" of criminal justice reform.

In her first week on the job for Soros, Tymas met Chloe Cockburn, then at the American Civil Liberties Union (ACLU) and later director of strategy on criminal justice for the Open Philanthropy Project (established by Dustin Moskovitz, a cofounder of Facebook, and his wife, Cari Tuna). They talked for hours about prosecutors at a Pret A Manger in Washington, D.C. Elections for local prosecutor were typically second-order races that voters skip or pay little attention to, uncertain about who is on the ballot and what they stand for. In a poll paid for by the ACLU, half of sixteen hundred likely voters said they didn't know the D.A. was elected. What would it take to change that?

Tymas and Cockburn were in touch with a group of death penalty opponents around the country who aimed to unseat prosecutors who sought execution frequently. In 2015, Soros funded successful campaigns to oust D.A.s in two districts in Mississippi and in Caddo Parish, Louisiana, which had the highest death sentence rate per capita of any county in the nation. The jurisdictions were relatively small, but the races showed it was possible to defeat incumbents known for overzealousness.

The method of selection for prosecutors in the United States has changed over time. The job was part-time and low status in the Revolutionary era. (George Washington persuaded his first attorney general, Edmund Randolph, to take a half-time post at half the salary of the cabinet by dangling the prospect of higher private fees to be earned on the side.) In state court, prosecutors were paid by the case or conviction, filing paperwork much like county clerks. Defense lawyers, not prosecutors, captured the early American imagination. In the Boston Massacre trial of 1770, John Adams took the unpopular assignment of representing eight British soldiers accused of murder following a Boston riot. Afterward he looked back on the trial as "one of the best pieces of service I ever rendered my country." In modern times, the characters of Perry Mason and Atticus Finch deeply etched the honor of the criminal defender into the culture.

As the nineteenth century unfolded, the authority of prosecutors grew, and so did the concern that the position was ripe for political patronage. Elections for district attorney date from 1832, when Mississippi changed its constitution to give local voters the power to elect district attorneys to make them more accountable. By the time of the Civil War, most states had followed Mississippi's lead. Today prosecutors are still appointed only in Alaska, Connecticut, Delaware, New Jersey, and Rhode Island. In the United States, electing D.A.s is the norm—yet worldwide, ours is the *only* country in which voters choose local prosecutors. Grand juries were preserved to issue indictments, but mostly operated as rubber stamps.

In the late-1960s moment of rising crime and urban rioting, candidates for D.A. started competing for the law-and-order mantle. Did D.A.s have to campaign on raising conviction rates and stiffening punishments to win? That's been the long-running assumption. But maybe it's wrong. Reviewing a data set of district attorney elections in the state of New York since the 1990s, Yale law professor David Schleicher found that "mostly, incumbents just win until they quit." Crime rates factored heavily into the popularity of mayors, but prosecutors (maybe because voters pay less attention to them) appeared to win reelection in the absence of a major crack-up or scandal.

Perhaps district attorneys beat the law-and-order drum because everyone else did it, or because they thought the rhetoric would help them move on to higher office. But they also mirrored their usually affluent and increasingly suburban social class. District attorneys are elected countywide in the United States, and in many places that meant a city plus its suburbs, where the number of voters swelled. "White suburbanites' power over local prosecutors and trial judges grew, even as those officials focused a larger share of their attention on crime in urban black communities," the late Harvard law professor William Stuntz wrote. In other words, the people who dominated the electorate weren't often directly affected by crime, either as victims or as perpetrators.

The partial exceptions to harsh law-and-order prosecution, over the last generation, were a few cities like Seattle and Milwaukee with long-serving D.A.s who emphasized drug treatment and rehabilitation rather than locking people up and throwing away the key. Another example was San Francisco, where Kamala Harris ran for D.A. on a "smart on crime" platform. In her 2009 book by that name, she pointed out that California prisoners offended after release at the alarming rate of seven out of ten, and she argued that criminal justice was failing on its own terms. The reentry and diversion programs she supported affected a small number of people. She steered a middle-of-the-road course on law enforcement as she rode her record to statewide office, first as California's attorney general and then as a U.S. senator.

Conservatives have traditionally used the position of D.A. as a springboard to higher office. Harris sees it as essential for Democrats to recruit progressive candidates, especially women and people of color. "I say that because these offices matter deeply to the well-being of the community," she told me, "and also because of the credibility you bring to criminal justice reform if you go on to become governor or senator."

With three wins in Mississippi and Louisiana, the time seemed right to go bigger. Maybe the political barriers to electing a new kind of D.A. could fall all over the country. Tymas launched an operation for local D.A. elections like the one the Democratic Congressional Campaign Committee ran for House races, working with the political consulting firm Berlin Rosen. "When we began the work, it had never been done on a national scale before," she told me. "We pick the race, figure out if it's winnable, and how to win. For every one race we decide to play in, there may be three or four where we go, meet with candidates, do opposition research, poll, and then reject it for any number of reasons. Nobody else is vetting the candidates like we are."

Chicago was an obvious draw. Local groups like SOUL and The People's Lobby wanted to unseat Anita Alvarez, the state's attorney allied with Mayor Rahm Emanuel. Aspects of Alvarez's record— among them, her support for mandatory minimums for gun possession—were straight out of the law-and-order playbook. During her tenure, prosecutors who had just won their first jury trial hung mementos on the bulletin board that greeted everyone who walked into the office. One pinned his tie to a picture of a young woman who was weeping—the defendant.

Fueled by Black Lives Matter, frustration was rising over Alvarez's refusal to file charges against a police officer who shot a seventeen-year-old, Laquan McDonald, sixteen times, killing him in the street. Along with Emanuel, Alvarez fought the release of the police dash-cam video of the shooting.

Alvarez had a charismatic challenger in the upcoming Democratic primary: Kim Foxx, an African American former prosecutor who'd grown up in Chicago's Cabrini-Green housing projects. Foxx shared the activists' goal of changing how prosecutors measured success. She said that when she worked for Alvarez, "I became very frustrated by what I found to be not the pursuit of justice, but the pursuit of convictions."

As energy among Chicago's organizers grew, Chloe Cockburn of the Open Philanthropy Project advised donors on $300,000 in funding for local groups. Then in November 2015 the video of McDonald's shooting was finally released (thanks to the persistence of a freelance journalist). The footage showed McDonald walking away from police rather than menacing them, contradicting the officer's claim that he fired in self-defense.

The video rocked the city. Alvarez ultimately indicted the officer who killed McDonald, but for the wounded communities of Chicago, it was too little, too late. Foxx proved to be a skilled and magnetic campaigner, and momentum swelled behind her. "Chicago has really determined, energized groups led by young people and people of color and they joined together and knocked on thousands and thousands of doors," said Rob Smith, one of the death penalty opponents involved from the beginning and the director of the Fair Punishment Project, a criminal justice reform group then based at Harvard. "If you are someone who believes the system is irredeemably terrible, then you are not pushing for any prosecutors," said Mariame Kaba, the longtime Chicago activist. "We said that if Kim got elected, it would not be, 'Yay, our job is done.' But we'd have an opening that we never had before."

Color of Change worked with local organizers on a new kind of campaign event: the textathon. "We watched the Sanders campaign use peer-to-peer texting, and it was exciting," Robinson said.

"There was this idea in the election world that you have to pay a lot of campaign workers to increase turnout, especially in a low-stimulus election. We decided to try to disrupt that. We asked our members to show up. Say one hundred to two hundred people, meeting in an innovation hub or the Malcolm X Center or a church basement. We got some of the spaces donated, plus enough Internet. We had laptops if people didn't have them. We could load up data for five hundred names, and people sent texts, using a script."

With polls showing Alvarez was beatable, Soros contributed $400,000 to create the Illinois Safety and Justice PAC, which also received $300,000 from the Civic Participation Action Fund, a nonpartisan funder that seeks to engage people of color in the democratic process. Foxx raised $3.8 million all told and defeated Alvarez in the March 2016 primary by almost forty points. "It was an amazing moment," Cockburn said. "We had a convergence of organizers who'd been working on justice and safety for years in Chicago, plus national groups bringing resources and expertise on prosecutorial reform, and the energy that had been building from Black Lives Matter for months and months." The activists and donors who'd invested in Chicago felt they'd cracked a code. Changing the model for prosecution could fast-track reforms that had so far eluded them. And major D.A. elections were winnable.

"If you follow the criminal justice reform movement, the last several years have been fairly optimistic," said Udi Ofer, director of the ACLU's Campaign for Smart Justice, which has received $50 million from Soros's Open Society Foundations. "We decriminalized or reclassified drugs in some states. We raised the threshold for a felony property offense." But in some places, "the number of people in prison and jails hadn't changed as much as the reforms would suggest." Ofer started in his job in October 2016, with an agenda to push toward cutting the prison and jail population by half.

The reformers looked around, asking which cities had promising candidates and local groups energized to back them against law-and-order incumbent D.A.s. A series of races on the November

2016 ballot in cities across the country took on the flavor of Chicago's contest. All told, the Soros contributions to fifteen races in 2016 and the year before added up to nearly $11 million. From 2015 to 2017, the Open Philanthropy Project directed about $6 million to political organizing around prosecutorial reform, and its cofounder Cari Tuna gave about $1.25 million more to five groups working on the issue. Harris County, Texas, which includes Houston and its suburbs, was a major target.

In July 2015, Sandra Bland, who was twenty-eight, died in jail in a neighboring county after she was pulled over for a traffic stop and couldn't afford to pay bail. Bland's death galvanized the Texas Organizing Project (TOP), a force statewide that previously concentrated on issues like housing, education, and healthcare. Kim Ogg, who was trying to become the first Democratic D.A. in Harris County in four decades, won the primary and came to TOP asking for support. "That race became our flagship issue for the 2016 election," Ginny Goldman, then the director of TOP, told me. Her group raised $1.5 million to get out the vote and a Soros-funded PAC gave Ogg nearly $900,000.

Bail reform became a major campaign issue for Ogg when a public interest group led by Alec Karakatsanis, a young Harvard Law School graduate, sued Harris County on behalf of people who couldn't make bail for offenses like driving without a license. The suit featured videos of hearing officers routinely setting bail in a matter of seconds, with no defense lawyer present. One officer on video raised the bail amount repeatedly because he didn't like how the defendant was speaking to him. Ogg won the election and directed her prosecutors to recommend the pretrial release of most people accused of misdemeanors. She also filed a brief in the bail reform suit on the side of the plaintiffs rather than the county and the sheriff's office. "We do not want to be complicit in a system that incentivizes presumptively innocent people to plead guilty," she wrote.

Five months after Ogg's election, Judge Lee Rosenthal (appointed to the federal bench by President George H. W. Bush) handed down a landmark opinion that declared Harris County's misdemeanor bail system unconstitutional. Rosenthal quoted Ogg's brief to full advantage: "The Harris County District Attorney emphasizes that 'holding un-adjudicated minor offenders in the Harris County Jail solely because they lack the money or other means of posting bail is counterproductive to the goal of seeing that justice is done.'"

The November 2016 election resulted in a string of victories for criminal justice reform. "Oklahoma passed a ballot initiative to re-classify many drug and property offenses and reinvest back into communities," Udi Ofer said. "California voters adopted parole reform. Marijuana legalization passed in four states." A dozen D.A. candidates won while promising reform, including Aramis Ayala, a former defense lawyer in Orlando, Florida, and Mark Gonzalez in Corpus Christi, Texas, who called himself a Mexican biker lawyer and had "Not Guilty" tattooed across his upper chest. Several of the newly elected D.A.s were minorities or women or both. Addressing the demographic imbalance of the nation's prosecutors was part of the reform agenda. Of the more than twenty-four hundred elected prosecutors in the country, 95 percent were white and 79 percent were white men, a study showed.

The progressive victories in D.A. races involved mobilizing relatively small numbers of voters. Kim Ogg won in Harris County (population more than 4.6 million) with about 86,000 votes and the general election with less than 700,000. For Mark Dupree in Kansas City, an ordained minister, the winning total was under 7,300 to become the first African American D.A. in Kansas. The reformers concluded they'd found a needle that was ready to move. "You can spend all the money in the world and not make change happen," Cockburn told me. "The country had to be primed for this, and Black Lives Matter set the stage. Maybe what the money does is speed up the change or make it go a little smoother. Maybe it's like high-octane gas."

Donald Trump's surprise victory overshadowed everything else on that same 2016 election night, and his presidency ushered in an approach to criminal justice wholly at odds with the reform movement. In his inaugural address, Trump turned a dark warning about "crime and gangs and drugs" into a frightening image of "American carnage." Never mind that the murder rate had dropped by half since 1980; Trump falsely insisted that it "is the highest it's been in forty-seven years." By blasting Chicago for its homicide spike and denigrating immigrants as criminals, Trump embraced a tactic that has helped Republicans win the presidency since Richard Nixon campaigned in 1968 on a promise to restore law and order. (John McCain and Mitt Romney didn't prey on fear of black and brown criminals. They lost their runs for president.)

For all Trump's fear-mongering, however, he had no authority over local criminal justice. County and city prosecutors handle as much as 95 percent of the national docket for felony charges. Include misdemeanors (so that we're talking about everything from homicide to disorderly conduct, with assault, domestic violence, drugs, and guns in between) and their share rises to 99 percent. (Federal prosecutors, working in U.S. attorney's offices and appearing in federal court, overlap with local D.A.s on drugs and guns; they also handle immigration violations and white-collar offenses.) It matters, too, that the states mostly spend their own money, $200 billion annually, for criminal justice (including about $80 billion just on prisons and jails). By comparison, in all the years from 1993 to 2012, the Department of Justice awarded states and localities a total of about $38 billion in criminal justice grants, or about $2 billion a year. In other words, the Justice Department has a big megaphone and some money to seed its ideas, but local D.A.s and state officials hold more sway.

What's more, despite his victory, Trump was increasingly out of sync with Republicans as well as Democrats on criminal justice. Polls show that Americans exaggerate the level of crime across the country but not in their own backyards, which suggests they could be receptive to local criminal justice reform. In a 2017 survey of a thousand people conducted for the ACLU, 71 percent said it's important to reduce the prison population—including 52 percent of Trump voters. When voters think about the price of incarceration, they're even less likely to support the sweeping tough-on-crime mantra.

Some conservatives have picked up on the dissatisfaction, assailing dubious policies for wasting money and inviting government overreach. At the 2015 Conservative Political Action Conference, one of the most prominent gatherings on the right, a panel called "Prosecutors Gone Wild" proved a hit; a reprise two years later drew an audience of more than one thousand. In a 2017 op-ed in the *Wall Street Journal*, the tax-cut cheerleader Grover Norquist ranked criminal justice reform near the top of "the conservative movement's most important recent accomplishments." Norquist argued that "America's reddest states" are proving that reform works, and he concluded that "strong conservative leadership has been essential."

Charles and David Koch, the billionaire financiers who have poured money into hard-right causes and candidates, began ramping up support for criminal justice reform around 2015. "I always say, it's not rocket science," the Kochs' point person on the issue, Mark Holden, told me. "It's not even political science. It's common sense." Holden has a personal connection to the issue: he worked as a prison guard on his summer and winter breaks from college at the University of Massachusetts. As proof of the power of second chances, he brought up a RAND study from 2014 showing that $1 spent on education in prison saves nearly $5 in future incarceration costs by cutting the rate of reoffending by more than 40 percent. "A lot of the things that will keep people out of prison to begin with is having a community around them—a mentor, an opportunity, education," he said. "Somebody to keep you on the straight and narrow. If people don't get that, or they get it and they don't take advantage of it, or they had a lousy education, and they go to prison, they need that even more coming out."

After the 2016 D.A. elections sank in, the conservative media focused on the funding from George Soros, a bogeyman to the right as much as the Koch brothers have been to the left. The Soros contributions to D.A. candidates made national headlines, first in *Politico* and then in conservative outlets like the *Washington Free Beacon*, Fox News, and the *Washington Examiner*. Governor Greg Abbott gave speeches railing at Soros for "messing with Texas." A prosecutor in Oregon, Josh Marquis, warned on the Heritage Foundation's news site of Soros's "staggering" campaign to swing the D.A. elections. Marquis (a Democrat) has dismissed out-of-control mass incarceration as an "urban legend" and served on the board of the National District Attorneys Association. "The police say there is a war on cops," he told me. "Many of us career prosecutors believe there's something of a war on prosecutors."

Some reformers see tension in relying on wealthy donors. "The activist groups are empowered to do their jobs by the money," Bill Lipton, the New York State director for the Working Families Party, told me. "It's great, but it also shows you how broken the democracy is."

When Eric Gonzalez ran for D.A. in 2017, he wasn't a candidate in the Soros mold. He represented a different test for the reform movement: Could it encompass—and benefit from—a career prosecutor who saw being an insider as a strength?

Activists in Brooklyn expressed faith in Gonzalez from the start. "We were one of the first to endorse Eric," Lipton said. "He walked the walk." The things Ken Thompson was renowned for, Eric implemented. At a spring 2017 event at the Brooklyn Women's Bar Association, Linda Sarsour, who organized demonstrations after Eric Garner was choked to death by a police officer on a Staten Island sidewalk, praised Gonzalez. "You're always there in the background, doing the work," she said, "doing right by us Brooklynites."

Gonzalez was, in fact, playing a behind-the-scenes role in New

York City's most important criminal justice reform effort. In the fall of 2016, weeks after he became acting D.A., Gonzalez got a call from Jonathan Lippman, the former chief judge of New York State. Lippman had a politically tricky request: he wanted Gonzalez to be the first D.A. to get behind the drive to close Rikers Island.

Rikers, which sits in the East River between Queens and the Bronx, was established in 1932. Inmates hauled the fill that expanded the size of the island to accommodate ten jails that now sprawl across more than four hundred acres. In 2014, the U.S. attorney in Manhattan called Rikers "broken," finding that teenagers were subject to attacks by other inmates, and spotlighting "rampant use of unnecessary and excessive force by staff."

Campaigns to close Rikers had sputtered in the late 1970s to early 1980s. The main sticking point was the massive number of inmates—more than twenty thousand at the high point in the early 1990s. Where else would the city put all those people?

But as arrests and crime fell in New York, the Rikers population dropped by more than half, to about ten thousand on a given day in 2016. A new coalition of groups, led by and representing people of color, saw opportunity. The most important one, JustLeadership USA, was founded by Glenn Martin, who went to college after being released from Attica prison, where he went for an armed robbery conviction. Their campaign, #CloseRikers, was about much more than the conditions inside the jail. Closing Rikers would be possible only if the population could be cut in half again, to five thousand, so that small jails in the boroughs could handle the load. In other words, #CloseRikers also meant #Decarcerate.

Marches and demonstrations to close the jail followed. Ambushed by protesters in Harlem, Mayor de Blasio dismissed their cause as impractical. But the Speaker of the New York City Council, Melissa Mark-Viverito, launched a commission to prove that it could be done; to chair it, she chose Lippman, one of the most prominent advocates for criminal justice reform in the state. Martin joined the commission while JustLeadership kept pushing from the outside. (Martin later left the organization amid allegations of sexual harassment.)

Lippman started calling the city's district attorneys because organizers saw them as crucial. "My pitch to the D.A.s was that Rikers was a stain on the soul of the city, and their support was critical for our credibility," Lippman told me. He started with Cy Vance, the D.A. in Manhattan, whom he'd known for years. Vance, a frequent presence at high-society galas and benefits, upstaged Gonzalez in much the way Manhattan tended to outshine the outer boroughs. He was a regular on the law school speaking circuit. (It didn't hurt that his office had more than $800 million in civil forfeiture funds to spend on projects of its choice, the result of criminal penalties paid by three international banks.) But Vance had so far disappointed criminal justice reformers. They'd had high hopes a few years earlier when he took the unusual step of opening his office's case filings to the Vera Institute for its review of racial disparity in prosecutions (Whitney Tymas's project). But when Vera found that at almost every decision point in the process, black and Latino people faced worse outcomes than whites, Vance didn't do much to root out the problem. "The D.A.'s office didn't really figure out how to systematically, purposefully reduce the disparities uncovered by the study—in case acceptance and dismissal, and bail and sentencing recommendations," said Nicholas Turner, the president and director of Vera. "They did respond by committing to improve diversity and provide training in implicit bias, but these things weren't tailored to address the problems the study found."

Vance was noncommittal in response to Lippman's bid for support to close Rikers. Gonzalez was next on Lippman's call list. The new D.A. had visited Rikers several times. He knew that about 75 percent of the people behind bars were there because they couldn't make bail. The remaining 25 percent were mostly people serving time for parole violations or after a conviction. Turnstile jumpers and marijuana smokers were still among them, but their numbers had dropped since 2010, when a devastating report by Human Rights Watch helped defense lawyers persuade judges to stop putting people in jail for an offense that some cities merely ticketed. Starting in 2012, the Bronx Freedom Fund and the Brooklyn Community Bail Fund helped reduce the numbers, too, by posting bail for thousands of misdemeanor defendants. So did a pretrial supervision program established by the mayor's office in 2016.

Nevertheless, about 4,250 people were still being held at Rikers on any given day for nonviolent crimes. Keeping them off the island was the place to start cutting the jail population. To reduce it to the level needed to close the jail complex, though, would also require changing bail practices for some felonies. Prosecutors would have to stop automatically making the standard demand for bail of $10,000 to $50,000 for people charged with gun possession (like Kevin) or $5,000 for the theft of a backpack.

Brooklyn was ahead of the game, compared with the other boroughs: per capita, it sent the fewest people to Rikers. Gonzalez had the power to do more on his own. He could direct his office to stop asking for bail for all nonviolent crimes, or do even more. But as the interim D.A., he'd just taken over a large organization with a strong internal culture, and he had caretaker status rather than an elected mandate. Some politicians or ideologues wouldn't have cared about that, but Gonzalez was neither. If he acted unilaterally, he thought, he would risk a backlash.

If #CloseRikers took off, on the other hand, Gonzalez would have political cover. "I knew that closing Rikers meant changing how we charge and how we think about bail," Gonzalez told me. "Those were things I wanted to do." He told Lippman he supported the campaign. The judge could take Gonzalez's backing to the other D.A.s in hopes of persuading them to join and then going public. "From the beginning, Eric said he was with us," Lippman said. "It was a big relief to me. I knew then I'd be able to get the law-enforcement community on board."

In the months that followed, #CloseRikers won over Vance and Darcel Clark, the new district attorney in the Bronx. "If you'd told me before we started that we could turn this ship around so quickly, I'd have said you were out of your mind," Lippman said. In late March, de Blasio, who'd been balking, decided at the last minute to host the press conference announcing the commission's findings. The mayor stood with Mark-Viverito to herald a "historic announcement": the city committed to closing Rikers over the next decade.

A few weeks later, Gonzalez announced that his office would no longer ask for bail in most misdemeanor cases. The policy didn't go as far as defense lawyers and activists wanted because it included a list of exceptions. (Prosecutors were still encouraged to ask for bail for people who were on parole, supervised release, or felony probation, had an open felony case or a history of violent felonies, or were charged with a domestic violence misdemeanor.) But in a reverse of the previous rule for all cases, line prosecutors would have to give a reason for demanding bail, rather than justify a decision to let someone go without it. In Chicago, Kim Foxx issued her own decree: release for anyone who couldn't make bail up to $1,000. Gonzalez's policy would be harder to implement because it wasn't as clear-cut, but it probably affected more people. None of the other boroughs had anything like it.

Gonzalez made headlines again that month by showing how local prosecutors could fight the Trump administration. As the Department of Homeland Security ramped up the detention and deportation of people with criminal records, the day-to-day charging and plea-bargaining decisions that state prosecutors made had enormous bearing on which immigrants were most vulnerable. While any undocumented immigrant could be picked up, the legal risk increased for people with certain criminal convictions. One rule of thumb was that being convicted for a crime that carried a potential sentence of more than one year made it much harder to fight a deportation order in immigration court. The same was true of a conviction for a crime of moral turpitude, a category that included drugs, domestic violence, and guns.

Gonzalez announced that his office would agree to shorter sentences for undocumented immigrants charged with nonviolent crimes and misdemeanors. He also hired two immigration lawyers to advise the assistant D.A.s on all the case-by-case decisions the new policy entailed—the first D.A. in the country to bring such expertise in-house, as far as I could tell.

Many prosecutors think it's not their job to worry about the consequences of a conviction beyond the sentence they ask for in court. But convictions have all kinds of ripple effects: they can cause the loss of a job, a university admission, a professional license, the custody of a child, or a benefit like public housing. Gonzalez's move to spare certain immigrants from the consequences of a conviction signaled a willingness to think more broadly about the scope of a prosecutor's job. "Maybe you've been taught that it's the defense that has the obligation to protect their clients' interests," Gonzalez said to a roomful of newly hired assistant D.A.s at a training that spring. "I don't think that's good enough. We have the obligation to make fair plea offers, and I want you to be mindful about immigration consequences when you do that. . . . We should not be burying our heads in the sand and saying it's not our responsibility to worry about this. I'm charging you that it is your responsibility."

Gonzalez also argued that treating immigrants fairly in court would build trust of law enforcement in their communities, easing the way for them to report crimes and serve as witnesses. This part was personal. After his half brother was killed, the investigation in the Bronx went nowhere. Then after two years, a pizza deliveryman walked into a precinct station and reported that he'd seen the shooting while he was making a delivery. The crime had been eating away at him; he'd also recently run into the killers and felt threatened. Finally, the police cracked the case and arrested two suspects. But before their trial, the deliveryman was deported to Mexico. Gonzalez and his family never knew why. They wondered if the shooters, or their lawyer, had reported him to make the case go away. Before the witness left the country, he identified someone else (the customer he was delivering to when the gun fired) who could identify the shooters. Still, with only one witness, the case was weaker, and only one of the two men was convicted.

Showing mercy to immigrants was good politics in Brooklyn, where more than one-third of residents were foreign-born. Two days after announcing the new policy, Gonzalez officially declared his candidacy for district attorney. An audience of several dozen supporters, including local union members and Hasidic leaders, gathered in Bedford-Stuyvesant, in a plaza encircled by a mosque and two churches, as a D.J. played Sugarhill Gang's "Apache." Ken Thompson's widow gave a laudatory introduction. Like a man determined not to screw up his debut, Gonzalez spoke every word from a script. "Today, Brooklyn is one of the safest large cities in the country," he said. "This is proof that the choice between safety and constitutional protections, especially in communities of color, is a false choice."

Gonzalez wanted to be a progressive and still respond to the traditional concerns of law enforcement. He wanted to be a force for evolution, not revolution. Given Brooklyn's history of diversion and relatively low incarceration rates, he could stick to this path and still run one of the most progressive D.A.'s offices in the country.

As the donors, activists, and local organizers who'd succeeded in 2016 looked ahead, they saw a chance to spur other cities forward. No one had come up with a slogan to match "law and order" or "tough on crime," and Trump's victory under those banners suggested they still animated the voters who made up his base. And yet, all over the country, D.A. candidates won by frankly and frontally attacking mass incarceration, wrongful convictions, and other markers of injustice. The public was primed by an array of forces—

Black Lives Matter, *The New Jim Crow*, the cost of incarceration, private prison corruption, untested rape kits, the haunting tales of innocent people behind bars, and, as a precondition, the drop in crime. How far could D.A. change go?

Two races in spring 2017 would raise the bar. One involved Stephanie Morales, who had won a special election two years earlier to finish the term of her boss, the previous district attorney, in Portsmouth, Virginia, a racially diverse city of about one hundred thousand. Morales, who is African American, was thirty-one and had four young children when she took office. Two months after her victory, a white police officer killed an unarmed black man suspected of shoplifting at Walmart. There was no video of the shooting, but there were witnesses, and most of them said the man had his hands up when the officer shot him in the face and chest.

Over the previous decade, fewer than a dozen white officers in the whole country had gone to jail for killing a black person. Knowing the challenge, Morales decided to try the case against the Portsmouth cop herself. When his lawyer introduced a police manual, arguing that his client followed the guidelines on the use of force, she asked if a McDonald's manual would exempt company employees from following the law. The jury convicted the police officer of manslaughter.

Running for a four-year term, after her two years in office following the special election, Morales drew a white male challenger who promised to "mend relationships" with the police. Whitney Tymas, George Soros's strategist, reached out to Morales on social media and channeled donations to her. Morales also got help from a PAC founded by activists, Real Justice. The funders encouraged Morales to run forthrightly on her record. "It was scary at first," she told me. "They did a whole mailer about the officer shooting. I didn't know how the community would respond. But then I thought, 'OK, go ahead. Prosecutors should be bold. If I win, I'll know people are really behind me.'"

Around the same time, the D.A. race commanding far more

attention nationally was taking shape in Philadelphia. With the position up for grabs in a special election (the previous D.A. had resigned after being charged with bribery), eight candidates declared for the Democratic primary, including Larry Krasner, a civil rights attorney.

No one like Krasner had ever been a big-city D.A. before. He joked that he'd spent his career "becoming completely unelectable" by suing the city's police department seventy-five times. But Krasner's record became a selling point in a city with the highest rate of imprisonment per capita of the nation's ten biggest metropolitan areas, a trail of wrongful convictions (often in cases in which prosecutors or the police concealed exonerating evidence), and a history of brutal and racist policing. If Brooklyn, for all its flaws, had been one of the better places in the country to be charged with a crime, Philadelphia had been one of the worst. Mistrust of law enforcement was wide and deep, especially in the black community, which had been scarred by police bias and shootings.

In the city of Frank Rizzo, the racist police chief and mayor of the 1970s, Krasner called the policing of marijuana "stupid," denounced the death penalty, and promised to end mass incarceration. To a historic degree, local groups, led by the Working Families Party, 215 People's Alliance, and Reclaim Philadelphia, mobilized to get out the vote. Separately, the Philadelphia Coalition for a Just District Attorney set policy goals. Color of Change supported all of this work. The ACLU hired formerly incarcerated people to knock on their members' doors to raise awareness about the election. Real Justice PAC, inspired by Bernie Sanders's presidential run, placed three staffers with Krasner's campaign. Through another PAC, Soros kicked in $1.6 million.

When Krasner won the primary in May, some of the supporters at his victory party chanted, "No good cops in a racist system." The *Philadelphia Inquirer*, which often backs Democrats, ran skeptical articles and a series of letters from readers under the headlines

"DA Candidate Krasner Faces Fear and Loathing," "After the Anti-Police Chants, an Opportunity in the DA's Race for the GOP?" and "City Prosecutors Not Celebrating Krasner's Victory." The *Inquirer* endorsed Krasner's Republican opponent. A local leader of the Fraternal Order of Police warned that if Krasner won in November, the results would be "catastrophic."

Eric Gonzalez's big test came on a hot and sticky night that July. With four of the other Democrats running in the primary, he arrived at St. Francis College in Brooklyn Heights for a forum sponsored by Color of Change and several New York advocacy groups. Gonzalez was the front-runner and expected his opponents to go after him. They'd all worked as prosecutors and then left the job, putting them in a position to criticize the D.A.'s office. Gonzalez was the only one onstage who would answer for its record.

A statuesque woman with a pink flower in her hair took the microphone when it was the audience's turn to ask questions. "My name is Hertencia Petersen, and I am the aunt of Akai Gurley," she said.

In November 2014, she explained, Akai Gurley was walking down a dark stairwell in his Brooklyn public housing project, unarmed, when he was killed by a bullet fired by Peter Liang, a rookie police officer, which hit Gurley after ricocheting off the wall. Liang said he had his gun out because the lights weren't working in the stairwell and he fired by accident when he was startled by a noise. But Gurley's girlfriend said that as she knelt by his side, trying to resuscitate him, Liang stopped briefly and then kept going down the stairs. The D.A.'s office prosecuted Liang for manslaughter, saying he'd been reckless. When he was convicted, more than ten thousand protesters hit the streets in Brooklyn, asking why an Asian American, the son of Chinese immigrants, was the first police officer in more than a decade to be convicted in a shooting. Two months later, Ken Thompson recommended probation and community service rather than prison for Liang, enraging Gurley's family and prompting a wave of protests from the other side.

"Akai was murdered," Petersen said now. She listed the names of three other victims of police shootings. "The Brooklyn D.A.'s office failed every last one of us."

One of Gonzalez's challengers, Marc Fliedner, had tried the case against Liang. Now he lit into Thompson's decision not to seek jail time, saying he'd quit over it. Petersen's voice rose. "What have you done since Ken Thompson's demise?" she asked Gonzalez directly. "You're running for D.A. What are your goals? What are your visions? Don't run on Ken Thompson's coattails. Run on your vision. Give the people of Brooklyn what you want for your family." The crowd whistled and cheered.

"Miss Petersen, what I can say to you is, I'm committed to doing the work," Gonzalez began.

"Why haven't you done it?" someone yelled from the crowd.

The moderator broke in, quieting the hall so Gonzalez could speak. But as he began, Petersen was back on her feet. "Do you think if it was Akai who had murdered Peter Liang, it would have been the same?" she called from her seat. "A life was taken. You are not understanding the pain of the family." She clasped her hands at her chest. "Don't try to pacify me."

"I'm not trying to pacify you," Gonzalez said. He didn't add that he knew something of what she was going through because of his half brother's death. He stayed on professional ground. "Ken Thompson believed he made the recommendation that was appropriate. I stood by his recommendation." While afterward his thirteen-year-old son would urge him to be more impassioned at the next debate, Gonzalez had managed to meet anguish with calm at this one. The crowd didn't turn on him. The debate went on.

Later in the evening, Gonzalez said he opposed mandatory minimum sentences for gun possession, rejecting outright the approach taken by Bloomberg and the gun control movement a decade earlier. "Especially for young people, we have diverted people charged with gun possession," Gonzalez said, underscoring his commitment to continue the programs his predecessors had nurtured. The moment showed that Gonzalez was willing to touch a third rail for prosecutors, out loud and in public: mercy for people whom the state considered violent felons.

Gonzalez was responding to the progressive tilt of the race, but he was also demonstrating why advocates like Danielle Sered had faith in him. He was willing to stick his neck out for people it was all too easy to condemn. "Mass incarceration is made or broken by a bunch of assistant D.A.s and their supervisors and the decisions they make between 10:00 a.m. and noon," said Sered, who'd worked closely with Gonzalez on Common Justice, her restorative justice program for young adults charged with violent felonies. "Eric was one of those assistant D.A.s for a long time. He understands where the levers that drive the use of jail and prison really are."

Gonzalez's rejection of zero-tolerance prosecution of gun charges also pointed to a way to reduce incarceration that went beyond dismissing or diverting misdemeanors. "No one thinks that prosecutors, even progressive prosecutors, will be lenient toward people who've committed serious violence, like murder or sexual assault," said Paul Butler, a former prosecutor and Georgetown law professor. "Gun possession cases, with people who haven't actually done anything violent, are a good place to start thinking about ways that prosecutors can enhance community safety while locking up fewer people and not contributing to racial disparities."

As the summer wore on, Gonzalez kept moving. With Vance, Clark, and the D.A. from Queens, he wiped out seven hundred thousand outstanding summonses for long-ago infractions like unpaid tickets. He celebrated the release of a man, after twenty-one years in prison, who said he had been coerced into confessing a murder—the twenty-third conviction in three years the D.A.'s office asked to be overturned. He urged federal Immigration and Customs Enforcement (ICE) agents to stay out of the local courthouses, where they sometimes surprised people and took them into detention. When an eighteen-year-old said two police detectives had picked her up and forced sex on her while she was in their van, Gonzalez held a press conference to announce charges against both detectives for rape and kidnapping.

The other candidates in the D.A. race made progressive promises as well. Pundits turned to the usual law-and-order rhetoric. "Stunning to see Brooklyn DA candidates competing to go softer on crime," tweeted Alyssa Katz, a member of the editorial board at the New York *Daily News*. "They all sound like they're running for Public Defender, not prosecutor," added Clyde Haberman, a former columnist for the *New York Times*.

The punditry, however, missed the degree to which Gonzalez, by building on the relationships he'd made during his career, also strengthened his ties to the establishment. In August, he won the endorsement of the police union, the Patrolmen's Benevolent Association. He sewed up the backing of the borough's entire delegation to Congress along with a list of City Council members and state legislators. He was on his way to raising $2 million, a huge amount for a D.A. candidate.

In the weeks before the election, progressive advocacy groups urged every candidate for D.A. in the city to reject campaign contributions from bail companies. In the past, taking the money had been routine; this time, Gonzalez gave back the $7,750 he'd received.

Gonzalez also came under fire for the limitations of his bail policy. An average of 160 misdemeanor defendants from Brooklyn were still held at Rikers each day. At a candidates' forum, one of Gonzalez's opponents made him answer for a $500 bail request for a homeless person accused of stealing cheese. "I grew up poor," Gonzalez started to answer, "and I understand that when we set bail on people who can't make it, we've in essence criminalized the fact that they live in poverty—"

"Then why are you still doing it?" someone in the audience yelled.

In early September, the public radio station WNYC broke a

story that called into doubt the biggest promise of the Thompson-Gonzalez tenure: the pledge to stop prosecuting low-level marijuana offenses. More than 80 percent of the people arrested for marijuana possession in Brooklyn, it turned out, were still being prosecuted. The D.A.'s office was still charging people for weed if they had a criminal record or were smoking in public. And whites and Asians were about twice as likely to have their marijuana possession cases tossed as blacks and Latinos, largely because of the arrest records from stop-and-frisk.

The vast racial disparity took Gonzalez by surprise. "As crazy as it sounds, we didn't keep track of those numbers," he told me later. "What surprised me was not the number of people of color arrested, because I obviously see that. What surprised me was that in other communities, the white neighborhoods of Brooklyn, the policing didn't reflect arrests there as well. It shocked me how much it was concentrated in the poor communities of color." To WNYC at the time, he said, "If it takes me to be more aggressive in declining to prosecute more cases, I'm willing to do that."

Gonzalez cruised through the primary a week later, more than forty points ahead of his rivals. He won the general election in November with 89 percent of the vote. In Philadelphia, Krasner got 75 percent. Voter turnout was up by nearly 70 percent from the last D.A. election. In a no-holds-barred victory speech before a jubilant crowd, Krasner promised "transformational change" for a system "that has systematically picked on black and brown people." He talked about ending mass incarceration and the death penalty and cash bail.

"This is what a movement looks like," Krasner said.

"I'm here to make sure that our criminal justice system becomes the fairest, most progressive system that we have while also making sure our families in Brooklyn are safe," Gonzalez promised.

6

TRIAL

IN THE MONTHS leading up to trial, Valerie Corder told Noura that the D.A. was floating a potential offer: would she plead guilty in exchange for a twenty-five-year sentence? Noura said no. She wanted a trial. She thought it would prove her innocence.

Corder didn't push her client to take the plea. She was the kind of defense lawyer who relished a fight. She had close friends in the criminal defense bar in Memphis, but she saw herself as more independent because she made most of her living in civil court. "I wasn't in the club," she said of the criminal courthouse, which houses the Shelby County district attorney's office.

The American adversarial model of justice promises to reveal the truth through "zealous advocacy," with the prosecution and the defense going at each other as hard as the rules allow. But as repeat players in a local system, defense lawyers depend on their relationships with prosecutors and judges, while clients come and go. The courthouse is a workplace, and the people who work there get to know each other. That's not necessarily compromising, but the temptation exists to accept a worse deal for one client in exchange for a break for another, or just to be liked. Corder saw herself as standing outside of the system, refusing to go along to get along. While Noura waited—her trial was postponed from January to fall 2008, and then to February 2009—Corder tried to ensure that she had every bit of evidence the state was obligated to give her.

In the United States, defendants didn't have the right to see evidence in the government's possession until the late 1950s. Before that, our American rules reflected those of early modern Britain, where people suspected of crimes were required to speak for themselves, without a lawyer, and had no right to learn in advance of the evidence against them, or even the charges. The element of surprise was deemed crucial to ascertaining the truth—until the nineteenth century, when the British courts changed course, requiring broad disclosure of the prosecution's case before trial, including a full list of witnesses, a summary of how they would testify, and the production of other investigative material, like police and lab reports. Germany and France imposed similar rules. Judges in the United States, by contrast, continued to emphasize that defendants might harm or intimidate witnesses if they knew they were planning to testify. "Trial by ambush," as it's called, remained the norm.

In 1957, the Supreme Court ruled that prosecutors had to give the defense one type of evidence: the prior statements of trial witnesses after they testified. Justice William J. Brennan, an Eisenhower appointee who became one of the era's leading liberal jurists, wrote the majority opinion in that case, and in a major speech at Washington University's law school in March 1963, he went further, criticizing the American practice of keeping the prosecution's case secret before trial. Brennan argued that it was "particularly ironic" that at the Nuremberg trials, conducted in the mid-1940s to bring Nazi war criminals to justice, Soviet prosecutors protested the American rules of evidence as unfair to defendants. Isn't denying access to the facts of the prosecution's case "blind to the superlatively important public interest in the acquittal of the innocent?" Brennan asked.

Brennan's speech was part of a sweeping argument for criminal justice reform. Led by Earl Warren, the consensus-seeking California governor chosen as chief justice by Eisenhower, the Supreme Court revolutionized the process the government must follow to convict someone of a crime. The Warren Court gave poor defendants the right to a free lawyer, barred the admission of illegally obtained evidence, and required the police to inform suspects in custody of their rights (the Miranda warning).

Two months after Brennan's speech, defendants won the constitutional right to see some of the evidence in the state's possession before trial. The ruling came in *Brady v. Maryland*, a 1963 appeal by an Air Force veteran, John Leo Brady, who'd been sent to death row for a murder committed four and a half years earlier. Brady's lawyers had argued previously in state court that prosecutors should have disclosed that a codefendant had confessed to the killing. The Warren Court decreed that before trial, prosecutors must turn over evidence that is "favorable" to the defense if it is "material either to guilt or to punishment."

The Brady rule became a tool capable of rebalancing the scales between the defense and the prosecution. It was imperative for the state to share proof with the defense "because police have unparalleled access to the evidence in criminal cases," Alex Kozinski explained in an influential law review article in 2015, when he was a judge on the U.S. Court of Appeals for the Ninth Circuit. (In 2017, Kozinski retired from the bench following highly credible accusations of sexual harassment by several women, including former law clerks.) The state is responsible for investigating crimes, and that means it largely controls the gathering of information. Police scour the crime scene, send what they find to a forensics lab, and receive the results; detectives usually interview witnesses before anyone else does. The Brady rule is supposed to ensure that if law enforcement agents turn up anything that could help the defense, they'll hand it over, so that all the facts come out.

For years, however, little attention was paid to enforcing the Brady rule, in part because it was so hard to prove it was being broken. Prosecutors decide what counts as "material" or "favorable"— in the heat of battle—while the judge and the defense have no way to see what they're holding back. It's as if prosecutors are tennis players calling their own lines when their opponents, and even the referee, can't see the other side of the court.

In 1985, the Supreme Court made it even easier for prosecutors to cheat. In a five-to-three decision in the case *United States v. Bagley*, the justices decreed that the defense had to do more than bring hidden evidence to light to prevail. To win a new trial, the defense also had to show that there was a "reasonable probability" that the jury would have reached a different decision if the evidence had been disclosed. If not, then the prosecution's failing would be excused as immaterial.

Justice Thurgood Marshall, in a dissent joined by Justice Brennan, explained the pitfalls of the Court's new standard. It asked the prosecutor to "perform the impossible task of deciding whether a certain piece of information will have a significant impact on the trial, bearing in mind that a defendant will later shoulder the heavy burden of proving how it would have affected the outcome." At worst, Marshall predicted, "the standard invites a prosecutor, whose interests are conflicting, to gamble, to play the odds."

Marshall's prediction has come all too true. When previously hidden evidence does come to light, prosecutors have reason to hope that judges will be prone to decide that it didn't really matter. For example, in 707 cases of prosecutorial misconduct between 1997 and 2009, many of them involving withheld evidence, the California courts reversed fewer than one-quarter of the verdicts. In a national study by the Center for Public Integrity, judges reversed only 18 percent of more than 10,700 convictions in which they found that misconduct by police or prosecutors occurred. In the rest, they ruled that the failure to turn over evidence was a harmless error: the jury would have convicted either way.

While many prosecutors treat their obligation to turn over evidence as sacrosanct and interpret it broadly, others limit what counts as material evidence and thus what they think they owe the defense. Gary Udashen, a defense lawyer in Texas who chaired the board for the state's Innocence Project, described an appeal he handled a few years ago in which evidence favorable to his client came to light after the fact, and the judge asked the prosecutor why she hadn't disclosed it at trial. "She said she didn't think that evidence was true, so it wasn't material," Udashen said. "Prosecutors may say something isn't true if it's inconsistent with the state's case." In other words, the prosecutor viewed the evidence as she wished to see it, rather than considering how the defense could use the information.

In recent decades, several states and an increasing number of district attorney's offices have tried to fix the flaws of *Brady* by opening the prosecution's files to the defense beyond the requirements set by the Supreme Court.

Tennessee has done nothing along these lines. Weirich's obligation was to follow the limited but crucial bedrock rule set out in *Brady*—to turn over evidence that was material to Noura's guilt and helpful to the defense before her trial. Back in 2005, soon after she began representing Noura, Corder started asking Weirich for the evidence the state was gathering. She filed motions asking for all the prosecution's Brady evidence and also—by name—for everything related to a witness named Andrew Hammack.

Hammack was Noura's age. She knew him as a friend of a friend who'd inherited some money from his father and lived with a couple of roommates, sometimes selling pot and making fake IDs. In the days after Jennifer Jackson's death, the police interviewed Hammack twice about the murder. Hammack's account filled in part of the time Noura said she was driving around alone. In the first interview, he said he called Noura twice between 11:00 p.m. and

1:00 a.m., and that she asked him to meet her at her house. He also said they spoke again later and that she told him she was waiting for him. In the second interview, Hammack added a third call, which he said Noura made from her home phone.

Hammack didn't actually go to Noura's house that night. Still, he was valuable for the prosecution: he was the only witness who could put Noura at the scene of the crime during the hours when Jennifer was murdered.

Noura said she called Hammack once in the hour or so after midnight. "He was going to stop by my house and see my kitten," she told the police. "I was supposed to call him when I got home." But Noura said she didn't reach Hammack again. Cellphone records showed that she called him at 12:55 a.m., as she said, and that she placed another call to him at 3:54. She tried him again, six times in quick succession, just before and after 5:00 a.m. But the phone records didn't establish whether Hammack picked up or whether the call went to voicemail. Noura also texted Hammack. The police recovered the content of her last three messages. At 4:05 a.m., Noura texted, "nothn sittn at erics" (the friend whose house she drove to); at 4:29 a.m., she wrote, "what r u doing"; and at 5:00 a.m., simply "answer."

The police collected Hammack's DNA, and it wasn't a match for the blood found in Jennifer's bedroom. Still, to Corder, Hammack presented a chance to sow reasonable doubt, not only by disputing his story but also by presenting him as a potential suspect. A week after the murder, Hammack's roommates came to the Memphis police station and reported that they didn't know where he was for part of the night Jennifer was killed, and that he got nervous when they asked him about it. They talked to Lieutenant Mark Miller, a lead homicide investigator, and gave him a pair of New Balance sneakers, which had reddish brown stains, and which the roommates said they'd noticed Hammack wearing the weekend of the murder. Miller had pictures taken of the shoes and then gave them back to the roommates instead of sending them to the lab for testing. But he did conduct a third interview with Hammack, who this time told a different story, saying that when Noura called him before 1:00 a.m., his phone was in a truck with a friend. Hammack said she then tried to reach him by calling the phone of a friend, named Ryan, while they were out at a party. Hammack said he agreed to meet Noura at her house but didn't go because he was drunk.

Corder saw Miller's decision not to test Hammack's shoes as shoddy police work. The discovery materials she got about him, from Weirich and Stephen Jones, the assistant prosecutor in Noura's case, seemed incomplete to her. She kept pressing. A month before the trial, Judge Craft instructed the prosecutors to turn over to Corder any exculpatory evidence they had.

When Corder didn't get any evidence related to Hammack, she filed a motion for sanctions against Weirich and Jones, an aggressive move that accused them of concealing evidence. That day, and again as the trial opened—the jury was selected on February 9, 2009—Jones told Judge Craft that he and Weirich had given the defense all the evidence they were obligated to provide. Corder still thought something was missing, but she didn't know what. The judge said that if the prosecution didn't turn over evidence that could help Noura, the defense would have "ironclad" grounds for a mistrial, and Weirich and Jones could be disbarred. Then he put an end to the wrangling and the trial began.

Weirich went first. She stood before the eight women and four men of the jury in a gray suit and white blouse. She knew how to command their attention. "There were signs," she began, puncturing the silence of the room. "When friends and family look back on the summer of 2005, they remember signs, flashes, warnings, indications, rumblings, before a volcano erupts. . . . Like the conversation that a neighbor overheard in the driveway: 'Give me the fucking money.'" Weirich's voice rose close to a yell. "'Give me my money.'"

Weirich let her damning words echo, and then spoke as if she were Jennifer Jackson. "Shh, shh, Noura, let's talk about this inside so the neighbors don't hear," she said. Returning to her own voice, she described the exchange she'd just voiced as "conversations a week before Jennifer Jackson's dead body was found in her bedroom, about rules Mom was laying down."

Oh my God, Noura thought. *This is what it's going to be like. I didn't talk to my mom like that. There was no money. And the neighbor she's talking about lived across the street and down a ways from us, so how could she hear us in our driveway?* It didn't make sense to her, but she had to sit silently and listen.

"There were signs," Weirich said again, "but nobody could anticipate a thirty-nine-year-old mother's dead body found crumpled in a corner of her bedroom, naked and stabbed repeatedly. Nobody saw that coming."

Weirich unspooled more of her story. Jennifer Jackson went to a wedding at the Calvary Episcopal Church on the night of June 4, 2005. "Meanwhile, across town, the defendant, her daughter, was out, hanging out with friends. She was with a bunch of teenagers." Weirich mentioned the parties Noura went to that night and a call she received from her mother at midnight, telling her to come home. "The next time anybody sees the defendant is at 4:04 in the morning when she's checking out at a Walgreens," the prosecutor continued. "She's bought a bottle of hydrogen peroxide, New Skin, Skin Shield, adhesive tape and other liquid bandages.

"Twelve-thirty to four. No one sees her."

Weirich ticked off more "signs." Noura had been wearing a long-sleeved sweatshirt the morning of her mother's murder, even though the day was hot. She'd answered, "Let me think," when the police asked her where she was the night before. She hadn't wanted to take off the white tape covering the cut on her hand. One of Noura's friends had told the police Noura called her mother "a bitch who needs to go to hell" at the party that evening. Weirich repeated the line twice.

When Weirich moved to the physical evidence, she told the jury how the police took pictures of the crime scene, collected blood samples, and gathered other evidence. "There were signs every-where," she said. It sounded as if the signs were present in the phys-ical evidence at the crime scene, though Weirich didn't directly misrepresent the facts by saying so. Instead, she addressed the emo-tional knot at the heart of the trial: the difficulty of blaming a daughter for her mother's death. "Nobody wanted to say the un-speakable," she said. "It was almost the answer of last resort be-cause no one, even the most hardened, seasoned homicide detective, wants to say the words that a daughter could kill her mother . . . for what?" She paused. "To get her money. To get that money that her mom was holding back for college."

With her motive now established, Weirich addressed the glaring weakness in her case: the lack of physical evidence. "You will hear from crime scene officers," she told the jury. "You will hear from the Tennessee Bureau of Investigation DNA expert about what she found and what she didn't find in a house where this young lady lived for five years. It was almost as if she had never stepped foot in there." Weirich paused. "Surely her blood's in there, isn't it? No." But that didn't matter, she urged. "It's not that easy, ladies and gen-tlemen . . . DNA is a wonderful thing, but it's not a freeze frame. It does not tell us what was left behind when a crime was committed. . . . It's not that easy. We can't take the easy way out with the science. If we could, we wouldn't need you. We wouldn't have to look at all the signs. . . . You've taken an oath not to ignore them. You won't be able to. And as difficult as it will be to wrap your heads around, there will be no other verdict that you can come to except that which is the most unthinkable: that the defendant killed her mother with premeditation, what we call in the State of Tennessee murder in the first degree."

Weirich sat down.

Corder didn't give an opening statement. She turned that task over to her cocounsel, Arthur Quinn, a stern man with a sharp manner of cross-examining witnesses. With little of Weirich's narrative skill or appeal to the jury's emotions, Quinn described the lack of physical evidence against Noura. "At the end of this case you'll be asking yourself who really did kill Jennifer Jackson," he told the jury. "It's still an unanswered question."

For the nine days of the trial that followed, the jury heard from more than forty witnesses for the prosecution. There was a great deal of testimony about the small cut on Noura's left hand, and the gap in her statement to the police, when she left out her 4:00 a.m. stop at Walgreens. The jury saw footage of Noura at the counter buying bandages and skin-care products and taking a paper towel from the clerk. Corder countered by stressing the before-and-after photos of Noura's white-tipped manicure, at the party Saturday night and the next morning at the police station. "Look at the nails," Corder urged the jury. "Could those hands have been in a brutal knife fight just hours before?" Corder tried to persuade Judge Craft to let her show the jury Jennifer's shopping list with the word "Band-aids" in her handwriting. But the judge refused to admit the list, saying that because it was undated, he questioned its authenticity.

By contrast, Judge Craft gave free rein to the prosecution to prompt more than a dozen witnesses to talk about Noura's character. One after the other, they described her partying, her sex life, and her drug use. They gave salacious details about Noura's behavior the summer after Jennifer's death. Perry, Noura's former boyfriend, described her climbing up a ladder and coming through a window into his bedroom. "We kind of made up for lost time, you know," he said archly. "Did she—did you all have sex that night?" Stephen Jones asked. Yes, they did, Perry said.

It was hard to see how the testimony bore on whether Noura killed her mother, but it reinforced the image of her as a girl who would do anything to fulfill her desires.

Noura could see that Weirich was good at drawing out witnesses, eliciting detail that made the conversations they described seem vivid and real. Weirich was respectful, organized, and in control. She didn't ask questions if she didn't know the answer.

On the stand, some of Noura's friends and family members swiveled away from the sympathy they had shown her after her mother's death, hardening against her. Witnesses, too, are subject to the hindsight bias (the tendency to think they knew it all along). Once they agree to testify for the prosecution, they're often on the side of proving guilt, arrayed against someone who often is accused of a terrible crime. The longer witnesses are in that position, "repeating the conclusion and its bases, the more entrenched their conclusions are likely to become," Keith Findley, the University of Wisconsin law professor, has written.

The neighbor who said she'd heard Noura demanding money from her mother testified that Noura had spoken "in a rage." Noura's aunts, who refused to speak with the defense before trial, turned up the drama in describing the argument Noura and her mother had in Florida over Memorial Day weekend. "Jennifer had had it with her," Cindy told the jury. "She didn't want her to move out, but she was eighteen, and could not seem to take her home-school tests after she was almost expelled from school. And she just wasn't listening to Jennifer or doing anything she was supposed to do." She described Noura as "sullen" and "very upset."

Listening to her aunts and other witnesses denigrate her relationship with her mother, Noura bit the inside of her cheek until she could taste blood. "It was almost like a physical experience," she told me. "Like if you stand stock still and let people hit you, and you can't throw up your hands to deflect their blows." The most painful witness was her uncle Eric. "He broke my heart," she said. When Eric was a teenager and Jennifer took him in, he was like an older brother to Noura. Now he was on the side of the prosecution, helping to supply the motive Weirich had promised the jury by testifying that he heard Noura and her mother argue over putting her father's assets into a college fund.

Eric, along with Noura's aunts, had a financial stake in the trial's outcome. Several months after Noura's arrest, they sued her for the value of her mother's estate, which totaled about $1.5 million, almost all of it from Jennifer's life insurance policy. Noura's lawyers asked her aunt Grace about the lawsuit because they wanted the jury to know about it. "For her to walk away with a pot of money after carrying out what she set out to do would be the biggest travesty of all," Grace said. If Noura was convicted of killing her mother, Tennessee law would prevent her from inheriting her mother's assets. Her aunts and uncle would get them instead. (Through their lawyer, Grace, Cindy, and Eric declined to speak with me.)

Grace admitted that she hadn't seen her sister and niece often over the years, but claimed that she and Jennifer remained close. "I love my sister and was always there for her." She helped Weirich by testifying that Noura told her she'd cut her hand on broken glass, not the explanation her friends said she'd given. "She said, 'Grace, any doctor would tell you that's a burn. I burned it cooking macaroni and cheese.'" Grace also made Noura sound ungrateful for the rent her aunts paid for her apartment over the summer. "She goes, 'I'm not living in a five- or six-hundred-dollar a month apartment,'" Grace testified. "'I'm used to living in a nice house.' So, she was not happy, and we then changed and upped and spent a lot more money to get her a nicer apartment."

Cindy's closing words were the most devastating. She recounted the conversation she'd had with Noura over the phone after her arrest. "I was taking care of her," she said, to explain why Noura called her from jail. "I would have gotten her lawyers or anything she needed if she had an alibi." She asked Noura to prove to her where she was on the night of Jennifer's murder.

"She said, 'I don't know.' And I asked her again, 'Where were you during all of this? Who were you with?' And she said, 'I don't know.' And then I never heard from her again."

On the last day of the prosecution's case, Weirich called Andrew Hammack to the stand. When she asked him if he and Noura were friends, he said they were "friends with benefits." It was one more reference to her sex life, and according to Noura, it wasn't true. But her lawyers didn't object. When Weirich led him through the night of June 4 and the crucial early hours of June 5, Hammack said he'd gone to a party with Ryan and that he'd had his phone with him all night. He and Noura talked between 10:00 p.m. and midnight, he said, or maybe between midnight and 2:00 a.m., and then again at about 4:00 a.m. Noura had asked him to "come to meet her at her house," Hammack told the jury.

"Was that a normal request of hers?" Weirich asked. "Did she normally call you and say come meet me at my house at five in the morning?"

"No, ma'am," Hammack answered.

Later, Weirich circled back to ask about the timing of Noura's calls. Hammack said they'd talked twice, and both times Noura asked him to come over.

"What time?" Weirich asked about the second call.

"Four-ish," Hammack answered.

When the prosecution rested its case later that day, Judge Craft asked Corder if she planned to call any witnesses. Noura was desperate to correct the jury's impression of her. She wanted to call friends who could testify on her behalf, and she wanted to speak for herself. "There were so many questions nobody could answer but me," she said. She wanted to tell the jury how rejected she'd felt by her aunts and to say that when Cindy asked where she was on the night of her mother's death, in that fateful call from jail, she didn't answer because she felt betrayed. "I said, 'I'm in jail! Get me out!' And Cindy didn't say, 'How? Where? Let me talk to somebody.' She was like, 'OK, answer my questions if you want to get out.' I felt like she didn't care about what was happening to me and it didn't matter what I said."

Noura also wanted to explain how alone she felt after her mother's death, living by herself for the first time, and to say that Wei-rich's "signs" that she wasn't grieving—the parties at her apartment, the visit to Perry's house—showed that she was casting about, how-ever she could, for human contact.

But putting Noura on the stand was a big gamble. She'd been on and off a heavy regimen of antianxiety and antidepressant medica-tion while she was in jail. Frustrated and angry about the trial, she was close to unraveling. Corder wasn't sure how Noura would hold up under cross-examination, and advised her to invoke her consti-tutional right to remain silent. "You never put your client on the stand in a reasonable-doubt case," she told me later. "She's not a professional witness. Amy Weirich is a professional examiner. Who do you think will win at that O.K. Corral?"

Corder also could have called witnesses to testify about Noura's character and her relationship with her mother. Bill Shelton and Ansley Larsson attended the trial and were disposed to portray Noura and Jennifer as loving and close. Eric's former girlfriend and other friends visited Noura in jail. These people had known Noura and her mother for years and could have told the jury that the argu-ments between them were the standard fare of adolescence. Corder also could have elicited testimony about the unsolved murder of Noura's father and the transfer of his cars and other property to Jennifer's house.

But Corder called no witnesses. "If the state hasn't met their burden of proof in proving this is the crime that was committed and this is the person who committed it, there is no defense to be put on," she said later in a television interview. It seemed like a pat answer, and I asked Corder to explain. "Everyone in that court-room wanted to know where Noura was in that window of time when her mother died," she said. "If you have no witness who can answer that burning question and provide an alibi, then there's very little we could have put on that would have helped." Weirich could have created further doubt in the jurors' minds by asking character witnesses why they didn't know where Noura was that night, Corder contended. Or the jury could have blamed the defense for making the trial stretch out longer. These explanations didn't make much sense to me. It probably would have been improper to ask character witnesses why they didn't know Noura's whereabouts, one former prosecutor told me, since they wouldn't be expected to be her keeper. When I ran Corder's reasoning by other defense lawyers, they were also puzzled, despite their reluctance to question her trial strategy since they hadn't been in the courtroom.

Back at the jail at night after her aunts' testimony, Noura saw news coverage of her trial, which was playing each day live on Court TV. Listening to other prisoners and commentators dissect her demeanor in court, Noura started to doubt her ability to advocate for herself. "So much of the trial was about my own emotions being examined, like how I didn't grieve properly," she said. "If I didn't cry, I was a stone cold killer. If I did, I was guilty. I thought, *Maybe Valerie is right. Maybe I'll make things worse if I testify. Maybe I can't help myself.*"

Rather than put on a case, the defense rested.

Stephen Jones, Weirich's assistant, gave the prosecution's closing statement. He used PowerPoint to lay out a timeline of Noura's movements on the night of the murder, highlighting the block of time when she was alone.

Jones dwelled on Hammack's testimony. "What did Andrew tell you?" he asked the jury. "What did Andrew tell you the defendant wanted him to do when he met her at her house? 'I want you to go inside with me. I want you to go inside with me.' Had she ever asked him to go inside with her? No. Six calls. 'I want you to go inside with me.' She needed a cover-up," he said, hitting each word hard. "Someone to go inside with her so that they could say, 'Yeah, I was with her when she found her mother's body. Oh, it was horrible.' But that didn't work out. Andrew didn't meet her there." So instead, Jones argued, Noura went to rouse her neighbor after she killed her mother, to fake the discovery of her mother's body in his presence.

When it was her turn to speak, Valerie Corder asked the jury to concentrate on the physical evidence—"the only thing," she reminded them, "that's not subject to revisionist history." One by one, Corder picked up the objects from Jackson's bedroom that the police had bagged—pillows, comforters, bed linens, a step stool—and piled them on one side of the courtroom. The point was that none of it implicated Noura. "We have the complete DNA profile . . . of someone whose blood was mixed with Jennifer's," Corder said. "None of Noura's blood is at the scene. But by golly, somebody else's is." She drove the point home: "Because they didn't find her blood there, they're going, 'Don't pay attention to the scientific evidence.'"

Corder argued that Weirich and Jones could have definitively established Noura's whereabouts by calling a cellphone tower expert, but didn't. She noted the state's failure to test the condom found on the floor and the hair found in Jennifer's hand. "Don't you want to know whose hair is in Jennifer's hands? Why doesn't the state want to know? Does it not fit with their theory?" Corder meticulously walked through each weakness in the state's case. She belittled the prosecution's theory as "We've got these few neutral things, look at them as evilly as possible. We've got all this exculpating evidence. Don't look at it at all."

But Corder said nothing that would paint a picture of Noura different from the one Weirich had created. "They're trying to make you dislike her," she pointed out, without trying to counter those feelings. It was a sharply analytical approach: all head, no heart. Perhaps inadvertently, Corder opened the door to interpreting the DNA evidence in a way that didn't exonerate Noura. "Either they indicted the wrong person, and they don't want to change their theory of the case now," she said, "or maybe more than one person killed Jennifer." It was possible, and it meant Noura could have been the accomplice.

The jury had just a few breaths to absorb Corder's presentation before Weirich rose for the last word—the state's rebuttal. She began with a bombshell.

"Just tell us where you were!" the prosecutor shouted, striding across the courtroom to where Noura was sitting, bending her knees to look her in the eye, and throwing up her hands in a gesture of impatience. "That's all we're asking, Noura!"

It was the question—the crucial question—that the defense had not answered. Noura blamed herself for that. "I thought she wouldn't have been able to say that if I'd taken the stand."

At this point, Corder rose to her feet. "Objection, Your Honor," she said. In 1965, in the case *Griffin v. California*, the Supreme Court ruled that a prosecutor may not suggest that a defendant has implicitly admitted guilt by deciding not to testify. The right to remain silent, enshrined in the Fifth Amendment, forbids "comment by the prosecutor on the accused's silence," the Court wrote. It's a basic tenet of American law and prosecutorial ethics: it's against the rules—a form of cheating—to insinuate to the jury that a defendant who didn't testify owes an explanation for her whereabouts or her conduct. Most prosecutors stay away from such aspersions. They want to fulfill their ethical duties and don't want to risk a mistrial.

In response to Corder's objection, Judge Craft called both lawyers to the bench so they could talk outside the jury's hearing.

"I want a mistrial," Corder said.

Weirich defended herself. "It's a quote from an aunt who testified," she said. She was referring to Cindy's testimony about Noura's call from the jail, though she hadn't framed her own words to the jury that way.

"That is an unfair comment on my client's right to remain silent, and it's a demand that she not remain silent," Corder countered. "She can couch it in whatever terms she wants, but that was grossly inappropriate."

Noura's trial had been one of the longest and most high-profile in years in Memphis. A mistrial would mean starting over. It would mean that all the time and expense and work of the jury, the judge, and the lawyers had been wasted. "All right," Judge Craft said.

"What I'm going to do at some point is to give the jury an instruction and at this time, I'll allow Ms. Weirich to proceed."

"This is just absolutely unbelievable," Corder said.

Judge Craft called the jurors to order and reminded them of Noura's right to remain silent. "When Miss Weirich opened her argument, she was not at all discussing or asking Miss Jackson a question," he said.

The judge was trying to unring a bell. But he also gave Weirich a chance to repeat her stinging phrase as she began her closing statement again. "As her aunt asked her," Weirich said this time, "just tell us where you were, Noura. We just have to know."

As she had at the outset of the trial, Weirich drew the jury's attention to her portrait of Noura. In contrast to Corder, she made a humble appeal. "There's one picture that keeps playing over and over and over in your head and it is nowhere in this courtroom. It is none of those four hundred exhibits," Weirich said, gesturing toward Corder's pile. "Nobody had that piece of evidence to bring you. You know the picture we're talking about. It's the picture of an eighteen-year-old, enraged, out of control. Noura Jackson, snapping.

"Do not be fooled, ladies and gentlemen," she cautioned, beckoning the jury toward her narrative and away from Corder's effort to sow doubt. "Do not be fooled."

The jurors deliberated for nine hours. When they filed back into the courtroom, Noura sat in a blue and white flowered dress with her hands folded in her lap. She tried to make eye contact with some of the jurors. They all avoided her gaze. When she heard the words "guilty of second-degree murder," her head fell.

Speaking to the press afterward, Weirich celebrated. "It's a great verdict," she said.

The prosecutors had a problem, though. Five days after the trial ended with Noura's conviction, Stephen Jones filed a new document with the court: an "omitted" witness statement, as he put it, to give to the defense. That statement was a handwritten note from Andrew Hammack that cast his own testimony in a new light.

In the note, Hammack added significantly to the story he'd told Miller—the one that differed from his trial testimony: he gave details about leaving his cellphone in the truck and going to the party with his friend Ryan. With the note in hand, the defense checked this part of Hammack's account and discovered it couldn't be true. Ryan hadn't been in Memphis on the night of the murder. He was visiting a college in Mississippi with his parents. (I tried to reach Hammack to talk to him about the discrepancies between his handwritten note and his other statements and testimony, but he didn't respond.)

The defense also learned from the note—for the first time—that Hammack said he was "rolling on XTC" that night, referring to the drug known as Ecstasy or Molly, a hallucinogen. To Corder, this was a big deal. She could have used the note to attack Hammack's reliability—and the prosecution's theory that Noura had called Hammack to engineer a cover-up. Would the jury have believed Hammack if they'd known he was rolling on Ecstasy that night? If they'd known that his alibi didn't hold up, would they have considered him more seriously as an alternative suspect, and faulted the police for failing to investigate more thoroughly when his roommates implicated him?

The police had had the note all along. Hammack gave it to Lieutenant Miller on June 13, 2005, the day Miller interviewed him, a little more than a week after Jennifer's death.

Stephen Jones would later say he found out about the note for the first time in the middle of the trial, when he saw a reference to it in Miller's write-up of his interview with Hammack. Realizing that something was missing from the prosecution's files, Jones sent an investigator to look in the police records. The investigator returned with Hammack's note. Jones said he tucked it into a flap of his notebook intending to give it to Corder—and then forgot about it until after the trial ended, when he was tidying up the cart of evidence. Now that he'd found the note and remembered its relevance, he said, he was handing it over.

To Corder, the note was Brady material. The prosecutors should have turned it over to her before trial. By failing to do so, she thought, Weirich and Jones broke a sacrosanct rule of their profession.

Corder also thought Judge Craft would agree with her. At a hearing during the run-up to trial, Craft said that "the prosecution's duty to disclose Brady material also applies to evidence affecting the credibility of a government witness." Noura's right to a new trial would be "ironclad" if the prosecutors violated her constitutional rights under *Brady*, Craft continued. Now, Hammack's note in hand, Corder asked the judge to make good on his word.

Instead, Craft denied Corder's motion for a new trial. The motive the prosecution established for Noura was "crystal clear," he said. "There was such a web of guilt woven around her" that Hammack's handwritten note "would not have affected the trial or the verdict." Craft said the prosecution's failure to disclose the evidence may not have been proper but wasn't intentional.

Rather than receive a new trial, Noura was ordered to appear for a sentencing hearing at the end of March. On that day, she listened for five hours as Weirich urged Judge Craft to impose a weighty punishment for second-degree murder in Tennessee: twenty-five years. She heard her aunts speak of their grief over losing their sister. Noura thought about her mother, and how her own right to grieve had been ripped from her. She was an orphan, but in the eyes of the law, that was her own doing.

Judge Craft imposed a prison sentence of twenty years and nine months. His next words felt to Noura like dirt she could never wash off. As if he were stating an incontrovertible fact, Craft said, "Noura killed the only person that really loved her."

7

THE GUILTY PLEA

KEVIN'S JOB INTERVIEW with UPS was scheduled for the day after his December hearing. He missed it because he mixed up the time and then didn't bother to reschedule. It seemed pointless to look for a job with his case in limbo. Sometimes he thought he'd be better off just getting it over with and going to prison. "You do your time," he figured, "and then you're done." But he kept going to his GED classes, working toward taking the test in the spring, and hoping to hear from YCP, the diversion program run by the D.A.'s office. Weeks passed without a phone call.

At the end of January, Judge Mullen announced her ruling. She would not allow Kevin's statement to the police to be admitted in court. If the case went to trial, the jury could still learn about the gun, but Officer Joseph could not testify that Kevin said he'd take the charge for the weapon.

Mullen's ruling—a victory for Kevin and his lawyer, Debora Silberman—was a rarity in the New York City courts, where hearings about suppressing evidence take place in only a tiny fraction of cases. What the prosecutors in the gun court, Caryn Teitelman and her assistants, did next showed the impact of Silberman's determination to challenge the evidence against Kevin before trial. Without Kevin's statement, a jury might be more reluctant to hold him responsible. After all, there had been four people in Chris's apartment that night. For the prosecutors, that weakness in the case came on top of another problem. When the gun was analyzed at the forensics lab, the mix of DNA found on the grip, near the safety, didn't include Kevin's. The prosecution couldn't use science to prove he touched the gun. Without Kevin's admission or his DNA, the case came down to the word of the police.

Teitelman thought she still had enough evidence to prove Kevin's guilt beyond a reasonable doubt. "We would have dismissed the case if we didn't think we had evidence going forward," she told me. From the point of view of a prosecutor, it was a fair judgment: Teitelman believed Officer Joseph. She also knew that if the Brooklyn D.A.'s office dismissed the case, there would be serious blowback from the police. At the same time, Judge Mullen's ruling gave Silberman a chance to renew her plea for diversion. Kevin would still have to plead guilty, but he'd have a chance to stay out of prison. Teitelman talked with the assistant prosecutors working the case and the supervising attorney for the geographical zone that included Brownsville. (The Brooklyn D.A.'s office divides responsibilities by area as well as case type.) The prosecutors considered, among other things, Kevin's age, his lack of criminal history as an adult, his GED classes, the fact that the police had come looking for Chris and not Kevin, and the recovery of the gun inside an apartment rather than on the street. Taking it all into account, they gave their provisional approval: Kevin would be one of the small number of defendants in the gun court to be screened for YCP.

To pass the screening, Kevin had to show he could follow YCP's rules: submit to random drug testing, do community service, check in with a YCP social worker in person every week, and work or go to school. YCP also included a nightly curfew of 10:00 p.m., weekends included. Kevin had to call in from home, which would take some getting used to, as he often saw his girlfriend at her house before she left for her night job in Manhattan.

The real sticking point for Kevin, though, was YCP's policy of asking prospective participants questions about their neighborhoods and networks before accepting them, ostensibly to determine whether they were gang-involved. He and other young people I talked to suspected they were being pumped for information that could be fed to the police or the D.A.'s office. For just about any young man in a poor neighborhood in Brooklyn, snitching was a dangerous betrayal. Just a whiff of it could put you in serious jeopardy.

Everyone knew people like Chris were being watched on social media. Gonzalez acknowledged as much. "In Brooklyn, one-half of 1 percent of the population commits 70 percent of the crimes," he said. "We have a very focused approach, by going after what we call the drivers of crime. There are thirteen thousand people we monitor in Brooklyn. We pay attention every time they get arrested. We monitor them on social media." The idea came from Cy Vance, the Manhattan district attorney, who launched a unit in 2010 to track what he called "crime drivers." Data-driven prosecution was supposed to be an advance, as CompStat, the NYPD's crime-mapping system, was for policing. An email system alerted prosecutors when someone on the alert list was arrested for any crime. Those people were subsequently more likely to have high bail set and more likely to go to prison than other defendants facing similar charges.

Vance said he intended to target people with repeat convictions, gang ties, or who'd refused to cooperate as witnesses. But only 25 percent of the people on the Manhattan alert list had a prior violent felony arrest and only 15 percent had such a conviction. The D.A.'s office could set an alert for anyone the Crime Strategies Unit decided was of interest. "No rules govern when you can be alerted when someone has been arrested," an official told me. "For example, it could be someone who was present at a shooting who doesn't have a conviction. Or if the person of interest had a case that got dismissed, the alert doesn't have to go away. You can keep it as long as you want."

YCP was not designed for gang members or for using partici-pants as informants. The D.A.'s office said the screening interviews with YCP applicants would be kept confidential. But Project Redi-rect, the stricter felony diversion program for people who were deemed to be involved with gangs, was known for funneling infor-mation to the police. As Kevin was being assessed for YCP, he had little trust that a program run by the D.A.'s office would keep his secrets. He didn't think diversion should entail giving up informa-tion. "You say I'm in this program to work on me, and then you're asking me who has guns in Brownsville? And you work for the D.A.'s office? No way," he said.

It's typical for prosecutors, not judges, to exert near-total con-trol over who gets diversion. But it's not typical for a D.A.'s office to run its own diversion program. Most of these programs are oper-ated by social-service agencies. Going for his screening, Kevin felt surrounded by law enforcement. He had to wait at the entrance to the building on Jay Street that housed the D.A.'s office, where police officers also went after making an arrest. Then he went through a metal detector and past a command center with two holding cells where detectives conducted interviews.

When YCP admitted its first participants in 1998, African Amer-ican and Latino churches took the lead, recruiting local mentors, but over time church participation dropped off, cutting important ties to the community. Defense lawyers worried about submitting their clients to YCP, with its prosecutorial bent. What would hap-pen to their records when the program ended? Would the police watch them indefinitely? If they wanted to stay out of prison, how-ever, defendants in the gun court had no other choice but to accept the direct oversight of an arm of the D.A.'s office. Successfully com-pleting YCP (or Project Redirect) was the only way they could earn the dismissal of the violent felony charge they were about to accept.

Working out of the same building as the D.A.'s office on Jay Street, YCP social workers had an especially difficult and ethically fraught task. Their job was to help clients improve their well-being and their prospects; the prosecution's job was to generate guilty pleas and clamp down in the event of any sign of trouble. "The whole program, I don't know what I think about it," a social work intern at YCP told me after spending several months there. "I learned a lot, but I had a lot of criticisms. It's a little manipulative. It's an alternative to incarceration, but it's in the D.A.'s office, and the D.A.'s office profits from every person who pleads guilty to be in the program. My constant fear was that the kids didn't feel they could be honest."

The social worker screening Kevin for YCP, Maksim Kreyngold, was a Russian immigrant with a kippah. He'd come to the United States in 1994 because being Jewish in Belarus felt increasingly isolating and precarious. His high school teachers let him out of class early in hopes that he could get home safely, but once a group of boys caught him and beat him, fracturing his spine. Kreyngold arrived in New York when he was eighteen knowing no English; he worked his way from language classes to courses at Hunter College. He became Orthodox, attended a yeshiva, then finished his B.A. at Touro College and got his social work degree. "I was searching a lot," he said of his early years in the United States. "I was lost. The worst part is you don't know what to do with your life. You're trying to prove you're a good person but they don't know you." Though he'd had a different upbringing from his clients, and his Russian accent sounded nothing like their speech, Kreyngold understood what it felt like to be treated as lesser and to fear being cast out. He wanted to build his clients up. He was trained to set a baseline for them, based on their competencies—emotional, organizational, and otherwise—when they came in the door. He tried to help them develop from where they were rather than from an abstract ideal of where they should be.

But Kreyngold also had to answer to his bosses and to the expectations of prosecutors. He was trying to walk a line, doing his job while shielding his clients. It wasn't easy.

At first, talking to Kreyngold to be assessed for YCP, Kevin thought he was being set up to fail. It was a hard time: at home in Brownsville, his act of loyalty toward Chris in taking the weight of the gun charge was being twisted into something sinister. Chris had also been charged the night the police came to his apartment, for the misdemeanor of hindering the prosecution, because he'd thrown the magazine out of the window. He got out on bail, but four months later he was caught with another gun, and this time he was charged with CPW2 and sent to jail on high bail.

Chris's girlfriend didn't seem to know about the second gun charge, and so she didn't understand why he was in jail and Kevin was free. She jumped to the wrong conclusion: that Kevin had snitched. The accusation put Kevin in peril. "She's promoting I'm out here snitching because I'm not in jail for the gun and her boyfriend is and people are believing her," Kevin told me. "I had to really bark at her. I was about to beat her up. That snitching thing is no joke. Especially where I live at, you could get hurt with people saying things like that. And then at the same time, you got YCP trying to make me a snitch. Are you serious? It was everything going on at once."

Kevin tried to explain that he was facing two years in prison and two years of parole, but he wasn't sure he was getting through. "It was up to the point I was about to mess up my case to prove to these people I wasn't snitching. You know you're not supposed to have your friends come to court if they're gang-related. It's not a good look. But I was willing to have them come so they could see me being offered two and two." Waiting for Kreyngold's decision on YCP, he told his friends he was in the program already so they would think he was facing consequences for his gun charge, imposing a curfew on himself to make it seem true.

Kreyngold didn't know any of this, and when Kevin wouldn't answer his questions, Kreyngold wasn't sure if he could trust him.

One day in the spring, he pressed a bit, trying to understand. Why had Kevin been around a gun? Was he gang-involved? They got into a real argument. "I was at the point where I said, 'I don't care if you keep me or not,'" Kevin said. "It could have gone really downhill."

Kreyngold could feel the temperature rising and decided to take a break. He wasn't discouraged, though. "I saw the real person," he told me later of the interaction. "You can work with that. He didn't get aggressive. He had a reaction and we spoke about it. I'm not going to give up on him. Are you kidding me? But I have to do my job. I have to know who you are a little bit. There's something about being able to admit what you did. It's like Yom Kippur. You start by admitting your sin. You do *tshuva*." The Hebrew word means something like repentance, and it's an element of atonement. "It's like a miracle. It builds rapport and trust, and then when they feel comfortable, they stop BS-ing you and you can really start to work with the kid."

Kreyngold still had to get approval to admit Kevin from the head of YCP and the prosecutors, and they were skeptical. Toward the end of April, Kevin had missed a court date: someone from a rival project was being sentenced that morning, for killing a man he believed killed his brother, and a lot of his supporters were expected to come to the hearing. Kevin didn't feel safe with them in the courthouse. He called Kreyngold and Silberman to tell them he couldn't come. Silberman explained his absence to the judge, and Kreyngold assured her that the YCP screening was moving ahead on schedule. But afterward, Kreyngold told Silberman he had to see more from Kevin.

Kevin and I met later that day at a diner a few blocks from the courthouse. We drank iced tea and he talked about a loss that was crowding out his other thoughts. A month earlier, he'd persuaded a friend to drive him more than six hours upstate to pick up his best friend, Travis, from a medium-security prison near the Canadian border. Kevin and Travis had known each other since kindergarten. When Travis had problems getting along with his family in middle school, he moved into Kevin's apartment for a few years. "My mom would introduce him as her son when he lived with us," Kevin said.

When he was thirteen, Travis was charged with conspiracy related to a shooting. He did stints at Rikers Island for assault and larceny, and then in the summer of 2014, when he was nineteen, he got shot, though not seriously wounded, while he was walking down one of the main streets in Brownsville. The shooting could have been connected to the fighting among the projects or it could have been random; Travis and Kevin weren't sure. Kevin's main feeling was relief—what if Travis had been paralyzed or killed? It could have been so much worse.

Around the same time, Travis got caught for a credit card scam. He'd been asking people on their way out of coffee shops to sign petitions and then trying to steal their credit cards or phones. He pled guilty a year and a half later and went to prison for nearly two years.

"He didn't want visits, the whole time," Kevin said. "I missed him." He'd made sure to answer his phone whenever Travis called. On the drive home, they talked about Travis's young daughter and how he should stay clear of anything that could violate his parole. "I'm trying to tell him, 'We grown now, man. No one goes around stealing phones or whatever. You got a child.'"

During his first weeks at home, Kevin thought Travis was doing a lot of what he was supposed to do. He saw his daughter and his mother. He looked for a job. Then he stopped answering Kevin's calls or texts. Over two days, Travis went on a spree with someone Kevin knew and didn't like. The pair robbed someone and posted videos of themselves on Facebook flashing $100 bills and bags of pills. Kevin didn't really know how to explain Travis's actions. Maybe it was the drugs. "I guess they just took over his body," he said.

The police came looking for Travis in a high-rise, knocking on his door in the early evening. Travis called his mother and told her he loved her. With the police still pounding on the thick metal, he tried to climb out the window and somehow make it to the ground safely, but he fell to his death. He was twenty-one.

Kevin was the one who called Travis's mother to tell her. "I'm like, 'He's gone.' I just had to tell her immediately straight. She started screaming." Kevin met her at the hospital to help identify the body.

Recounting the story at the diner, Kevin seemed wrung out. When he came downtown, he usually wore bright durags, red or blue or gold, which he took off for court or his YCP meetings. (The colors didn't mean what they used to, Kevin and other young men told me, now that gangs like the Bloods and the Crips no longer ran their neighborhoods.) Today his hair stayed pulled back in a pony-tail under his gray hoodie. He had a cold and his throat was scratchy. He'd talked through Travis's death with Kreyngold, who he felt un-derstood, but he couldn't shake a deep sense of futility verging on despair. "What can you do about it?" he said. "If everyone's not on the same page, you can't make a change. You can try but it's a dead end. Some people look at it like you got to try. I wish that I didn't have no beef with anyone anymore. But I can't make that happen. I can tell you, it's pointless."

Kevin was steeling himself for Travis's funeral the following Fri-day. He worried about missing a summer-job orientation, to be held on the same day, which he had to attend to get into YCP. Another scheduling conflict loomed: his next court date was supposed to take place on the day of his GED test. Middle-class teenagers can typically find a way around obstacles like this, since if they have a good excuse, they get to reschedule. In Kevin's case, Kreyngold changed the date of the summer-job orientation, but the GED test proved to be unmovable. Kevin could take it again, but first he'd have to go through six more months of classes. Discouraged, he decided to quit school for the time being. His upcoming summer job would cover him with YCP.

"Today I see my brother for the last timeee," he wrote on Face-book, on the day of Travis's funeral, above a picture of the two of them, their younger faces open and expectant. "My mind all over the placeee rest up Beloved."

The jury trial has an essential place in the American Constitution. The founding fathers saw juries as a means of achieving fairness and truth and as "a shield against tyranny," as Jed Rakoff, a federal district court judge in New York and a former federal prosecutor, has written. Thomas Jefferson called trial by jury "the only anchor, ever yet imagined by man, by which a government can be held to the principles of its constitution." Article III of the Constitution guarantees the right to a jury in trials of all crimes (except impeachment) in the state where they are committed. The Sixth Amendment repeats this promise and adds the right to a speedy and public trial "in all criminal prosecutions." The founders gave the right to trial by jury such primacy because "they were unwilling to trust the government" to mark it in a plain old statute, Justice Antonin Scalia wrote. More than other features of America's constitutional structure, the jury offered direct democracy, with lower requirements of property ownership than most forms of government service. "Juries were, in a sense, the people themselves, tried-and-true embodiments of late-18th-century ideology," Yale law professor Akhil Amar wrote in his book *America's Constitution*. "Trials were not just about the rights of the defendant but also about the rights of the community." They brought ordinary Americans into the courthouse and gave them responsibility for the most important decisions that happened within it.

Plea bargains, on the other hand, have no cherished spot in the Constitution. They are nowhere to be found.

For close to a century after the nation's founding, trials and juries dominated American courts. They were short and cursory. There was no right to counsel for people who couldn't afford one (that would not come in ordinary state cases until 1963), so defendants often didn't have lawyers to challenge the evidence against them. But the framers would have easily recognized the process, which relied on juries to establish guilt and on judges to determine punishment. That began to change following the Civil War. In the late nineteenth century, caseloads grew along with rising crime, and the plea deal, negotiated outside of public view, began to replace the open courtroom battle of the trial. One scholar mourned the "vanishing jury" as early as 1928. The plea rate for felonies hovered at 80 percent until the mid-1970s.

What happened next—the true disappearance of the jury and the trial—was a function of the rising power of prosecutors. Intent on putting more people in prison to fight the crime wave of the 1980s and 1990s, state legislators and Congress increasingly favored three-strikes laws (which set a long sentence following a third conviction) and mandatory minimums, with penalties dictated by the charge rather than by a judge's decision at sentencing (that way, a lenient judge couldn't undermine the will of the legislature). By 1994, every state had at least one mandatory minimum law and most had several. State criminal codes also expanded, allowing prosecutors to stack up multiple charges and penalties for a single offense. Congress also locked in mandatory minimum sentences as it added new offenses to the federal criminal code. (Another popular approach, "truth-in-sentencing," cut off early release by curtailing the authority of parole boards.)

This was the period in which imprisonment rates in the United States and Europe diverged. In the early 1970s, the scale of incarceration in the Northeast, the Midwest, and the West Coast was comparable to the scale in Sweden, Denmark, and Norway. Over the next thirty years, the Scandinavian numbers stayed low while the American numbers shot up. "In the span of a little more than three decades," William Stuntz wrote, "Americans first embraced punishment levels lower than Sweden's, then built a justice system more punitive than Russia's."

Though it wasn't framed this way, the turn in the U.S. toward harsh punishment stripped authority from judges and handed it to prosecutors. This is crucial. Prosecutors decided whether to charge a crime in such a way as to trigger a mandatory minimum or three-strikes penalty in the first place. And there were more of them: from 1990 to 2007, the number of prosecutors across the country jumped by 50 percent, from twenty thousand to thirty thousand. Crunching the numbers for thirty-four states in a previously overlooked state-court database, and excluding marijuana arrests because they rarely resulted in prison, John Pfaff, a Fordham law professor, found that in the 1990s and 2000s, the total number of felony filings grew substantially, and the number of filings per arrest—the link in the chain controlled by prosecutors—doubled. (Perhaps reflecting the greater drop in crime in big cities, another data set from seventy-five major metropolitan areas shows only a modest rise in felony filings. It doesn't include the number of filings per arrest.) Conviction rates per arrest also increased slightly over the same period. Crucially, so did prison admissions—another factor that prosecutors heavily influence and that obviously contributes to mass incarceration.

With the power prosecutors gained to threaten prison time came the power to strike a harder bargain—and they used it to settle cases with plea bargains, negotiated outside the courtroom. Plenty of prosecutors were drawn to the profession by the prospect of live combat at trial. But plea bargains forestalled tricky legal fights and seemed the only way to cope with towering court dockets. Plea bargains often take weeks or months to achieve—a long time in the life of a defendant, but in terms of time spent in court, a small fraction of the many hours lawyers and judges put in for a trial. Replacing trials with deals benefited judges and defense lawyers as a means of coping with their workload, along with prosecutors, as the University of Chicago law professor Albert Alschuler pointed out decades ago.

And so the criminal justice landscape reconstituted itself, making way for a feature that distorted the original design. It's called the trial penalty, and it's become so common in the criminal courtroom that we hardly register it anymore. Here's how it works: A defendant who takes the prosecutor's offer and pleads guilty gets a break at sentencing compared with the length of the sentence for the top charge. A defendant who refuses the prosecution's offer and goes to trial gets socked for it if he loses. The right to trial is undisturbed in theory; in practice, invoking it comes with a heavy price. Judge Rakoff quantified the crushing trial penalty for federal drug cases: "In 2012, the average sentence for federal narcotics defendants who entered into any kind of plea bargain was five years and four months, while the average sentence for defendants who went to trial was sixteen years."

Trials remain the public face of the American justice system and a pillar of its legitimacy. They inject drama into true-crime stories in the news, and in movies and books. Of course, they haven't vanished entirely: in a tiny fraction of cases, jurors listen to both sides, do their best to follow the judge's instructions, and decide whether the state has proved guilt beyond a reasonable doubt. But in many states, upward of 95 percent of criminal convictions are obtained through guilty pleas. The rate in some states, including New York, is as high as 98 percent.

For almost everyone summoned to a courthouse in a criminal case, the reality is the one Kevin experienced. The criminal code gives prosecutors a menu of options (second degree, third degree, fourth degree) for crimes like burglary, sexual assault, or criminal possession of a weapon. "If the menu is long enough—and it usually is—prosecutors can dictate the terms of plea bargains," Stuntz wrote. Defense lawyers are often reduced to tactics like stalling and begging, judges are incidental, and the jury never shows up. "The outcome is very largely determined by the prosecutor alone," observes Rakoff, one of a handful of judges who write frankly about the shortcomings of the system they oversee. He calculated that of the 2.2 million Americans now in prison, more than 2 million are there "as a result of plea bargains dictated by the government's prosecutors, who effectively dictate the sentences as well."

Formally speaking, judges have the power to reject plea deals. In practice, they almost never do. As the last stop on the assembly line, judges inspect for major defects, but they feel the pressure to move the product to delivery.

"I'd much prefer the defendant plead guilty to a misdemeanor than a felony," I heard Judge Suzanne Mondo tell Teitelman and an assistant prosecutor one day as I sat listening, getting the feel of gun court. Judge Mondo was talking about the slim man standing before her, a twenty-year-old named Zamir, who shared an apartment in a Coney Island housing project with his grandmother. The police had searched their home after getting a call from an informant they wouldn't identify. They found an unloaded gun, along with a small amount of marijuana and a few pills, and arrested Zamir, who had no criminal history.

Since his arrest, Zamir had voluntarily enrolled in and completed a diversion program. He was also taking a year-long course in plumbing and pipefitting. Still, Teitelman consulted briefly with her assistant and told the judge, "I can't imagine a misdemeanor is appropriate with this set of facts," She didn't say why. As a result of her decision, Zamir was sent to jail for thirty days, with a felony conviction that would remain on his record, hurting his job prospects and affecting his housing. When I talked to Zamir after he got out of jail, he said he was barred from returning to his grandmother's public housing unit and couldn't find work in the trade he'd trained for. "I can't get the jobs I wanted," he told me. "This has ruined things for me. That's how I feel right now."

Kevin knew that if he went to trial and lost, he'd go to prison for at least three and a half years—and that the Brooklyn D.A.'s office would demand more time, not because Teitelman would suddenly conclude he deserved it but because she had to signal to other defendants that they would pay a price for the time and resources a trial required. That was how the trial penalty worked. In the gun court, Teitelman's power to prosecute CPW2 and unleash the threat of a heavy sentence meant that about 250 plea bargains took place in the gun court's first year and a half, compared with nine trials—three of which led to acquittals, a significant loss rate for the D.A.'s office.

Plea bargains are supposed to be a type of contract, which means they have to be agreed to freely, voluntary rather than compelled. Rakoff called this conception of the plea deal "a total myth." Yale law professor John Langbein has gone even further, comparing plea bargains to torture, arguing that the purpose of both is to produce a confession. "There is of course a difference between having your limbs crushed if you refuse to confess, or suffering some extra years of imprisonment if you refuse to confess, but the difference is of degree, not kind," he wrote. "Plea bargaining, like torture, is coercive."

In medieval times, Europeans made torture victims repeat their admissions publicly. This was supposed to prove that a confession was voluntary, though anyone who recanted could find himself questioned under torture again. American judges require defendants to answer yes, also publicly in the courtroom, to a series of questions before accepting a plea: "Has anyone threatened you, or forced you, or pressured you to plead guilty against your will? Do you waive your right to appeal voluntarily, of your own free will and choice?" Nancy Gertner, who spent seventeen years as a federal judge, compared the scripted exchange to a Kabuki ritual. " 'Has anyone coerced you to plead guilty,' I would ask, and I felt like adding, 'like thumbscrews or waterboarding?' " she wrote after leaving the bench. " 'Anything less than that—a threatened tripling of your sentence should you go to trial, for example—doesn't count.' "

The Supreme Court banned coerced confessions in federal court in the late nineteenth century and in state court in 1936, in the case *Brown v. Mississippi*. The police, the justices ruled, aren't allowed to make you talk by hurting you or threatening consequences for your family. They drew an analogy between a coerced confession and an "involuntary" plea. And in 1968, they struck down a federal kidnapping statute that allowed for the death penalty only if a defendant took his case to trial, so a defendant had an overwhelming incentive to accept a plea and avoid execution. But the justices stopped short of saying that the threat of a death sentence made plea agreements coercive. Instead, Justice Potter Stewart wrote, the statute was "evil" because it "needlessly encourages" guilty pleas.

Ten years later, in *Bordenkircher v. Hayes*, Justice Stewart returned to write the opinion that did more than any other to set plea bargaining on its current course. The defendant, Paul Hayes, stole a check from a local business in Lexington, Kentucky, and forged the signature so he could use it to pay for $88.30 worth of groceries. Hayes lived with his diabetic mother and four of his fifteen siblings, working as a horse groom to support the family, which also received welfare. The check forgery carried a sentence of two to ten years in prison. A decade earlier, Hayes probably would have gotten the minimum two years for pleading guilty, but prosecutors were getting tougher on repeat offenders by 1973, and Hayes had been convicted of a sex offense as a teenager and of a robbery when he was in his early twenties. As a result, the prosecutor thought he should serve five years for the bad check. And if he refused to plead guilty, the prosecutor threatened to add a charge under the state's three-strikes law—with a mandatory life sentence.

Hayes took the case to trial. The prosecutor made good on his threat. Hayes lost and was sentenced to life.

When Hayes appealed, the Supreme Court rejected his argument that his life sentence arose from a " 'vindictive exercise of a prosecutor's discretion.' " The threat of severe punishment could discourage the defendant from asserting his trial rights, but that was an " 'inevitable'—and permissible—'attribute of any legitimate system which tolerates and encourages the negotiation of pleas,' " Justice Stewart wrote for the majority (in part quoting a previous ruling). Plea bargaining flowed from a "mutuality of advantage" to defendants and prosecutors, he assumed.

The ruling had enormous consequence. "*Bordenkircher* is the single biggest wrong turn the Supreme Court has taken in criminal law," Rachel Barkow, a law professor at New York University, told me. "If you asked me what's the one thing the Supreme Court could do to fix our current system, I'd say it would be to overturn it. The Court made a terribly wrong assumption that prosecutors wouldn't just wallop people. But they do. There has to be oversight of prosecutors. But now, when people plead guilty, they often have to agree to waive their appeal, so they can't contest anything. There would be so many more cases where problems would surface that would outrage people if it weren't for those waivers." Consider the degree to which convictions dwarf appeals. More than a million people are convicted of felonies each year, not to mention the many more who plead guilty to misdemeanors. The total number of appeals annually is seventy thousand.

Plea bargaining "'is not some adjunct to the criminal justice system; it is the criminal-justice system,'" Justice Anthony Kennedy said for a majority of the Supreme Court in 2012, quoting William Stuntz. Why didn't this make things better? It's the lure of the plea deal that entices prosecutors to reflexively file the maximum charge or pile on additional charges that inflate the penalty to an excessive degree, like the life sentence Paul Hayes received for forging an $88.30 check.

Plea bargaining has become the silent engine of our criminal justice system. As Albert Alschuler, a University of Chicago law professor who has written about plea bargaining for decades, told the writer Amy Bach, "Once you get used to it, you don't even notice the injustice."

For the most part, district attorneys and their representatives have fought for as much leverage in plea bargaining as they can get. Rachel Barkow points out that the *Congressional Record* is replete with testimony from Department of Justice officials lobbying for stiffer sentencing laws—not because they think most people should do the maximum time but because the threat of harsh punishment bends defendants to their will.

The National Association of Assistant United States Attorneys, which represents federal prosecutors, resisted sentencing reform throughout the Obama administration, calling mandatory minimums the "cornerstone" of battling drug traffickers and armed criminals. As attorney general, Jeff Sessions made this view a defining principle of his Justice Department. "When a criminal knows with certainty that he is facing hard time, he is a lot more willing to cooperate," Sessions said that February in a speech at the Heritage Foundation. "When the sentence is uncertain and up to the whims of the judge, criminals are a lot more willing to take a chance." Sessions may be right that defendants knuckle under because of mandatory minimums. But he was celebrating a burdening of the right to trial that can make innocent people conclude they have no choice but to plead guilty—as some number have done when faced with the choice between five years and life in prison, or the death penalty.

Writing about Paul Hayes and the stranglehold of plea bargaining more than a decade ago, Stuntz laid out a road not taken—a path that courts ultimately didn't take, which would have led away from mass incarceration. What if the Supreme Court had struck down Hayes's life sentence as disproportionate to his wrongdoing, in violation of the Eighth Amendment's ban on cruel and unusual punishment? Stuntz wanted to set limits on the threats that prosecutors can make in plea bargaining. "If the threatened sentence is disproportionate—if any reasonable judge, given the authority to decide, would have declined to impose it—one should not trust the fairness of the conviction and sentence the threat produces," he argued. "Plea bargains will be fair and just if, but only if, the threats that induce them are fair and just."

Hayes's life sentence was also wrong, Stuntz argued, because he was treated far worse than other people who committed similar crimes. Stuntz's solution was to require states to keep track of charging and sentencing patterns, so that judges could ask prosecutors to show that the sentence they threatened had been imposed in a reasonable number of similar cases. The idea was to provide a check on disproportionality, and push the system toward moderation, by making it more transparent.

Paul Hayes was a twenty-nine-year-old black man when he was sentenced to life. If racism fueled the prosecutor's willingness to throw the book at him, maybe a right to proportionate and consistent punishment would have protected him. "Prosecutors rarely intentionally discriminate against defendants based on race," Professor Angela J. Davis wrote in 2017. Yet a number of studies, she points out, have documented racial bias, often unconscious, in the life-altering decisions prosecutors make. Researchers have found that black defendants in various settings—Wisconsin, Manhattan, Virginia, and the federal courts—were more likely to receive plea offers with jail or prison time and less likely to have charges reduced or dismissed. There is a persistent and nagging black-white gap in the criminal justice system, and it can't be explained away by neutral factors. To take one of many examples, prosecutors were more likely to charge defendants with offenses that carry mandatory minimum sentences, Sonja Starr and M. Marit Rehavi concluded in the *Yale Law Journal* after analyzing a large dataset of federal cases.

What would happen to plea bargaining and heavy dockets if prosecutors could no longer threaten a longer sentence to avoid trial? Felony prosecutions make up less than 20 percent of the criminal docket in New York, so there might well be slightly more trials, but that's a benefit, given how low the trial rate has fallen. Trials help keep prosecutors and their law enforcement partners honest by forcing them to meet a high burden of proof. Prosecutors could keep the docket moving by screening cases with greater care at the outset, and dropping the ones that don't hold up. They could also refrain from piling on charges they don't plan to stick with—and probably don't really believe are warranted. There's evidence that the public would approve of the change. A judge in Ohio asked jurors in twenty-two trials to write down the sentence they thought the person they found guilty deserved. On average, their recommendations were nearly two-thirds lower than the minimum penalties in the federal guidelines.

Plea bargaining in the United States diverges from the practices of other countries. In Europe, prosecutors typically have a duty to pursue the truth rather than to win convictions. The system isn't adversarial, designed to achieve a fair contest between two sides; it's inquisitorial, designed to achieve faithful application of the law. In Germany, for example, prosecutors investigate and turn over their file of evidence to the court, subject to inspection by defense counsel. The judge then effectively takes over, becoming responsible for seeking as well as evaluating evidence. Prosecutors don't bargain over charges and their decisions are subject to review or appeal. They're not invested in winning. They can even choose to appeal convictions on behalf of the defendant. In France, prosecutors and judges serve in the same branch of the legal system and go back and forth between the two roles. The British system is adversarial, but prosecutors are required to follow charging standards and other guidelines. Their work is overseen by the director of public prosecution, an appointed official.

In general, guilty pleas aren't obtained by the threat of a harsher penalty, Erik Luna and Marianne Wade found after studying the role of prosecutors in six European countries. In other words, there's no penalty for going to trial. "Most European professionals are aghast at plea bargaining practices reported in the United States," Luna and Wade found. For example, European prosecutors were shocked by the case of Weldon Angelos, a twenty-three-year-old music producer in Salt Lake City who was caught in 2002 selling $350 worth of marijuana to an informant a few times. He had no criminal record, but the FBI said it had evidence that he belonged to a gang. Angelos had guns in his house and car, at least $18,000 in cash, a $16,000 rental car bill (which the prosecution thought came from trips to buy marijuana in California), three pounds of marijuana, and duffel bags with marijuana residue in them. Rob Lund, the federal prosecutor handling the case, offered Angelos a fifteen-year plea deal, warning him that because of the guns, he'd face a mandatory fifty-five-year minimum if he was convicted at trial.

Angelos took the gamble. He went to trial and lost. Judge Paul Cassell asked the jurors who convicted him to write down the sentence they thought he should serve. Most proposed penalties in the range of five to fifteen years. Cassell had no choice but to impose the full fifty-five.

Discussing the case, Luna and Wade listed the punishments Angelos probably would have received in five other countries: a maximum of five years in prison in Germany; two to four years in Britain; three and a half or less in Poland; one year or less in Sweden; a fine of 350 euros in the Netherlands.

Angelos's story has a coda. Paul Cassell resigned from the bench in 2007, and afterward he cited Angelos's sentence as a chief reason. "I sometimes drive on the interstate by the prison where he's held," Cassell said, "and I think, 'That wasn't the right thing to do, and the system forced me to do it.'" Back at his previous position as a law professor at the University of Utah, Cassell helped mount a clemency campaign, asking for mercy for Angelos from President George W. Bush, who rejected his petition, and then from President Obama, who took no action.

In May 2016, Rob Lund, the prosecutor, went to see Angelos in prison. Lund thought that the fifteen-year plea deal had been fair given the combination of the guns, the gang, and the large quantity of drugs. "I had to charge the most serious offense possible," Lund said. "I made the lowest offer I could." Lund never wanted Angelos to get stuck with anything like fifty-five years. "The sentence was disproportionate to the conduct. At the time, I wrote a detailed letter spelling out the consequences of going to trial. I said, 'This is crazy. This kid can't go to trial.'"

The fifteen years were nearly up now, and in the intervening time, attitudes toward marijuana had shifted. Lund watched states from Colorado to Massachusetts to Florida legalize the drug or make it medically available. Later, he read studies finding it to be less harmful than alcohol for brain development. Lund looked into Angelos's prison record and saw that he'd taken advantage of the opportunities available. He went to see Angelos in prison and concluded that he'd reformed. "He was very mature and open with me and extremely humble."

By now, Lund had a new boss: a U.S. attorney who was amenable to reconsidering Angelos's sentence. And Lund was in a better position to push for it. "By then I'd served sixteen years and I had more juice to do something," he told me. "Hopefully, I was a wiser prosecutor, too." Concluding that Angelos was a low risk to reoffend, Lund filed a motion that allowed for his release. Angelos got out that May. He was grateful that Lund made sure he was free in time to see his oldest son graduate from high school.

When I talked to Angelos a year and a half later, he was working on a book and a documentary film about his experience. Overall, he had mixed emotions about his prosecutor. "He was aggressive at trial, and the whole thing was a nightmare to me," he said. "But when he came to see me in prison, that changed my opinion. He seemed sincere. Meeting him was good for me because it made me see him in a different light."

In the week after Travis's death, Kreyngold told the prosecutors that he was ready to admit Kevin to YCP. Teitelman and her assistants weighed whether the gamble was worth taking, and whether they could sell it to the police and to the supervising attorney for the zone that included Brownsville.

Chris's case factored into the prosecutors' thinking. They'd offered him the standard plea deal in the gun court: two years in prison and two years on parole. With the multiple charges and his previous record, Chris would get no chance at diversion. He took the deal and went to prison upstate.

For a year, Teitelman and her assistants had insisted that Kevin deserved the same punishment. Kevin and Chris were each caught with a gun, and that was good enough for the prosecutors. They didn't really try to figure out who the gun belonged to, or whether both young men were truly culpable or high-risk. It was common in Brooklyn for the police to find a gun in a group of young men, and common for the person who took the weight to be the youngest one there or the one without a serious criminal record. A shooter could lean on someone else to be the carrier, and that person would go down for the crime of possession. The police and the prosecutors knew it, too, but it didn't change the drive to put more people in prison in the process of getting guns off the streets, to use the favorite phrase of police, prosecutors, and the mayor.

Kevin, however, now had three things going for him he didn't have at the outset. He had Kreyngold in his corner, ready to admit him to YCP. He had Judge Mullen's decision to keep his admission about the gun out of the evidence the prosecutors could present at a trial. And now, in spite of Kevin's efforts to shield him, Chris was in prison for his subsequent gun charge, which helped satisfy the police.

In the year since he'd been arrested, Kevin had gotten tired of waiting, tired of having charges hanging over his head, and he'd thought more than once about pleading guilty just to get it over with. But his patience, and Silberman's and Kreyngold's efforts, were about to bear fruit. Teitelman and her assistants modified their offer: for pleading guilty to attempted CPW2, Kevin would receive a two-year prison sentence like Chris, but crucially, it would be suspended while he participated in YCP. If he successfully completed the program over the course of a year, he wouldn't go to prison and his conviction would be erased from his record. Here was the rare offer of diversion for a crime the state deemed violent. Teitelman felt the risk was worth taking. "This was the right thing to happen in this case," she said. "Now you have a twenty-year-old kid in a rigorous program with the chance for a clean slate at the end."

Still, Silberman worried about the two-year sentence hanging over Kevin: if he got arrested before he finished YCP, he'd do the time. She had other clients who'd failed out of Project Redirect, the other diversion program run by the D.A.'s office, for suspected gang members, with its unannounced home visits and ankle bracelets. "I had a client do eight years for failing Project Redirect," Silberman said. But YCP had a better record, and given all the power prosecutors wielded in gun court, Silberman felt she'd done the best she could for her client.

In early June, Silberman, Kreyngold, and Kevin met at the courthouse for his fifteenth court appearance in a little over a year. "I'm ready," he said on the elevator. "I've been ready for so long." It was a relief to be out of limbo and to have in place the limits imposed by YCP—a real curfew, drug testing, and an order for no further contact with the police—so that his friends and the neighborhood could see that he hadn't gotten off scot-free, that he wasn't a snitch.

The assistant prosecutor was waiting on the nineteenth floor. Kreyngold gave the lawyers copies of his latest report on Kevin. It noted Kevin's compliance with the curfew, praised his mother for being "very helpful throughout," and laid out a plan for Kevin to do a hundred hours of community service at a local recreation center over the summer.

But when Kevin's case was called, Judge Suzanne Mondo refused to take his plea. Years earlier, Mondo had accepted a plea to a conditional discharge for a man charged with selling cocaine and having a loaded gun in his apartment. When the man was later charged with gang assault, Judge Mondo got the tabloid treatment in the *New York Post* for being a "soft judge" who'd delivered "junk justice." Kevin represented a risk Mondo didn't want to take. She sent Silberman and the assistant prosecutor out of her courtroom, and they hurried down the hallways and then to courtrooms on other floors in the building, looking for another judge—any judge—willing to accept Kevin's plea. It seemed strange, but that was how gun court worked.

An hour or so later, Silberman came back with a name of a judge willing to take the plea: Joseph Gubbay, who oversaw the drug treatment court on the fifteenth floor. While the lawyers and social workers sat in the front row, Kevin waited in the back of Gubbay's courtroom as the judge listened to progress reports about rehab and outpatient therapy. Each defendant who got a good report, for following the mandated course of treatment, got a round of applause.

As the minutes ticked by, Kevin's eyes closed. Close to 1:00 p.m. he heard his name and roused himself to stand before Judge Gubbay with Silberman and Kreyngold.

From the bench, Judge Gubbay scanned Kreyngold's report. "If he successfully completes YCP, the case will be dismissed entirely," the judge summarized. "If he's not successful, he faces a minimum of two years incarceration and two years post-release supervision."

The judge asked Kevin if he was making his plea voluntarily, if he understood the consequences, and if he agreed to waive his right to appeal, all as dictated by the prosecutor. Kevin said yes to the litany of scripted questions. "We are incredibly grateful to Your Honor for taking the case," Silberman said. "We thank the D.A.'s office for this opportunity."

The judge nodded and focused on Kevin for one last minute. The deal was done. Judge Gubbay had played no role in making it happen, but he could use the occasion to impress the stakes of the guilty plea on the young man before him. "I want you to know the court has no wiggle room whatsoever," he told Kevin. "If you fail the program, you go to jail."

8

THE NEW D.A.S

A FEW WEEKS after Eric Gonzalez won the Democratic primary in September 2017, he walked out onto the stage of an airy lecture hall at Harvard with six other district attorneys for a Q-and-A session called "A New Vision for the 21st Century Prosecutor." The school year was only a few weeks old, and some of the first-year law students who'd come to the event, wearing hoodies, T-shirts, or polos, exchanged names as they took their seats. The prosecutors, dressed in dark suits, introduced themselves to each other, too. They represented cities and counties west to east, in California, Colorado, Kansas, Wisconsin, Florida, and New York, and most had been in office for less than a year. They'd come to Harvard to swap ideas, recruit elite law students, and test the reform movement they'd joined.

Mark Dupree, the new D.A. for Kansas City, Kansas, got the first question. At thirty-four, Dupree unseated the three-term Democratic incumbent in the 2016 primary by a margin of nearly twenty percentage points. He was a former defense lawyer and the first African American to be elected D.A. in his state. "Mark, you said earlier today that you've been flipping cabinets"—turning things upside down—"to make changes," said the moderator, Harvard law professor Alex Whiting. "Talk about your journey."

"I'm a minister, so tell me if I'm talking too much. Or just say amen," Dupree said to laughter from the audience. "I was eight years old when I saw my first body. When I was twelve, I ran home after someone was shot beside me. Then I found out education can change things. I met my first lawyer when I was fourteen. Then I shadowed a judge. He was a short man with an Afro. They said 'rise' and everyone rose and it blew my mind. That changed the entire trajectory of what I wanted to do." Dupree paused. "Before I ran, maybe 15 to 20 percent of the community knew what the D.A. does. Everyone got mad at the police but didn't know anything about the office behind it. So now we go to neighborhood watch groups, we go to schools, we go everywhere we can so people know what we do and we can be held accountable for the use of the discretion and power we have."

Tori Verber Salazar, who took office in 2015, introduced herself as the first woman to be elected D.A. of San Joaquin County, California. Her main recommendation to students who wanted to be prosecutors was to volunteer in a prison. "It will change your life," she said. "As a prosecutor, you'll have such a big stack of cases you won't even know if it's a man or a woman whose case you're looking at. You're a court processor. Going inside a prison made me stop and look at each person as an individual."

Melissa Nelson, the Republican state attorney in the Florida district that included Jacksonville, talked about starting in her office as a young line prosecutor and then leaving in frustration for private practice. The elected state attorney Nelson had worked for, Angela Corey, was one of the most aggressive in the country. In 2011, she charged Cristian Fernandez, an abused twelve-year-old, as an adult, for first-degree murder in the death of his two-year-old brother.

(The children had been left alone. After Cristian called his mother to say the toddler was hurt, it took her eight hours to bring him to the hospital.) Nelson joined the team of lawyers defending Cristian, who faced a life sentence. "I had the opportunity to become an adversary to my old office," she told the Harvard students. Nelson helped negotiate a seven-year sentence for Cristian and then ran against Corey with the support of prominent members of Jacksonville's bar. Nelson won the Republican primary in 2016 with nearly two-thirds of the vote.

"Now I think you have a Harvard law grad in your office?" Whiting asked.

"She decided to return to her hometown," Nelson said. "Her resume was incredible. Before she walked in, we thought something must be terribly wrong. Her reason: she wanted to do service. She was right."

In their first months in office, the newly elected D.A.s were caught between the entrenched bureaucracies they'd inherited and the impatience of the advocates who'd worked to elect them. It was easier to see what was wrong than to fix it, especially in large offices. Business as usual, however unacceptable, had the force of institutional inertia behind it. The task at hand felt huge and largely organizational. The D.A.s sounded less like politicians than overwhelmed executives, trying to right the ship—and the fundamentals—without capsizing it.

Onstage, the D.A.s grappled with a central dilemma: how to recalibrate the many decisions their assistant district attorneys made each day—about bail, charging, and plea bargaining—that still turned on discretion. Line prosecutors and their supervisors held the trajectory of a person's life in their hands every day. As the boss, you could sweep into office with lofty statements of principle, but changing the judgment calls made in court and redefining what it meant to get it right was not so easy. Over time, examples of how you wanted it done would accrue, and you could hold them out as the desired result, but it would take time, effort, and a deft hand at office politics. Assistant D.A.s were trained to be risk averse, which meant erring on the side of locking people up. Changing that mindset often meant confronting opposition from within the ranks and dismantling the basic building blocks of an office, including training, supervision, and rewards.

Advocates pushed for more, faster. "They won't let you get away from them," Foxx said, with wry affection, of the activists who'd gone from campaigning for her to tracking her work. The advocates knew that as elected officials, the D.A.s needed their constituencies to compel them to take an axe to the status quo. No one knew how long their window of opportunity would last. What if the crime rate rose, or a high-profile case went wrong?

In New York, three local groups started Court Watch NYC, which sent volunteers to observe arraignments and other proceedings in Brooklyn and Manhattan. When they saw something they didn't like, they called out Gonzalez and Cy Vance on Twitter. When they tweeted about a $1,500 bail request for a man accused of stealing four bars of soap, Gonzalez had to answer for it on the radio. He said the man had outstanding warrants for his arrest, which showed his "unwillingness to come to court." Was that enough, in Brooklyn, to send someone to jail?

If the new D.A.s had to contend with disappointment for being cautious, they could also pay a price for going too far. The cautionary tale on this front involved a star of the reform movement in Florida who picked an unwinnable fight.

Aramis Ayala, elected in the district that includes Orlando in 2016, was Florida's first black state attorney. Ayala didn't campaign in opposition to the death penalty, but once in office, she had to decide how to charge a man accused of killing his ex-girlfriend and the police officer who'd tried to arrest him. In Florida, which has typically had around 350 people on death row and lists sixteen "aggravating" factors that allow prosecutors to seek execution, the murder of a young woman and a cop made for a quintessential death-penalty prosecution. The mother of the young woman did not want Ayala to seek execution; the husband of the police officer did. In March 2017, Ayala concluded that the death penalty didn't serve as a deterrent and announced that her office would no longer seek it in the double murder—and to be consistent, not in any other case.

Ayala's declaration set off a volley of criticism. The Orlando police chief attacked her for sparing an accused cop-killer. "If there was ever a case for the death penalty, this fits," he told the press. Then the fury against Ayala spread statewide. Governor Rick Scott, a Republican, accused Ayala, a Democrat, of defying the law by refusing to enforce it. He issued orders that stripped Ayala of the pending double-murder prosecution and twenty-eight other murder cases, handing all of them to a prosecutor in another district who supported the death penalty. The Florida legislature piled on, slashing $1.3 million of Ayala's budget to reflect the cost of the cases she'd lost.

Scott's move was an unusually aggressive use of executive authority, but the governor had an unusual statute on his side: a state law that gave him the power to reassign cases from one prosecutor to another if, for any "good and sufficient reason, the Governor determines that the ends of justice would be best served."

When Ayala sued Scott to get her cases back, the Florida Supreme Court ruled against her, five to two. Ayala's "blanket refusal" to seek the death penalty "does not reflect an exercise of prosecutorial discretion," the majority wrote. "It embodies, at best, a misunderstanding of Florida law."

In the beginning of September, Ayala backtracked. Instead of continuing to refuse to impose the death penalty, she appointed a group to advise her on when it was appropriate. "Unfortunately, a lot of people only know me for that," she said of the struggle. "But there certainly is more to me as a person, as a lawyer, as a prosecutor."

Ayala's travails showed that the new generation of reform-minded D.A.s needed help. That was the underlying purpose of bringing them to Harvard. It was one of a string of gatherings convened by a group called Fair and Just Prosecution, which its executive director, Miriam Krinsky, described as a supportive network and concierge service for D.A.s with aspirations for reform.

Krinsky had fifteen years of experience as a federal prosecutor. She'd led a major investigation of violence in the Los Angeles jails in 2012 and then gone to the sheriff's office to help implement reforms. Krinsky wanted to spare the new D.A.s from having to solve every policy problem from scratch, by helping them pool resources and ideas.

Krinsky also encouraged the prosecutors she worked with to serve as a counterforce to state D.A. associations that followed the old law-and-order script. With Trump in office, her group fought the resurrection of the war on drugs at the Justice Department. In May 2017, Attorney General Jeff Sessions directed his corps of five thousand federal prosecutors to bring the most serious available felony charge in as many cases as possible. The instruction overturned Eric Holder's directive, put in place four years earlier, which told prosecutors not to trigger mandatory minimum penalties against most nonviolent drug offenders.

Sessions's memo took the Justice Department back to unleashing the full might of the top charge against anyone involved in a drug conspiracy, no matter how low in the hierarchy. It was the same power Caryn Teitelman wielded in the Brooklyn gun court, but the severity of federal sentences made it even more crushing. In response, about two dozen D.A.s, including Gonzalez, Dupree, and nearly all the others who came to Harvard, signed a letter rejecting Sessions's memo as "an unnecessary and unfortunate" return to the past with "no certain benefits" and "significant costs."

In opposing Sessions's memo, the D.A.s found they could call for mercy and stand on safe ground politically. Many of them came from cities where suspicion of the Trump administration ran deep. The D.A.s had on their side members of Congress from both parties, the ACLU, and even the Koch Foundation. They were singularly well positioned to provide a counterweight to federal prosecutors, whose national association backed Sessions's draconian policy.

A few months later, Sessions threatened to withhold federal funding for so-called sanctuary cities, which he viewed as shielding immigrants from ICE's plan to step up detentions and deportations. Many of the prosecutors working with Krinsky, along with more than a dozen police chiefs and sheriffs from largely Democratic cities, spoke out against the attorney general again. In court, in a brief circulated by Fair and Just Prosecution, the law enforcement leaders argued that "entangling" local policing with ICE would sacrifice community trust, making it harder for them to prevent and solve crimes. Again, the prosecutors and police chiefs had a singular place in the debate. They could make opposing ICE's tactics a matter of public safety and they could make it personal: their own crime-fighting efforts were on the line.

The fights with the Trump administration underscored why criminal justice reformers were turning to cities for leadership. But the focus on local D.A. elections went beyond Trump. The Justice Department had proved an unreliable partner for wholesale reform during previous presidencies, too.

Barack Obama talked about mass incarceration and unfairness as a young senator. He made the first visit by a sitting president to a federal prison. He banned solitary confinement for juveniles in the federal system, invoking the tragedy of Kalief Browder's case in the Bronx. But Obama's stated commitments translated into relatively meager accomplishments, two law professors, Rachel Barkow at NYU and Mark Osler at the University of St. Thomas, argued in a 2017 law review article. For example, Eric Holder and Loretta Lynch, Obama's attorneys general, pushed states to change their bail practices but didn't address the rising rate of federal detention. Obama tried to fix the pardon process but largely failed, and his overall rate of granting petitions for clemency—5.3 percent—was higher than George W. Bush's, but barely better than Bill Clinton's, and far behind the five presidents from Lyndon Johnson to Ronald Reagan.

Barkow and Osler also showed that Obama's Justice Department blocked reform on multiple fronts. When Congress reduced harsh sentencing for the possession of crack rather than cocaine—a racially infected legacy of the war on drugs—the Justice Department balked at applying the new sentencing scheme to people who had already been sentenced. After backing one bill that would have reduced mandatory minimums, but failed to pass, the Justice Department in 2013 opposed a stronger bipartisan bill that would have effectively eliminated them. Federal prosecutors argued that the change would make it too difficult to obtain guilty pleas and cooperation, and the bill died in the Senate. Finally, after Obama asked a presidential council of advisors for recommendations to strengthen forensic science—a discipline riddled with faulty findings and lack of rigor for common methods like analyzing bite marks, hair, and handwriting—the Justice Department rejected the council's findings. "The message the Department sent," Barkow and Osler wrote, "was loud and clear: whatever the science says, we find this evidence valuable to our law enforcement agenda, so we will continue to use it."

Barkow and Osler's central point was that Obama fell short of his own goals because he deferred to federal prosecutors, who were invested in "maintaining a status quo" that favored their interests. Despite efforts by Obama's civil rights division and police reform initiatives, the Justice Department as a whole wasn't ready to be a beacon of change.

The D.A.s who gathered at Harvard had to second-guess their offices' past decisions and at times constrain their own power. Unlike federal prosecutors, however, they'd been elected to do that and more. They had no competition from the Justice Department and also no playbook.

After the Harvard panel, the prosecutors mingled at a reception, giving their cards to students who expressed interest in a summer job, and then walked to dinner at a nice restaurant. At a corner table, they passed plates of corn pancakes and Wellfleet clams and discussed the parts of their jobs they'd figured out—and the parts that remained a puzzle. At meetings of their state D.A. associations, these prosecutors sometimes felt like pariahs. This convening, by contrast, offered a warm bath of affirmation and peer support.

The D.A.s talked about messaging. Christian Gossett, the Republican D.A. of Winnebago County, Wisconsin, said he worried that the national reform movement seemed like a liberals-only cause. Responding, Andrew Warren, a Democrat in Tampa who had courted Republican voters to defeat a longtime incumbent, said he often framed his agenda in terms of conserving resources. "You talk about cutting back on the low-level prosecutions through diversion so you can concentrate on the serious crimes."

Melissa Nelson said people in unexpected places felt the harshness of the system. Seeking support in the mostly white and conservative counties around Jacksonville, Nelson gave a speech to a group of professionals one night. "I assumed they had no contact with the system," she said. "I was wrong. I heard vivid stories from some of them about their personal involvement and the impact."

Eric Gonzalez said he found that the message of fairness had stronger appeal than he thought it would. When Brooklyn's conviction review unit recommended freeing people, some of the recommendations turned on violations of rights rather than exonerating evidence. "We've said on the record in court, 'We can't tell you this person is innocent, but we can tell you he didn't receive a fair trial.' We've overturned twenty-three convictions now, and it's about to be twenty-four. We're getting widespread support throughout the community. It shocked the other D.A.s in my state."

"Can I visit?" Mark Dupree asked. "I want to do it. I'll need support."

The first conviction review units (also called conviction integrity units) were created more than a decade ago, in Dallas, Texas, and Santa Clara County, California. The units arose in response to exonerations achieved by the Innocence Project, bringing the work of investigating past errors and misconduct inside the D.A.'s office. At least thirty-three offices had a conviction review unit, and their work accounted for 269 exonerations across the country. At their best, the units helped generate policies for preventing future wrongful convictions (like opening files to the defense or improving police procedures for witness IDs).

At the Harvard dinner, it was clear that a conviction review unit was high on the list of priorities, along with reducing cash bail and marijuana prosecutions, wiping out old summonses and bench warrants, and increasing access to diversion for mental health and drug treatment and for young people.

The D.A.s compared notes on other priorities, sensitive to the political pitfalls and legal quirks of their cities. They started talking about Kim Foxx's decision earlier that year to unilaterally raise the threshold for felony theft in Chicago and the rest of Cook County to $1,000 in stolen goods, from $500, as state law provided. (Meanwhile, in Knoxville, Tennessee, the D.A. was charging shoplifters with felony burglary—and demanding high bail—when they stole goods worth as little as $40.)

The D.A.s were intrigued by Foxx's boldness. Christian Gossett, however, pointed out that in Wisconsin, if he adopted Foxx's approach to shoplifting he would face staff reductions. State funding for attorney slots was based on a formula that credited felonies at almost four times the rate of misdemeanors (and gave no weight at all to cases disposed of through diversion without a charge). "The whole system benefits from overcharging," Gossett said.

Budgeting affected the group in other ways, too. The level of funding for their offices mattered, and so did the source of the money. Prosecutors' offices and local jails are largely funded by county budgets. Prisons are funded by the state. That means prosecutors get the political benefit of sending people to prison without bearing the financial cost locally, giving them an incentive to seek more severe punishments.

The D.A.s also talked about the challenge of cleaning up after sloppy predecessors or inheriting hostile staffs. Some couldn't easily fire people because of civil service protections. Mark Dupree, who'd replaced about half of the lawyers in his office, called himself blessed. "Do you feel you're held to a different standard as the first black D.A.?" Gonzalez asked him. The table quieted for the answer.

"Yeah," Dupree answered. "It's to be expected. And then there's the fact that I'm not a conservative. Everyone is expecting me to fail." He shrugged. He sensed a degree of grudging respect, too. "Some of the deputies and officers are saying I lit a match under the good-ol'-boy network."

The exchange on race picked up the thread of another conversation I'd heard a few months earlier at a meeting in New York of the Institute for Innovation in Prosecution, funded by the Manhattan D.A.'s office, which brings prosecutors together with academics and other experts. There, Paul Butler, a Georgetown law professor, gave a presentation based on his new book, *Chokehold*, about the policing of black men. Butler said his experience as an assistant prosecutor—working for Eric Holder in Washington, D.C., in the 1990s—confirmed his feeling that "if you had too many concerns locking up black men, this was not the work for you. I didn't call the defendants 'cretins' on my first day, but it didn't take long." He asked the prosecutors in the audience whether they thought the values and orientation of their profession had changed. He used the words "white supremacist" to describe the system many of them uphold.

Karen Friedman Agnifilo, chief assistant D.A. in Manhattan, spoke up, telling Butler his negativity felt alienating. "A white supremacist—that's a type of person I don't identify with," she said. "If people want to join forces, I wish there was a better way to reach out and make us feel part of the cause."

Kim Foxx was listening, and she stood up to respond. "We need to be honest in these conversations," she said. "Blacks and Latinos need to talk about what it's like when most of the defendants look like you, and the other prosecutors don't, but they watch *The Wire*. I've been in the room, and heard people say of the defendants, 'They're not your kind.' I say, 'Wait, I'm from Cabrini Green. I'm from the projects.' People like me usually don't feel comfortable in a prosecutor's office. I left for that reason. But first I stayed as long as I could because I thought, 'If I'm not here, who will look at cases the way I do? What will happen to this kid jammed up on assault and battery?'

"Some of my communities are struggling so hard, they know nothing else than to call the police—until it's their son," Foxx continued. "We're conditioned to believe our safety is tied to a system that has oppressed so many of our people."

For years, at Georgetown, Paul Butler has discouraged progressive students from becoming line prosecutors. He thinks they're seduced into locking people up—as he was when he started out in the same job—and if they try to resist, they don't wield enough power to make a real difference in court day to day.

Butler has a colleague at Georgetown, Abbe Smith, who directs a criminal defense clinic and wrote an article in 2001 with the provocative title "Can You Be a Good Person and a Good Prosecutor?" In the piece, Smith answered her own question: "I hope so, but I think not." She explained, "At its best, there is a clarity and consistency in a narrow, letter-of-the-law approach and perspective of prosecutors. . . . At its worst, however, there is a kind of moral fascism." Smith wanted to turn on its head the presumption that prosecutors are the ones who "wear the white hats," while defense lawyers are amoral. The lesson is that lawyers who only see themselves on one side or the other of the defender-prosecutor divide tend to be tribal. They band together, either as champions of the underdog or as guardians of victims and public safety.

The movement to reform prosecutors' offices depends on a more open view. "I say, we need good ethical people, who understand the crisis we have with regard to mass incarceration and racial disparity, to be defenders and to be prosecutors," said Angela J. Davis, who directed the D.C. Public Defender's Office before joining the law faculty of American University. She tells her students: "We need people to do criminal justice better."

That has to be the right answer: as long as we have an adversarial system, we will be in urgent need of prosecutors who are committed to social and racial justice. When I take my turn giving law students advice, I tell them that the devil is in the details of the particular office they choose to join. It's not just about whether the office has a progressive bent or a strong ethical code. It's also about how much discretion they'll have as line prosecutors.

In 2016, an assistant district attorney in Boston, Adam Foss, gave a TED talk about using his discretion, at the age of twenty-nine, to divert rather than arraign a teenager named Christopher who'd stolen thirty laptops from the store where he worked. He returned most of them, did many hours of community service—and then went on to become a bank manager (making more money than he did, Foss added, to the delight of his audience). "No one can tell us how to prosecute our cases," Foss said. "The decision about Christopher was exclusively mine." When I asked Foss about this a few months later, he explained, "I had an African American supervisor, who saw the world as I did, and he gave me discretion."

Many young prosecutors, however, remain frustrated by how little discretion they are able to exercise. Recruited to work for Manhattan D.A. Cy Vance by a top official who assured him the office was intent on reform, Jarvis Idowu found himself clashing with his supervisor over bail. In one case, Idowu wanted to waive bail for a man who'd been arrested for stealing two closed-circuit cameras from the hallway of his apartment building. It was the man's first arrest, and he said he'd asked the landlord to take the cameras down, because he didn't want surveillance outside his door, and then removed them himself when the landlord refused. The supervisor overruled Idowu, and he had to ask the judge for $10,000 in bail even though he thought the amount was unwarranted and unaffordable. After that, he kept trying to ask for low bail in felony cases but was reversed every time.

"I kept pushing, but there's no meaningful space for different perspectives here," Idowu told me. "If you're willing to adopt the office culture, the way the old guard has been doing things for the last thirty years, you'll be fine. But if you want to do something else, they'll strip away all your discretion." He'd heard Paul Butler speak, and had felt pangs of recognition and self-doubt. "You have to be hyperaware of the mental gymnastics you'll do to make yourself feel like a good person," he said. "We all have to go home feeling like we're doing the right thing. So you'll tell yourself, 'I'm making progress. I got bail set at $5,000, not $35,000.' But then the person still winds up at Rikers. I find myself trying to take an inventory, asking, 'Am I actually doing good here?' It's a hard belief to maintain." A few months later, Idowu told me he'd been fired for being insubordinate. He went to work with Adam Foss to design and run a training program in progressive prosecution—the kind of instruction they both wished they received. That fall, they tried out the training for the first time, with newly hired prosecutors in the Philadelphia D.A.'s office.

When Larry Krasner was elected district attorney for Philadelphia, a couple of months after the Harvard event, he joined his peers under the umbrella of Fair and Just Prosecution.

More than the others, Krasner had immediately found himself at war with the police in his city. Rank-and-file cops circulated the hashtag #notmyDA on social media. Soon after his victory, Krasner gave a talk about the use of force to the city's black police union, a group separate from the Fraternal Order of Police. He said there could be "issues" about training the police to aim at a suspect's chest and torso, though he added that didn't mean an individual officer who opened fire in this manner "did anything wrong." Without attending the speech or hearing it, the president of the Fraternal Order of Police lit into Krasner's remarks as "dangerous and despicable," accusing him of seeking to endanger officers' lives.

The fight was on. If the adage held true that a D.A. alienates the police at his or her peril, then the antipathy would soon sink Krasner. But the police weren't Krasner's base. Their critics were. The air of defiance extended to the executive suite of the D.A.'s office, where Krasner cleaned house, firing thirty-one people office-wide and installing a new leadership team. "When the pirates take over the ship, some of the crew is going over the side," Krasner said.

I grew up in Philadelphia, and I had special reason to pay attention to Krasner: his new team included my sister Dana as a policy adviser. Like her boss and almost everyone in his inner circle, Dana had never been a prosecutor. She'd worked as a civil rights and defense lawyer for more than a decade. On her first day of work, with a mix of disbelief and delight, she texted me a picture of her official ID card from the D.A.'s office.

When I asked Krasner what kept him up at night, he sounded as impatient as the activists who elected him. "There's so much to do, moving forward and also backward," he said. "We want to look at the decisions made by judges or the previous administration we feel were unjust at the same time as we look at our pending cases. It just seems difficult to wrap your arms around all of these issues. And an injustice that goes on day after day is a harm, to a victim or an innocent person or someone else. You almost feel like you're in an emergency room full of people, with too few doctors triaging as fast as they can."

For his unbridled determination, Krasner got love from criminal justice advocates and liberal TV hosts like Chris Hayes and Samantha Bee. *The Nation* praised him as "the most radical DA in the country." Bernie Sanders sat down with him for a roundtable discussion, filming a video to post online. Like Sanders, Krasner was willing to blow things up in order to put them back together. He didn't think he had a choice. Given Philadelphia's history, it would take revolution, not evolution, to make the D.A.'s office a progressive institution—and that was precisely his plan.

Watching the newly elected D.A.s as Krasner joined the mix, it seemed to me that they could afford to be bolder because they had each other as guides and prods. It was easier to throw off the constraints of precedent and institutional sclerosis if you could borrow an idea a peer in another city had tried. The give-and-take also reduced the overwhelming scale of the whole enterprise; no one had to reinvent every single feature on his or her own. The D.A.s made me think of skaters, dashing one after the other onto the ice. It was an ensemble performance: when one successfully landed a daring combination of jumps and spins, the others learned the steps and followed. "It's very helpful," Krasner told me. "We have examples of policies we can steal and try, with knowledge about how they work. For example, in Chicago, Kim Foxx changed retail theft into a low-level offense to empty the jails. So we can do that knowing there has been no cataclysm."

Sure enough, two months into his term, Krasner announced that the theft of retail goods valued under $500 would be treated as a summary offense in Philadelphia (maximum punishment ninety days in jail, a $250 fine, and restitution). He also rolled out guidelines for reducing cash bail for nonviolent crimes. Like Gonzalez, Krasner said prosecutors could still ask for bail in such cases, but he made it clear that release was what he generally expected, and his policy applied to a larger share of cases. Next Krasner announced that he was adopting Gonzalez's approach to minimizing the consequences of low-level charges for undocumented immigrants, thanking the Brooklyn D.A. at a press conference. In April, Philadelphia announced it would close its dangerous and decrepit jail because the population had fallen by a third over two years (from eight thousand to fifty-four hundred). The jail closure fulfilled a longtime goal of the mayor, and the city reaped the savings.

Krasner also entered a thicket involving life-without-parole sentences for juveniles. In a pair of rulings in 2012 and 2016, the Supreme Court ruled that such punishments would often be unconstitutional if they were mandatory. "Mandatory life without parole for a juvenile precludes consideration of his chronological age and its hallmark features—among them, immaturity, impetuosity, and failure to appreciate risks and consequences," Justice Elena Kagan wrote for a majority of five in the 2012 case *Miller v. Alabama*. "It prevents taking into account the family and home environment that surrounds him—and from which ʻ.e cannot usually extricate himself—no matter how brutal or dysfunctional." Everyone sentenced to life without parole as a juvenile got a new hearing. But it wasn't at all clear when, if ever, they would be released. "We think appropriate circumstances for sentencing juveniles to this harshest possible punishment will be uncommon," Kagan wrote, but didn't rule out a life sentence, or even say whether a sentence of several decades should also be rare. Many D.A.s responded to the Court's rulings by asking for new sentences in the range of forty to sixty years or longer—an effective life sentence.

Kim Foxx had recently navigated one of these cases. Addolfo Davis was convicted in 1990 of double murder, along with two fellow gang members, when he was only fourteen. In September 2017, Foxx weighed in on the side of mercy, asking the judge reviewing Davis's mandatory life sentence to consider the differences in brain development between children and adults. It was a major reversal for the state's attorney's office, which opposed any reduction in Davis's punishment at a resentencing hearing two years earlier. Foxx's stance was enough to win the approval of a new plea deal, which secured Davis's release in 2020.

Krasner had Addolfo Davises coming out of his ears. Because of the harsh practices of his predecessors and local judges, more than two hundred juvenile life sentences were pending for review in Philadelphia—more than anywhere else in the country. Krasner set up a committee to look at the cases one by one, taking into account the inmates' prison records as well as their age at the time of conviction and the circumstances of their crimes. In the first batch of eight to go to court, Krasner asked for sentences of twenty-one to twenty-nine years, which translated into release for time served. The punishments already imposed, he argued, were enough.

But Pennsylvania's sentencing guidelines set thirty-five years as the minimum for a juvenile convicted of first-degree murder. In five of the eight cases, judges rejected the lesser sentences Krasner proposed: a setback for the new D.A. and a reminder that there were limits to his power. Some members of Krasner's team recommended increasing his sentencing offers to bring them into line with the judges' expectations. Krasner refused. In his first year in office, only one of the one hundred people in Philadelphia released from juvenile life sentences had been rearrested, and he'd been resentenced before Krasner took office.

As winter turned to spring, Krasner and Gonzalez launched experiments with the potential to touch every aspect of the operations of their offices. Their differing methods offered a comparison between two types of innovative D.A.s: the consensus-builder in Brooklyn and the barn-burner in Philadelphia.

On January 22, two days after his inauguration, Gonzalez welcomed five dozen outsiders to the office for an initiative called Justice 2020. Gonzalez's new director of policy, Jill Harris, put together the group, and it reflected her background at the Legal Aid Society and the ACLU. There were a few representatives from the police department, but service providers, defense lawyers, religious leaders, and community organizers dominated. The reform movement had a seat at the table—a lot of seats in fact.

The group would work over the next four months on a set of recommendations for what Gonzalez should accomplish over the next two years. "I need you to think that just because something hasn't been done before doesn't mean it can't be done," he told them at the outset.

Six weeks later, in March, Krasner simply started doing what hadn't been done before. He didn't officially gather stakeholders, didn't build consensus internally, didn't start with trainings. He sent a top-down memo to the supervising attorneys in his office. The memo had no title, but it could have been called "Your Job Just Changed: If You Don't Like It, There's the Door."

Do not charge marijuana possession, regardless of weight, he instructed his assistant district attorneys. Do not charge sex workers who have fewer than three convictions. Offer more diversion, not after charges and a guilty plea, but out of the system entirely—including for some cases of gun possession, drunk driving, and marijuana distribution.

Krasner's instructions weren't actually hard-and-fast rules. Rather, he framed them as a set of presumptions. He wanted his assistant D.A.s to exercise more discretion, not less. "Previously, we roboticized them. Someone else told them how much the case was worth," he told me. "That's about politics—about defending yourself in the newspaper if something looks like a disparate or bad outcome. I think that's entirely contrary to doing justice."

An assistant prosecutor could go against the guidance in the memo only with the approval of a supervisor (or, in some cases, a top deputy). As Krasner's dramatic downward shift on charging and plea bargaining sank in, career prosecutors found themselves unable to wield power in the way they'd been trained. Parole and probation were one early flashpoint. Along with the highest incarceration rate in the Northeast, Pennsylvania had the highest rate and number of people on parole of any state. In Philadelphia, an astonishing number of residents—one in twenty-two—were under supervision, while half the people in the city's jails were being held on accusations that they had violated the terms of their supervision. Statewide, a third of inmates were in prison on parole or probation violations (at a cost of $420 million a year). Some were in custody for using marijuana—while Krasner had instructed his line prosecutors not to treat using marijuana as a violation of supervision, he couldn't stop judges who continued to do so.

To chip away at the number of people being supervised, Krasner asked the Philadelphia probation and parole department to send him the names of ten thousand people who could exit supervision early. "We said, 'You tell us, based on your criteria, who should be off supervision—say, the people who haven't caused a problem for the last three years,'" Krasner said. The department came back with criteria that would apply to only about a thousand people. Krasner did what he could on his own by setting a new standard for punishing violations of the conditions of supervision, instructing prosecutors to stop asking for jail time for minor infractions, and permitting them to ask for no more than two years in prison for major violations without approval from a top deputy.

As the clashes between the old guard and the new continued, a stream of supervisors were reassigned or resigned. Krasner encouraged the exodus. Appearing before the Philadelphia City Council to ask for a budget increase, he complained of inheriting "a Grade-B District Attorney's Office." The insult was unmistakable. At a meeting a few days later, a career prosecutor, with tears and anger, said Krasner was wrecking the office he and his colleagues had built. Krasner wasn't in the room and he didn't apologize later. If morale was low for a time, so be it. Eventually he'd have his own hires to lead. "It's difficult," Krasner acknowledged when I asked about translating his vision to the day-to-day reality in court. "You're talking about multi-generational training in the other direction."

There were survivors who helped make change. They walked a line, trying to satisfy the new boss without renouncing all the work they'd done before his arrival. Paul Goldman, a prosecutor in juvenile court for sixteen years, specialized in the process that determines which teenagers between the ages fifteen and seventeen are charged as adults. He started when fears ran high of the teenage superpredator, a myth of the 1990s. When teenagers were charged with crimes that Pennsylvania law treated as serious, ranging from shootings to muggings, the D.A.'s office tried to keep them in the adult system—four hundred or five hundred a year, Goldman estimated. Later, as crime declined, the number dropped to about two hundred annually.

Goldman said he always believed that prosecuting teenagers under the age of eighteen as adults was "a sensitive and controversial thing" and should only be done when "absolutely necessary." Working for previous D.A.s, he allowed, meant that "my own goals and thoughts, what I wanted to do with cases, has probably been molded to a certain extent, so that our unit would survive." Now Goldman was at the head of the juvenile unit. In the first year of Krasner's tenure, the number of teenagers prosecuted as adults fell by about 40 percent, and the number of fifteen- to seventeen-year-olds waiting in adult jail before trial because of high bail dropped by half or more. Krasner's team hailed Goldman as one of the supervising attorneys who'd successfully navigated the transition. But there were only a handful like him in the office. The other supervisors in the juvenile unit were rotated out or left before the year was out.

In his groundbreaking memo, Krasner tried to hurry change and make it stick. He instructed his prosecutors to make plea offers below the bottom end of Pennsylvania's sentencing guidelines in nonviolent cases. If the guidelines called for a maximum of two years or less in prison, they were supposed to seek house arrest, probation, or diversion. This policy, too, was a presumption, not a rule, and it didn't apply to many major felony charges. Still, Philadelphia prosecutors were giving up the threat of prison in many cases in which the state allowed them to levy it.

Krasner also made an intriguing symbolic move. He told his prosecutors that every time they asked a judge for a prison sentence, they had to state the cost of incarceration, calculated at $42,000 a year, and justify it. Some judges and assistant D.A.s called the directive a gimmick, but Krasner's rationale was that cost should be central to sentencing decisions and the public should know it.

Of all the challenges prosecutors face, perhaps none is larger than their responsibility to victims. In modern law, victims don't press charges. The state plays that role on behalf of all of us—that's why the prosecution is called "the people" in court. In the 1980s, the victims' rights movement emerged in American politics because victims too often felt sidelined and even ignored. Since then, if not before, some prosecutors have used victims to justify severe punishments (and, at worst, score political points). For some victims, the more retribution, the better. Others, though, have been served by a kind of reconciliation. It's called restorative justice, and while it's been relatively rare in the United States, that's something the new D.A.s could start to change.

In its basic contours, restorative justice brings victims and perpetrators together in hopes of a deep form of reckoning and resolution. Sometimes it includes an apology or the payment of restitution. These features are ancient and in a sense familiar. The Hebrew Bible calls for restitution for property crimes. Native American communities used aspects of restorative justice centuries ago, and the Maori of New Zealand and the English in medieval times had their own systems for it. It's common sense that some victims and accusers have healing things to say to each other. Paying restitution to the person who suffered from a crime, or to her family, may be more useful and meaningful than paying a fine to the state.

Outside native communities, restorative justice in the United States dates to the 1970s in theory and the 1980s in practice, but has mostly been confined to offenses like teenage shoplifting and vandalism. The victims' rights movement has had other priorities, and liberal criminal justice reformers have mostly been wary of ceding influence to victims, who may prefer distance and retribution to intimacy and answers. Pursuing the elusive goal of closure is deeply personal: there's no right way to do it. Practitioners like sujatha baliga, who started a restorative justice program in California for teenagers that offers a path to diversion before charges are filed, talk about being equally dedicated to victims and the people accused of harming them.

Research backs up the idea that restorative justice can help repair the damage of violent crimes. (There have been enough studies to produce a metastudy about the benefits.) The possibility of a connection for victims made sense to Melissa Nelson when she became a state attorney in Florida. "When terrible things happen to you or someone you love, you're intertwined with that other person, the person who is responsible, for the rest of your life," she said. "You think about them all the time and what they did."

When Nelson was elected, one Jacksonville family was locked into an intense and untraditional battle with the state attorney's office. The case involved the murder of a young woman named Shelby Farah. On a Saturday evening in July 2013, James Rhodes walked into a Metro PCS cellphone store in Jacksonville and asked Farah, the clerk at the cash register, for the money inside. She gave it to him, and then Rhodes shot her in the head. She was twenty years old. He was twenty-one.

Felled by her grief, Shelby's mother, Darlene Farah, tried to learn everything she could about her daughter's killer. With the help of a private investigator, Farah learned that Rhodes had been abandoned by his parents and had mostly grown up in a state boys' home, where he'd been sexually assaulted. When Rhodes's lawyer approached Farah to say that he was willing to plead guilty in exchange for a life sentence, Farah went to pray with her pastor and decided to support the plea. She didn't want Rhodes to face capital murder charges. "The state raised him," she said. "How can they say now that they want to kill him?"

Angela Corey, the aggressive state attorney who was Nelson's predecessor, insisted on seeking the death penalty for Rhodes. When the trial prosecutor showed Farah's son, Caleb, a video of his sister's killing, Caleb broke with his mother, moving out of her house and calling for Rhodes's execution. I reported on the case for the *New York Times Magazine*, and Farah told me she felt the prosecutors were trying to punish her. She supported Nelson in the election, and after she won, Nelson agreed to a life sentence for Rhodes.

Farah wanted one more thing: to talk with Rhodes. He'd thanked her in a letter, and now she wanted to meet him face-to-face. Caleb had come around to accepting the life sentence, and he wanted to meet Rhodes, too. So did Farah's second daughter, Nycole. After Rhodes's sentencing, the family went to Nelson's office and spent about an hour talking with him in the presence of his lawyer and a prosecutor. "I told him I don't want him to feel like his life was over," Farah said. "I told him I want him to get his GED. I told him we are carrying on Shelby's legacy out here, but I can't carry it on in prison, and if she'd known about his situation and his childhood, she would have tried to help him."

Rhodes told the Farahs that all he ever wanted was a family, and if he'd had a mother like her, he would not have ended up where he was. He said he was sorry. "He looked at us. He said he knows sorry isn't going to bring Shelby back and if he had a choice, if he knew Shelby could come back if he took his life, he would do it." Caleb asked to lead the group in prayer. "We all held hands and he prayed for, among other things, James's safety in prison," Rhodes's lawyer said. "It was a moment I'll never forget. I believe James felt forgiveness and a measure of peace."

Farah was grateful, and though Melissa Nelson had been anxious about the meeting beforehand, she thought of its emotional power later that spring when she hit a dead end in prosecuting another difficult case. This time, forty-three years had elapsed since the senseless murder at a grocery store of its owner, Freddie Farah (no relation to Darlene), as he stood at a counter. Reopening the cold case, the police tracked fingerprints on three items from the store to a suspect: Johnie Miller, who was seventeen at the time of the crime and had since become a popular street performer in New Orleans. Questioned by investigators, Miller said he hadn't done it. Nelson had an eyewitness who could identify him—but she died while he was in jail awaiting trial. "She was the link between the prints and the killer," Nelson said. "Without her, we were up a creek." She feared that if she proceeded to trial, Miller would profess his innocence and would be believable. She worried about the effect that would have on Freddie Farah's widow, Nadya, and their four adult children.

Nelson consulted with Lauren Abramson, who ran a restorative justice program for teenagers charged with property crimes in Baltimore. She thought about how many times she'd seen victims feel burned by the traditional process of plea bargains or trials. "We set up this adversarial system, and the person closest to the defendant is the defense lawyer, often telling them, 'Stay quiet, don't talk.' The lawyers are doing their job, but there's nothing here that advances the cause of restoration of the victim. I think most people leave very unsatisfied."

Nelson felt her office had a good relationship with Nadya and her children. The prosecutors explained that because the available evidence against Miller was weak, they planned to offer him a guilty plea for the time he'd served. Would it help them to talk to him? One of Farah's sons, Robert, had grown up asking police officers what happened to his father. He still wanted to know. "Robert said, 'Melissa, I want to ask him why. I want to know if my dad said something.'"

Nelson expected Miller's lawyer to reject her proposal. "We have no witnesses, so they know we can't make the case, and that means we have no leverage." But Miller said yes. "Then we had this meeting and he surprised all of us."

Miller said he recalled every detail of the crime, which he'd never spoken of. He knew Farah as a kind man who gave sweets to children. He couldn't justify the killing to himself. He didn't minimize the harm he'd done, and over and over again, he apologized.

Farah's wife said that she knew Miller didn't need to do this, thanked him, and accepted his apology. Nelson found herself crying. Afterward, the Farahs sat in court when Miller pled guilty. He was released after less than a year in jail. "He came clean with a lot of questions that I had for him and once he did that, I know it sounds crazy, but it kind of relieved me," Robert Farah said to the *Florida Times-Union*. "Am I upset that he is not spending time? I'd rather him answer my questions and give me the answers that I have been looking for all my life than to have him sitting in jail without anything."

Encounters like these restore victims by giving them control. They ask the questions. They decide whether and how to forgive. Danielle Sered's program in Brooklyn, Common Justice, was achieving results that impressed Nelson: 90 percent of the victims who were invited to participate chose to participate and agreed to have the person who hurt them go through the program in place of a prison sentence. Less than 7 percent of the people who'd done the harm had to leave the program because of a new conviction.

Nelson asked an advisory committee she'd created to figure out how she could continue what she'd started with the two Farah families. "We won't impose it on a victim," she said, "but I'd like to get to a point where we offer something like these meetings to victims as an option. That's our hope."

PART TWO

THE QUALITY OF MERCY

9

THE APPEAL

NOURA DREADED THE move from jail to prison after her conviction. In the weeks following her sentencing in March, she checked the list each week for the transport van and felt relief when she wasn't on it. Then, one morning in May, a guard who'd been kind throughout her stay roused her at 5:00 a.m. Time to go.

Noura begged to wake up two friends and say goodbye. She gave them a stack of candy bars, ramen noodles, and bags of chips, which she'd bought from the commissary but couldn't take with her. They gave her a couple of plain white T-shirts. In the intake area, she was given the clothes she had been wearing when she first arrived. They'd been sitting in a zipped nylon bag and smelled like garbage. She was supposed to wear them during the trip. Noura had gained weight and could no longer button the jeans. Moving slowly, she got onto the white van in jail pants.

They drove for three and a half hours to the state's classification center for female inmates in Nashville, where she would spend the next three weeks. Compared with the Memphis prison it looked surprisingly benign, even a little like a community college, with a brick façade and white columns at the entrance and porcelain sinks in the bathrooms. Noura could let herself in and out of her cell.

But Noura couldn't stay in Nashville. It was just for processing prisoners and assigning them to their long-term placements. Noura was sent to the Mark H. Luttrell Correctional Center, on the outskirts of Memphis. What she heard about it from other women scared her. "People said there were rats and it was really ghetto and they had no AC," she said. When she got off the bus, she saw only steel and concrete. There were padlocks on the cell doors. "You hear people talk about prison as caging human beings. In Memphis, that image is real."

Noura had learned to avoid drawing attention to herself—to look down, tuck in her shirt, and stay out of arguments. She caught a break when she was assigned to room with Melissa Barnett, who'd been convicted of killing her father and didn't judge Noura.

Still, the facts and media attention surrounding Noura's conviction made her a subject of gossip. It also brought her to the attention of Pat Culp, who ran a ministry at the prison called Women Empowered to Become Self-Sufficient. Culp taught a class called Journey to Success, which she persuaded Noura to join. Most programs in the prison focused on reentry services for women serving short sentences, but Culp nurtured a smaller group who were locked up for the long term. She was one of the few people Noura encountered who didn't probe about her past. "It's not part of my ministry to ask anyone about their charges," Culp said. "I knew nothing about Noura or her trial."

Noura soon became part of the team of volunteers Culp recruited for a cherished annual event: Winter Wonderland. "Before Christmas, we turned the gym into a shopping mall," Noura said. "For a week, it felt like we were free." Volunteers brought food from the outside, like submarine sandwiches or fried chicken or nachos. The prisoners received vouchers so they could buy goods, donated by local merchants and nonprofits, to give their families. And they made and sold small gifts, like string bracelets, which Noura bought by the dozen with money friends like Bill Shelton put in her commissary account. When her friends pointed out she had more bracelets than people to give them to, she said she was acting in the spirit of her mother, who loved to buy in bulk at Sam's Club, and then hand things out—a polo, a bathrobe—when people came over.

Noura signed up for every class Culp offered. They covered problem-solving, domestic violence, parenting, resumes, job interviews, and other life skills. They chanted a refrain: "Fearless action indicated through hope"—FAITH. Noura was trying to move past anger and resentment. She wasn't there yet, nor was she resigned to life in prison. But she wanted to find a little peace, and her relationship with Culp helped. She took a GED course, graduating first in the class in the summer of 2010 and giving the valedictorian speech in a cap-and-gown ceremony, with Ansley Larsson and two other friends from the free world at the ceremony. She took cosmetology classes, and she got a job as a hallway worker, mopping floors and emptying trash for 17 cents an hour.

In the classes, Noura got to know other long-serving prisoners. They called themselves "old-heads." Many were black and grew up poor. Noura found herself on the other side of a social divide she knew from childhood. "When I was growing up, especially in East Memphis, I had a single parent, so I was different from everybody else whose parents were high-school sweethearts, and whose mothers never worked," Noura said. "And I had a foreigner for a father. So my whole life I did everything to try to fit in, and I never did. Then I went to prison and everyone thought I was this privileged person with this perfect life, and that I had the life that everybody I grew up with had. So I didn't fit in there, either."

The old-heads' stories were laced with cruelty and regret. Octavia Cartwright, Noura's cellmate one fall and winter, was nineteen when she broke into a home in 1999 with a man she knew from high school. He was looking for money to buy drugs. Octavia was reeling from the aftereffects of a rape; she'd also been beaten and neglected by her alcoholic mother as a child, according to court papers she filed. The man used a pair of scissors to stab a woman who was inside, and Octavia hit her with the butt of a gun as they dragged her around the house. The victim eventually recovered from her injuries but said the attack traumatized her. The man, who is white, was awarded bail of $30,000 and got out of jail. Bail was set at $100,000 for Octavia, who is black, and she couldn't pay it. Admitting to planning the crime, he pled guilty and received a twenty-five-year sentence. Octavia was offered the same deal but didn't want to take it. "There was a lot of manipulation from him and I thought people would see that," she told me. "Twenty-five years seemed so long and I knew people with the same charges or even murder who didn't do time like that." Lee Coffee, the Shelby County prosecutor who opposed Noura's indictment and later became a judge, was the prosecutor at Octavia's trial. He piled on the charges and the judge sentenced her to ninety-one years. When I met Noura for the first time in prison, she told me more about Octavia's case than her own. "Everyone wants to make a big deal about me," she said. "I'm the poster child for 'this could happen to you.' For scaring white people about what could happen to their daughters. But injustices have been happening in the black community. Why aren't we horrified by that? What are we going to do about it?"

Because of the length of their sentences, the old-heads obsessed about filing appeals in court. Often it was like throwing yourself against a wall, agonizing and fruitless. As Noura talked with her lawyer, Valerie Corder, her friends cautioned her not to get her hopes up. In the appeal, Corder raised several issues about Weirich's handling of the trial. The first stop was the Tennessee Court of Criminal Appeals. A panel of judges ruled against Noura in December 2012, more than seven years after she first went to jail. About the first accusatory words of Weirich's closing argument—"Just tell us where you were. That's all we're asking, Noura!"—one judge said it was "certainly dramatic" but not improper. The other two thought that Weirich's remarks were improper but didn't affect the outcome of the trial. All three judges said Weirich and Jones should have turned over Hammack's handwritten note, but that it likely wouldn't have benefited Noura's defense. Despite the warnings from the old-heads, she was crushed.

Amy Weirich, meanwhile, was on her way to new heights. In January 2011, Bill Gibbons, her boss and the elected district attorney for Shelby County, left to join the administration of Tennessee's Republican governor. At forty-five, Weirich was tapped as Gibbons's interim replacement, becoming the first woman to hold the post, though she told me she didn't spend much time thinking about that. When she ran for election in 2012 to serve out the remaining two years of Gibbons's term, Weirich benefited from her reputation for being "tough as nails." A defense attorney who was among her admirers lauded her as the best trial lawyer in town. In courthouse chatter, her victory in Noura's case was cited as the proof.

Like many large metropolitan areas, Shelby County, made up of Memphis and its suburbs, had more Democrats than Republicans, and it was also majority African American. The area has long been fractured by race, with a history of control by white politicians and business owners. Founded on the backs of slaves, Memphis was the capital of a cotton empire, connected by the Mississippi River to one slave port in New Orleans and by railroad to another in Charleston. Nathan Bedford Forrest, the Confederate general and Ku Klux Klan leader, invested in the railroad and championed local ordinances that benefited the slave trade, from which he profited. His statue stood at the center of a city park until the end of 2017. When the Reverend Martin Luther King Jr. was shot and killed on the balcony of a Memphis hotel in 1968, he'd come to support a strike by sanitation workers against a segregationist white mayor who dug in to fight their demands for better pay and working conditions.

The city also had one of the highest violent crime rates in the country. Segregation and racial inequality never really abated, and for part of the 2010s, Memphis ranked first among large metro areas for poverty and child poverty, with a growing gap between white and black residents. In that environment, Weirich's law-and-order message gained traction. Noura followed the election closely and watched Weirich coast to victory. She felt that she'd helped fulfill the ambitions of her worst enemy. It seemed increasingly clear that her only hope lay with the Tennessee Supreme Court. "There was nowhere to go after that," she said. "It was the last stop."

Corder was determined to get Noura's case before the court. In her petition, she argued that Weirich had violated Noura's constitutional rights at the trial in two major ways. The first was Weirich's failure to turn over Andrew Hammack's note. The second was Weirich's demand, in her rebuttal, that Noura tell the jury where she was on the night of her mother's murder. Judge Craft should have granted Noura a new trial, Corder argued, and the court of criminal appeals shouldn't have dismissed Weirich's closing remarks as a harmless error that hadn't affected the verdict.

The five Tennessee justices controlled their docket, with complete discretion over whether to grant the review of Noura's petition or leave the ruling of the criminal appeals court in place. Corder poured herself a glass of champagne when she received word in April 2013, in the form of a two-sentence order, that the Tennessee Supreme Court would hear Noura's appeal. She called the prison warden to ask her to tell Noura and then printed out the brief she'd written for Noura's earlier appeal and took out her red pen: she had to cut it to meet the state supreme court's page limit. Oral argument—Corder's chance to make her case in person—was scheduled for November 6.

Corder decided that the best way to demonstrate the impact of Weirich's rebuttal would be to show the video of it to the justices. She looked at the court's rules: they barred the submission of a recording of any trial proceedings. She submitted the six-second clip anyway as an exhibit. No one objected.

On the day of the argument, Corder got to the historic court-house in Nashville early in the morning and arranged to set up a screen and a DVD player. Standing at a wood lectern, she faced the five justices, who sat before a carved archway flanked by Corinthian columns. "Miss Jackson's appeal contends she did not receive fundamental due process," she began. She brought up Hammack's missing note and suggested that prosecutorial misconduct was "evident" in Weirich's closing rebuttal to the jury.

Corder pressed play. Amy Weirich appeared on screen, striding toward Noura in the trial courtroom and shouting, "Just tell us where you were! That's all we're asking, Noura!" Corder stopped the tape.

"Was she saying that to the defendant?" one of the justices asked.

"Yes, Your Honor, she was."

"That's the defendant in the far left-hand corner?" the justice asked.

"Yes, Your Honor," Corder answered again.

The chief justice broke in. He instructed a clerk to dim the lights. "And now perhaps you could replay that," he said to Corder.

The lights went down. The justices watched the video again.

Corder left the courthouse elated.

Sometimes, in the months before the Tennessee Supreme Court's decision, the full weight of everything Noura had lost would hit her. She'd been in prison for a third of her life—eight and a half long years. She had friends but no family. "We'd go on lockdown," which meant being confined to a cell for days, "and after it was over everyone would call their mamas. Except me. I had a friend from Alabama. Her mother sent her a card every day for a week before her birthday. I saw that and I thought about how when I went to overnight camp just for a week, my mother wrote out cards and mailed them before I left so I would get one every day. I went to that camp for five or six years. She did that every time." Noura tried to imagine someday rebuilding her family by having a child of her own. "I was raised by a single parent, and I didn't always know what I wanted to be, or who I wanted to be with, but the one thing that has remained constant in my life is that I wanted to be a mother."

Her endometriosis made her fear that would never happen. Without sustained medical attention, it worsened over the years in prison, causing pain and potentially threatening her fertility. Even if she got better somehow, her biological clock was ticking away, and with all the credits for good time she could muster, she still had as much as a decade left to go on her sentence.

Even as she struggled with her health and her emotions, Noura thought about the mantra her mother recited in hard times: "Sadness, anger, resentment, acceptance, and healing"—S-A-R-A-H. Noura tried to pull herself toward the last two stages. She thought her mother would have wanted that for her. She moved with some of the other old-heads to a wing of the prison called the Annex. She could sign in and out of the building on her own to go to work, the most freedom she'd had since her arrest. She'd become Culp's teaching aide and assistant. She had a landscaping job, which included painting lines in the parking lot and cutting the grass on the prison grounds, including a stretch next to a path called the Shelby County Green Mile, where people in the free world jogged and biked. She joked to her friends that the job was a white girl's dream: she could get a tan.

Several months passed without word from the Tennessee Supreme Court. The delay was unusual and coincided with an election year. Weirich was running with strong Republican support, this time for a full eight-year term. On August 7, 2014, she sailed to victory with 65 percent of the vote. "When Amy won that second election, it kind of defeated me," Noura said. Also, two state supreme court justices had retired and the Republican governor chose conservatives to fill the vacancies. "Everyone was so pessimistic for me because one of the justices who retired was the most liberal and she was the vote I would be looking for." Noura tried to stop thinking about her appeal. "I was just waiting for the paperwork denying me. We all were, and I was trying to accept defeat." She found herself backsliding to anger. Written up for smoking and not signing in, she lost her place in the Annex.

Back in a padlocked cell with a new roommate, Noura didn't go to dinner one night. She wanted a bit of time to herself. It was August 22, a couple of weeks after the election. She was sitting on the toilet in her cell when she saw her name scroll across the bottom of her cellmate's TV screen. The sound was turned off. Noura lunged to turn on the volume. The announcer spoke words she'd taught herself not to hope for: "The Tennessee Supreme Court has granted Noura Jackson a new trial."

She screamed for someone to let her out of her cell, but the guards were at dinner with the prisoners. Finally, someone heard her and opened the door. Noura waited for her friends on the breezeway between the cells and the dining hall. She found Octavia, and two other friends, Michelle and Shayne, who worked as prison law clerks, helping people who were trying to file petitions but didn't have lawyers. "They were crying. I was crying. Michelle said, 'You're the only person I know who won at the supreme court. It never happens. We couldn't believe it.'"

The court's ruling was unanimous and it was scathing. The justices said that by looking straight at Noura and demanding, "Just tell us where you were!" Weirich "implicitly encouraged the jury to view Defendant's silence as a tacit admission of guilt." Commenting on a defendant's decision not to testify "'should be considered off limits to any conscientious prosecutor,'" they continued. "Given that 'the impropriety of any comment upon a defendant's exercise of the Fifth Amendment right not to testify is so well settled as to require little discussion,' it is not at all clear why any prosecutor would venture into this forbidden territory." Judge Craft's instructions to the jury to disregard what Weirich had just said probably compounded the problem, by further emphasizing Noura's decision not to testify. They also noted pointedly that Weirich was "doubtless well aware" of this rule, citing three previous cases in which appellate judges criticized her and her office for making prejudicial statements to the jury.

Normally, courts give one reason for reversing a conviction, and stop there. This was different. The justices turned to Hammack's note. "The record on appeal also establishes that the prosecution violated Defendant's right to Due Process," they wrote. "This separate and flagrant violation of Defendant's constitutional rights also merits our consideration and independently entitles Defendant to a new trial." In the fifty-one years since the U.S. Supreme Court's ruling in *Brady v. Maryland*, the Tennessee Supreme Court had reversed only one other conviction because the prosecution had failed to turn over evidence. But this time, the court said that the note was material and could have altered the verdict.

The fifty-two-page opinion ended with a rebuke of Judge Craft. "In this case, the trial court repeatedly permitted the introduction of evidence concerning Defendant's alcohol use, drug use, and sex life," the justices wrote. "The prejudicial effect of this evidence may well have outweighed its probative value." The justices cautioned that in the event of a new trial, Craft should reconsider his approach.

"This Supreme Court opinion is what every lawyer hopes for," Corder told the press.

Of course, the Tennessee justices didn't free Noura. They simply rewound the case to the moment when she was charged with murder. Weirich announced that she would prepare to try Noura a second time. "I disagree with the Supreme Court's ruling," she said. "Our primary concern is continuing to speak with Jennifer Jackson's family and getting justice for her and them."

The stakes were high for those who'd welcomed the trial verdict. Grace, Cindy, and Eric were still suing Noura for her mother's estate. Weirich's reputation was on the line as well. With everything she'd put into the case and reaped in return, she had every incentive to insist on Noura's guilt. She also had the same problem she'd had since the outset of the case: she lacked another suspect. The police hadn't solved Nazmi Hassanieh's murder or identified the person whose DNA was found in the blood spattered in Jackson's bedroom.

Bill Shelton, who continued to visit Noura in prison, had wanted for years to turn the tables on Weirich. In the Tennessee Supreme Court's opinion, he saw an opening. The state's Board of Professional Responsibility, an arm of the state supreme court, has the mission of "protecting the public from harm from unethical lawyers." Soon after the court's decision, Shelton filed a complaint with the board against Weirich, attaching the entire opinion in *State v. Jackson.* "As the TN Supreme Court concluded, Weirich violated 2 of Noura Jackson's constitutional rights," Shelton wrote in block print. "Now she publicly disagrees with the Court's ruling. If not swiftly and strongly disciplined, why should we not expect more constitutional violations from her and/or her office?"

It wasn't the first time such questions about a Shelby County prosecutor had surfaced.

When Amy Weirich became district attorney in 2011, her mentor was Tom Henderson, the director of criminal trial prosecutions. Henderson joined the office back in 1976. During his early years working there, the courts ignored obvious misconduct by senior prosecutors in the office. In 1980, a Vietnam veteran murdered two people in Memphis. The police learned he had post-traumatic stress disorder and a drug addiction. That evidence remained buried even as a prosecutor told the jury the veteran's claims of mental impairment were "baloney." When the files were opened more than a decade later, the state and federal appeals courts said the concealed evidence wouldn't have made a difference—and affirmed the man's death sentence.

In 1985, a woman who killed her abusive husband said she was provoked by his cruelty, which included sleeping with other women and telling her the details. This time, the Shelby County prosecutor didn't turn over explicit letters between the husband and one of his girlfriends, which backed up the wife's account. When the letters came to light on appeal, the wife's death sentence was affirmed nonetheless. In a dissent, a single federal judge wrote that the prosecutors "covered up the love letters while lying to the trial court," and concluded, "This set of falsehoods is typical of the conduct of the Memphis district attorney's office during this period." Several lawyers and judges also told me that cheating on the Brady rule was a regular practice for a few prosecutors in Shelby County at that time, mostly tolerated or ignored by their peers as well as the courts.

Henderson was known as the most skilled trial lawyer in the office. "I was meant to be a prosecutor," he would say later. "My original plan was to stay here two years, get some trial experience and then go into practice and make a lot of money. I was going to defend the downtrodden and oppressed, but as a prosecutor I saw that the downtrodden and oppressed in the criminal justice system are the victims, not the defendants. They're the only ones who didn't do anything to be here." Henderson named his three sons after Supreme Court justices. Two were obvious choices, John Marshall and Joseph Story, foundational figures in the early United States; the third was Roger Taney, a strong supporter of slavery best known for writing the discredited 1857 opinion in *Dred Scott* that said black people could not be U.S. citizens.

In the early 2000s, judges and defense lawyers started to question whether Henderson himself was withholding evidence. Courts twice found that in earlier capital murder cases, when the defendant's life was on the line, Henderson did not give the defense all the evidence he should have. One of Henderson's lapses resulted in a mistrial, and the defendant was later acquitted. In the other, the defendant was found guilty and a state appeals court let the verdict stand.

Then in October 2012, a couple of months after Amy Weirich won her first election, one of the biggest cases of Henderson's career blew up on him. A thirty-year-old named Michael Rimmer had been arrested in 1997 and charged with killing his former girlfriend, Ricci Ellsworth, while she worked the night shift as a motel clerk. The police couldn't find Ellsworth's body, but a trail of her blood ran from the motel bathroom to the office, where about $600 was missing from the cash register. Rimmer's past made him an obvious suspect: he'd gone to prison a decade earlier for raping Ellsworth. And the DNA in blood found on the seatbelt of a car he drove could have been Ellsworth's, medical examiners said.

The police had a lead from an eyewitness that pointed in a different direction, however. An army sergeant who pulled into the motel's parking lot that night said he saw two men with blood on their knuckles, as if they'd been in a struggle, standing next to a car with an open trunk. Shown an array of photos, the sergeant didn't pick Rimmer. Instead, he pointed to another man who was wanted for a different stabbing.

Henderson decided the ID was a false lead and didn't tell Rimmer's lawyer about it. Instead, he sought and won a death sentence for Rimmer. But in 2012, a Tennessee judge, James Beasley, reversed the murder conviction. Judge Beasley said that Henderson "purposefully misled" the defense about the eyewitness statement and ID that remained buried in the state's six-thousand-page file, finding Henderson's claims that "he knew of no evidence exonerating or exculpating" Rimmer to be "blatantly false, inappropriate, and ethically questionable."

It was a remarkably clear-cut finding of wrongdoing. Sometimes prosecutors omit evidence without meaning to, or it's the police who are to blame, because they don't turn over all the material in their investigative files. Judges are generally reluctant to say a prosecutor has broken the Brady rule on purpose; it's hard to prove intent and easier to give the prosecutor the benefit of the doubt. Judge Beasley didn't take that out. He made a point of saying that Henderson acted intentionally, misconduct many district attorneys say they won't tolerate.

Henderson had helped Weirich rise through the ranks by developing her talent and vouching for her. When Judge Beasley's damning finding hit the courthouse, the news traveled through the Memphis bar. Weirich backed up Henderson. He said he'd forgotten the eyewitness ID and she said he was guilty merely of "human error." "That's it," she told the local press. "End of story. Period."

The Tennessee Board of Professional Responsibility didn't see it that way. The board investigated an ethics complaint against Henderson—much like the one Shelton would bring against Weirich—and in 2014 made him the kind of offer he was used to making: he could go to trial, or he could plead guilty to violating his ethical responsibilities in return for a public censure.

Henderson pled guilty, and Weirich offered only praise, calling him a "dedicated public servant." Though they understood the power of loyalty, to some members of the local bar Weirich's stance was jaw-dropping. "Amy basically stood up on TV news and said he didn't do anything wrong," a local judge told me. "That's the equivalent of a defense lawyer standing up with a client who got convicted and saying, 'No, he didn't do it and he's not going to prison.'"

Weirich kept Henderson in his role as trial supervisor, which reinforced a culture of impunity in her office. "It's disturbing when a prosecutor with a history of failing to disclose evidence has the job of overseeing the next generation of lawyers," said Ronald Wright, a law professor at Wake Forest who studies the organizational culture of prosecutors. One former assistant district attorney told me that Weirich's unwillingness to grapple with Henderson's misconduct, plain for all to see, "made it clear that, quite honestly, she doesn't believe that ethical violations are important."

When Henderson retired in 2016, Weirich offered praise for his "incredible teaching skills." When I asked her about her decision to keep Henderson in a position of honor and trust, she said, "The message it sends to prosecutors, to everybody, is that prosecutors are not perfect. This office touches over 200,000 cases every year and mistakes are going to be made, but there's a huge difference between a mistake and misconduct, and there was nothing in what happened to Mr. Henderson that rose to the level of my taking any further action. It was hard enough on him personally and professionally. There was no reason for me to do anything else."

A district attorney sets the tone for her office, influencing, however subtly, how prosecutors will resolve the tension between sharing evidence and scoring a win. The Brady rule depends on an honor system—that idea of prosecutors as tennis players who will make the right calls when no one else can see the lines. It's ripe for abuse and offers little possibility for recourse. It also operates quite differently from the process for disclosing evidence in civil suits, in which both sides are entitled to review relevant documents and to depose each other's witnesses. "If the civil plaintiff, who seeks primarily the payment of money, must share his evidence in advance of a trial," wrote Miriam Baer, a Brooklyn Law School professor and former assistant United States attorney, in a 2015 article in the *Columbia Law Review*, "then surely the prosecutor, who seeks the defendant's loss of liberty or life, ought to suffer the same obligations."

Yet in many courthouses, the practice of criminal law is far looser than civil practice, even though liberty rather than money is at stake. "When I entered law practice at the age of fifty-seven after a lifetime of being a professor, what surprised me most was the irresponsibly aggressive conduct of prosecutors," the former U.S. solicitor general Walter Dellinger wrote in June 2017, describing a case in which prosecutors failed to disclose key evidence. "Many, of course, strive to do justice. I was shocked by those who do not."

It bears repeating: for most prosecutors, cheating is unthinkable. Nevertheless, one of the most disturbing features of our system is that we may never know the number of hidden-evidence cases. Since 95 percent or more of cases end in plea bargains, defendants often have little chance to see or test the prosecution's proof. Many waive their right to appeal, and if not, they need diligent lawyers to comb through files for previously missing evidence. "The Catch-22 of *Brady* is that you have to find out they're hiding something to have a claim," says Kathleen Ridolfi, the lead author of a study of wrongful convictions for the Northern California Innocence Project. "How many do we miss?"

That question has loomed especially large for federal judges. They used to have a relatively free hand in overturning wrongful convictions through the "Great Writ" of habeas corpus (a means of challenging the basis for detention since 1305). Since 1996, however, they've been constrained by a law called the Antiterrorism and Effective Death Penalty Act (AEDPA). Signed by President Bill Clinton in the wake of the Oklahoma City bombings to speed up executions, AEDPA forced federal judges to defer to the previous determinations of state courts except in narrowly circumscribed instances. If the state appeals courts rejected an appeal, even in cursory fashion, federal judges were often bound to do the same. "The collapse of habeas corpus as a remedy for even the most glaring of constitutional violations ranks among the greater wrongs of our legal era," the late Judge Stephen Reinhardt of the U.S. Court of Appeals for the Ninth Circuit wrote in 2015.

AEDPA is one more reason that a D.A.'s office can get away with a pattern of playing fast and loose with the rules. In research published in July 2017, the Fair Punishment Project at Harvard singled out Weirich, along with Leon Cannizzaro and Tony Rackauckas, the district attorneys in New Orleans and Orange County, California, for numerous allegations of misconduct in their offices between 2010 and 2015. The Fair Punishment Project's director, Rob Smith, calls these district attorneys "recidivists who are repeatedly abusing their power. Under Cannizzaro and Rackauckas, multiple murder cases have unraveled when judges found that prosecutors failed to disclose evidence that mattered for mounting an effective defense." (Press officers for the three district attorneys questioned the validity of the findings.)

The concern that something was amiss in Shelby County has extended to Weirich's own conduct. At the end of 2014, a judge ordered her to testify about her handling of a 2005 trial, in which a man named Vern Braswell was convicted of killing his wife. On appeal, a defense attorney and a prosecutor who was new to the case—one of Weirich's own employees—found in the files a manila envelope, about half an inch thick, labeled with a sticky note that said "Do not turn over to defense" or words to that effect, dated 2005 and signed with Weirich's initials. What was written on the pages inside? The answer became a mystery. The prosecutor who found the envelope didn't want to open it without permission from his supervisors. When he went back to look for it later, he said, the envelope was gone.

Weirich spent four hours in the witness chair answering questions about the disappearance. Leaning forward to make her points, her legs pressed together and her hair closely framing her face, she said she'd turned over everything she was legally required to turn over and knew nothing about the envelope. "A couple of people say they saw this envelope," she told the press after the hearing. "I don't recall that envelope and nobody can say what was in it."

A few weeks after the Tennessee Supreme Court reversed Noura's conviction, a federal judge dismissed her friend Octavia's petition. At first she didn't tell Noura. She didn't want to bring her friend down. "We were close," Octavia told me on the phone from prison. "I love her and I don't like to push my woes on people when they're having a good moment in life." As cellmates, they stayed up till 3:00 a.m., cooking sweet potato pie and chicken quesadillas and making handmade cards with glitter, stickers, and other arts and crafts supplies they were allowed to buy. Every Monday, on the night before the transport bus came, Octavia would tell Noura that if she wasn't there for the weekly headcount on Tuesday, she would come back for a visit someday. When Noura finally found out that Octavia's appeal had been denied, she wept. "I hated that for her," she said. "I really, really did." Octavia wiped away Noura's tears. Though neither of them spoke of it, Octavia would probably never be released.

Noura didn't want to say it out loud, but she was starting to imagine the possibility that maybe she wouldn't be there for count the following week. Maybe she'd get to go home, wherever that was. The Tennessee Supreme Court ruling entitled her to a new bail hearing. She'd been behind bars for more than nine years, for a crime the state was back to square one in proving. Noura had heard of a few women whose convictions had been overturned. They'd soon gotten out on bond.

It took three months before she had her first court date, and when it took place, her case was right back in front of Judge Craft. Corder had warned her that this would happen, but standing there, Noura could feel her confidence seeping away. The only action Craft took was to schedule another court appearance in January, two months away. The lack of urgency made her think "that nothing would be easy or simple for me."

Corder wanted Weirich and the Shelby County district attorney's office off the case. When prosecutors are accused of breaking basic rules, like the Brady rule, and courts criticize them directly, they're often asked to step aside for another prosecutor, because their personal stake in reinstating a conviction could cloud their judgment. Since Weirich was now the district attorney and everyone in the Shelby County D.A.'s office worked for her, Corder wanted her recusal to extend to the other prosecutors there as well. At the January court date, Weirich agreed to step aside but said her office would give Noura "another fair trial." Corder balked. She asked Craft to appoint a special prosecutor outside of Shelby County and to grant Noura a bond hearing. He put off a decision again until the middle of February. More time was passing: it had been six months since the Tennessee Supreme Court reversed Noura's conviction and almost ten years since her mother was killed.

A few days before her February hearing, Noura was told she would soon be bused to the jail, and she went to the office of the prison chaplain to make a phone call. While she was there, guards came in and shut down the office, strip-searching everyone and escorting them back to their cells. They were told that a box addressed to the chaplain's office had gone missing. The chaplain was on leave for a few weeks, and the guards suspected that someone was trying to smuggle in cellphones.

Culp was covering for the chaplain for a few weeks. Though she wasn't there the day the box was delivered, she was questioned. "They wanted to know who asked me to pick up things from the mail room," Culp said. "They did ask me if Noura was the one who asked me to go to the mail room. She wasn't. But I think I was called in because of my relationship with her. The investigator seemed to be focused on Noura, and it did seem to be as if he was trying to get me to admit I had knowledge of Noura getting that box or sending me to the mail room for it."

Passing contraband in prison was a felony. If Noura was implicated in a scheme to smuggle in cellphones, prosecutors could ask Judge Craft to keep her behind bars for years without retrying her for the killing of her mother. Was it crazy to think she was being set up?

Noura couldn't discuss what was happening with the old-heads. She was told to pack and get on the bus to court. She did it warily. Five years earlier, she'd been scared to make the trip in the opposite direction, from county jail to prison. Now she didn't want to go back. In prison, she had Culp and Octavia and the rest of her friends. In jail, she'd be forbidden from calling or writing to them and they wouldn't be allowed to contact her, either. She'd have to face the questions about the contraband, along with the next phase of the murder case, without the people she trusted who knew the system from the inside. But she had no choice. The bus was waiting. This time, she didn't get to say goodbye.

10

DIVERSION

DIVERSION WAS SUPPOSED to be Kevin's lifeline, but his chance almost ended a few weeks after it began. A few weeks after his guilty plea, he walked through the park near his house and stopped to watch a game of dice. It was the first time he'd been out at night since the accusation by Chris's girlfriend that he'd snitched began to circulate, threatening him. Now that he was in YCP, the rumors were fading.

Kevin was glad to be outside. It was around 9:00 p.m., an hour before his curfew. Some of the people playing dice were smoking marijuana. Mindful of his next drug test, which could come at any time, Kevin held only a regular cigarette. Suddenly, the cops were upon them, squealing to a stop at the curb and moving fast. The people playing dice scattered, but Kevin stood still. *Why should I run? I'm not doing anything wrong.*

The police took him into custody, charged him with loitering, and sent him to central booking for the night.

It was a bullshit charge, in the language of the Brooklyn courthouse. But by getting arrested, Kevin had violated the terms of his plea agreement. When Judge Gubbay said Kevin had no wiggle room, this was what he meant: any tangle with the police, and he would go to jail.

When a YCP client got arrested, the case was routinely flagged for the D.A.'s office, so a prosecutor could call the precinct and tell them whether to set a high bail that would hold the person in jail. But in Kevin's case, there was a glitch of some sort, and no one called the D.A.'s office or YCP about his arrest. Kreyngold learned about it from Kevin, who missed his 10:00 p.m. curfew check-in because he was being held and called Kreyngold the next day to explain. Kreyngold took note of Kevin's honesty and show of trust. "In my head," he said, "I gave him a gold star."

The next day, Kreyngold met with Kevin and asked if he'd been smoking pot when the police came and just didn't want to say so. Kevin said no. Kreyngold asked him to take a drug test. Kevin passed. Kreyngold didn't think Kevin deserved jail time, and he didn't want to jeopardize his good standing with the prosecutors or the judge. His job was all about gauging when his clients were making progress, and when he could tell they were, he hated to see them derailed. Kreyngold checked Kevin's rap sheet. It showed no new arrests, but he warned Kevin that the one from the dice game could pop up in the system at any point. Months earlier, Debora Silberman, Kevin's lawyer, had given him a similar warning: "The minute you do anything, the minute you jump that turnstile, the D.A. and the judge will say, 'He got arrested again.' We don't want to give them an inch."

The arrest weighed on Kevin. "They'll see the violation when I go back to court in September," he said. "I don't know what happens then."

First, though, came summer. Kevin loved being outside in the long daylight hours. With Kreyngold's help, he joined the city's Summer

Youth Employment Program, which offered jobs that paid fourteen-to twenty-four-year-olds $11 an hour to work up to twenty-five hours a week. Kevin's job, as a counselor for kids in a summer program at the nearby community center, was comfortable and familiar. The kids he was assigned to were from the Brownsville projects, like him, and he usually knew one of their older siblings or their mothers. The kids looked up to him, he said; he felt like the "cool counselor."

With his first paycheck, Kevin got a phone to replace his old one, which had died after months of blinking on and off. But the new phone didn't work with the family plan his mother paid for, so he had to resell it at a loss. His girlfriend complained that he was hard to reach. Still, they settled into a pattern: Kevin would go home after work in the afternoon, tired from running after the campers, sleep until his curfew call with Kreyngold at 10:00 p.m., go back to sleep till midnight, and then see her when she came over after her evening shift in Manhattan. She usually came every other day. He stayed in more than he had in the past.

It was easier to stay out of trouble that summer, more than any other time Kevin could remember since childhood. He and his friends were getting older, and twenty-one felt different from sixteen or even nineteen. More people had jobs. Kevin still wanted the respect of his peers and to be known for standing up for himself, but he was determined to steer clear of conflict rather than lean into it. "I can't remember the last time I actually had a fight," he told me one day with a note of surprise. He was figuring out how to stop short of a physical altercation.

In some ways, Brownsville was changing along with him. In 1993, seventy-four people were murdered there, a staggering total for an area of its size. In 2010, the year Kevin turned fifteen, the number was down to twenty-eight, but Brownsville was still New York City's murder capital. In 2017, the number dropped to nine. The total for shootings, at thirty-one, also represented a historical low, and a drop of more than a third from the previous year.

Kevin noticed the difference. Brownsville had once been as violent as any crime-ridden city in the developing world. Now it was safer than the wealthy parts of New York were a generation ago. (Twenty-three people were killed in one precinct on the Upper West Side in 1993.) In his book *Uneasy Peace*, the New York University sociologist Patrick Sharkey argued that across the country, the most disadvantaged city residents have gained the most from the steep decline in crime. Because homicide is the leading cause of death of young black men, its decline improved their life expectancy as much as ending obesity would in the United States. Black children have also benefited: the gap in academic achievement between them and white students has narrowed the most where violence has fallen furthest.

It's common to chalk up variation in crime to changing levels of wealth. But Brownsville has remained poor. What changed?

Certainly the policing tactics that have succeeded throughout New York City—crime mapping and hot-spot policing made possible by the data system CompStat, and the shutting down of outdoor drug markets—played a role. In Brownsville, though, people both needed the police and had reason to be wary of them. Older residents remembered when a group of dirty cops known as the Morgue Boys roamed their precinct in the late 1980s and early 1990s, using the drug epidemic as an excuse to raid, steal, and make false arrests. More recently, stop-and-frisk alienated a lot of residents. No one I met in Brownsville had a good word to say about Omnipresence, a policing strategy introduced in 2014. During the day, officers stood like sentinels at the perimeter of the high-rises. At night, they lit up the neighborhood, wheeling powerful floodlights into parks and squares and parking their cruisers, lights flashing, at major intersections.

Looking at a crime drop only through the lens of law enforcement, however, offers a misleading view. Other elements are often more crucial to a community's well-being, including what sociologists call social cohesion: trust and communication among the people who live there, fostered by the organizations that serve them.

In the 1990s, the sociologist Robert Sampson led a watershed study of almost nine thousand residents of more than three hundred neighborhoods in Chicago. His team conducted extensive surveys and made street-level observations, driving around in an SUV with video cameras mounted on the back that taped people's interactions on thousands of city blocks. "I joke that we should have patented what we were doing—it was an early form of Google Street View," Sampson said. The work showed a link between the level of violence and what he called "collective efficacy"—the strength of people's ties to each other and their willingness to come together to address a threat or make something good happen. Holding demographics constant—across income, education, race, and single parenthood—Sampson showed that crime varies enormously by the level of interpersonal connection. (So does health: another study found that after a lethal heat wave in Chicago in 1995, social cohesion accounted for a death rate that was ten times lower in one poor Chicago neighborhood than in the similar one next to it.) "It makes sense if you think about it," Sampson said. "In most communities, there's no cop on the corner. Family ties and community cohesiveness go way beyond police and incarceration. Something else has to strengthen the social fabric."

Chicago's 2016 homicide spike was concentrated in highly segregated neighborhoods where Sampson found the reverse dynamic: weak and fraying social ties. The outbreak of murders also coincided with a free fall in the rate at which the police solved violent crimes. The Chicago police solved 70 percent of homicides in the 1990s, compared with just 17 percent in 2017. The rate for solving nonfatal shootings fell to 5 percent in the same year. By comparison, the national rate for solving murders is 60 percent. In big cities where violent crime has significantly declined, the solve rate for homicides in 2016 ranged from 45 percent in Philadelphia to the mid-fifties in Houston and to around 70 percent in Los Angeles and New York.

In Chicago's plummeting solve rate, Sampson saw eroding trust between the community and police. Impunity for shooters makes witnesses afraid to come forward, giving the police fewer leads to follow—a downward spiral. Research also shows what we called 'legal cynicism' is higher in low-collective-efficacy and high-disadvantage neighborhoods. So another way to think about it is that residents are reacting to the inability of police to solve crimes or larger problems."

Sampson also found that the increased presence of nonprofit organizations in a community strongly predicts more collective action. Patrick Sharkey, the NYU sociologist, has quantified this effect. Collecting data from 264 cities over twenty years, Sharkey found that each addition of a community-based nonprofit group accounted for a drop of approximately 1 percent in the murder rate. "Considering that this segment of the nonprofit sector grew by about 25 organizations for every 100,000 residents in New York and elsewhere, community-based organizations appear to deserve more credit than they get for contributing to the fall of violence," he wrote. "While police departments remain crucial to keeping city streets safe, community organizations may have the greatest capacity to play a larger role in confronting violence."

In his analysis, Sharkey included many kinds of nonprofit groups, working on neighborhood development, drug treatment, job training, and youth enrichment as well as crime prevention. When organizations like these work well, they throw off crime prevention as a kind of by-product. "It's surprising how broad the activities are that contribute," Sampson said. A community group may start by cleaning up the park or converting a vacant lot into a playground. A safer space means more adults are out and about, providing supervision and deterring crime with their presence, even though that wasn't the goal of cleaning up the park or building the playground.

Historically, Brownsville had few resources compared to the rest of the city and a low number of arrests per homicide. By 2016, the neighborhood was beginning to attract more resources, though still not as many as other parts of the city. The newcomers included Anthony Newerls's group, BIVO, and the Brownsville Community Justice Center (BCJC), which recruited local businesses to employ some of the young people they served. The city was supporting both of them. Elizabeth Glazer, the director of the Mayor's Office of Criminal Justice, was a former prosecutor with a vision for preventing crime that went beyond the standard law-enforcement tools. "She has been obsessive about this," said Sampson, who served on an advisory board Glazer created. "She's trying to measure New York City neighborhoods, recognizing from the beginning that it's not just about law enforcement, that you have to look at how a broader range of services are integrated into the community."

Glazer introduced me to Eric Cumberbatch, director of the city's Office to Prevent Gun Violence, who grew up moving around the city with his four brothers. (His father struggled with drug abuse and his mother was a teenager when he was born.) Cumberbatch told me that sending people to prison for gun possession was not the most productive approach. He was focused on helping young people find jobs and supporting an effort called Cure Violence operating in eighteen sites around the city. The aim was to train and dispense outreach workers and "credible messengers" from the community—people with gang and criminal histories—to press for the peaceful resolution of neighborhood conflicts and prevent retaliation after a shooting. Longtime community activists in Brooklyn had more hope for Cure Violence than anything else the city had funded in a long time. It was "people policing themselves," Paul Muhammad, a representative on a community board, told me.

Cure Violence had to coexist with the police and their approach to gangs. In June 2018, Chief of Detectives Dermot Shea testified at a public hearing about a database with 17,500 people the police suspected as gang members. Shea said the database had been cut in half during the de Blasio administration, but city documents showed that during the same period, only 1 percent of the people who'd been added were white. For the first time, Shea explained how the police put people on the list. The criteria included posting on social media with known gang members or a police report that someone was frequently hanging out at a "known gang location." Shea called the database a "vital tool" given that half the murders in the city over the past year involved a gang member as victim or perpetrator. "We do not want to start at square one each time one of these groups commits violence," he said, "without knowledge of who they or their associates are."

Lawyers and social workers at Legal Aid and Brooklyn Defender Services were dubious of the large number of people in the database and the quality of information that got them there. "We see people added to the database based on recycled information from low-level contacts," said Anthony Posada, supervising attorney of Legal Aid's Community Justice Unit. "There's no requirement of a conviction before you get on it. When someone goes on parole, they're looked at as a source of information. That's how the police cast a wide net. It makes it incredibly difficult to be integrated back into your community if you're still treated as guilty and gang involved even if that's far from true."

The NYPD had another means of targeting gangs called Ceasefire, launched in 2014. It wasn't clear how people were being identified for Ceasefire, other than a vague link to the gang database, according to Shea. But once you were on the list, you got a letter warning you that the police were watching and threatening that if you or "any member of your crew" got into trouble, "the District Attorney's Office will take a hard stance on plea positions for even the most minor offense."

Community activists and nonprofit leaders, however, saw Ceasefire as a problem. Its tactics of intimidation made it more difficult for them to work with people in the same high-risk pool. "Ceasefire uses people's backgrounds against them," said Andre T. Mitchell, who operates Cure Violence sites in Brooklyn as the founder of the group MAN Up. "You're forever looked at as a perpetrator, and that's unfortunate, because people should be allowed to grow and develop. We treat their backgrounds as a positive. We ask them to use their experiences and influence to talk down situations that could lead to very violent outcomes. They're part of the solution rather than the problem. That's where we get a lot of our success."

The successes of Cure Violence looked real. A 2017 study by researchers at John Jay College found a significantly larger drop in gun injuries in New York City neighborhoods with Cure Violence than those without. Trust in the police also increased. At one Cure Violence site, more than a year passed in a large housing project without a shooting. Cure Violence didn't get all the credit. The neighborhood also benefited from expanded afterschool programs, non-profit offerings, and more light towers and cameras. Whatever the mix of reasons, for a time, people put away their guns.

Talking about the decline in shootings in Brownsville in the summer of 2017, Kevin didn't trust it to last. Cure Violence wasn't operating in his neighborhood and he'd never heard of it. He'd felt in danger for as long as he could remember, and it would take more than a few months for him to believe that this was more than a lull. Besides, the peace wasn't exactly total: one day at his summer job, Kevin heard about gunfire grazing the leg of a baby near the subway stop on Sutter Avenue; on another day, a friend of his who'd moved to the Bronx came home for a cookout and got caught in crossfire. "You can't sleep on it," Kevin said of the relative calm. "It don't mean it can't happen later on or tomorrow. I don't put nothing past nothing."

Still, as the summer's rhythm took hold, Kevin began to unfurl from the crouch he'd been in since Travis's death a few months earlier. "I'm doing well," he said toward the end of July. "Working every day."

He was walking in downtown Brooklyn, wearing a blue Adidas shirt, jeans, white sneakers and a white durag, on his way from his weekly appointment with Kreyngold to the office of his bail agent a few blocks away. Since his phone broke, he'd missed a few of the weekly calls he was supposed to make to the bail agency. He figured he'd stop by and explain, no big deal. After all, he'd called in weekly for more than a year, and he hadn't missed a single court date.

The office had bare walls, two desks, and a couple of metal folding chairs. Two bail agents, older white men in jeans, looked up when Kevin walked in. One wore bifocals. The other had a pair of handcuffs dangling from the belt below his paunch.

Kevin gave his name and explained about his phone. The bail agent with the handcuffs looked back at him, expressionless. "If I was a female, I'm sure you'd find me," he said. He typed for a moment, looked at his computer screen, and turned back to Kevin. "You're twenty-one years old."

"I'm not making any excuses," Kevin said. "I'm not arguing with you. I know I was supposed to check in. That's why I'm here now, making it right."

"He's only here because I called him," the other bail agent said bitingly. "He's not here because he decided to come in. He didn't have some epiphany."

"I figured that," the first agent said.

"What?" Kevin asked, looking from one of them to the next. "I've been on y'all thing for a year. I just pled guilty. I pled guilty to the program a month ago. I don't know why I'm still on bail."

"Ask the judge."

"I'm still here," Kevin said. "It is what it is." He walked out and exhaled slowly in the elevator, his head down and his eyes on the floor. "I really don't like those people," he said under his breath. His earlier buoyancy was gone. In the annals of injustice, this encounter with the bail agents barely registered. But it was deflating for Kevin—it didn't feel like a small thing.

The hassles accumulated that summer. Despite the promised cutback to stop-and-frisk, one day in September police stopped Kevin at the Broadway Junction subway station, where he switched trains to go downtown. It was about 10:00 a.m. on a weekday and the cops asked Kevin for his ID, suggesting he was truant. Kevin usually carried his ID in his wallet, but that day he'd forgotten it. He told the police he was twenty-one. He suggested they call his mother, or Kreyngold, whom he was on his way to meet. The police refused and made him wait for hours while they ran his name to look for outstanding warrants.

Policing tactics seemed to be shifting here and there, however. On another evening, Kevin was driving with a friend in his neighborhood when they spotted a car following them. It was unmarked, but Kevin and his friend had seen it before and made a note of it. To test their theory that cops were driving it, Kevin's friend made a turn at a stop sign without using his signal—asking for trouble, no doubt, but also an act of young bravado. Sure enough, plainclothes officers pulled them over. Kevin's friend told them he didn't signal because he wanted to know why they were following him. They told him not to be a wiseass and ordered him and Kevin out of the car so they could search it. The police checked his license, which came up clean, found nothing of interest in the car, and let them drive away without a ticket.

Kevin thought the police chose to follow the car because he or his friend was being watched. He didn't know how people got onto the list for surveillance or how the cops used it. But the monitoring on social media was obvious. Posting your whereabouts and your social network on Facebook was doing the cops' work for them. After he got arrested for the gun charge, Kevin got a friend request from an account he didn't recognize. He clicked on the notification and saw the face of a police officer he knew—one of the cops who'd arrested him in Chris's apartment. "He's black, so he stood out. This was his real Facebook, with his name and pictures of his kids and his house."

Kevin's intimacy with some of the plainclothes detectives wasn't entirely a bad thing. One day after Travis's death, Officer Joseph stopped at the basketball court outside Kevin's building and called him over. He wanted to offer his condolences. "He knew Travis used to live with me. He said, 'I'm sorry for your loss. That situation was crazy. But you're in a program now and you're doing good. You're gonna be OK.'" The night Kevin got arrested for loitering at the dice game, Officer Joseph happened to be at the precinct and tried to intervene with the arresting officers, suggesting that they give him a ticket instead of booking him. It didn't work. Kevin and his friends noticed, though, that the cops were no longer busting people for small-time marijuana sales. "They leave them alone. Or if they see someone with weed, they'll tell you, 'I don't care about that.'" Sometimes the cops let other minor infractions slide, too. "Even a knife—they'll take it but they won't arrest you for a petty thing like that anymore." In a sense, it was the opposite of broken-windows policing. Let the little stuff go to build trust. Maybe the one you let off the hook now will help you solve a bigger crime later.

Perhaps it was a coincidence, but Officer Joseph seemed to be following the script for civic engagement Elizabeth Glazer laid out for me. As Mayor de Blasio campaigned for reelection, patrols in Brownsville began to include scooters and bikes. Glazer's office produced the Mayor's Action Plan for Neighborhood Safety, which connects police called "neighborhood coordination officers" with other city agencies to work on issues like the use of public space in and around housing projects. The officers could still make arrests, but they also held meetings where residents could ask for help with anything from drug deals to garbage collection and double-parked cars.

Brownsville also had recently gotten a new commanding officer, Deputy Inspector Rafael Mascol, an African American in his mid-fifties who grew up on Long Island and now lived east of the city. I first heard about him at the Brownsville Community Justice Center, when a social worker told me about asking Mascol to pull the police off the corner during a block party so people could come and go without feeling watched. Mascol did as she asked. He also pointed out young people he thought needed BCJC's services, so the staff could reach out. "He prefers us to get to the young people before they commit crimes," said Andre Mitchell of MAN Up. "When you speak to him, you feel like he's the man who lives down the block," Digna Layne, a resident advocate for one of the Brownsville projects, told me. "He will give you his cell number and he will answer any time of night."

I met Layne at a meeting of the 73rd Precinct, attended by about sixty people and held at a senior center. It was the week before Thanksgiving, and the crowd, which was mostly elderly but included community advocates and a handful of children and grandchildren, sat at round tables with pumpkin centerpieces. Anthony Newerls, director of BIVO and president of the precinct community council, welcomed everyone and introduced four new police recruits. (As an icebreaker, they answered *Jeopardy!*-style questions about local landmarks and street names.) Staff members from BIVO and the BCJC talked about working with young people.

"You mean the shooters?" someone in the audience called out.

"I don't know what you're talking about," the BIVO staffer answered firmly. "We deal with high-risk youth. We work on aggression and preventing violence, ways for them to resolve conflict. We're growing. If you know a young person like that, whatever their interest is, send them our way."

When it was Mascol's turn to speak, he started with good news. "We have the lowest crime in Brownsville ever. We have the lowest homicides in the history of this area. We are very thankful for every person we've saved." He gestured toward the new recruits. "The work these men will be doing, and have been doing, is what's brought us to this place right here."

Mascol wanted to make it clear, though, that they still had work to do. "Last month, my heart was broken, because we had eight arrests of juveniles. Eight arrests." He shook his head. "That's how I know we're not there yet."

When he was done speaking and shaking hands, Mascol and I sat down to talk. Promisingly, precincts in which the NYPD rolled out an initiative linked to the Mayor's Action Plan were showing a greater drop in crime (7 percent) than those without it (4 percent). What did Mascol think was working?

He began with a traditional crime-fighting answer, ticking off the units focused on narcotics, gangs, and gun violence suppression. Then he expanded the circle to include the neighborhood coordination officers, the violence interrupters of Man Up, and BIVO and the BCJC. "The housing developments have been beefing for as long as we can remember, but we've made so much headway on that issue," he said. "In the developments, the young people battle it out, but when they go to those organizations"—BIVO and BCJC—"they know they can't do that. Maybe they find out something about each other they didn't know before."

In a 2010 survey, 70 percent of Brownsville residents named guns, gangs, and drugs as their community's top problems. In November 2017, nearing his one-year anniversary as commanding officer, Mascol could say that the number one crime in Brownsville was neither violent nor drug-related. It was credit card fraud.

Guns still preoccupied him, however. "Two years ago, we took 265 of them off the street in the 73rd," Mascol said. I asked about Anthony Newerls's distinction between likely shooters, who carried guns for offensive purposes, and less-dangerous carriers, who carried them as defense or got arrested as part of a group that had a gun and stepped up to take the charge. "I've had so many people give me so many reasons why they have a gun," Mascol said. "Two weeks ago, a guy who'd gotten beat up was walking home by himself with a gun. He doesn't want to be a victim. He gets arrested for the gun. Is he a bad guy? I don't know. He could shoot someone or someone could take it from him."

Should most people go to prison for having guns? I asked. "That's not my call," Mascol replied. "My call is to get the gun off the street. The prosecutor decides how to charge him. The justice system decides the penalty."

When I asked Mascol what he would do to further reduce gun

crime in Brownsville, he didn't call for more arrests or more prison. He focused instead on the swiftness and certainty of punishment. It frustrated the police to arrest someone for having a gun and then see him back out on the street as the case ground on and on in court. "Trials should begin in three months," he said. "If there's anything I'd do, it would be to speed up the justice system. No year or two years of waiting." Swift and certain consequences mattered most in cases involving victims, but Mascol thought it would also deter people from carrying guns. Whatever time they should do, it should be done when they got caught, so they'd leave the neighborhood when everyone could make the connection between the crime and the punishment.

Mascol's concept of swift and certain consequences is a venerable and underappreciated approach to deterring crime. The word "deterrent" first appeared in English in 1829, in a book about punishment by Jeremy Bentham, the British philosopher and father of utilitarianism. He believed that a law's success could be measured by whether "the desired effect is produced by the employment of the least possible suffering." For Bentham, the desired effect was the prevention of crimes, not retribution—the gut-level and often more popular motivation. It should be the overarching purpose of punishment.

Bentham and another Enlightenment thinker, the Italian philosopher Cesare Beccaria, proposed that punishment deters crime when it is swift, certain, and proportionate. It has to be severe enough to discourage other potential criminals, but following utilitarian principles, a penalty that is more severe than necessary to achieve its goal is useless or worse, since it's hurting the people it affects without helping anyone else. Beccaria argued that certainty was the most powerful element of deterrence. "One of the greatest curbs on crime is not the cruelty of punishments, but their infallibility," he wrote. "The certainty of punishment even if moderate will always make a stronger impression."

A corrupt version of Beccaria's philosophy was used to justify the country's turn toward mass incarceration in the 1990s. "When a potential criminal knows that if he is convicted he is certain to be sentenced, and his sentence is certain to be stiff, his cost-benefit calculus changes dramatically," Senator Phil Gramm of Texas wrote in 1993 to push for mandatory minimum sentences. Gone was Bentham and Beccaria's emphasis on moderation. And as the rate for solving murders fell, certainty of punishment waned as a reality for perpetrators: the lower their chances of getting caught, the less mandatory minimum penalties would deter them. People also have to know how the law works to be deterred by mandatory minimums. Many don't.

Severity, nevertheless, was the only element of deterrence that politicians could attain with the stroke of a pen. In a time of rising crime, they overvalued increases in punishment. And, of course, the mandatory punishments didn't operate on their own. They took discretion away from judges (after conviction) and handed it to prosecutors (at the charging phase). Discretion is stubborn—stop it in one place and it will pop up in another. Otherwise, the law would fall hard on people who don't seem to deserve it (and who more often happen to be well-off and white).

Is there a better way to use punishment to achieve deterrence? Perhaps the most promising model was created in a Honolulu court in the early 2000s. A judge named Steven Alm started overseeing people on probation for felonies like burglary and drug dealing. As part of their supervision, they had to take drug tests for meth-amphetamine. According to the rules, one failed or missed test meant their parole would be revoked and they'd go back to prison for five to ten years.

In reality, as Alm soon learned, the people coming before him could fail or miss a drug test as many as ten times before he learned of it. Probation officers saw the punishment as far too severe for the violation. So when people failed the first or second or even the ninth time, the probation officers didn't impose the threatened consequences. Judges tended to tacitly go along, presumably because they also weren't eager to send people to jail for years for screwing up one drug test.

Judge Alm, a former prosecutor, didn't think it made sense to look the other way and then arbitrarily crack down. "You wouldn't bring up a child that way," he thought. "You'd have clear rules, and clear consequences for breaking them, and those consequences would happen right now, not in the sweet by-and-by."

Judge Alm set up a pilot project called Hawaii's Opportunity Probation with Enforcement, HOPE for short. He came up with a script that he read to people assigned to HOPE: from now on, every time they broke a rule of probation they'd be arrested on the spot and go to jail within seventy-two hours. Not for years, but for days. Smoke meth before your baby's first luau, the judge said, and you will miss it "because you decided to miss it when you decided to break the rules."

After receiving Judge Alm's warning, the HOPE participants were tested for drugs every week, more frequently than they had been before. If they failed a single test, they briefly went to jail, as Judge Alm had promised.

Judge Alm's divergence from the practice of the other judges created the conditions for a natural randomized experiment, the gold standard for empirical research. How did his HOPE participants fare compared to defendants with similar convictions who were experiencing probation as usual?

Four years after HOPE launched, the public policy professors Angela Hawken and Mark Kleiman did that study. The results aligned with Judge Alm's instincts. The HOPE group committed fewer violations with every additional month they were on probation, whereas for the probation-as-usual group, the violation rate rose, "as if they were learning how much they could get away with,"

Kleiman wrote. Six months in, Kleiman and Hawken found that the HOPE participants were 79 percent less likely to fail a drug test and 55 percent less likely to be rearrested for a new crime.

Replicating the results of the HOPE study has been tricky, but the implication of the program is this: if punishment is swift and certain, it need not be severe at all. Or conversely, as Kleiman and Hawken put it, "Severity is the enemy of swiftness and certainty, because a severe penalty will be more fiercely resisted and requires more due process to support it."

The problem is that severity is the weapon prosecutors have come to wield above all others.

Project Fast Track, de Blasio's big plan for getting guns off the streets in New York, promised speed, certainty, and severity. The mayor and the D.A.'s office said the Brooklyn gun court would process cases, from start to finish, in six months. This was what the police wanted.

It wasn't happening. Two years after the gun court opened, 40 percent of its 851 cases remained on the docket. Gun possession cases inched along more slowly, on average, than they had before the new court launched. On a typical day, I saw one defendant plead guilty while the cases of dozens of others were shuffled along to the next court date, with unresolved questions about the legality of a search, or the status of DNA testing, or the availability of evidence like video footage, or the timing of a mental health assessment.

DNA testing was a major source of delay. Around the time the gun court launched, New York City started testing every gun the police found. No other big city did DNA testing on that scale. It was expensive. The medical examiner's office got an extra $8 million (a 10 percent increase in its annual budget) to pay for fifty-five new employees plus training and equipment. Still, the testing took months.

Another source of delay was the prosecution's newly stiff and initially uncompromising demand for serious time—two years in prison and two years of parole—in exchange for a guilty plea. Two years upstate was a lot, especially for people without a previous felony conviction. Delays, in the form of requests for discovery, for example, were one of the only ways to fight back. To pressure people to plead up front, the D.A.'s office made what they said were best and final offers at the outset. As cases sat on the docket, however, prosecutors sometimes came around on deals, like Kevin's, which they'd ruled out earlier.

As the gun court failed to live up to its speedy billing, the NYPD began mocking the name "Project Fast Track" internally. ("We never should have called it that," one source in the department told me. "Big mistake.") Mayor de Blasio stopped talking about it: for all the fanfare of the initial City Hall press conference, the whole thing soon dropped off the radar.

As for certainty of punishment, from 2016 to the beginning of 2018, close to half the gun arrests in Brooklyn ended with a decision not to prosecute or a dismissal. There were also a tiny number of acquittals. People who got caught with guns in Brooklyn were somewhat more likely to be convicted than they had been before the gun court opened, but if nearly half the cases still ended without a conviction, it was hard to imagine that a lot of people were being deterred from having a gun on that score alone.

The gun court did deliver, however, on de Blasio's promise of increased severity. After it opened, felony convictions rose in Brooklyn (more than they did in the other boroughs) and a higher percentage of people who pled guilty went to jail or prison—two-thirds in 2016 compared with just over half before the gun court opened.

Ken Thompson signed on for sending more people to prison for gun possession when he agreed to Project Fast Track. Eric Gonzalez didn't undo the deal. From his point of view, it mattered that Brooklyn was still far less likely than Manhattan to send gun carriers to prison for two years or more. In a mark of his evolution-not-revolution style, Gonzalez quietly increased the size of YCP (from forty-four admissions in 2015 to sixty-three in 2017). He could get behind cracking down on gun possession as long as Caryn Teitelman didn't have to insist on prison when a defense lawyer like Debora Silberman argued persuasively on behalf of a compelling client.

I saw severity every time I went to court. One man with a previous conviction for gun possession—from 1989—was held at Rikers for ten months on $15,000 bail. When the lab results showed that his DNA was on the gun, the prosecutors offered a deal of twelve years. Several months later, the man pled guilty in exchange for five years in prison followed by five years of parole.

Often, the process itself was the punishment. One day, I watched as a twenty-three-year-old who had recently moved to New York was charged with a felony over a gun he bought legally in Florida: the police found the firearm in a suitcase in his car with the rest of his belongings. His case was dismissed a year later—after nineteen court appearances and a great deal of stress for his elderly mother, who felt responsible for bringing him to New York—when a judge found the police didn't have good reason to stop the car, so the search that revealed the gun was unconstitutional.

Another morning, a seventy-year-old man shuffled forward, leaning on a cane. He had been diagnosed with early-onset dementia and Parkinson's. In April 2016, neighbors called the police to complain about noise coming from his sister-in-law's basement, where he was living and throwing a party. The police found a gun lying on a makeshift bar. A conviction would almost certainly mean he'd lose the green card he'd gotten nearly thirty years earlier when he immigrated from Jamaica, and if he was no longer a legal permanent resident, he'd be deported. His lawyer asked the prosecutor to drop the charges in light of her client's mental condition, but he refused, insisting the man remembered more than he was letting on. The case dragged on for more than a year, with twenty court appearances, until he was found unfit to stand trial. According to his therapist, the stress of the arrest and the days the man spent at Rikers (he couldn't make bail right away), and frequent court appearances caused his mental functioning to decline. At the end of 2017, he had a heart attack. His lawyer asked for a dismissal in the interest of justice. The D.A.'s office objected.

The day before his September court date, Kevin was told that he'd failed his random drug test for YCP. He was incredulous. "I haven't smoked weed in five going on six months now," he said. "My system is beyond clean." He went straight to Kreyngold, his YCP social worker. "I'm like, 'I know I don't smoke weed and I'm not going to jail for this.'"

The protocol was for Kreyngold to accept the lab results and report them to the judge. But Kreyngold decided to retest Kevin himself. They went into the bathroom, Kevin peed in a cup, and he was right: his urine was clean. "I asked Max, 'How is that possible?'" Kevin said. "He said the guy at the lab probably looked at it wrong. I'm like, 'Yeah, and he was about to get me into a lot of trouble.'"

If a YCP client got rearrested or otherwise broke the program's rules, the D.A.'s office imposed sanctions—including ankle monitors—on its own, without a court order. The monitors, cumbersome boxes attached with thick Velcro straps, could be required for weeks or months, including for participants who were showing up at YCP, proving that they were in Brooklyn and not going anywhere. For many participants, the monitors were objects of loathing and embarrassment. One nineteen-year-old cut his off and wound up in jail for weeks as a result. Kreyngold had done his job at YCP for years before the monitors were introduced, and he'd concluded they were "modern-day shackles," as he put it. "For a young person who is still developing and maturing, to put a monitor on them is degrading and makes them feel caged. It's not helping us with compliance or completion. It doesn't help the kid understand the mistakes that were made or how to reflect on that. Instead of using the tools of social work, it's choosing the punitive side."

Prosecutors could also ask judges to set high bail in order to send YCP participants to jail for a new arrest. "Sometimes young people don't think out the entire consequences of their actions, and they need to be reminded," Teitelman said. "Sometimes it takes seeing what jail is like." Some parents and girlfriends thought brief jail stints had the effect of getting participants back on track; others objected.

YCP held participants to a higher standard than the people around them. If they smoked weed or jumped a turnstile with their friends, the police would run their names and arrest them while letting the others go. Some defense lawyers and social workers thought the police targeted their clients, raising questions once more about the watch list in Brooklyn and the extent of surveillance.

The D.A.'s office saw itself as patient and forbearing, allowing for second and third chances. "We recognize there's a learning curve," Teitelman said. "If you catch another gun case, or a serious assault, then OK, you're getting indicted right away and going to prison. But that's not this." A short stay in jail was for "violating curfew ten times, say, or failing more than one drug test. By the same token, when people are doing well we praise them along the way. It's important for a courtroom full of people to see that and for the participants to hear it. We don't want people to fail. We want them to succeed. That's the goal in diversion." Still, nearly one in five YCP clients failed.

For the social workers, reporting a minor infraction or failed drug test was high stakes. Kreyngold wrestled with the consequences as he wrote his report for the court about Kevin later that summer. Kreyngold started with the positives: Kevin's summer job, his clean drug tests, his compliance with the curfew. But he couldn't leave out Kevin's arrest. What if the prosecutors or the judge found out and felt hoodwinked? So he settled on a bland description. Kevin had notified him about a "negative police encounter," Kreyngold wrote, which YCP was still in the process of investigating.

Kevin tensed up in the days before court. He dreamed that his teeth were falling out. "Pray for Brownsville," he posted on Facebook, though the violence was still in abatement. "It's no backwoods out here." On the way to court, he steeled himself for the possibility that he'd go straight to jail. He reminded himself how close he'd come to graduating from high school. *I could have been in college right now,* he thought.

In the elevator, his lawyer, Debora Silberman, her hair a little wet from her morning shower, tried to set him at ease, chatting about flying to Houston to see her family. Kevin said he'd never been on a plane. He wanted to see other parts of the country, but he also still hadn't made it to the one specific destination he had in mind: the trampoline park Sky Zone. It was only twenty-five miles from his apartment.

Inside Judge Gubbay's courtroom, Kevin waited nervously, knee bouncing, in a maroon tracksuit. His hair was in a topknot and he had small diamond studs in his ears. He listened to Judge Gubbay urge a man making uneven progress in recovery not to give up. The clerk called Kevin's case just after noon. He went to stand before the judge with Silberman and Kreyngold. The prosecutor stood across from them, but his role was minimal. Kreyngold was the voice of the D.A.'s office.

"This is the first update since the plea?" Gubbay asked. Silberman answered yes. Kreyngold vouched for Kevin's compliance with YCP's rules and brought up Kevin's hope of getting his GED, which they'd been discussing.

"YCP will help him make connections so he can achieve that," Gubbay said. He looked at Kreyngold's report and then at Kevin. "There's a reference on page two: you had an encounter with the justice system?" he asked.

Kevin, whose hands were clasped behind him, pressed a thumb into one of his forefingers.

"It has not been borne out yet?" the judge asked.

"Correct, Judge," Kreyngold said.

"And YCP is looking into it," Gubbay continued, "but at this

point, I see no prejudice to the defendant. He's moving forward."
He nodded at Kevin. "Very good." Gubbay asked the prosecutor if
he had anything further. The answer was no: the D.A.'s office would
rely on Kreyngold. The anticipation was over. No jail.

Outside, leaving the courthouse, Kevin walked fast. "The system, the system, the system," he said, shaking his head. "It's so
crazy. Like that right there: they arrest me for nothing but then
somehow it doesn't show up. It should have but it didn't. They always tell you to follow the rules, but then how do you know? You
can get in a lot of trouble for nothing, like me and that drug test,
but then you do something and they don't even catch it."

11

THE ALFORD PLEA

ON FEBRUARY 13, 2015, Noura returned to Judge Craft's court-room for the first time since her conviction. Finally, six months after the Tennessee Supreme Court's decision to give her a new trial, she was getting a bail hearing. She wore a thermal undershirt under an orange prison top and navy blue pants. Her hair was loose to her shoulders and dark brown, the blond streaks long gone. Ansley Larsson and Bill Shelton sat on the benches in a group of about a dozen of her friends, wearing wristbands with "Free Noura Jackson" printed on them.

To Noura's relief, Weirich wasn't in court. A deputy prosecutor from Shelby County stood up to represent her. "Our office is going to voluntarily recuse itself," she said. The Tennessee district attorneys' conference would appoint a special prosecutor to take over.

A new lawyer, Michael Working, had joined Corder in representing Noura. Noura called him "a mercy junkie," meant as a compliment. He came to see her regularly in prison, and when she told him about the troubles of her friends on the inside, he tried to help them, too. Working practiced criminal law at his own firm. He had a wife and two kids, an itch to perform as a storyteller at local clubs on open-mike nights, and a sense of gratitude that came from knowing his life could have veered off course, landing him in a place like that of his clients.

Twenty years earlier, when he was eighteen and a high school senior in Maryland, students on the football team hazed his younger brother. They bound, gagged, and blindfolded him, and poured urine on his head. A couple of days later, Working and his brother waited for one of the ringleaders in the locker room. "My brother confronted him about what had happened, and he jacked my brother into the locker and was beating on him. I ran over and pushed him off, and he stumbled over his bag of equipment on the floor and hit his head on the cement wall when he fell." His injuries weren't serious, but Working was expelled and criminally charged—initially with the felony of assault with intent to kill. In the end, he was allowed to plead guilty to the lesser charge of battery and receive a sentence of probation, which didn't block him from going to college and then law school. Working identified with Noura. "I've relocated a thousand miles from where I grew up to start my life over," he told me. "But doing Noura's case brought me real close to who I was and how things could have turned out for me."

Standing up in court to ask for bail for Noura on multiple court dates, Working asked Judge Craft to at least reinstate the $500,000 bail he'd set before her first trial. In the years since, Noura had amassed a record of good behavior in prison and that should count in her favor. Craft, however, kept postponing his decision. In his view, Noura's years in prison made the question of her release less urgent, not more. "Miss Jackson has been in jail for nine and a half years, since September 2005," he said. "This is not an emergency."

A month later, D. Michael Dunavant, a district attorney from a rural area northeast of Memphis, was appointed as Noura's special prosecutor. Dunavant told Craft that to prepare for trial, he needed the help of seventeen members of Weirich's staff. Corder and Working objected. What was the point of Weirich's recusal if seventeen people who worked for her remained on the case? Craft ordered another postponement. When Corder and Working asked him again to set a bond for Noura, he again refused, delaying the bond hearing until mid-May and saying he would push it back further if he thought Dunavant didn't have enough time or resources to prepare.

While the lawyers argued and Craft delayed, Dunavant continued to investigate the box of contraband cellphones missing from the prison. Neither the old-heads nor Culp could remember a high-level inquiry like this before. "The investigation was quite lengthy and it was quite biased," Culp told me. "I felt like they thought I was covering for Noura. But I would not have lied for Noura if she had done anything wrong."

The box was eventually tracked to its sender, who turned out to be a former prisoner. She and Noura weren't in prison together and didn't know each other. She'd been close to an old-head named Candace, who was questioned and then taken to solitary confinement. "I was locked in a cell alone with nothing for over two months except when they would handcuff me and take me to a tiny room where I was locked in with a TDOC [Tennessee Department of Corrections] investigator who would threaten me with outside charges unless I told him that N was involved somehow," Candace told me via email. "All of which is in violation of TDOC policy and a blatant violation of my right to due process." Candace said it wasn't the first time she'd been locked up during a pending investigation. "I am no model inmate. My disciplinary record is extensive," she wrote. "It was beyond anything I had experienced before, though. I know it sounds harsh but I honestly feel like I was mentally and emotionally tortured during those two months. . . . It was just anything to break me down emotionally, all the while telling me if I would just say N knew about the package it could all be over."

Candace and another prisoner were criminally charged for bringing the cellphones into the prison. They each got two years tacked on to the end of their sentences. None of the old-heads could remember criminal charges or added time for contraband before. (Dunavant, who has since become the U.S. attorney in West Tennessee, declined to comment on the contraband investigation when I asked him about it through a spokesperson.)

Later, Noura learned that because of the contraband investigation, Dunavant had gotten transcripts of her phone calls from jail. They gave him a window into her loneliness and the fear of a second trial that was beginning to gnaw at her.

In prison, in the bubble of elation after her conviction was reversed, Noura insisted that she wouldn't take a plea offer. She knew how much the old-heads wanted her to stand up to Weirich and take her case to trial. "The people on the inside, they looked at me like I was the freedom fighter, the one that could make a difference. Because I had Amy dead to wrong. The Supreme Court said so."

But then "slowly but surely," she started to break down. "Every time I would call Ansley, I would cry. I was like, 'This is miserable. I can't stand it here. I don't want to be held here. How can they keep doing this?' Because here I was, halfway through my twenty-year sentence, with the Supreme Court overturning it, with a huge group of supporters, and I couldn't even get a bond. I was my own worst enemy because they knew how miserable I was getting. I was emotionally unraveling and they used that."

On May 19, the day before Noura was due back in court, prosecutors met Corder and Working at a Memphis coffee shop. They wanted to make a deal: they would reduce Noura's sentence to fifteen years if she pled guilty to voluntary manslaughter.

Determining how long Noura would stay locked up if she took the plea wasn't a matter of subtracting the years and months she'd already served from the fifteen-year total. Tennessee had a complicated method for awarding good-time credits that shortened the court-imposed sentence. Noura's lawyers called the Tennessee Department of Corrections to ask what would happen if she took the fifteen-year plea. Meeting with Noura at the jail, they reported that she had enough good-time credits to be released that day.

As they all remember it, Noura said, "No, I won't take the deal, because if I do they'll never figure out who killed my mom."

"Honey, they'll never say it was someone else," Working said.

Corder told Noura she didn't have to be a martyr. She added this: "Look, you want your mom to come back, and that's not going to happen. And you want people to think that you're innocent, but here's the thing: the people that already think you're guilty are going to think you're guilty. And the people that believe in your innocence, they believe in your innocence. You want to have a baby. That can happen. You want to have an education. That can happen. You want to have a chance at a life. That can happen. Let go of the two things that can't happen and hold on to the three that can."

Noura knew that her friends in prison would feel that a guilty plea was an act of betrayal. She felt that way herself.

But she could go free, her lawyers promised. She could restart her life.

The prosecutors' offer was good only until the hearing the next day. If Noura didn't take it, they would make sure she served every day of her twenty years.

The American criminal justice system was built to prevent the conviction of the innocent. "Better to let ten guilty people go free than to convict one innocent person," the eighteenth-century English jurist William Blackstone famously wrote. The principle served as a founding ideal, and confidence in its achievement ran high for much of the country's history. In 1923, Judge Learned Hand, a towering figure in the law, dismissed the conviction of the innocent as an "unreal dream." Justice Sandra Day O'Connor was nearly as confident seven decades later. "Our society has a high degree of confidence in criminal trial, in no small part because the Constitution offers unparalleled protections against convicting the innocent," she wrote in 1993.

No longer. "Twenty or thirty years ago, people commonly said that it was almost impossible to convict an innocent person in this country, because our constitutional protections are so strong and there are so many Supreme Court cases that protect the accuracy of criminal trials," University of Virginia law professor Brandon Garrett, author of the book *Convicting the Innocent*, said. "Then came DNA testing and the Innocence Project, and that blew up everyone's understanding of how criminal justice works in this country." Since the first DNA exoneration, in 1989, more than 450 people have been cleared based on the science, which provides an unmatched degree of certainty about what physical evidence shows. The DNA revolution also opened a door to roughly eighteen hundred exonerations that didn't rest on genetic material.

Exonerations tend to expose bad police work, including suggestive photo lineups, coerced confessions, and misplaced reliance on jailhouse informants. They also reveal prosecutors being blinded by tunnel vision and breaking the rules to nail down a conviction. Chillingly, prosecutors may be more likely to withhold evidence when proof of guilt is uncertain. If you think the suspect did it but you don't quite have the goods to convict, you may be tempted to put a thumb on the scale. In 2002, James Liebman and Jeffrey Fagan of Columbia Law School reviewed about five thousand death sentence appeals across the country—cases in which execution was on the line. They found that 351 convictions were ultimately overturned in state courts and that in about 20 percent of the three hundred cases in which they could determine the reason for the reversal, the state failed to disclose evidence. "Our analyses reveal that it is in close cases—those in which a small amount of evidence might tip the outcome in a different direction—that the risk of serious error is the greatest," they wrote.

About 18 percent of exonerations—DNA and non-DNA, death sentences and other penalties—involve defendants who pleaded guilty. At first this finding is confounding: why would someone who didn't do it say they did? If the prosecution has evidence suggesting they're innocent, wouldn't they already know about it?

Writing for the *New York Review of Books* about why innocent people plead guilty, Judge Jed Rakoff blamed the "prosecutor-dictated" system of plea bargaining itself. A prosecutor can wield the threat of a heavy sentence like a sledgehammer. "The typical person accused of a crime combines a troubled past with limited resources," Rakoff writes. "He thus recognizes that, even if he is innocent, his chances of mounting an effective defense at trial may be modest at best. If his lawyer can obtain a plea bargain that will reduce his likely time in prison, he may find it 'rational' to take the plea."

In a wrenching case in West Virginia, a nineteen-year-old named Joseph Buffey was caught in the vise Rakoff described. In December 2001, Buffey was arrested for breaking into three businesses in his hometown, Clarksburg. Questioned by the police, he admitted to those crimes. Then they started asking him about a far more serious one, which had taken place the next morning: the robbery and rape of an eighty-three-year-old widow who lived less than half a mile from the Salvation Army store that Buffey had broken into. The victim was the mother of a police officer, and she'd noted details of the crime so that she could tell her son. She said there was a single attacker, describing his clothing and the knife and flashlight he carried. A bandanna covered part of his face, but she saw his bare white legs.

Buffey is white, and since he'd been nearby causing trouble, the police interrogated him for more than nine hours about the robbery and rape. At 3:25 a.m., they turned on a tape recorder. Buffey hadn't eaten since lunch. When they asked again about the elderly widow, he said he "broke into this old lady's house," but denied the rape. When the detectives pressed him for details relating to the crime, like where in the house he encountered the victim, he got them wrong. Even when prompted, he couldn't say where the victim's house was. He described coming in through a window but couldn't remember which side of the house it was on (in fact the assailant entered through a sliding glass door at the back). He couldn't independently come up with any inside knowledge of the crime.

Minutes after Buffey's admission, one investigator asked, "What are you scared of?"

"You really want to know the truth?" Buffey said. "I didn't do it." He told the police he "made up a story" because they were "breathing down my neck, telling me I did it."

The detectives decided Buffey was lying. A seventeen-year-old friend he committed the break-ins with, high on opiates when he talked to the police, implicated Buffey in the rape. The police sent the victim's rape kit to the state forensics lab for DNA testing. Buffey told his appointed lawyer, Thomas Dyer, that the test results would clear him and that he had an alibi: After he left the Salvation Army, he went to a motel and spent the night with his friend and his sister. Dyer called the prosecuting attorneys repeatedly over the next months to ask about the results. The prosecutors told him there were no results yet. In the meantime, they made a plea offer: if Buffey pleaded guilty to the rape and robbery, they would drop the other charges against him, mostly related to the break-ins. Dyer told Buffey that given his youth, he had a good chance of serving only fifteen years in prison.

Dyer's billing records showed he spent little time investigating the case. He didn't go to the crime scene or try to confirm Buffey's alibi. "There wasn't a lot to investigate," he later testified. "The Buffeys were the preeminent crime family for four or five generations in central West Virginia," Dyer said when I spoke to him. "If your name was Buffey, you were instantly, by the world around you, associated with criminal conduct. There weren't any people in law enforcement or the community who were presuming Joe Buffey was not guilty."

Dyer said that when he asked Buffey if there was any point in waiting for the DNA results, Buffey answered, "All I can tell you, Mr. Dyer, is that they're not going to find any DNA." Yet Dyer didn't take Buffey's statement as an indication of innocence. "The opposite," he said. "Much of communication in life is nonverbal. Here's this guy with his silent smile. At the time he pled guilty, there was zero question in my mind that he was guilty. None. If I'd had any, I'd have insisted we wait on the DNA results." Buffey later testified that he repeatedly told Dyer he was innocent.

Bad advice from defense lawyers—or sometimes little advice or attention at all—contributes to wrongful convictions, too. "The adversary system assumes that each side has adequate counsel," my grandfather David Bazelon wrote in 1973, when he was chief judge of the Court of Appeals for the D.C. Circuit. "This assumption probably holds true for giant corporations or well-to-do individuals, but what I have seen in 23 years on the bench leads me to believe that a great many—if not most—indigent defendants do not receive the effective assistance of counsel guaranteed them by the 6th Amendment." The point sadly holds true today, especially in states without well-funded public defender offices. Stephen Bright, former director of the Southern Center for Human Rights, has seen the damage firsthand and thinks prosecutors share responsibility for it. "Today, the United States Department of Justice, state district attorneys, and state attorneys general," he has written, "take every advantage of the ignorant, incompetent lawyers foisted upon the poor."

By the time of the final plea hearing and sentencing, the prosecutors still said they didn't have the DNA results—six months after the case began. Buffey pleaded guilty to the rape and robbery. Apologizing to the victim by name, he said, "I am really sorry for what I did and I just—I just made bad choices. I do realize that I did wrong. I do realize that I need to be punished for it." People in Clarksburg—a small town of just sixteen thousand people—were still reeling from the heinous attack. Instead of the 15 years his lawyer had predicted, Buffey was sentenced to 70 to 110 years.

In his first year in prison, Buffey filed a petition himself, arguing that he was coerced into making a false confession and asking to find out what happened with the DNA results. He finally received the report the following year from the state forensics lab—and it said he was not the source of the male DNA in the seminal fluid taken from the victim. What's more, the DNA report had been completed six weeks before Buffey's final plea hearing.

If the case had gone to trial, Buffey's conviction would have been easily reversed—a no-brainer given the Brady rule. But the Supreme Court has never said that prosecutors must turn over evidence that could establish a defendant's innocence before he or she pleads guilty.

In 2008, six years after Buffey's conviction, the Innocence Project and a West Virginia lawyer took his case. After a long battle, Buffey's new lawyers won a court order to run the DNA from the rape through CODIS, the national criminal justice database, and the search produced a match: the source of the DNA was a man named Adam Bowers. At the time of the rape, Bowers was sixteen and lived a few blocks from the victim. He'd also been accused of trying to rape another woman in October 2001, and he was in prison for another break-in and assault.

In May 2015, Bowers was found guilty of the rape and robbery Buffey was still in prison for. It seemed that he'd finally gotten the break that would free him. Except that David Romano, the Clarksburg special prosecutor brought on to handle the case after the Innocence Project came on board, remained unconvinced of his innocence. "He told three officers he was in that house," Romano told me. He went on to say that false confessions "only happen when someone is of low intelligence or something else has overcome their will." Romano didn't think a nine-hour interrogation like Buffey's could overcome the will of someone innocent. But Romano was wrong. There are many scenarios for false confessions. "Many involve people who are vulnerable because they are mentally ill, or juveniles, but in many other cases people have no limitations like that," said Brandon Garrett, a University of Virginia law professor. "They're just worn down by the questioning, and they thought they could clear up the misunderstanding once they get out of the interrogation room." Hauntingly, innocent people are susceptible to the false hope that the truth will come to light later.

Romano doubled down, arguing in court that Bowers and Buffey committed the crime together, communicating through hand gestures and whispers so the victim wouldn't know there were two assailants. (The victim could not be asked about this new theory because she now suffered from dementia.) Buffey's DNA was not found because he wore a condom, the prosecutors conjectured. "I don't think the DNA evidence points away from him," Romano told me, echoing Amy Weirich's response when I asked her about the DNA in Noura's case. No one can stop a prosecutor from this kind of misleading insistence.

Buffey's case went to the West Virginia Supreme Court, and in 2015 he finally won a unanimous ruling from a conservative bench. "Fundamental principles compel the conclusion that a defendant's constitutional due process rights, as enumerated in *Brady*, extend to the plea negotiation stage of the criminal proceedings," the court wrote. But Romano wasn't through: he used his power as a prosecutor to go after Buffey once more, this time by charging him with statutory rape for a relationship he'd had, before he went to prison, with an underage girl. She said she'd consented, and with Buffey she had a daughter, whom she was raising. If he'd been convicted, he would have had to register as a sex offender for life and give up contact with his child. Romano offered a deal: he could plead to one count of robbery, in connection with the original charges, as well as the burglaries he'd always admitted, get out of jail, and avoid registering as a sex offender. He took a plea deal to the original robbery, still saying he didn't do it, and in 2016 returned to his family.

For all the professed commitment to protecting the innocent, American law gives it very short shrift. Once a prosecutor wins a conviction, new evidence of innocence won't necessarily result in a new trial. "There is no basis in text, tradition, or even in contemporary practice (if that were enough) for finding in the Constitution a right to demand judicial consideration of newly discovered evidence of innocence brought forward after conviction," Justice Antonin Scalia wrote in 1993. He went even further when a man named Troy Davis, convicted of murder, tried to avoid execution based on the statements of three witnesses who came forward after his conviction to say someone else had confessed to the murder. The Supreme Court has never held, Scalia said, "that the Constitution forbids the execution of a convicted defendant who has had a full and fair trial but is later able to convince a habeas court that he is 'actually' innocent."

Many courts around the country have agreed that prosecutors must share Brady evidence with defendants before they plead guilty. After all, if Brady is a trial right, and more than 95 percent of convictions are obtained through guilty pleas, then Brady is a dead letter. But the Supreme Court has never said this, and a few lower courts are holding out. The U.S. Court of Appeals for the Fifth Circuit (which covers Texas, Louisiana, and Mississippi) has repeatedly ruled against people like Joseph Buffey, decreeing that the right to Brady evidence comes into play only when there is a trial. In 2017, a man named George Alvarez asked the Fifth Circuit to reconsider. Alvarez pled guilty after a guard accused him of assault while he was in jail for public intoxication and burglary. After the plea, Alvarez discovered that the police department all along had a video that proved he didn't assault the guard. He spent four years in prison for the assault. Released after the Texas Court of Criminal Appeals decided that he was actually innocent, Alvarez sued based on the video and won a $2.3 million damages award.

A three-judge panel on the Fifth Circuit reversed the judgment, taking away the $2.3 million award. The reasoning was simple: "Alvarez did not have a constitutional right to exculpatory evidence when he pleaded guilty." Alvarez then asked the entire Fifth Circuit to reconsider (a second layer of appeal called en banc review). His petition attracted the opposition of Trump's Justice Department. Ignoring the reams of evidence about how one-sided plea bargaining has become, the Justice Department urged the Fifth Circuit not to extend the Brady right to the period before trial, reaching back to the Supreme Court's decision in *Bordenkircher v. Hayes* to make a see-no-evil claim: defendants are to be presumed capable of "intelligent choice in response to prosecutorial persuasion."

It fell to a dozen former state and federal prosecutors from around the country, in their own brief, to point out that "neither reason nor evidence" supported the Justice Department's assurance that innocent people won't plead guilty. "It is not by tricking defendants, but by making pleading a sensible option for innocent and guilty alike, that the plea-bargain system exacts its greatest toll," the former prosecutors wrote. They sided with Alvarez. In 2018, however, he lost his second appeal to the Fifth Circuit by a vote of 13 to 3.

In jail, talking to her lawyers, Noura worried about the prosecution's fifteen-year offer. Did she really have enough good-time credits to get out? She didn't know exactly how the calculations worked, but she knew they could be tricky. She wished she could talk to her friends in prison.

Corder and Working assured Noura that they'd checked and double-checked her good-time credits and sentence expiration with the Tennessee Department of Corrections. For the prosecution's benefit, the fifteen-year deal would make it look like she wasn't just pleading to time served, but she'd get out straightaway. They were her lawyers. She was supposed to trust them. And she'd grown increasingly afraid of a second trial. She distrusted the new prosecutors in light of the contraband investigation. Judge Craft seemed implacably against her. (In a later TV interview of a sort judges rarely grant, he said, "There's no question that she committed the murder in my mind.") Noura was desperate to go home, to wear real clothes and eat real food and drive a car and go to a store. "I just wanted out so bad," she said. "I thought, 'People will have to forgive me.' I felt like I was fighting for everybody, and then in that one moment of selfishness, you know, it's like the forbidden fruit. It was right there, and I bit it."

The next morning before dawn, her hands shackled on the bus from the jail to the courthouse, Noura felt cold. The cuffs left white marks on her wrists because her skin was so dry. She thought, *I'll never have to do this again.* She thought it over and over again as she walked in a chained line of prisoners, asked for toilet paper, and had to use the toilet in front of other people. *I'm going to walk out of here and never come back.*

Noura waited for an hour and a half with about thirty other women in a large holding cell underground. A guard came over to say he'd heard she was taking a plea.

If he knows, it must be for real, she thought.

When it was her turn to go up to the court, the bailiff who came for her was Sergeant Nichols, who'd been there the day she was arraigned. Nichols steered her into a small room next to Judge Craft's courtroom, away from the media, and took off her handcuffs and shackles so she could sign the papers for the plea. Noura could barely breathe or think. "You get to go home," she remembers Nichols telling her. "That's all that matters."

Larsson and Culp were there with Working and Corder. They hugged her and stayed while she signed her plea agreement. It took two or three tries because there were mistakes in the paperwork. Noura was taking an Alford plea, which allows a defendant to acknowledge that the state has enough evidence to convict her while she still maintains her innocence. The state would still treat her as guilty and her criminal record would say she'd been convicted of manslaughter. Still, an Alford plea allows a defendant to save face. For someone who has a chance of being released, the plea is like a bitter pill, hard to swallow but a cure for the ill of imprisonment. They're not uncommon for resolving Brady violations, and Noura had made making an Alford plea a condition of her agreement. For the prosecution, an Alford plea offers an essentially cost-free way to dispose of cases in which guilt may have become harder to prove with the passage of time. Some of the witnesses who testified against Noura nearly a decade earlier were no longer available or willing to cooperate, Dunavant would tell the press later that day.

After Noura signed the papers, it was time to move to the court-room next door to take the plea before Judge Craft.

"We can announce today that the defendant is prepared to enter a plea of guilty to the lesser included offense of voluntary man-slaughter," Dunavant said, "and agree to a sentence of fifteen years. We believe that we could have sustained our burden of proof be-yond a reasonable doubt and yet, as a result of these settlement negotiations we believe that this is, in fact, in the best interest of the State of Tennessee and the victim's family. And so we are submit-ting that to the court for approval, based on the defendant's volun-tary entry of the plea."

Corder spoke for Noura: "We remind the court that my client maintains her innocence, but does agree to the negotiated settle-ment as a resolution to these charges."

To create the proper record, Judge Craft described the prosecu-tion's case against Noura. As he spoke, she flipped open the plea agreement she'd just signed. It said she was pleading to fifteen years at 60 percent parole eligibility. Since she'd already served nine years, she would be eligible for a parole hearing immediately.

But that wasn't the same as being released. Noura turned to Working, who was sitting beside her, and asked about the sentence once more. "Trust me, babe, you're flat," he said. "You're flat." (To flatten a sentence is to complete it, based on the number of days you've served and your credits.)

Unsure what to think, Noura heard Judge Craft calling her to stand before him. "All right, come around, Ms. Jackson," he said, beckoning.

After asking her full name and how far she'd gotten in school, Craft instructed Noura to look at the paper she'd signed. "This paper contains all of your rights under the United States and Tennessee constitutions regarding this offense. Although you have these rights now, you're going to have to waive or give up these rights in order for me to hear this guilty plea. Do you understand that?"

"Yes, sir."

Craft ran through the rights she was giving up, including the right to a jury and the right to put on witnesses and testify. He reached her sentence and read it aloud: "Fifteen years at a 60 percent parole eligibility." Noura would immediately be eligible for parole, he agreed—but then cautioned, "There's no guarantee that you'll get parole. So we are not promising that you're going to be released when you enter this plea."

Noura looked at Larsson and Culp, who looked back at her, frowning. She wobbled one more time. Everyone was here, expecting her to accept the deal her lawyers had made for her. How angry would the prosecutors and the judge be if she tried to back out now?

Craft continued. "You also are pleading guilty saying you're not guilty under an Alford plea," he said. "The United States Supreme Court said that you could plead guilty to something you say you didn't do if you think it's in your best interest that if you went to trial you might be convicted and you might get more time. So you need to understand, is that why you are pleading guilty?"

"That's the only reason why," Noura said. She wanted to say it out loud.

"You're afraid if you went to trial you might get more time and basically you think it is in your best interest? You're trying to cut your losses, is that right?"

"Basically, yes."

"OK. All right," Craft said. "You also need to understand that this is a guilty plea, and so, even though it is under Alford, it counts as a guilty plea and it is going to be on your record from now on. Do you understand that?"

"Yes, sir."

Craft explained that having a record meant Noura couldn't own a gun. He also made sure she understood that she was waiving her right to appeal. Then he asked, "Are you entering this plea freely and voluntarily, without any threats or pressures, or promises that we haven't talked about?"

"No, sir," Noura said. She was giving the wrong answer and she knew it. She felt scared and obstinate, and the old-heads had told her that unless she gave the correct answer to this question, her plea would be invalid. Noura was afraid to stop the process, but maybe Judge Craft would have to stop it now.

But no one seemed to notice. "You're doing this because you want to?" Craft continued.

Noura felt defeated. "Yes, sir," she said.

Afterward, alone with her in a small holding room, Noura's lawyers told her to smile. "You're about to be a free woman," Working assured her. After saying goodbye, he told the reporters gathered outside that Noura had agonized over taking the plea but it was too good to pass up. "She would have fought an additional ten years on principle. But who wants to give up their thirties on principle?"

Noura went back to the jail, where she gave away her possessions. The guards said she could be released at any time. But days passed, and the computer didn't show a release date for her. Noura read the paper that listed her good-time credits again and again, trying to figure out the holdup. She called Larsson every day, and on the fourth call, Larsson picked up and said, "Oh, baby." Noura had been right to doubt. She didn't have enough credits to wipe out the fifteen-year sentence. It would take more time to earn them. She would go back to prison for another year and three months.

Working felt he'd made the worst mistake of his legal career. He and Corder told Noura to withdraw the plea. They would hold a press conference to explain and start preparing for trial. (Later, when I called the Tennessee Department of Corrections, a spokeswoman told me that the staff did not remember giving Noura's lawyers information that was "erroneous or misleading in any way.")

But Noura didn't want to make her lawyers look bad after everything they'd done for her. In prison she'd come to prize loyalty above almost anything else. She also felt dread about the uncertainty of a new trial. Her lawyers told her to think it over. "I didn't have any friends to find in jail. I couldn't call my friends in prison. I literally went inside of my cell and looked out the window."

Noura decided to leave the plea deal intact but asked to transfer to a different prison: she felt sick about facing her friends, who would be mystified about why she'd been duped into taking a bad deal. She'd given in to the prosecutors and she didn't even have her freedom to show for it.

But Noura was sent back to her old unit anyway. Some friends were kind; others pulled away. "After the plea, in prison, that was my lowest point. You keep falling down and getting up, and I'd conditioned myself for that, but this time I fell down and I was pissed. The thing that I hated the most was that during my whole incarceration I had been many things. I had been angry, and outraged, and hurt, and confused, and lonely. But one thing I had never been was bitter. I had never been bitter the whole ten years I had been incarcerated. I fought that bitterness for the last fifteen months."

At the end of the year, a few days after Winter Wonderland, the Tennessee Board of Professional Responsibility announced it was filing ethics charges against Weirich and Jones for their failure to turn over Hammack's note and a separate charge against Weirich for her improper rebuttal to the jury. Bill Shelton had been right to complain about the prosecutors' conduct, and the board recommended that the prosecutors each agree to a public censure. It was a slap on the wrist, but Weirich and Jones refused to accept it. That meant a panel of lawyers would be appointed, to hear the board's case against them, at a formal trial.

On a warm, bright morning in August 2016, Noura was taken to a room at the perimeter of the prison. A friend who'd gotten out the previous year had sent her a sleeveless blue dress, and she changed into it, gathered her hair into a topknot, and put on hoop earrings and ballerina flats. As she walked through the gates, TV cameras caught her hugging Larsson, who'd come to pick her up and take her to stay at her house.

Later that day, Noura issued a statement. She thanked her friends and her lawyers, and continued:

> Today I enjoyed small pleasures you all take for granted, like a good cup of coffee, the smell of fresh flowers, painted toenails, and a trip to Target. In the next chapter of my life, I plan to honor my mom by forcing the State of Tennessee to identify the person whose complete DNA profile was mixed with my mother's blood in her bed. I have been greatly disappointed in the justice system, but I still hope for justice in the upcoming ethical misconduct trials of Prosecutors Amy Weirich and Steve Jones.

In the car, Noura asked to drive by the house where she'd lived with her mother. "Everyone in prison talks about going home," Noura told me, "but it was different for me. I didn't have my old home to go back to. I decided I needed to see it." Looking out the car window, her eyes filled with tears. The house had been repainted, the shutters were stained an unfamiliar dark brown, and a boat was parked in the driveway. "Do you want me to do anything?" Larsson asked.

"I want you to keep going," Noura answered.

She'd gotten used to her mother's absence in prison, but now it hit her all over again. She remembered realizing, eleven years earlier when she first went to jail, that she relied on her mom so much that she didn't know her own social security number. Now she needed health insurance and a job and a driver's license. She had a place to live, but everything else felt uncertain. She would have to make her own way.

12

THE DISMISSAL

ONE DAY IN October, after his weekly meeting at YCP, Kevin waited for his friend Michael outside the D.A.'s office in downtown Brooklyn. They'd grown up together in the project and stayed in touch after Michael moved into a new apartment in one of the other developments, though the beefing meant they couldn't be seen together. Michael was the type to stay out of a fight, but he'd been charged with having a gun the previous fall. Like Kevin, he pled guilty and got the chance to avoid a prison sentence—three and a half years for the maximum gun possession charge, in his case—by completing YCP. They'd both come to see Kreyngold.

Walking to the subway together, Kevin and Michael took out their phones to watch a Facebook video from that morning. It showed a guy they knew. He was sitting on a bench in the hallway of the courthouse when another guy entered the frame and punched him. A fight ensued, court security officers broke it up, and both men were taken away in handcuffs.

The video was going viral among their friends. It was funny, horrifying, and a serious loss of face for the guy who got jumped. He was a "main factor," Kevin said—a heavyweight in his gang. Beating him up meant humiliating the rest of the crew along with him. They'd have to retaliate, and the violence would ensnare him even though he wanted out. "He's one of the people who wants to change his life around," Kevin said of the person who'd gotten jumped, "but I don't know if he can. I tell him, you can't do stuff and then walk away."

Kevin took comfort in telling himself that he wasn't in so deep. He could get out of his tight circle in Brownsville if he wanted. He was pretty sure of it. Maybe it would be as easy as moving to Queens with his girlfriend. It was hard to know for sure, though. Maybe he would have to move farther away, upstate. "I want to go where no one know me," he said to Michael. "It's too much here. Brownsville is ignorant."

I'd heard Kevin say this a bunch of times before. The place he came from limited him, though it was also a source of identity and pride. On Facebook, a regular supply of dark-humor posts made the rounds among his friends: "Brownsvillians got so much love & unity when we go against outsiders." "Im from Brownsville where niggas hear gunshots & argue about what type of gun it was." The affection and insults, irony and resentment circled back to the small-town nature of the projects, to the comfort of being known and the difficulty of feeling stifled. It was hard to break away from the fixed image everyone had of you, hard to imagine yourself differently when it seemed like your friends and family never would.

Having YCP in common gave Kevin and Michael a reason to talk about finding work. Waiting for the subway, Michael said he'd just gotten his OSHA certification, required for construction jobs in New York, by taking a two-day health and safety course. Kevin knew other people who'd recently gotten OSHA certified. He'd been planning to take the course as well, but missed his chance earlier in the summer.

"I've been applying for mad jobs," Kevin said. He'd filled out applications at local stores in Brownsville and franchises like Dunkin' Donuts, where he'd worked after he left high school, but he couldn't seem to get a call back. The one response he'd gotten was from UPS, which he'd reapplied to, for a seasonal driver's assistant. The work was as needed, and in the weeks since, Kevin hadn't heard anything more. Michael suggested calling his interviewer back, so Kevin pulled out his phone and made the call. The interviewer told him to be patient. "It's whenever the driver needs someone," he said when he got off the phone. "It could be today or next week or the week after that."

If he couldn't find a job, Kevin could fulfill YCP's mandate—get a job or go to school—with another GED course. He was still frustrated by missing the test in the spring, at the time of Travis's death. At Kreyngold's suggestion, though, he'd signed up for a course in Red Hook, a part of Brooklyn where he could be anonymous, which felt better than going back to the place where he'd already taken it. It turned out he was too old for the program.

Plus, he needed money. His mother was working two jobs, one as a health aide and one in retail, to cover the household expenses for Kevin's brother, sister, and niece. Kevin couldn't remember the last time his mother had bought something for herself. He didn't know what she'd buy if she could. He could count on her in a fix, like when she bailed him out of jail, but she needed him to be self-sufficient. "She knows I can be on my own," he said, "so it feels weird to ask her for money."

Before Kevin and Michael split up, several blocks from the projects, I asked Michael how he felt about YCP. "It keeps me focused," he said. Around this time, another YCP participant told me he didn't want the program to end: he was afraid of losing the structure and his weekly meetings with Kreyngold, whose advice and encouragement he'd come to rely on.

Did YCP, however irritating and cumbersome, ease the way to a better life, maybe outside of Brownsville? Kevin considered this as we walked away from Michael. "This program really helped me," he said first. Then he backed off. "It did and it didn't. Every little thing I did could get me in trouble." He thought some more and then revised this statement, too. Before he got arrested, when he'd been working at Dunkin' Donuts, he sometimes ran into friends on the way to work and called in sick to hang out with them. He could imagine feeling the same temptation now but not acting on it, because acting on it would cause problems with YCP and because he was out of the habit. He'd made use of the program. "Now I'm not outside. I'm not in the streets. At night, people call me to come out. I'll be chilling in the house with my girl."

More than 4.6 million people in America currently live under court supervision, more than twice the total in jail or prison. Just under 4 million of those are on probation; another 800,000-plus are on parole. It's a net of social control. The number of conditions people must comply with can range between ten and twenty even though studies show that a lighter touch is better. A violation of one of those conditions, even a small one like traveling out of state for a night without permission, can lead straight to jail. Over the last decade, states started to balk at the sprawl and the cost, and a majority have tried to rein in and improve probation, parole, and other forms of court supervision.

Yet supervision still has all kinds of pitfalls, racial disparity chief among them. In 2014, the Urban Institute studied probation violations in Portland, Oregon; Dallas; Cedar Rapids, Iowa; and New York City. The study found that in all four places, probation was revoked for African Americans more often than for whites to a degree that couldn't be explained by differences in criminal history or the number of probation violations. The judges and probation officers interviewed for the study, however, distanced themselves from the problem, saying racial bias existed in other parts of the system, like arrest and sentencing. No one wanted to be held responsible, and there was always someone else to blame.

When parole is revoked for a violation, the result can seem arbitrary and even perverse. The Brownsville Community Justice Center, one of the programs the police singled out for praise, had a youth advocate on staff named Cadeem Gibbs who was on parole for five years following a six-year sentence for an armed robbery. In 2014, Gibbs was invited to a training by the National Council of Elders, a group of veteran civil rights organizers, at Alex Haley Farm in Tennessee. He asked his parole officer for permission to travel out of state and was told to come back for written approval. When he returned, the officer wasn't there; Gibbs decided to make the trip anyway because he didn't want to miss the opportunity. When his parole officer found out, he sent Gibbs to Rikers for four months. Then in the spring of 2018, a week before his term of parole was finally set to expire, Gibbs learned that at the administrative hearing he had because of the 2014 violation, four months had been added to his term of supervision along with the jail time he'd done for going to Tennessee. No one had told him.

At this point, Gibbs was a budding entrepreneur. He'd left the justice center to start a social enterprise initiative, the Roundtable Project, with the mission of raising consciousness about issues that impact the black community and starting businesses to serve as resources for it. "I'm trying to address the problems that cause people to enter the system but they keep pulling me back into it, pulling me backward," he said. His lengthy term of parole was literally blocking his advancement. His experiences showed that despite the national effort to lighten the touch of parole and probation, the system could still be senselessly harsh. Parole was beyond the reach of the Brooklyn D.A.'s office (though in some states prosecutors can step in and recommend more prison time). The process for revoking parole in New York didn't take place in front of a judge in open court. It was a closed-door administrative proceeding at Rikers, decided in a small windowless room by a hearing officer who represented the parole board.

People under supervision often have to pay for it. Forty-four states impose user fees for probation or other forms of supervision, and forty-nine allow charges for ankle bracelets (sometimes the money comes out of user fees they already impose). Almost every state has increased its fees since 2010. Supervision may also come with conditions, like classes on anger management or drunk driving, which entail additional fees. A 2016 *New York Times* investigation found fees as high as $5,000 for classes relating to a single offense. Sometimes the charges for "offender-funded" justice are levied by private companies, which contract with the state to run their supervision programs. "Private e-carceration," as Michelle Alexander calls it, allows the same corporations that run bail agencies or private prisons to keep making profits from monitoring and surveillance. In 2014, Human Rights Watch examined private probation practices in courts in three states and found that many delegated "a great deal of responsibility, discretion, and coercive power" to companies subject only to lax oversight and regulation. Acting like "abusive debt collectors," the companies wring money out of their mandated customers to the point of financial ruin.

Or jail. In 2017, a company called Providence Community Corrections agreed to pay total damages of $14 million to about 29,000 people in Tennessee who'd been jailed or threatened with jail because they couldn't pay their probation fees. The company had a contract with Rutherford County to collect the money. As part of the settlement (in a lawsuit led by Alec Karakatsanis, the lawyer who successfully sued Harris County over misdemeanor bail) the county agreed to stop contracting with private probation companies and to waive fees for low-income people. Providence Community Corrections went out of business.

In 1983, 150 years after Congress banned debtors' prisons, the Supreme Court declared it unconstitutional to confine people because they can't afford court fines or fees for services. But to this day, people are jailed when they fail to pay charges for court-mandated "services." The Supreme Court has never set limits on when a judge can find that a defendant is "willfully" refusing to pay.

No matter how poor you are, prosecutors can argue that you have the wherewithal to find the money, and a judge can go along. In a district in central Florida, the cost of diversion ranges from $360 to $720 plus a $50 "prosecution fee," which goes straight to the D.A.'s office. The prosecutor's office posts a notice on its website. "Pretrial diversion is a voluntary program, funded entirely by the fees paid by the participants," it reads. "Therefore, fees are not eligible for reduction or waiver."

In New York City, supervision could cost $125, if it came with a class for shoplifters, or $1,000, for domestic violence prevention. But YCP, funded by the D.A.'s office, was free. Kevin was short on money that fall, borrowing from his mother or girlfriend even for small expenses, like taking the subway or buying a cheeseburger. Despite the promise of work from UPS, no one called. Or at least he didn't think he got calls—it was hard to be sure since his phone wasn't working properly. He couldn't afford a new one. To follow up on the other job applications he'd submitted, he checked his email on his mother's laptop or a computer terminal at the library. No bites. Kreyngold tried to help, without much success. YCP wasn't an employment agency.

Kevin's break came from a girl in his building who worked for a company near JFK airport that shipped packages in and out of the country. They had openings. Kevin sent an email right away and got a call fifteen minutes later. In a sign that New York's job market was tightening, he was hired to start after Thanksgiving. His job was to inspect packages for contraband, including explosives, weapons, and drugs. The starting pay was $11 an hour, with the promise of a raise to $13 in January. Kevin took the 7:00-a.m.-to-3:00-p.m. shift, which meant leaving his house around 5:30 a.m. He took the subway to the last stop, hopped in a van, and then walked the last half mile. Often he worked till 5:00 p.m. for overtime pay. The work wasn't fun, but he could listen to music on his headphones and call his girlfriend on breaks. Most of his coworkers were older than he was. It was easy to keep his distance, and he liked that. No entanglements.

Now that he was working, Kevin was seeing his friends from Brownsville even less than he had over the summer. "By the time I get to my house it's seven," he told me. "I've got three hours till curfew but I go straight in the house. I've been on my feet all day checking boxes." His friends were occupied, too. "Some people are in school, some are working, everybody doing something."

At his next court date, Kevin's lawyer, Debora Silberman, and his social worker from Brooklyn Defender Services, Rebecca Kinsella, looked him up and down with approval. "I'm happy for you," Kinsella told him. They'd been working with him for a year and a half. Kevin called them his team. He looked better—more purposeful—to them than they'd seen before. "You seem energized," Kinsella said. "I look at you, and you're different. It's like your face is clear."

"I'm happy for me, too," Kevin said. "It's the fact I'm about to get off this program. I got a super-good report. The time is flying. I took a clean urine test. I'm doing what I got to do. It feels good. Like with this check I got coming, I can get a new phone. And I'm saving for getting my girl a ring. Not a marriage ring, but a ring she'll like for our anniversary."

Silberman patted him on the shoulder. "Saving money, having goals—you get to see the fruits of your efforts," she said.

In court, Silberman pointed out Kevin's work uniform, a yellow security vest, to Judge Gubbay. The vest was like a shield: Kevin wore it home after work and found that when he walked through Brownsville, the police didn't hassle him. Judge Gubbay congratulated him and set his next court date at the end of February. If Kevin stayed on track, he could complete YCP by then. His odyssey would be over. He'd no longer be a violent felon in the eyes of the state. His conviction would be dismissed and sealed.

Along with working and following all the rules of YCP, Kevin had one remaining hurdle: eighty hours of community service. He regretted not doing it earlier. Kreyngold nudged him at their weekly meetings and gave him suggestions for places near his house where he could complete it. But with a full-time job, the community service was hard to schedule. Kevin didn't want to risk losing his job to work for free.

In mid-February, with two weeks until court, Kreyngold wondered if Kevin was playing games with community service and talked about extending his time in YCP. "Kevin is Kevin!" he told Kinsella and Silberman. "He is doing well for the moment he is in. But he is capable of so much more. Just has to mature quickly. He will come to realize it one day. But I cannot enable him." Kreyngold knew I was following Kevin's case, but the rest of the D.A.'s office wasn't paying attention, and he didn't feel pressure to get Kevin through. If anything, he was being told not to cut his clients any slack.

A few days later, Kevin called Kreyngold from the bus, and a woman sitting near him heard him tell Kreyngold that he needed to find a place where he could do the community service at night. When he got off the phone, she gave him the number of an agency for people with developmental disabilities. He called and set up times in the evening and on weekends when he could do cleaning and maintenance.

Kevin's court date was now eleven days away. After work, he went straight to the agency and spent his evenings mopping floors and unclogging drains. He knocked off another thirty hours over two weekends. "It's crazy but I can't complain," he told me. "I'm going to finish."

On his last day in YCP, after his final curfew call, Kevin told his mother he'd made it, and she started to cry. "She believed in me, but she didn't know," he said. "She just didn't think, like, a whole year, staying out of trouble, curfew, can't smoke—she thought I was going to mess up. She really wasn't down on me, but she had it in her head, it could happen."

For his court date, Kevin took the day off from work and put on a red wool hat, black jacket, and matching black and red sneakers. "I Am No Longer State Property," he posted on Facebook as he left home. In his final report to the court, Kreyngold wrote that over his year in YCP, Kevin "became a responsible and hardworking young man." Kevin remembered the beginning, when they'd butted heads. Kreyngold didn't believe he'd succeed in completing the program then, Kevin thought, and the doubt fueled him. Before he came to trust his social worker, he was merely driven to prove Kreyngold wrong.

As he approached the door to Judge Gubbay's courtroom, Kevin found Silberman and Kinsella in the hallway. He told them he was helping his mother with the rent for the first time, chipping in $200 a month. He was planning to get a learner's permit and then his driver's license. He said he and his mother were talking about buying a car together. He was talking about sorting out his GED and then taking classes at Kingsborough Community College, where he could earn an associate's degree.

"It's been almost a two-year journey for us," Silberman said to him outside the courtroom. "It's been a long time. We've had clients in your position and they have not been as successful as you've been. We hope that you're proud of yourself. We really appreciate that this has not been easy."

"It was but then it wasn't," Kevin said. "I knew I was going to finish."

"You and you alone made the choice to finish. And when you set your mind to it, you did. I hope that also shows you, Kevin, that you are someone who, when you set your mind to something, you're able to achieve it and do it."

"Yes yes yes yes yes," Kevin answered.

He held the door to the courtroom for Silberman. About two dozen people sat on the benches inside, waiting for their own cases to be called. Teitelman wasn't in the room; she didn't need to be. But she'd gotten an email about Kevin's completion of YCP and remembered how hard Silberman had pushed for diversion instead of prison. "We want this outcome," Teitelman said of Kevin's case. "We want the dismissal."

At ten to noon, a clerk called Kevin's name for the last time. Judge Gubbay congratulated him and called for a round of applause. Kevin felt tired and a little giddy. As the room echoed with clapping, he ducked his head, smiling a little but embarrassed to let it show. Then he set his mouth in a hard line, straightened his shoulders, and walked out the door.

13

THE ETHICS TRIAL

SIX MONTHS AFTER her release from prison, Noura Jackson was back in court. This time, she'd come as a spectator, sitting on a bench with her friends Ansley Larsson and Bill Shelton and her lawyer, Michael Working. The man on trial was Stephen Jones, the prosecutor who'd found Andrew Hammack's note and then, he claimed, forgotten about it until the jury verdict against Noura was over and done. Jones was the one in the hot seat at the front of the courtroom. His wife sat on a bench in the back, hands clasped.

Noura had come, she told me, because she wanted to see for herself that "prosecutors can't just do what they did to me." Jones's trial would be a moment of vindication. And yet no matter how many times she reminded herself that he was the one on trial, she felt jittery and on display. She'd taken care with her makeup that morning—a skill she'd perfected in prison—and she was wearing delicate ceramic earrings Larsson had made by hand, black to match her blouse. The night before, she'd dreamed that she was back in prison and couldn't get out. It wasn't just a dream, of course. It was also a memory.

Noura felt unsettled, too, being back in Memphis. After living with Larsson for a few months, she'd moved to Nashville to live with her girlfriend, whom she'd met in prison. They'd found a small house with an alarm system, which Noura needed in order to feel safe, in a development with plenty of trees and rolling green hills. When she and her girlfriend told the landlord about their prison records, he said he believed in second chances. They paid three months' rent up front along with the security deposit.

Moving in, Noura grew close to her girlfriend's extended family, especially her teenage daughter. She also made a good friend who had a three-year-old son and a new baby. Looking after the kids, Noura thought often about having her own child, but she didn't feel stable enough yet. In the meantime, her endometriosis was flaring up. If it got worse, she faced the prospect of a hysterectomy and losing the chance to get pregnant someday. Her felony record could stand in the way of trying to adopt.

At home, sitting out on her back patio, drinking coffee and smoking, Noura was racked by loss, past and future. Worrying about whether she could ever become a mother, in spite of her endometriosis, she thought of her own mother. "She's the one person who would understand, because I'm her child, and that would be her grandchild. And she's not here."

Her thoughts of her mother were now bound up with her decision to plead guilty, and they filled her with remorse. "On paper, I'm the killer," she said. "Even though I maintain my innocence, that's what the cops look at. So, somebody's just getting away, and I helped make that happen. There's this sense of guilt because I traded all of these things to be able to wake up free, but I'm not even free. Like, my body's here, and I'm here, but I'm still very much a prisoner in my own head. You know, I'm still the girl that killed her mom. I'm the girl that sold out." The plea deal tortured her. She regretted it over and over again, reliving the decision and doubting herself. "I didn't really realize how much I was sacrificing. I didn't know. And sometimes I still find more things. Like, daily, like even just now."

There wasn't much Noura could do about any of this, so she made it bearable by cooking and caring for her girlfriend's family, especially the three-year-old. Noura made him cheese sandwiches, helped him learn to use a toilet, and planned his birthday party.

As she sat in court in Memphis, her life in Nashville receded before the figure of Stephen Jones. He wore a dark suit and rimless glasses, his mouth set in a line, as reporters and camera operators from the local TV stations ran wires and set up microphones to tape the proceedings. By going to trial first, before Weirich, Jones was effectively testing the waters for his boss. Weirich's trial was scheduled to follow two months later. If Jones lost, she could avoid the spectacle of facing trial by agreeing to the public censure recommended by the Tennessee Board of Professional Responsibility. And if Jones won, would the board lose its nerve about trying her?

Krisann Hodges, the lawyer for the Board of Professional Responsibility, took her place at the front of the courtroom just after 9:00 a.m. It was her job to argue the case against Jones before a panel of three judges. In their day-to-day lives, the panelists were Memphis lawyers. They depended on their law licenses for their livelihoods, as Jones did, and they were part of the same social network. One of the judges was even a former Shelby County prosecutor. In other words, Jones's judges were his peers.

The three men, all white, listened poker-faced as Hodges launched into her opening argument. "Today the board will present to you a case involving the responsibilities of a prosecutor," she said, "and the injury that can occur when a prosecutor does not live up to the high duty we expect from a person holding this position."

Hodges laid out the board's theory for Jones's culpability. The Tennessee Rules of Professional Conduct for lawyers went beyond

Brady, imposing a broader responsibility on prosecutors. Rule 3.8 instructed them to "make timely disclosure to the defense of all evidence or information known to the prosecutor that tends to negate the guilt of the accused or mitigates the offense." The words came from a set of model rules of professional responsibility developed by the American Bar Association (ABA) and adopted in some form by almost every state.

Rule 3.8 didn't require proof that a prosecutor withheld evidence deliberately to hold him or her responsible. This was a sore spot for some prosecutors who thought findings of ethical violations should be reserved for the rare situation with smoking-gun evidence that a prosecutor cheated on purpose. For years, the National District Attorneys Association (NDAA) has urged judges to use the term "error" rather than "prosecutorial misconduct" unless they find that a prosecutor deliberately committed a misdeed. A broad conception of misconduct "feeds a narrative that prosecutors are corrupt, which is poisonous," said Joshua Marquis, a longtime district attorney in Oregon, who served on the board of directors of the NDAA.

These tensions were an undercurrent at Jones's trial. In her opening statement, Hodges went through the moments at Noura's trial that could have prompted Jones to remember Hammack's note undermining his testimony. Back then, in Judge Craft's courtroom, the homicide investigator who questioned Hammack about the night of the murder was Jones's witness, and Jones asked him a series of questions about what Hammack said. Jones also listened as Weirich questioned Hammack. Finally, at the end of the trial, it was Jones who used Hammack's testimony to make the damning claim that Noura engineered a cover-up. "Despite the obvious goal posts in the case, Mr. Jones forgot and forgot and forgot to turn Hammack's note over to the defense," Hodges said.

Jones's lawyer, Brian Faughnan, swept away any hint of blame when it was his turn to speak. "We are here because Steve did the right thing," he began. "From Jones's perspective in the middle of the trial," Hammack's note was just "one piece in a 450-piece puzzle." Once Jones found the note, he recognized he'd made a mistake and turned it over. "The kind of prosecutor we should go after in the state is the kind that would deep-six that document," Faughnan argued. "Steve is not that prosecutor. He does not need to be punished to send a message. He should be praised as an example of what a prosecutor should do in a big case."

It was a strong defense. When Jones was sworn in as his own chief witness, he portrayed himself in the terms his lawyer laid out—as an exemplar of the legal profession. Sitting in a straight-backed chair, without the usual barrier of a desk or a lectern between him and the judges, Jones took back the authority that the proceedings threatened to diminish. At the time of Noura's trial, he'd been the lead counsel in more cases than he could recall, he said. In the D.A.'s office, he served not only as a prosecutor but also as the legal advisor to Weirich and the other lawyers on staff. "I'm responsible for training," he said. Jones conducted trainings in person and was also responsible for keeping up with developments in the law. "I read every appellate opinion that comes out of the state courts, and I pull out what I think are issues that a prosecutor needs to be aware of and compile it in a Word document and then I email out every attorney in my office and then all the attorneys across the state."

In other words, Jones was the in-house expert, trusted to educate Weirich and her office on the finer points of law. He held himself out as particularly knowledgeable about the Brady rule. And for good reason, it seemed: Jones was the author of an article in the *Memphis Law Review* called "A Prosecutor's Constitutional Duty to Disclose Exculpatory Evidence."

Yet on the stand, Jones made a series of striking errors about *Brady* and a prosecutor's duties, mangling the law because he apparently didn't know it. "The word 'favorable' is not used in U.S. Supreme Court opinions defining the *Brady* doctrine," he said in response to a question from his own lawyer. But the most important passage of *Brady* states: "We now hold that the suppression by the prosecution of evidence favorable to an accused upon request violates due process." In eighteen subsequent Supreme Court opinions defining and applying *Brady*, "favorable" has appeared more than eighty times.

Jones incorrectly described a prosecutor's obligation to turn over exculpatory evidence. "I think the definition for exculpatory is what sometimes as a prosecutor we'll refer to as the SODDI defense: Some Other Dude Did It," he said. "Not only some other dude did it, but this defendant couldn't have done it." This narrows a prosecutor's duty to disclose to a small slice of smoking-gun evidence. The Tennessee courts, by contrast, have repeatedly held that "exculpatory" means any evidence that's material and favorable to the accused or could impeach a witness for the prosecution.

Jones's misstatements of law belied his presentation of himself as a legal expert. They were also self-serving: he shrank the doctrine to diminish his own obligation to disclose evidence, and the significance of his failure to do so. Perhaps the judges on the panel would have questioned Jones's credibility if they'd seen his mask of professionalism slip, but strikingly, no one exposed his misstatements at the trial. They skipped by, unnoticed.

On the second day of the trial, Judge Craft sought to further boost Jones's reputation, appearing as a character witness for him. It was an ill-advised step for the judge to take given his personal stake in defending the guilty verdict and his decision not to declare a mistrial when Hammack's note surfaced, according to ethics experts I consulted. But Craft chaired Tennessee's Board of Judicial Conduct. He had little to fear. And he went all out, calling Jones "Mr. Boy Scout" ("By that I mean he just, like, is nerdy as far as every dot and tittle must be perfect"). Craft admitted he'd never seen Jones try a case other than Noura's. Still, Craft said that when he had heard Jones was accused of intentionally withholding evidence, "I almost laughed because it's like—it's like accusing Mother Teresa of not caring for the poor."

———

"Who exactly is going to prosecute prosecutors?" Alex Kozinski, the former federal appeals court judge, asked, in a 2015 law review article that commanded the attention of the national press as well as the legal community. The answer, almost always, has been no one. To understand why, you have to start with another wrong turn by the Supreme Court.

In 1969, a federal judge found that a prosecutor in Los Angeles named Richard Pachtman had elicited false and misleading testimony from his chief witness at the murder trial of a man named Paul Imbler, who turned himself in for a robbery and was then arrested for the separate killing of a grocery store owner in a holdup. Because of the judge's finding against Pachtman, Imbler was released from death row. He sued Pachtman for damages, seeking compensation for the decade he spent behind bars.

Pachtman wasn't a clear-cut villain. After the trial, he'd continued to look into the murder. When he found new evidence that helped Imbler, he brought it to light. The courts that heard Imbler's suit dismissed it. In 1975, the Supreme Court heard oral argument in the case to consider, for the first time, whether prosecutors could be sued based on the federal civil rights law called Section 1983. That's the law that allows people to go to court if they think the state deprived them, in any setting, of a constitutional right.

Police and other law enforcement officials enjoy *qualified* immunity from civil rights suits. They win as long as the court finds they performed their duties in good faith and didn't violate clearly established constitutional rights. In *Imbler v. Pachtman*, however, the Supreme Court gave prosecutors something more: *absolute* immunity. No matter what they did wrong—concealing evidence, presenting perjured testimony, pressing charges without evidence—they would be shielded from civil rights suits, so long as they acted in the course of preparing or trying a case. Absolute immunity makes it virtually impossible to sue prosecutors individually for anything they do in the scope of their jobs.

The Court's vote in *Imbler* was unanimous. Writing for the majority, Justice Lewis Powell said that prosecutors must be free from the threat of a lawsuit to be "vigorous and fearless" in exercising their "wide discretion" about presenting evidence, trusting witnesses, and pressing hard at a trial.

Powell's words have not worn well. Absolute immunity is literally a get-out-of-a-lawsuit-free card for prosecutors. "They can be as reckless and self-serving as they want," Kozinski wrote, "and if they get caught, nothing bad will happen to them." When prosecutors withhold evidence or let witnesses commit perjury, they're subverting the system they're supposed to serve.

In *Imbler*, Powell promised that giving absolute immunity to prosecutors would not "leave the public powerless to deter misconduct." Even if prosecutors couldn't be sued for a civil rights violation, they could be charged and punished criminally for violating people's constitutional rights. And, Powell claimed, "a prosecutor stands perhaps unique, among officials whose acts could deprive persons of constitutional rights, in his amenability to professional discipline by an association of his peers."

Kozinski made mincemeat of Powell's faith in criminal penalties for prosecutors. "Despite numerous cases where prosecutors have committed willful misconduct, costing innocent defendants their lives," he wrote, "I am aware of only two who have been criminally prosecuted for it; they spent a total of six days behind bars."

Two cases. It's galling, when you stop to think about it. But mostly we don't. The impunity of prosecutors has barely registered with the public. When a police shooting is caught on video and appears to have no justifiable cause, the outrage is plain for all to see. The wrongs of prosecutors, cloaked in the customs and legalisms of court, far more often escape notice.

In the years since *Imbler*, the Supreme Court has not recognized its error. Indeed, in 2011, the justices made it harder still for people wronged by prosecutors to collect damages from them. This time, in the case *Connick v. Thompson*, Justice Clarence Thomas wrote the majority opinion in a hotly contested case in which the court split five to four, conservatives versus liberals.

The story of *Connick v. Thompson* was cinematic. John Thompson was about to be executed in 1999 when his lawyers made a last-ditch effort to save his life. They sent a private investigator back to the crime lab archives, and for the first time, she was allowed to search through old filing cabinets for something, anything, that might spare Thompson. In a corner of the room, in a file that didn't have Thompson's name on it, she unearthed a microfiche copy of a lab report. It was an analysis of the critical piece of physical evidence, a bloody swatch of cloth, which had been used to convict Thompson of a robbery—an outcome that influenced his separate conviction for murder and his subsequent death sentence. The hidden analysis showed that the blood on the cloth was type B. Thompson's blood was type O.

With Thompson's conviction thrown into profound doubt, a former New Orleans assistant district attorney came forward to say that five years earlier, one of the prosecutors in Thompson's trial confessed to hiding the blood analysis before dying of cancer. Nonetheless, District Attorney Harry Connick Sr. argued that the withholding of evidence was not a Brady violation.

The Louisiana courts disagreed with Connick, and in 2003, Thompson was finally freed. Blocked by *Imbler* from suing any prosecutors individually, Thompson sued Connick's office for damages. A jury awarded him $14 million, $1 million a year for each year he spent on death row. Connick's office appealed, and the case made it to the Supreme Court.

Thompson's theory was that Connick's office deprived him of his constitutional rights by failing to train its lawyers about their obligation to turn over evidence. Prosecutors weren't following the Brady rule, and it was an institutional failure. In the ten years before Thompson's conviction, during Connick's tenure as D.A., the

Louisiana courts threw out at least four other convictions because of Brady violations, and, in 1995, the Supreme Court overturned the death sentence of another defendant prosecuted by Connick's office. These cases showed a pattern.

In the jury's eyes, Connick's record added up to what courts call "deliberate indifference," and that was the rationale for awarding Thompson $14 million. Or as Justice Ruth Bader Ginsburg put it in dissent, Thompson won based on "testimony that Connick's office had one of the worst *Brady* records in the country."

Justice Thomas's majority opinion brushed that record aside. The jury award could not stand because Connick didn't have reason to know he wasn't adequately training his prosecutors about what the *Brady* decision required. The pattern of previous Brady violations in New Orleans wasn't similar enough to the concealment of the blood analysis in Thompson's case to put Connick on notice. Like Justice Powell before him, Justice Thomas pointed out that prosecutors who violate their ethical duties can be sanctioned, suspended, or disbarred. But that was no consolation for John Thompson. The Supreme Court's decision, he later wrote, freed prosecutors "to do the same thing to someone else today." He continued:

> I don't care about the money. I just want to know why the prosecutors who hid evidence, sent me to prison for something I didn't do and nearly had me killed are not in jail themselves. There were no ethics charges against them, no criminal charges, no one was fired.

John Thompson died in 2017 at the age of fifty-five. The outcome he described remains numbingly normal. After *Connick v. Thompson*, prosecutors are nearly untouchable. A 2006 study of almost thirteen hundred accusations of misconduct showed that none resulted in professional discipline. The Northern California Innocence Project identified sixty-seven prosecutors whom judges found more than once suppressed evidence or committed other misconduct. Only six were publicly disciplined.

The evidence overwhelmingly shows that the Supreme Court's faith in professional discipline is misplaced. That's not surprising when you think about the insular culture of a local courthouse. It's one thing for a judge or a defense lawyer to criticize a prosecutor within the traditional bounds of a hearing or a trial, and another to threaten her professional standing by blowing the whistle on her. The upshot, according to a 2011 *Yale Law Journal* article, is that "those who are in the best position to discover prosecutorial misconduct—judges, prosecutors, and defense attorneys—routinely fail to report it."

Trying to understand the reluctance to stamp out ethical lapses, I looked into a rape case in California. It started as a story about a judge reversing a conviction after finding that the prosecutor failed to turn over important evidence at trial. Then the tale grew wilder. Without clear authority, the prosecutor started issuing warrants to search the homes of relatives of the defendant. The judge ordered the prosecutor to stop. He kept going. The judge called the prosecutor's behavior "disturbing." Finally, the D.A.'s office reassigned the case and dropped the rape charges. Yet the judge did not report the prosecutor to the California Bar Court, which has the power to discipline lawyers in the state. When the Bar Court opened a case anyway, the judge testified with some reluctance. "It was hard for me," he said. "The other judges in my court all thought he was a whiz kid. I had colleagues who testified for him as a character witness."

In the end, the California Bar Court came down hard on the prosecutor, finding that he'd abused the power of his office and taking away his law license for four years. This was the rare case, then, in which professional discipline had real bite. It was also a case in which the panelists who decided the prosecutor's fate weren't local lawyers. They were judges of the Bar Court, set apart professionally. And the prosecutor's trial took place in another city, at a remove from his network.

That's not how it was done in Memphis with Amy Weirich and Stephen Jones.

Jones testified that he was alone in his office, hard at work on a Sunday in the middle of Noura's trial, when he realized that something related to Andrew Hammack was missing from the prosecution's files. He sent an investigator to the police department to look. On Monday morning, the investigator came back with Hammack's handwritten note. Jones read it, he said, but didn't do an in-depth analysis, didn't compare it to Hammack's other statements. Hammack wasn't his witness. Weirich was the one who was about to take his testimony. And so, Jones testified, he decided to hand the note over. "I was going to give it to the defense, and I was going to give it to Amy. She was going to deal with it. It was for her to think about the details."

So far, so good. Letting Weirich and Corder determine the note's value was the prudent thing to do. Except Jones didn't do it. According to his own account, he tucked the note into his trial notebook and left it there.

Did that mean he deprived Noura of a fair trial?

The Tennessee Supreme Court had said yes. Jones, however, insisted that Hammack's note had no significance. "It wasn't a bombshell, it was a nonissue," he said.

"Did you dismiss the impeachment value of the statement?" Hodges asked a minute or two later.

"I just wanted to make sure that it wasn't something that would mean I couldn't prosecute the case," Jones answered.

This was another misleading statement. Neither the Brady rule nor Rule 3.8 say that a prosecutor has a duty to disclose only if he determines the evidence leaves him unable to prosecute the case. But Hodges didn't call Jones on his misstatement. Instead, she asked a different question: "Mr. Jones, isn't the problem here, though, that you did not identify it as Brady material and therefore didn't produce it immediately to the defense?"

"The problem is that I forgot all about it," Jones said. "I had never intended not to give it to the defense."

It was a smart answer. To find him guilty, the judges would either have to find that Jones was lying or agree to damage the reputation of a fellow lawyer who made an innocent mistake that he did his best to correct.

Hodges exposed a chink in Jones's credibility when she asked him to describe telling Weirich about Hammack's note after he rediscovered it.

"I don't remember exactly when I talked to her about it because I was—she was not there when I found it," Jones answered, and then he started to meander. "So when I found it, I immediately went to work on, you know, figuring out how—I knew I was going to disclose it, but I didn't know if I should file it. Eventually I decided I should file it, and, you know, I told her at some point."

"But that was something of a memorable conversation between you and Ms. Weirich?" Hodges asked.

"Not really," Jones answered. "You know, I knew I intended to give it, I knew I should have given it, I knew I made a mistake," he said, lapsing into confusion. "I knew I was going to file it and disclose it to the world, I knew it was going to be litigated, you know, the motion for a new trial, and there was nothing that she—I mean, frankly I wasn't seeking her input because there was nothing to get her input about."

I've told a lot of prosecutors Jones's story. They've all found it hard to believe that an experienced prosecutor who rediscovered pertinent evidence after a big trial wouldn't remember consulting with his cocounsel—the lead prosecutor in the case—about what to do next. Here's a typical response from Jesse Evans, chief assistant district attorney in Cobb County, Georgia: "I don't want to cast aspersions on someone I don't know, but I don't see how someone could say they omitted evidence and then found it and forgot to tell. That would have been a big deal for me. That would be a loss of sleep."

At Jones's trial, however, the judges were gentle with him. "The problem is with me, not you," Leland McNabb, the former prosecutor on the panel, said when Jones apologized for giving an unclear answer. "I'm not trying to suggest you're not being forthright," a second panelist said when he asked Jones how he copied files for the defense.

Noura found the judges' solicitude hard to bear. They were giving Jones the benefit of the doubt. She'd never gotten that from Judge Craft.

I've spent some time describing discipline for prosecutors because on two occasions when they've been punished, statewide reform has followed. These changes have ended the blind reliance on prosecutors to call their own lines when no one can see if they're cheating.

The rules have been rewritten in Texas, a state with more than three hundred wrongful convictions over the last three decades. One of the people exonerated was Michael Morton, a supermarket manager from the Austin suburbs who spent almost twenty-five years in prison for the murder of his wife. DNA evidence freed Morton in 2011, but his lawyers also discovered that the police had collected evidence that suggested they had arrested the wrong man. The prosecutor, Ken Anderson, hadn't turned it over to the defense at Morton's trial. As a tale of innocence, Morton's story was familiar, but it sparked outrage among Texans, perhaps because Morton was white and middle-class. "I was just some guy living in the suburbs," Morton said. "Just like them. Married with a kid. Had a job. Had a mortgage."

Two years after Morton's exoneration, Texas did something never done before in the entire country: it put a prosecutor behind bars for withholding evidence. Anderson, who had since become a judge, pleaded no contest and left the bench. He lost his law license and was sentenced to ten days in jail.

In the aftermath, Texas enacted a groundbreaking law, called the Michael Morton Act, which was a giant leap toward transparency. It bound prosecutors to share their case files and provide nearly all the evidence in them to the defense—material or not, admissible or not—"as soon as practicable." If not, a prosecutor could face discipline. A lawyer "need only be negligent" to get into trouble. "Don't get burned," a prosecutor in Harris County cautioned on the website of the Texas District and County Attorneys Association. "If there is any conceivable way in which information or evidence could be considered favorable to the defense . . . don't stop to wonder whether the information or evidence is material and admissible. Just disclose it."

Laws like these, requiring what's called "open-file discovery," direct prosecutors to hand over nearly everything in their files so that defense lawyers can see for themselves. Once the defense makes a request for evidence, prosecutors don't make tricky calls about whether it's favorable or material to guilt or innocence. The laws protect confidential information and witnesses, and make exceptions for sensitive material, like a victim's medical record.

Kim Ogg, the reform-minded district attorney in Harris County, called the Michael Morton Act the single most important development in her thirty years of criminal practice. Gary Udashen, a defense lawyer and president of the state Innocence Project, concurred. "For twenty-five years, I never had prosecutors give me exculpatory evidence. Not once. *Brady* was meaningless in Texas. The Michael Morton Act changed the whole landscape. Now every prosecutor in the state is nervous about being caught withholding exculpatory evidence." In Harris County, Dallas, San Antonio, and Fort Worth, prosecutors have joined the movement to establish conviction review units, in order to ferret out the misconduct and errors of the past. The result has been more exonerations than in any other state.

North Carolina took a similar path. In 2004, five exonerations from death row spurred the legislature to pass the first open-file law in the country. Prosecutors must share "any other matter or evidence obtained during the investigation of the defendant." Nonetheless, in 2007 a high-profile rape case against three Duke University lacrosse players fell apart amid allegations that Michael

Nifong, the elected district attorney of Durham, concealed DNA evidence that was helpful to the defense. Nifong was disbarred and sentenced to one day in jail. In 2010, an investigation of the state crime lab found that analysts, under pressure to help win convictions, altered or withheld test results in at least 230 cases over sixteen years. The state legislature responded by strengthening the open-file law.

Prosecutors in North Carolina resisted the open-file mandate at first but have since come around. In a study published in 2016 in the *Washington and Lee Law Review*, 91 percent of prosecutors and 70 percent of North Carolina defense lawyers reported that the open-file law worked well. Old arguments about the virtue of trial by ambush, and the insurmountable risks of disclosure, have largely faded away. "Prosecutors can have blind spots," Benjamin David, an elected district attorney in North Carolina, told me. "We get so convinced that the defendant is guilty. We really can't be the architects of deciding what's helpful to the defense and what's not. Now they decide. In the end, that's liberating."

When I talked about open-file with prosecutors who hadn't practiced it, they were still often wary. They didn't believe that it could be liberating to give up the power to hold back information, or that witnesses could be protected. In New York, with the exception of Brooklyn, which has a long-standing open-file policy, district attorneys have opposed changing the state's law on the disclosure of evidence, which allows prosecutors to reveal no more than the Brady rule requires as late as the brink of trial. (It's routine for the defense to get a packet of evidence the *morning* of trial in New York.) Asked why he saw open-file as a nonstarter, given the success other states have had in sharing information while keeping witnesses safe, the president of the New York D.A.'s Association claimed that his state was one of the safest for witnesses in the country. "So why do we always feel that what we're doing is wrong and we have to modify it to what someone else is doing?" he asked.

That mindset helps explain why open-file is the law in only six states. Fifteen states have narrow discovery laws like New York's. The rest lie somewhere in between. Federal prosecutors are bound by a policy that goes beyond *Brady*, but not all the way to open-file.

Among the reformer D.A.s, the push is on for prosecutors to adopt open-file on their own. "I want the defense to have everything I have," said John Chisholm, the district attorney in Milwaukee. He saw benefits in departing from the traditional adversarial model. "A lot of times, you show them what you've got, and it tells them they don't have a chance. Or on the flip side, they can call you and say: 'I've found something out you might not know. Would it change your mind?' And then we can talk."

Darryl Brown, a University of Virginia law professor who has studied the issue, sees a "slow but steady march" toward greater disclosure, but he also sees resistance rooted in the bias people have to keeping the status quo. "You're comfortable with the familiar," he said, "and you can't imagine it could work another way." It's one example, among many, in which the quality of justice a person receives depends on the place in which he or she is accused of a crime.

In January 2015, Amy Weirich formalized a policy she called open-file. "It was really putting on paper the practice of this office as it already was," she told me. "The practice was to give to defense counsel what we have in our file." She added a caveat: "Now, there's always exceptions. There might be material in our file that can't be disclosed."

Defense lawyers and former prosecutors told me, however, that Weirich's office was neither transparent nor consistent. "The people who view a trial as a game continue to look for ways to hold things back," one former prosecutor in her office said. "You can say you have open-file, but if the file isn't complete, it doesn't really matter," another told me.

The gap was particularly evident in Shelby County's juvenile court. In 2012, after a long investigation, the Justice Department found systematic violation of the constitutional rights of teenagers in the juvenile court, as well as discrimination against African Americans. The Justice Department appointed Sandra Simkins as a federal monitor to oversee changes the county and the court agreed to make. Five years later, Simkins submitted a troubling report showing that some problems hadn't been fixed. She said that prosecutors regularly sought guilty pleas by asking to transfer teenagers to adult court—a serious step—without disclosing crucial evidence to the defense. The teenagers were effectively being coerced to plead in the dark. Simkins emphasized the "extraordinary gravity of the consequences" and the disproportionate impact on black teenagers.

A few days after Simkins's report became public, the mayor, sheriff, and juvenile court judge of Shelby County asked the Justice Department to end the federal monitoring. "It is time to terminate the agreement and allow all sides to stand together to praise the work that has been accomplished," the three officials wrote. When I asked Weirich about Simkins's findings, she said, "I don't know the specifics," but "we follow the law."

In the last few years, however, examples have mounted of Weirich herself cutting corners in major cases—including prosecutions that led to death sentences. Beyond Noura's case, courts called out Weirich's conduct in exceptionally strong language. The barrage of judicial criticism began a few weeks after Stephen Jones's ethics trial, when the United States Court of Appeals for the Sixth Circuit reversed the conviction of Andrew Thomas, a man Weirich tried for murder in 2001. At his trial, where she sought the death penalty, Weirich asked the state's pivotal witness (Thomas's girlfriend at the time of the shooting) if she had "collected one red cent" for testifying against him. The witness said no—even though she'd received $750 from the FBI for cooperating in a parallel federal case against Thomas, who maintained his innocence for the murder.

Weirich said there was no record of the $750 witness payment in the case file she received from federal prosecutors, who backed her up on this point. (They had reason to do so, since they collaborated on the case and continued to work together.) At the oral argument before the Sixth Circuit, however, the state conceded that the file contained a receipt for the payment. Did that mean Weirich knew about it? The Sixth Circuit didn't answer the question, but the judges said Weirich certainly should have known, since she repeatedly questioned Thomas's girlfriend about her "purportedly high-minded" reasons for testifying. "Any competent prosecutor" would have carefully reviewed the file, the appeals court said, to make sure nothing in it suggested the witness was lying, and a careful review would have revealed the receipt.

Around the same time, Weirich and Jones testified privately in a challenge to the murder conviction and death sentence of a man named David Ivy. The case involved the discovery of a letter, not given to the defense at trial, in which a gang member said Ivy had been framed. Weirich's and Jones's testimony about the letter remained sealed.

In October 2017, eight months after the ruling for Andrew Thomas, the Tennessee Court of Criminal Appeals threw out the double murder conviction of Joshua Bargery in Lake County, around a hundred miles from Memphis. One of the problems with the case involved a Memphis police officer who agreed to testify for the defense. He planned to say that the victims were killed in the same manner as in other crimes linked to a gang called the Mexikanemi, which Bargery's lawyers argued had committed the double murder. When the Lake County prosecutors saw the Memphis cop on the witness list for the defense, they called Weirich. She called the Memphis police chief to ask why one of his men was testifying for the defense. The chief spoke to the officer, who felt pressured and pulled out. In reversing Bargery's conviction, the appellate judges called the interference by Weirich and the Lake County prosecutors "inexplicable and improper."

Later that summer, the Tennessee board started an investigation into Weirich's conduct in Vern Braswell's case, the one in which the mysterious manila envelope with Weirich's initials went missing. A few months later, the state Court of Criminal Appeals issued an unsettling opinion in Braswell's appeal. "The olfactory perception of the missing sealed manila envelope is not pleasant," the judges wrote. But they stopped short of granting Braswell a new trial. "The Petitioner bears the burden of proof in this post-conviction case. Through absolutely no fault of the Petitioner or his post-conviction counsel, there is no evidence that any Brady material was inside the now missing sealed envelope. Accordingly, we must conclude that the Petitioner is not entitled to relief."

Weirich had been right: no one could prove what was in the missing envelope.

When I interviewed her, I asked whether she'd considered opening a conviction integrity unit, an early step many district attorneys take if they're serious about reform. "We have not," Weirich said. "Our entire office is a conviction integrity unit."

On the morning of March 2, 2017, the lawyer-judges of the Board of Professional Responsibility found Jones not guilty. His account, they said, was "entirely credible." Witnesses had spoken to his "integrity and candor." The panel refused to stain Jones's ethical record for a mistake they called "inadvertent." His elevated status in Weirich's office continued unchanged: he remained her legal advisor and training director.

Weirich called a press conference to praise the result and announce that the board had agreed to dismiss the charges against her in exchange for a private reprimand. She would be spared the embarrassment of a trial. The board also agreed, Weirich declared, not to appeal the panel's finding of not guilty in Jones's case, even though it usually appealed such rulings to the Tennessee courts. She ended on a grand, if elliptical, note: "Today is a validation that no matter the sacrifice, it is imperative every day and always to do the right thing for the right reason."

For Noura, the board's decision was like a light going out. She'd dared to hope that the legal profession would stand up for her, that other lawyers would want to draw a clear line between themselves and Weirich and Jones, between ethical conduct and cheating. "It wasn't a mistake, like you're driving and it's night and you can't see and you hit someone," she said. "It was on purpose." And yet Noura felt she was the one whose reputation had taken another beating.

The Tennessee board's decision attracted the attention of Nina Morrison, a lawyer at the Innocence Project who helped represent Joseph Buffey in West Virginia and Michael Morton, the suburban supermarket manager whose exoneration had such profound effect in Texas. She is a friend of mine, and she said she was disappointed to see one more bar committee "give prosecutors every benefit of the doubt." Wondering if there was anything to be done for Noura, she looked up the law on DNA testing in Tennessee. To her surprise, the state gave people who'd been convicted the right to petition to retest evidence even if their cases were over and done.

Maybe the Innocence Project could win Noura the chance to retest the physical evidence from her mother's bedroom, including the condom on the floor and the hair in Jackson's hand that had never been analyzed. Morrison asked one of her colleagues, Bryce Benjet, if he would take Noura's case. He said yes. Maybe there was still some chance, after all this time, to identify Jennifer Jackson's killer.

That was what Noura said she wanted, but the Innocence Project's intervention carried serious risks. What if, despite her protestations of innocence, her DNA was found in the evidence taken from the bloody scene of her mother's murder? If there was any reason to worry, this was the moment for Noura to pull back.

On my next trip to Memphis, Morrison asked me to sound out Noura about reopening her case. I watched her closely as I asked if she wanted to talk to Morrison and Benjet. She answered in a burst, eyes widening. "Yes, yes, yes," she said.

14

REFORM

IN MAY 2018, Eric Gonzalez stood at a podium in a sunny banquet hall at Brooklyn Law School to announce the results of Justice 2020, his initiative to set goals for his first two years in office. He looked more at ease in front of a crowd than he had at the outset of his campaign for D.A. a year earlier. A two-person camera crew was on hand to record the event, and the budget covered freshly brewed coffee with pastries and fruit. The group who worked on Justice 2020 from outside the D.A.'s office—activists, clergy, service providers, and defense lawyers—shared tables at the front of the room with Gonzalez's leadership team, which included new faces, another sign of change. Behind them sat rows of supervising attorneys and assistant D.A.s. In the end, whatever goals Gonzalez announced, whatever directives he gave, the implementation of them would rise or fall on the efforts of the line prosecutors who went to court every day.

Beaming, Gonzalez welcomed everyone, and then switched into the more serious mode in which he was still at his most comfortable in public. "We are going to protect public safety," he began, "but we are also going to be far less punitive." He mentioned his brother's death and the toxic relationship people in his neighborhood had with the police when he was growing up. He mentioned how much crime had fallen since then without claiming credit for prosecutors or police. "I don't think anyone understands the totality of why crime has been reduced so much." Then he made his pitch. It was time to do things that previously seemed unrealistic. "We have a mandate," he said. "The real cultural shift I'm going to be asking prosecutors in my office to make is considering jail as the last option. The alternative is jail. The alternative is not a program."

I'd heard a version of this a few months earlier from one of the people in the audience that day. Adam Mansky, director of criminal justice programs at the Center for Court Innovation (CCI), the force behind many of New York City's diversion efforts. On a visit we took to the Red Hook Community Court and Brooklyn's young adult court, Mansky told me about talking to D.A.s and city officials over the last two decades and hearing them treat diversion as inessential—nice if you could afford it as an extra. Now he felt on the verge of a breakthrough. The campaign to close Rikers forced the issue of reducing incarceration. The city started measuring CCI's effectiveness in terms of how many people were being diverted from prison along with how many were reoffending. Mansky was in talks about expanding CCI's programs for misdemeanors and even adding diversion for people charged with violent felonies, which previously no one wanted to fund. "We shouldn't be working on a few cases off to the side," he told me. "How many people should be locked up, as the only option? Fifteen percent? Ten percent? Whatever the number is, it's much lower than we recognize." There was no reason to settle for islands of mercy in a sea of cages.

The audience in the banquet hall was in a good position to hold Gonzalez to this. It was time to take a big step forward on the road New York had been traveling since the crime wave of the 1980s.

From 1988 to 1993, when crime peaked, felonies accounted for tens of thousands more arrests than misdemeanors in New York City. After that, misdemeanor arrests shot up because of broken-windows policing. For example, in 2011, there were more than 310,000 misdemeanor arrests and fewer than 110,000 felony arrests. After that point, misdemeanor arrests, too, began to fall as stop-and-frisk ebbed. Fewer people entered the system. Over the last few years in Brooklyn, significantly more cases have ended in dismissals.

Over the last two years, about 93 percent of people in Brooklyn charged with misdemeanors, and 86 percent of those convicted, did not go to jail. Of those originally charged with felonies, about 73 percent avoided jail or prison. Of those convicted of felonies, more than half did. The outcomes were the fruits of plea bargaining—the work of defense lawyers and the discretion of prosecutors.

Gonzalez was starting from a manageable baseline. From here, it was possible to imagine effective crime control focused on assessing people's needs rather than treating them as walking threats. Brooklyn, with its head start and its dynamic reform movement, could show the country how to keep communities safe by solving problems rather than serving up punitiveness. Making diversion the norm, and proving this would benefit communities rather than harming them—this could be the transformation that would spread.

There was a ways to go, however. On days when I went to criminal court in Brooklyn, I still regularly saw flashes of indifference and cruelty. A teenager was rejected from diversion because he didn't have stable housing. One prosecutor demanded a fine for a homeless person who couldn't pay it. Another sought unaffordable bail for a girl coming out of foster care who'd gotten into a fight. The everyday machinery of prosecution ground on, impervious to change at the top. It would take serious patience and stamina to change the system on a large scale. It would require further shrinking the number of people who entered in the first place. But that meant recognizing a truth that didn't have much traction yet in the D.A.'s office or elsewhere. Even if people didn't go to jail, for minor offenses they often still got way too entangled in the system's net. There was senseless cost and hassle and strain. For some people who get arrested, the best response is nothing—no criminal-justice engagement at all.

Gonzalez had just started a program to route people arrested for small amounts of drugs out of the courts and into treatment, without charging them. He believed that his staff was ready for this kind of cultural shift. In an internal survey, more than 90 percent said they shared his vision of progressive prosecution. While Gonzalez didn't face the same internal resistance as some of the other reform-minded D.A.s, some people in his office were still wary of change. At the Justice 2020 rollout, Gonzalez's chief of staff, Leroy Frazer Jr., a prosecutor for almost forty years, stood up to express the doubt some prosecutors felt about Gonzalez's plans. "We've been successful in getting crime down by holding incarceration over people's heads," he said. "If we get the message out there that prison is a last resort for us, aren't we going to open the gates? Won't crime go back up?" It's not easy to let go of long-held assumptions and the way you've always done your job.

As the event broke up, Lisa Schreibersdorf, the irrepressible and longtime executive director of Brooklyn Defender Services, button-holed Gonzalez. Speaking quickly and in a low tone, she asked him to intervene in a case that she saw as a test of his commitment to change.

Nearly two years earlier, a man nicknamed Kiki had been arrested for taking a laptop from the basement of a house in West Midwood, near Brooklyn College. Kiki, then twenty-eight, was born in Haiti, lost his mother when he was three years old—she died giving birth to his younger sister—and came to the United States with his father and sister in 2004, when Haiti was engulfed by a coup. They lived with various relatives and friends for a few years. Then they had to find their own place and soon they were evicted. Kiki wound up homeless at eighteen. Struggling with depression, he started drinking.

Late one night, Kiki went to McDonald's to buy food, and spotted a liquor store across the street. Though he was hungry, he spent his money there instead.

Sometime later, looking for a place to wash himself, he saw a house that he thought was empty. "It was like 4:00 a.m.," he told her, "and from what I seen I thought the house was abandoned." The area around it was strewn with trash and debris. He opened a basement window and climbed in. He didn't see any furniture, but there was a working shower. "I hadn't taken a shower in a week or two. I was smelling and when you aren't clean on the streets everything is worse." Afterward, he noticed a backpack on the basement floor, and there was a laptop inside. Kiki took it and sold it the next day for $800, using some of the money to buy food, alcohol, and marijuana and giving some of the money to his father and his sister.

It turned out that the house wasn't empty: a husband and wife had recently moved in and were renovating the place. The wife was pregnant, and when she learned the laptop was stolen, she realized she'd been home when a stranger entered her house. The police dusted for fingerprints and arrested Kiki, whose prints were on file from a marijuana arrest. The couple told the prosecutors handling the case that they felt frightened and violated. They wanted Kiki locked up. "We took a hard approach," the bureau chief for the D.A.'s office, David Klestzick, said. "Listen, it was a strong case. We had fingerprints. We got video surveillance showing that he entered the home. And he confessed." The top charge was burglary of a dwelling in the second degree. New York allowed the crime to be charged as a violent felony, with a mandatory prison sentence of three and a half years and a maximum of fifteen years, on the theory that a burglar who goes inside a home can encounter someone inside, creating the *risk* of violence even though none actually occurred. Many state criminal codes don't define violence as actual harm or injury, so people are locked up for "violent felonies" who haven't hurt anyone. Reformers have long tried to persuade the New York legislature to take burglary of a dwelling out of the category of violent crimes with mandatory prison time, but as is, the crucial decision about punishment remains in the hands of prosecutors at charging.

At Kiki's arraignment, the prosecutors made a take-it-or-leave-it offer— two years in prison followed by two years' parole. Accepting it would have made Kiki deportable, since he had a green card but not citizenship, not to mention he'd have a felony conviction and have to do the prison time. He turned the offer down. At the next court appearance, the prosecutors escalated their offer to four years in prison and three years parole in exchange for a plea to a higher-level felony. For a year, they wouldn't budge.

Kiki's lawyer at Brooklyn Defender Services, Scott Hechinger, asked a social worker to do a mental health evaluation, and it showed that Kiki suffered from depression and other trauma-related problems. He started to go to counseling. "It felt good, getting to talk to someone," Kiki said, stroking the slight beard on his chin. "I needed the help." The social worker wrote a report about Kiki for the court, and the prosecution's offer came down, but only to two and a half years.

Over the series of court appearances that followed, a gradual transformation took place. Kiki stopped drinking. He showed up for court on time, clean-shaven and neatly dressed. He moved in with the woman he was dating. He started working, cleaning up city parks for $13.50 an hour. Klestzick, the supervising prosecutor, noticed. "I was going to court every time, and I saw it myself, in how he looked physically, and how he acted. He started to look like a responsible guy."

When Gonzalez announced his plan to spare immigrants who committed nonviolent crimes from deportation, Hechinger, who was the director of policy at Brooklyn Defender Services as well as Kiki's lawyer, argued to the prosecutors that the policy meant they should give Kiki a break. Klestzick and his assistants agreed. They changed their plea offer to a nonviolent felony charge and six months at Rikers followed by six months' probation. "We started to look at who the defendant was because of the new immigration policy," Klestzick said. "He didn't really have a record. He wasn't a problem in the community." The couple whose home Kiki entered still wanted him to go to jail. "I get it," Klestzick said. "She's home when he comes in the house, and she's pregnant, and that's a tough thing knowing someone violated your personal space." Klestzick felt that six months in jail was "reasonable and fair and immigration-friendly."

To Hechinger, however, a felony conviction and six months in jail still seemed destructive. It would cost Kiki his job, give him a criminal record, and disrupt the life he was building with his girl-friend, who was seven months pregnant. Wouldn't Kiki be less likely to commit another crime if he could solidify his newfound stability rather than lose it? Hechinger wanted the D.A.'s office to agree to transfer Kiki's case to mental health court. The judge could then order Kiki into treatment and require him to report back for an extended time—diversion with accountability. But the victims were opposed and Klestzick held the line: the answer was no.

That was why Schreibersdorf, Hechinger's boss, sought out Gonzalez at the Justice 2020 event. She'd written him a long email about the case; now she asked him, face-to-face, to take a close look at it. I watched Gonzalez listen and nod. He had reasons to back up Klestzick, who had twenty-two years' worth of experience in the office and was his good friend. Sparing Kiki from jail entirely went beyond Gonzalez's immigration policy. At the same time, the case represented a chance to do what Justice 2020 promised: reduce in-carceration with little evident risk to public safety. How prosecu-tors exercise their discretion changes in just this way: case by case, by example. Gonzalez could use this case as a model for supervisors and line prosecutors to follow going forward.

The stumbling block for Gonzalez was the couple. They refused to meet Kiki so there was no chance for reconciliation. "Historically, we do not put people into diversion over the objections of our victims," he told me. "We just don't." But he'd read Schreibersdorf's email and found it compelling, and later that day, he reviewed Kiki's minimal criminal record and looked at the photos of the trash outside the house. Gonzalez decided it was credible that Kiki thought the place was abandoned. He decided to agree to the outline of what the defense wanted: no jail time and court-monitored treatment in mental health court.

Klestzick and Hechinger finalized the deal the day before Kiki's baby was born. "It was the biggest relief," Kiki told me, knotting his fingers together with his hands at his chest. "Not to have jail over my head—it had been so stressful, and now that was done and I could be with my girl and my daughter."

Gonzalez and I talked about the case a month or so later in his office. He was leaving early to throw out the ceremonial first pitch at a Mets game, but he didn't rush. He said he knew what it felt like to be the family member of a crime victim, because of his half brother's killing. He didn't want the couple to feel shunted aside; he also wasn't going to do as they wished. "Often I think victims feel like the justice system doesn't care about them," he said. "But I thought, 'You're asking us to take this person out of treatment and cause him to lose his job and maybe his housing. You're asking us to set him up to do the next crime.'"

The couple wasn't happy about the decision, Klestzick told me, but he'd come to see resolving the case without jail time as a template for the change he wanted to make. "To me, this was a completely new way to approach cases. For a case that absolutely impacts public safety, like a shooting, jail might still be the best option. But that's a very small percentage in the end. With every case, we should now be asking, 'What are we trying to accomplish?'"

———

Kim Foxx had a saying in Chicago: "You can't fix what you can't measure." In the spring of 2018, Foxx made data public to an unprecedented degree, releasing seven years of detailed information about felony cases. She wanted experts and interested observers to sift through the information, and she also analyzed it internally. When her review showed that prosecutors were wasting resources by overcharging for shoplifting, she raised the threshold for felony theft to $1,000. In the first year of this new policy, the number of people charged with felony theft for shoplifting plunged by more than 70 percent, from about 2,500 a year to about 720.

Gonzalez was also using data to track his progress. Often, when I talked to him, he would open a binder full of statistics and run his finger down the page. In July 2018, the office touted a 91 percent plunge in prosecutions for possessing or smoking marijuana, with only eight cases resulting in a misdemeanor conviction over the previous six months. Arrests for marijuana were down by 60 percent—perhaps in part because the police knew that if the cases wouldn't be charged, they could no longer collect overtime while they waited for a prosecutor to screen them ("collars for dollars," it's called).

Admissions to Rikers for misdemeanors were down, too, from about 30 percent of cases pretrial, the year before Gonzalez's bail policy went into effect in spring 2017, to around 5 percent a year and a half later. Manhattan adopted a bail policy like Gonzalez's in 2018. The Rikers population dropped from almost 10,000 to about 8,000. It wasn't low enough for the #CloseRikers campaign to succeed and the harder work of reducing bail for felony charges remained to be done. But with a statewide bail reform bill stalled in the legislature, the D.A.s were helping to make change bit by bit.

They were responding to the activists, who kept pushing from the outside, the defense bar, which pushed from the inside, the observers from CourtWatchNYC, who posted on social media about the day-to-day problems they still saw. Some judges seemed to feel the pressure, too. One day, for the first time I saw a judge release a defendant without bail over a prosecutor's objection. The assistant D.A. stood her ground for a beat, her mouth open as if she was about to protest. Then she looked over at the man who was about to go free. He seemed too surprised to smile. The prosecutor raised her eyebrows. Next case.

In the gun court, change was halting. One day in the spring of 2018, Debora Silberman scanned the file of a new client and recognized the name of the cop who'd made the arrest. The New York *Daily News* had just run an article about him—he'd been sued twenty-three times for bursting into people's homes, costing the city $280,000 in settlement payments. Silberman asked the line prosecutor how the D.A.'s office could continue to rely on this cop. A few days later, the gun charges against her client were dropped without explanation. "The disheartening question is how my client could be arrested in the first place by this officer," Silberman said. "Our clients' civil liberties can be curtailed for jaywalking, but when an officer repeatedly engages in misconduct and even breaks the law, the system looks the other way." The same thing happened again a few months later: Same cop, charges against three defendants dropped, and still no admission of a problem from the D.A.'s office.

At the same time, Silberman and other defense lawyers were getting better offers for their clients. Taking into account the high number of dismissals (and small but telling share of acquittals), about 30 percent of defendants arraigned on felony gun charges in Brooklyn went to jail or prison in 2017. In the D.A.'s office, Teitelman told me she was responding to the defense lawyers' stepped-up efforts to lay out for her why their clients deserved a second chance. But for most of Gonzalez's first year in office, YCP and Project Redirect didn't seem to be a priority for him. When social workers like Maksim Kreyngold succeeded in helping their clients, they often seemed to do so in spite of their boss, the chief of youth diversion for the D.A's office, who would come to court to personally demand jail time for participants who were arrested on minor charges or who displeased him.

Then in November 2018, the chief of youth diversion put an ankle monitor on a YCP participant, M., who'd been rearrested for a misdemeanor assault a few weeks before he was scheduled to graduate from YCP with a stellar record. (I'm using M.'s first initial to protect his privacy.) He'd completed a college-level course at The New School and spoken on panels about youth incarceration at other New York universities. Kreyngold objected to the monitor; he thought it was unwarranted and cruel.

At M.s' next court appearance, his Legal Aid lawyer, Roy Wasserman, protested. Arguing that the D.A.'s office had no authority to make M. wear the monitor, Wasserman showed the judge, Joanne Quinones, the contract M. had signed to be admitted to YCP. It said nothing about electronic monitoring. Quinones asked to see the chief of youth diversion, and when he arrived, she gave him a remarkable dressing down. The D.A's office had infringed on M.'s constitutional right to liberty, Quinones said. "I'm very concerned about this," she continued. "It's serious." She ordered the ankle bracelet removed immediately.

The chief of youth diversion still had the power to fail M. out of YCP, and for a moment, he seemed ready to use it. M. would then have to serve the entire prison sentence he'd received nine months earlier, for his guilty plea to gun possession and burglary charges. "He'd do three and a half years," Pichardo said. In the back of the courtroom, M.'s grandmother gasped.

In the end, the chief backed down, and M. went home free of his ankle monitor, relieved though also upset at how he'd been treated. Soon after, Gonzalez appointed a new chief of youth diversion. The D.A.'s office asked Mark Kleiman, the NYU professor who'd studied the HOPE project in Hawaii, to help redesign and expand YCP and Project Redirect. It would take time to know what all of this would yield. But the goal, Gonzalez said, was to create the conditions for a turning point in people's lives.

In Philadelphia, Larry Krasner was trying to solve a difficult problem of transparency. It involved disclosing particularly sensitive evidence: the personnel records of cops who'd lied on the job.

When Krasner took office, a leak to the press revealed the existence of a secret list created by the previous D.A. The list reportedly contained the names of dozens of cops deemed to be potentially unreliable witnesses, because they had a history of bias, being under federal investigation, using excessive force, violating someone's civil rights, lying on duty, or giving false testimony ("testilying," as it's called).

Krasner's team searched the office filing cabinets and found a large brown folder with a typewritten label, "Damaged Goods." Inside were the names of more potentially compromised police officers. The lawyers pulled all the relevant files they could find and moved them to a locked room on the 17½ floor, a tucked-away space with low ceilings and no windows. Over the next several weeks, they read through the files to make their own list, based on their assessments of whether an officer had committed serious misconduct.

A defense lawyer could use a finding that a cop had lied on duty to argue to the jury that he or she couldn't be trusted on the stand. Did that make the police personnel files on the 17½ floor Brady material, which had to be disclosed? The Supreme Court has never addressed this question, even though evidence that a cop has lied or committed other misdeeds "can mean the difference between acquittal and conviction, between life and death," as the lawyer Jonathan Abel observed in a 2015 *Stanford Law Review* article, titled "*Brady*'s Blind Spot."

Opening up police personnel records can cost some officers their livelihoods. If their past wrongs suggest they shouldn't be called as witnesses, why are they on the beat? In some states, defense lawyers have access to police personnel files. In others, police unions have fought successfully for laws that sealed them. New York has one of the strictest secrecy laws in the country. In March 2018, *BuzzFeed*

News was leaked five years of disciplinary records and reported that more than three hundred NYPD officers kept their jobs after committing "offenses serious enough to merit firing." *BuzzFeed* made the records public. Talk of changing the secrecy law still went nowhere.

In Philadelphia, Krasner wanted a new, carefully vetted database of cops with a record of serious misconduct, as well as a policy for disclosing their records to the defense and for dealing with past convictions that might be tainted. He tapped the head of the conviction integrity unit, Patricia Cummings, for the project. She came from Texas, where D.A.'s offices in Dallas, Fort Worth, and Houston had taken steps to disclose past police misconduct. Cummings collected policies from these cities and others. "We were hoping to get more buy-in from the police, and we wanted to show them we weren't crazy," she said.

Cummings settled on requiring disclosure if a police officer had a record of not being truthful on the job (for example, falsifying information in a police report or on the witness stand), committing a civil rights violation, or using excessive force. She wanted to make sure every line prosecutor handling a case involving a cop who'd been flagged knew about his or her record at the outset. Some cities kept a "do not call" list (as in do not call these cops to testify), which prosecutors were expected to check before trial. In the many cases that ended in guilty pleas, however, a police officer's dubious record was never exposed. Cummings was intent on doing more. Working with the IT staff, she and her team developed an alert system. When a prosecutor charged a case and entered it into the computer network, an alert would pop up if the arresting officer had been flagged. If the alert said the cop had a record of lying, the prosecutor was instructed that he or she probably shouldn't testify. If the alert noted an infraction like drunk driving, the prosecutor could put the officer on the stand but was obligated to disclose the information to the defense at the first court appearance.

When I talked to Cummings, about a hundred officers were in

the database, out of about sixty-three hundred cops in the city—and the police were balking at giving the D.A.'s office more personnel files to review. Krasner's quest for transparency was in danger because the police didn't trust him. They were learning how risky it was to be on the receiving end of prosecutorial power.

In November, the Fraternal Order of Police sued Krasner, the mayor, and the police commissioner over the database, saying they were damaging the reputations of individual cops without a fair process. Krasner's response was to hit back by asking for the personnel files of 4,500 more officers.

Krasner also pressed Philadelphia's mayor Jim Kenney. In the summer of 2018, protesters set up an encampment outside the downtown office of Immigration and Customs Enforcement to challenge the renewal of a contract with the city that gave ICE access to the city's database for tracking criminal cases (called the Preliminary Arraignment Reporting System, or PARS). The PARS contract was due to expire at the end of August, and Krasner had a say in whether to renew it, as did the mayor. In mid-July, before Mayor Kenney took a position, Krasner announced that he had no intention of signing a new contract with ICE. "The monster we have in the White House says we won't let you have 1.6 million bucks, which is money that would otherwise go to the city," Krasner said in an interview with NBC. He argued that it was worth giving up the funding to ensure that immigrants trusted the police enough to report crimes and serve as witnesses. Krasner added, "We know that most of the time the people getting deported have not been convicted."

Two weeks later, Mayor Kenney said the contract was off.

By the end of 2018, the jail population in Philadelphia was at its lowest point in more than a quarter century. The number of people being held because they couldn't afford bail had fallen and so had the number held for violating probation and parole.

In the courts, however, Krasner faced his share of setbacks. Some local judges didn't agree with his approach and found ways to blunt it. In October 2018, the Pennsylvania Supreme Court sided with a Philadelphia judge who refused to toss out a death sentence that Krasner said was tainted by the substandard performance of the defendant's lawyer at his 2005 trial. Krasner's office argued that only district attorneys, with their "wide grant of prosecutorial discretion," had the power to decide whether to "continue to seek the death penalty." By a vote of 6 to 1, the state supreme court justices (five of whom were Democratic appointees) said that until a verdict was reached, Krasner was right, but afterward, he was wrong. "We note that the Philadelphia District Attorney's Office, through the exercise of its prosecutorial discretion, actively sought and obtained a death sentence," the court wrote. "It cannot now seek to implement a different result based upon the differing views of the current office holder." Otherwise, "every conviction and sentence would remain constantly in flux, subject to reconsideration based upon the changing tides of the election cycles." Krasner could not undo the verdicts and sentences of the past without a court's approval.

In other cities, local officials also dug in against change. In the year after a federal judge found the bail system for misdemeanors unconstitutional in Harris County (in and around Houston), fourteen county judges (all Republicans) spent nearly $7 million of taxpayer money appealing the ruling. For the most part, the appeal failed, but bail reform hit a rough patch anyway. The county judges started granting low cash bonds to higher-risk defendants (with criminal histories and a record of failing to appear in court), releasing them without supervision or reminders to return to court. "It's like when you want something to fail," the lone Democratic misdemeanor judge protested. "Bail is being politicized, leaving practitioners caught in the middle," Kim Ogg, the new D.A. who'd sided with the plaintiffs in the lawsuit, told me. "That's us and the defense lawyers."

For a time, it looked as if the resistance to bail reform would derail it. The number of missed court appearances shot up. The system appeared to teeter on the edge of chaos. Then the November 2018 elections rolled around. All the judges who'd sued to stop bail reform lost, in a sweep that took out every Republican judge in Harris County. The lesson was sinking in: Standing in the way of criminal-justice reform could be politically dangerous.

As I followed the ups and downs of the new D.A.s, it was easy to forget about all the proseutors who still followed the traditional playbook. But my reporting on Amy Weirich in Memphis reminded me.

In August 2017, I published a story about Noura's case in the *New York Times Magazine*. Weirich's response was Trumpian—she turned on the press, which meant me. She said I'd written the piece "to push an agenda of pro-crime, anti-police, anti-prosecutors," and she used her office Twitter account to fire off a series of posts with the hashtag #ProCrimeNYTimes. Weirich's social media campaign didn't go anywhere, but it made me wonder anew about what motivated her. When I talked to people in Memphis who liked and respected her, they said she prized her professional reputation, saw herself as an advocate for victims, and put loyalty to colleagues above cleaning house. I could understand all of that but only from a distance. The single time I interviewed Weirich, she insisted on doing it over the phone rather than in person, sounded guarded and impatient, and stuck to sound bites. I came away with little insight. I tried to talk to her again, but I didn't get anywhere.

In fall 2018, Weirich tried to reposition herself. She announced an event to expunge minor criminal records and restore drivers' licenses to people who'd lost them because they owed court fees. Hundreds began showing up early in the morning at a Baptist church in Memphis, forming a line that wrapped around the block. Most left disappointed. "It was basically printing off the paperwork you owe," one man told the local press. "At least they are trying to address the need," said Josh Spickler, executive director of Just City, a local criminal justice reform group. "But only a few people are served and everyone goes away angry," In an op-ed in the *Daily Memphian* that December, Weirich wrote, "I have never considered putting people in jail as the central part of my job description." Yet Memphis continued to have a far higher rate of incarceration than other cities of its size and composition. "The jail population for Shelby County is higher than anytime in recent memory," Spickler told me, "and the primary driver is length of stay, which is longer than ever because of the extremely punitive plea offers from her office."

In December, Sandra Simkins, the federal monitor for the juvenile court, released her final report. The Trump administration had abruptly terminated the Justice Department's oversight in Shelby County, so this was Simkins's last chance to weigh in. She came down hard on Weirich's office for its part in the juvenile court's continuing "blatantly unfair" practices. Prosecutors continued to demand the transfer of cases to adult court, Simkins found, without turning over evidence. Since Weirich's 2014 election, the number of juvenile cases transferred each year had nearly doubled, from forty-seven to ninety-two. Eighty of those ninety-two teenagers were African American. "The combination of prosecutorial gamesmanship and the prosecutor's refusal to provide discovery (in contrast to all other Tennessee Counties), is a toxic combination for African-American youth," Simkins wrote. Weirich responded by saying that Simkins was "absolutely wrong." Restyling herself in a newspaper op-ed, it seemed, didn't mean rethinking her hardball tactics.

Weirich was also contending with rising discontent in her office. She irritated some of her staff when she told an assistant D.A. to leave the courthouse because her skirt was too short, and then followed up with an office-wide memo about proper skirt length and shoe style. When women protested that they were being singled out,

Weirich sent a second memo requiring men to keep their ties knotted and forbidding all staff from using earbuds at their desks. Feeling micromanaged and belittled, line prosecutors eyed the exits. When a single position opened up at the U.S. attorney's office in Memphis, more than two dozen Shelby County assistant D.A.s applied for it.

The continuing presence of Stephen Jones also bothered Shelby County prosecutors who wanted the office to raise its ethical standards. After Stephen Jones's trial, the Tennessee Board of Professional Responsibility issued an opinion to clarify the rule obligating prosecutors to disclose all the evidence they have that "tends to negate the guilt of the accused or mitigates the offense." Quoting a 2009 ethics opinion by the American Bar Association, the board said prosecutors had an ethical obligation to turn over evidence as soon as they reasonably could—not only if they decided it was material but, more broadly, "so that the defense can decide on its utility."

The Tennessee board opinion gave Noura some solace. Maybe the next prosecutors who withheld evidence wouldn't get away with it. Before the new ethics standard was finalized, however, all but one of Tennessee's thirty-one elected prosecutors (including Weirich) wrote a letter to the board denouncing the rule. They called it a "trap" and a "Pandora's box." Using Supreme Court Justice Robert Jackson's canonical words about the high calling of prosecutors, they argued that the best protection against abuse of power is a prosecutor's "sensitiveness to fair play and sportsmanship."

In other words, trust prosecutors to be their own watchdogs. It was a stunning argument coming from a group that used the threat of criminal penalties to induce good behavior. The Tennessee D.A.s were making an argument—*trust us to police ourselves*—they would never have accepted from defendants.

In New York that summer, state lawmakers made a bold move to force more accountability on prosecutors. In June 2018, the legislature established the first-ever independent state commission on prosecutorial misconduct. The commission had the power to issue subpoenas, hold hearings, and recommend that prosecutors be censured or fired. Perhaps the best evidence that a commission was needed came from an investigation by the media organization ProPublica, which looked at ten years of appeals, identifying thirty cases in which judges found that New York City prosecutors committed misconduct serious enough to require a new trial. Only one of these prosecutors was dismissed, demoted, or sanctioned in any way. Several got raises and promotions.

The New York District Attorneys Association lobbied hard to stop the misconduct commission, threatening to sue and to boycott it. Gonzalez stayed out of the fight until a few days before the deadline for Governor Andrew Cuomo to sign the bill, when his spokesman tweeted, offhand, that the office opposed it. I had trouble squaring this position with Gonzalez's bid to be a national leader for reform. The commission had the potential to serve as a new model for holding prosecutors accountable.

When I talked to Gonzalez over the phone a week after Cuomo signed the bill, he was waiting for amendments the governor had promised. Principally, Gonzalez wanted the commission to refrain from addressing complaints about a prosecutor while a case was pending so that it couldn't be used as a tool for chilling investigations, a change the governor promised to make. "Privately, I've already told some of the other D.A.s that once it's fixed, I'll do my part to make it successful," he said. "A lot of prosecutors don't want to hear that there should be additional oversight, but for me it comes back to the perception that people are not treated fairly in our criminal justice system. Our system depends on people believing that it is fair and just. Having this form of oversight will strengthen their belief in the system, so it's important for the commission to succeed."

Gonzalez hadn't jumped out in front of a contentious political fight. He might never be the guy to do that. ("I'm a deliberative type of person, in case you hadn't noticed," he told me.) Krasner, by contrast, kept being that guy. In November 2018, he quit the Pennsylvania D.A.s Association, taking 30 percent of its budget with him and making a remarkably pointed statement about the politics of incarceration across the urban-rural divide. "We have a motivated bunch of rural counties—motivated—who want to have our Philadelphians, often black and brown Philadelphians, in their jails," he said in a speech about why he was leaving. "Because it gives them power, it gives them money."

As I was finishing this book, I made a list of cities and counties where the D.A. was taking steps to reduce incarceration and make the system more just. The reform movement suffered setbacks at the polls in the 2018 primaries, as progressive candidates lost in Las Vegas, Sacramento, and San Diego. But in November, a slew of others won, in Boston, Western Massachusetts, Durham, Birmingham, Dallas, San Antonio, Contra Costa County, and St. Louis County, home of Ferguson. Adding to my list, I found that about 40 million Americans, more than 12 percent of the population, lived in a city or county with a D.A. who I thought could be considered a reformer, even if progress was just beginning.

There were surely other D.A.s, in smaller cities and rural places, who I could have included but didn't know about. They mattered, especially because it was in rural America, not major metropolitan areas, where the jail population was still rising. Because of past harsh practices in cities, black and Latino communities still bore the brunt of injustice and overpunishment, but mostly white areas were burdened, too.

In my reporting, I met small-town prosecutors who had scant resources, but a distinctive advantage—they could get to know defendants over time.

Cassie Devine has been a prosecutor in Nashua, New Hampshire, for thirty years. She grew up nearby, in Manchester. When Devine's three children were young, she took an assignment in the juvenile court so she could be home when they got out of school.

Jesus Cortes Rodriguez was twelve—a couple of years younger than her third son—when he came across Devine's desk for the first time for breaking some windows at a local middle school. He stood out to her because he seemed to have no guile. When the police showed up at his door, he admitted what he'd done.

Nashua was an old mill town of eighty-five thousand without much serious crime. If you were a repeat offender, you got to know the police and the prosecutors, and they got to know you. Over the next few years, Jesus got arrested repeatedly for fighting and then for selling drugs. The appeal of a local gang blotted out everything else. "I came from a strong family, and we loved each other, but for me to do good was embarrassing," Jesus said. "Doing wrong, that was more thrilling and cool." To prove himself, Jesus stabbed and beat people from a rival gang, then took a beating from his own gang as a hazing ritual.

Devine switched to adult court around the time Jesus turned eighteen. Files with his name on them kept reaching her desk. He'd grown tall and lanky, and the police knew him by his gang name, Stretch. Mostly he was getting picked up for small-time drug sales. But then came an accusation that he'd robbed another teenager over a drug buy and threatened him with a machete. "Someone owed me money when I was on drugs. My friend showed up with a machete, and I took the machete and said, 'Now give me all the fucking money.'"

Devine weighed the fact that Jesus was accused of holding the machete up outside a car window, not against the victim's neck. She decided to drop from felony charges down to a pair of misdemeanors—she had the discretion—and agreed to a six-month jail sentence followed by probation. She hoped that Jesus would benefit from supervision. "She had me in the system and I got put on probation, and she had a closer eye on me," Jesus said. "The thing I remember she said when I pled guilty and got sentenced was about my friend who I'd grown up with. She'd just gotten him five to ten years in prison, and I clearly remember her saying, 'You see what I'm doing to him right now? This could be you if you don't change up your life.'"

Jail, threats, and supervision were the only tools Devine had at the time. New Hampshire was stingy about spending on drug treatment and mental health counseling, and that made the court system the place where struggling people landed. Devine knew that almost everyone who passed through the courthouse would come back if she urged the judge to send them away, but she also knew that if she took a chance on a defendant who turned around and hurt someone, she'd have that on her conscience. Her successes—people with significant records whose crimes abated—were rare.

Months after Jesus got out of prison, she had to add him to the failure column when he was arrested for possession of crack cocaine. At this point, he was nineteen. She yelled at him: she'd taken a chance on him and he'd blown it. He was shipped off to Berlin, hours away upstate, for two years in prison. Inside, he decided he wanted to get out of the gang. Leaving led to a fight with three gang members who slammed him against the concrete. His cheekbone was fractured and he got six stitches above his eye.

The beating was captured—twelve brutal minutes of it—by the prison's security cameras. Devine refused to watch the tape.

When Jesus got out, he didn't rejoin the gang, but he was still rearrested twice within a year, and the second time it was for intent to distribute cocaine and marijuana—his third set of drug charges as an adult. In New Hampshire, that meant real prison time: seven to fifteen years. Jesus was twenty-one and had a girlfriend, Arianna, who was three months pregnant. At his bail hearing, Devine told him he was doing a life sentence on an installment plan. These were the moments when she felt like her power was for naught.

In prison, Jesus had heard about a new drug court in New

Hampshire. In 2015, in response to the crushing toll of the opioid epidemic, the state began to route a small number of people caught with drugs to county drug courts, where instead of prison they got treatment, cognitive therapy, and help with education and housing. In exchange, they agreed to take drug tests, attend group meetings, comply with intensive monitoring, and perform hundreds of hours of community service. With their intensive demands, drug courts set many people up for failure, sometimes triggering longer sentences for those who struggle to stay in treatment. "I heard nothing good about it," Jesus said. "But I thought, 'I'm going to fuck up again.' I debated. I did want to see my son born. Drug court was a way for that to happen. I thought, 'I'll ask Cassie Devine.' I didn't think she'd accept me. But my attorney came back and said that Cassie agreed: 'She thinks you've got it this time.' "

Jesus didn't understand why. "I don't know what got into her head thinking to give me another chance. I was looking to play the system." He wondered if Devine saw something in him that he didn't. "She pretty much knew my whole life," he said. Now she was handing him an exit ticket. It made him think: was he ready to change?

Devine was actually more willing to take a chance on Jesus than she was confident he would come through. She'd sent three people to drug court who'd later died of overdoses, and she'd seen many others fail out. But Jesus passed his drug tests, went to his classes, satisfied all the conditions. Tracking his progress, Devine felt like this was her purpose. You could be a prosecutor for three decades and people could still surprise you.

I met Jesus in the spring of 2017, in the middle of his fourteen-month term in drug court. It was evening, and he'd just changed out of the work clothes he wore for the landscaping job he'd recently started. "Clean money, not fast money," he said. "Hardworking money." He and Arianna had a small studio apartment. She worked at the desk of a Radisson hotel, and they scheduled their hours so they could switch off taking care of their baby, Massiah. Jesus was also taking night classes at his old school to get a high school diploma. His graduation was coming up in June. He'd been asked to be the class speaker.

Six months later, Jesus graduated again, this time from drug court. Arianna dressed Massiah in an outfit that matched his father's: navy pants and a blue button-down shirt with a gray vest. Jesus was one of eight drug court graduates, bringing the total in Nashua to just thirty-two over three years. When Jesus's name was called, last among the graduates, Devine walked to the podium. She was the person he'd chosen to speak on his behalf and the only prosecutor in the room. In a simple black suit, with a pair of glasses perched on top of her head, Devine said, "I have a long history with Jesus, but when you're in my line of work, that's not something anyone wants to hear." She sketched his path from juvenile court to prison. She talked of her frustration when he got out of the gang and prison, only to boomerang back in. She shook her head. "I would wave my mother finger at him and he just didn't listen."

Jesus leaned forward, listening now. "I've been a prosecutor for thirty years," Devine said. "I've seen a lot of horrible things. Today is one of the happiest days of my life."

In her first decade on the Supreme Court, Justice Sonia Sotomayor became its fiercest voice for people, like the ones in this book, who are suspected of or charged with crimes. She proved herself, again and again, to be a tireless protector of our basic rights. In one unforgettable dissenting opinion in 2016, *Utah v. Strieff*, she described just how much those rights are at risk of being snuffed out, first for people whom police and prosecutors view with distrust, and then for the rest of us.

Utah v. Strieff involved an illegal police stop. In December 2006, the Salt Lake City police got an anonymous tip that a house was being used for drug sales. An officer watched the house for a few hours and saw more people going in and out than he thought was typical. One of those people was a man named Edward Strieff. The officer stopped Strieff on his way out of the house (without seeing him go in or knowing how long he was inside), ran his license, and discovered he had an outstanding warrant for a minor traffic violation. The officer arrested Strieff, searched him, and found a baggie of methamphetamine.

The prosecution conceded that seeing Strieff come out of the house wasn't a sufficient basis for stopping him. But the trial court ruled that the drug evidence could be admitted against him anyway, saying the officer made a "good-faith mistake." The Supreme Court agreed, by a vote of five to three. The officer's discovery of the warrant for the traffic violation, Justice Clarence Thomas said, made up for the problem with the stop. Dissenting, Sotomayor wrote of the majority's decision:

> It says that your body is subject to invasion while courts excuse the violation of your rights. It implies that you are not a citizen of a democracy but the subject of a carceral state, just waiting to be cataloged. We must not pretend that the countless people who are routinely targeted by police are "isolated." They are the canaries in the coalmine whose deaths, civil and literal, warn us that no one can breathe in this atmosphere.

Sotomayor grew up in a housing project in the Bronx. In her first job out of law school, she worked as a prosecutor in the Manhattan D.A.'s office. She took the position, she told a packed auditorium at Yale Law School in the spring of 2017, because Robert Morgenthau, the legendary district attorney of Manhattan, said he could offer her "the opportunity to do more good for more people than anyone else."

Sotomayor spent five years in Morgenthau's office. At Yale, she said two things that were in tension with each other about the experience: she loved the job, and yet over time, being a prosecutor taught her that the criminal justice system "accomplishes nothing we think of as its purpose," Sotomayor told her audience. "We think we're keeping people safe from criminals. We're just making worse criminals."

We think we're keeping people safe. We're just making worse criminals. Sotomayor summed up how the criminal justice system continues to operate in most of the country. The bipartisan reform movement is about tearing down that kind of system. What comes next has to make the law of more value to the people it touches directly. Witnesses and victims often come from the same neighborhoods as the perpetrators and sometimes *are the same people.* They have to trust police and prosecutors in order to help them solve crimes. The system we should rebuild is one in which justice and mercy reinforce each other, in which success is measured by fortifying communities, not by putting people away in demand of an eye for an eye. Keeping people safe means making fewer criminals, and fairness is essential to that equation.

We can make incremental progress if we stop doing the stupid stuff, like weighing people down with court dates and convictions for smoking weed or playing dice or jumping a turnstile. (If it's a good idea to arrest poor people for not paying their subway fare, why don't we do the same thing to middle-class and wealthy drivers who blow through E-ZPass toll stations?) We won't get where the country needs to go, though, until we rethink the harder cases, too. Guns are dangerous, and when young people feel the need to carry them in neighborhoods like Brownsville, it's a warning sign: something is wrong. But that something is a lot more complicated than casting out the "evildoers" who carry pistols. Getting guns off the streets makes for a good slogan for city leaders, a seemingly unassailable political goal in the context of gun control. It's harder to help people than to lock them up. It's also almost always, in the end, far more pragmatic and worthwhile.

The movement to elect a new kind of prosecutor is the most promising means of reform I see on the political landscape. That doesn't make it a panacea. In her forthcoming book *Prisoners of*

Politics, Rachel Barkow argues that serious criminal justice reform means minimizing the role of politics and elections in crime policy, not playing the political game differently. She fears the reform movement could fizzle, especially if crime rises. I think and hope otherwise, and this book shows why, but it's a risk worth acknowledging.

Another challenge for the movement is figuring out how demanding to be. In reporting on D.A.s from Eric Gonzalez to Kim Ogg to Kim Foxx to Larry Krasner, I've mapped the variations from evolution to revolution. It's a mistake, I think, for reformers to impose a purity test. It's the job of activists, however, to have high aspirations and to be impatient.

The movement for prosecutorial reform can't just install new D.A.s and count on them to do the job differently. Some activists talk about co-governing. They mean taking part in policy discussions and also watching in court and tracking data for the outcomes they care about. When D.A.'s offices operate as a black box, cloaking the exercise of discretion, they weaken the social compact. Revelations of wrongful convictions and concealed evidence are so unsettling because they show the government wielding its raw power in ways we usually cannot see. Prosecutors have to commit themselves to performance measures like reducing incarceration, racial disparity, the rate of reoffending, and findings of misconduct. They have to commit to increasing community satisfaction with local justice—and then show how they score.

By focusing on prosecutors in this book, I've risked giving short shrift to all the other actors who determine the fates of people caught up in the system—lawmakers, judges, defense lawyers, cops, prison officials and guards, probation and parole officers. I hope I've shown, though, that how they do their jobs matters. It can mean everything to have a lawyer like Debora Silberman, a social worker like Maksim Kreyngold, or a prison volunteer like Pat Culp in your corner. At the same time, a prosecutor like Amy Weirich can destroy a life, especially if a judge like Chris Craft waves off her errors. The Supreme Court has taken wrong turns by letting prosecutors withhold evidence they should share and allowing them to impose plea bargains that are not freely bargained for. Perhaps most of all, the Court is to blame for creating the conditions for prosecutorial impunity. And the legal profession is at fault for fostering it. The leniency that prosecutors have demanded and received from state disciplinary committees is a breathtaking departure from the exacting standards that prosecutors too often impose on the rest of us.

The legislative branch has a major role to play in criminal justice reform. State lawmakers have begun charting a way forward—in Kentucky and New Jersey on bail reform, in Texas and North Carolina on open-file discovery, in Illinois in rejecting mandatory minimum sentences for gun possession, and in New York in creating the first-ever commission on prosecutorial misconduct. At the end of 2018, Congress joined them by passing a package of sentencing reductions and improvements to prison conditions. The bill, called the First Step Act, affected a small number of the relatively small share of federal cases. But it was the product of a bipartisan push from the ground up, and if the new law lives up to its name—if it's the first step to something greater—then it matters more than its size.

The criminal justice system is ungainly and massive, and rerouting it is like turning an ocean liner. It's a behemoth, at once mighty and monstrous. There is much steam built up to keep it going along its current course, and many levers to pull to steer it in a different direction. Somewhere along the way, the balance of power between the prosecution, the defense, and the judiciary shifted. We have to readjust it. The stakes are so high—the well-being of so many communities and the trajectory of so many lives. Public safety depends on our collective faith in fairness and our view of the law as legitimate.

As a journalist, I've never felt a greater sense of urgency about exposing the roots of a problem and shining a light on the people working to solve it. I feel a great sense of possibility. We have to fix the broken parts of America's criminal justice system. And we the people have the power to do it, with our votes.

EPILOGUE

IN SEPTEMBER 2017, Noura flew from Nashville to New York to tape an episode of a podcast called *Wrongful Conviction*. She was nervous about the interview and asked me to come with her to the studio. The host, Jason Flom, greeted her in a black Guns N' Roses T-shirt, black jeans, and black-framed glasses. He told Noura he was a founding member of the board of the Innocence Project. He didn't mention it, but he was also a mega-successful music executive who could take credit for launching Kid Rock, Lorde, and Katy Perry.

Flom, who was fifty-six, usually interviewed people who'd been formally exonerated, but since the Innocence Project was representing Noura, he'd made an exception. He put her at ease by taking for granted that she was telling the truth. "This story just really shocked my conscience, and you lived through it," he said to her a couple of minutes into the taping.

"Unfortunately, yeah," she answered. "There were times when I didn't know if I would make it to the other side." I could hear the relief in her voice: this was different from talking to a reporter, trained to ask skeptical questions. Flom was fully in her corner. They talked for more than two hours.

Afterward, Flom left the studio with us. When we walked past the entrance to the Broadway theater where the musical *Hamilton* was playing, Noura stopped to ask about the show, and Flom offered to get her tickets. When she went home to Nashville, they started talking on the phone. He brought her back to New York that winter for job interviews at a few nonprofit groups that worked on criminal justice reform. She didn't get a position, but Flom, who has helped several exonerees get on their feet, encouraged her to move to New York anyway, and keep looking for a job or go to college. Noura would have to leave the job she had, at a small company in Nashville that sold granite countertops. She worried about giving it up—it had taken her months to find—and about leaving her girlfriend and extended family.

But Flom's consistent presence, in one phone call and text after another, made Noura think she could trust him. Moving to New York was a chance to get out of the place where she could always meet someone who'd seen her face on TV, stamped guilty for murder. She could forge a new identity and a life she'd never otherwise have. Being in New York reminded her of her mother and the weekend trip they'd taken to the Plaza Hotel when she was sixteen. Her mom had talked dreamily about living on a sailboat in the harbor and working on Wall Street. Flom said he would pay Noura's rent and future tuition and support her until she got on her feet. On her next visit to New York, Flom came through with the tickets to *Hamilton*. She decided to take him up on his big offer, to take the chance.

At the end of February, Flom threw a joint birthday party for himself and Noura at a pool and ping-pong hall near Gramercy Park. Lawyers and interns from the Innocence Project, along with some of their exonerated clients, mixed with employees from Flom's company, Lava Records, and other people from the music industry.

Flom's twenty-three-year-old daughter and eighteen-year-old son were there, hugging Noura and introducing her to friends.

Noura and I went to visit a few colleges the next day. She was anxious about venturing back to the classroom, in her early thirties and with a prison-issue GED. As we walked over the glass-windowed bridge above Lexington Avenue that links the buildings of Hunter College and into a space outside the library, Noura stopped at the tables where student groups advertise events. She queried the students about their academic credentials. "Did you get As in high school? What did you get on the SAT?" she asked. "Do you think I'm smart enough to go here?"

Looking for an apartment, Noura didn't know the city well enough to prefer a particular location, but she had two strong desires. She wanted to live by herself, no matter if that meant renting a tiny studio. After all the years in prison with cellmates and without privacy, she craved a space of her own. She also wanted the security of a doorman. Her fear that a stranger could break in, vivid since her mother's death, remained strong. She and Flom found a building in Brooklyn she loved, with a one-bedroom apartment that even had a small balcony. In April, she and her girlfriend drove her belongings from Nashville to New York. They had a rocky parting, and afterward, sitting among piles of boxes, Noura felt overwhelmed and alone. "I'd been surrounded by this big noisy family in Nashville, and I felt important to them, and in New York I was just one person in a million." Then she heard the buzzer for the entry door and let in a guy who'd come to install her flat-screen TV. It had broken on the journey, but he said he'd help her get a new one. They talked for hours, and he invited her to dinner and for a private visit at the Metropolitan Museum of Art, where his wife worked. She could find kindness in the city.

A few days later, I stopped by Noura's apartment and we got out her laptop and scrolled through the options to sign up for health insurance. She was determined to find good medical care for the first time since her arrest. Once she had insurance, she navigated her way to a specialist who could treat her endometriosis. At her first appointment, she learned that she needed major surgery. She scheduled it for the first available date, at the end of July.

In May, Noura and Flom spoke at a summit called the Business of Equality held at the headquarters of Bloomberg, the media company. They talked about mass incarceration and the courage and resilience of people who are mistreated by the criminal justice system. Also on the program were Chelsea Clinton, the designer Diane von Furstenberg, and the actress Ashley Judd. The next evening, she had a benefit to go to for the Innocence Project. It was a gala, so Flom gave her money to buy an outfit. She went to Bloomingdale's, where she found a black silk gown and crocheted cardigan. Just before closing time, she asked the saleswoman to help her find a pair of black heels in her size. As they waited for a clerk to bring the shoes from another floor, the lights started to go out. No one else was left in their part of the store. The saleswoman hurried to ring up the dress and the cardigan and directed Noura to a staff exit, but when she got out of the elevator, she couldn't remember which way to go. She went back to the floor where she'd been. It was dark and empty. She took the elevator to the ground floor and tried to get out through the front doors, but they were locked. She called Flom, who told her to call the police. But what if they looked up her criminal record, and arrested her for being where she wasn't supposed to be?

Noura had people who loved her, and a silk gown in her shopping bag, but she couldn't shed the sense that she would always be a convicted felon, an object of suspicion, a pariah. She felt panicked and terrified. She ran back into the store, found an emergency exit, and pushed open the door. The shrill sound of a fire alarm filled her ears and her head. She stepped onto the pavement and took off running.

That June, Kevin's mother flew to Atlanta to visit cousins. She posted pictures on Snapchat of the flight—the first of her life. The visit stretched on for more than a month, and though she hadn't quit her job, it wasn't clear when she would return. Her relatives had a spacious house with an arcade room. "I don't know if they're semi-rich," Kevin said. "But my mother told me if I wanted to come, I could."

In some ways, the timing seemed perfect. Kevin had quit his job inspecting overseas packages after an argument with his supervisor. He was still seeing his girlfriend but didn't see why that should keep him from traveling. He was still trying to decide what to do next: get his GED and take community college classes, find a new job, get out of Brownsville? He'd only gone out of the state twice, once to Ohio with the CASES program and once to a water park in Virginia with his family when he was younger. Leaving for an extended period, or even for good, was a fantasy of safety and freedom. "I could go anywhere I want without watching over my shoulder. Go and come as I please." Still, he hesitated. He didn't know these cousins and they didn't know him. "To my mother, I'll be like, 'All right, I'm gonna come,'" he said. "But then I'll be skeptical about going down there."

Besides, he liked having the apartment mostly to himself. His brother was in and out, off to a basketball program one week and then barely home the next. His sister and his niece came to visit from Harlem but didn't stay long. It felt like a step up to Kevin. "I know how to live by myself," he said. "I know how to pay the rent and all that." He sounded older than when we'd met two years earlier, thoughtful and aware but also feeling his way forward and having a hard time planning. He'd gotten his learner's permit and was ready to take the road test for his license, but then he lost the permit and didn't replace it.

One night while his mother was away, after Kevin went to sleep, he heard banging and people shouting, "Police! Police! Police!" The cops broke down the door. The first one who came into Kevin's room flashed his shield, and another one behind him had a rifle. "Get on the floor!" he yelled. "Get on the floor!" Kevin obeyed.

"Put your hands on your back." He did that, too. The officers hand-cuffed him in his own room. They said they had a search warrant because the NYPD had been told that Kevin had guns in the house. That was all it took—one informant.

The officers sat Kevin in a chair, still handcuffed, while they tore through his room. The bed, flipped upside down. The dresser draw-ers, tossed onto the floor. The closet, emptied. No gun. When the cops finished, they moved to every other room of the house. His mother's room, turned inside out. His niece's room, toys thrown everywhere. The bathroom. The kitchen. The police rifled through everything.

Kevin tried to tell them there was nothing to find. "I said, 'I'm not trying to hide no guns in here. First of all, my niece be coming back and forth. Second of all, that's never on my agenda to have guns inside my house.' They kept trying to scare me: 'Oh, we'll find something. We're gonna kick your mom out of her housing.'"

Before they left, the police said something else, too: they men-tioned his prior record—the gun charge—and Ceasefire, the police- and prosecutor-driven effort to target people suspected of being connected to gang-related violence for extra measures of enforce-ment. It seemed to mean nothing that Kevin's indictment had been dismissed and was supposed to be sealed. The police clearly knew about it. ("We get lists of people we're supposed to seal, but pulling them all up in the data system isn't easy because of how bad the court data is," an official in the NYPD told me.) Kevin was also likely still on a watch list at the D.A.'s office.

Kevin's understanding was that there were forty people on his side of Brownsville identified by Ceasefire and another forty from the other side. His description of the consequences of being on the list matched the city's threats about coming down hard on minor offenses. "If a shooting happened, they could come up and take us in for questioning if they want to," he said. "It's like we're all on punishment. You can't chill in the park. They told us if they catch us jaywalking, smoking weed, if we're sitting on the park bench the wrong way, like on top of it with my feet on the seat, I could get arrested for that."

When I talked with police and prosecutors about Ceasefire, they thought Kevin must have done something else to get onto the list. Did he hang out regularly with a gang or a crew that had been involved in a recent shooting?

It was a question about guilt by association. There had been an uptick in violence in Brownsville, as Kevin predicted the previous summer. Eleven murders in the year to date, up from six in the first half of 2017. Thirty-eight shooting victims, up from twenty-nine.

One of the shootings that summer took place at a cookout Kevin helped host to remember Travis, his best friend who'd died. People of all ages came, as many as a hundred. One of them opened fire. Kevin wasn't sure who or why. "I don't even know, man. Everybody coming from every different project. This project probably has a beef with that project."

Was this what got Kevin onto the Ceasefire list? No one he knew could say, and I don't know the answer either. But I can tell you that the police did not find a gun in his apartment.

Cleaning up the mess the cops made after they left, folding clothes and picking up toys and putting away food, Kevin thought about how his past was following him. "Of course I don't like it, but then what could I do about it?" he said. "So I just gotta separate myself more. Just keep going down the path I been going on." Kevin liked the image, the sense of forward movement. He could see himself striding down that path, even if he didn't know where it led.

Recovering from the surgery for her endometriosis over the summer, Noura mostly stayed home, appreciating the quiet of her apartment. She quit smoking, accomplishing one major goal. With Ansley's help, she made her place comfortable and personal, with a small elephant sculpture over a corner desk and a wall hanging of a delicate iron-grill gate. It helped remind her that wherever you go, a door can open. A picture of herself with her mother and her grandmother sat in a frame by the door. Noura made herself cups of hot chocolate in a small espresso maker and walked to get what she needed day to day. "The guy with good mangos has a cart down the block, and there's a food truck that the richest or the poorest person will eat from," she said. "I love how nobody belongs here. It's everybody's street or area and there's no wrong or right way to feel or act or dress or be."

Noura still wanted to go to school, and in November she applied to a community college, with the goal of transferring to a four-year school once she'd proved to herself she could handle the coursework. "I hope to study Public Affairs," she wrote in her application. "I really want to work in the field of Social Justice Advocacy. There is a strong need for the people in my chosen field to have a deep understanding of the intricacies of how criminal and social systems work together and against one another. I have that kind of experience." She ended, "If you'd asked me five years ago, I wouldn't have been able to tell you about the future I can now see." When she was accepted, she wrote me a thrilled email: "I GOT IN!!!!"

One day around the same time, she worked for hours on her case with her lawyer at the Innocence Project. Afterward, she couldn't stop thinking about it, out of hope but also guilt. "I feel it's selfish as hell of me in a way," she told me. "The people on the inside need the pardons."

Among all the people accused of crimes I've known, Noura had the most success at making people want to help her. She thought that race, class, and gender played in her favor, and so did I—no one was offering Kevin a fresh start. Noura only felt good about the position she'd come to be in when she imagined she could extend a lifeline to people like the ones she'd left behind in prison. She wanted to do more speaking engagements; she liked to feel she could touch people, and had a lot to say about how incarceration affects women and their families. She got the most animated about raising money for Pat Culp's prison ministry in Tennessee. She was full of ideas about how she could help, and she'd settled on organizing the best present she could think of for Winter Wonderland, the Christmastime event she'd planned and lived for in prison. She wanted to provide a bag with soap, shampoo, and conditioner to all twelve hundred women in the prison. It would all have to smell really good, to make you feel human and a little cared for. Each bag would have to be identical so that no one would fight or feel slighted.

Noura wanted to bring the bags in person, to be cleared to volunteer in the prison, to help Culp with her ministry—and maybe to take it over someday, when Culp was ready to retire. She wasn't sure she should dream about that. She had to make a life in New York, and she didn't know if she could ever get cleared to volunteer in a Tennessee prison. But she knew the women there and what they needed better than she knew anything else.

AUTHOR'S NOTE

This is a work of nonfiction. The characters and scenes depicted in it are real. To protect the person I call Kevin, at his request I've changed his name and the names of his friends and the police officer who arrested him. There are no other pseudonyms in the book.

Emily Berl took the photograph on the book's cover for a project on Coney Island. Her subject is a rapper who uses the professional name Charge G By Code. He can relate to Kevin's experiences with law enforcement. "All day, as a youth growing up, they just run you down and try to lock you up for no reason," he told me. Charge G works nights at a T.J. Maxx distribution center in Pennsylvania. "As a rapper, I like metaphors," he said. "In life, if you follow someone, you could fall off a bridge. But I try to build a bridge and cross over." Lately, Charge has focused on developing the talent of young people, whom he has helped feature in music showcases in Brooklyn, New Jersey, and Philadelphia. He also told me about his son, who is a few years younger than Kevin and grew up in Brooklyn. "He graduated high school in June, and he's going to Kingsborough Community College to study computers. He has already done things I couldn't do."

ACKNOWLEDGMENTS

I'm so grateful to work with Andy Ward, my amazingly thoughtful, astute, and deft editor, and Elyse Cheney, my fierce, caring, indomitable agent. At Random House, I also thank Susan Kamil, Tom Perry, Chayenne Skeete, Greg Kubie, Joe Perez, Maria Braeckel, Matthew Martin, Benjamin Dreyer, Barbara Fillon, Leigh Marchant, Susan Corcoran, Nancy Delia, and Erin Richards.

At the *New York Times Magazine,* I'm indebted to Jake Silverstein and Ilena Silverman for making everything I write better. Thank you to Rob Liguori and Cynthia Cotts for their expert research on Noura's story. I'm grateful to Harold Ko, Robert Post, and Heather Gerken for making Yale Law School my second work home for the past decade. Lincoln Caplan is the kind of mentor we should all aspire to be and great fun to teach a class with. I love taping *Slate*'s Political Gabfest with David Plotz and John Dickerson every week. Thank you also to our producer, Jocelyn Frank, and our researchers, Izzy Rode and Bridgette Dunlap.

Jack Hitt, Alvin Melathe, and Veralyn Williams have been fabulous to work with on developing a podcast related to this book. (It's also called Charged and follows stories from the Brooklyn gun court.) The appendix, "Twenty-One Principles for Twenty-First-Century Prosecutors," is the result of a collaboration with Miriam Krinsky, Lauren-Brooke Eisen, and Jake Sussman—I'm so glad I got to work with all of you.

New Haven, where I live, has a big supply of smart and generous people, and Beverly Gage, Kishwar Rizvi, Kica Matos, Jake Halpern, Myra Jones-Taylor, and Jenn Marlon have been stalwart and generous in their friendship and willingness to talk through the ideas in this book. So have Rachel Gross and James Sturm, from a distance. Judith Resnik, Reva Siegel, and Linda Greenhouse are my feminist godmothers. Paul Shechtman, Denny Curtis, Vanessa Grigoriadis, Deborah Rhode, Laura Fernandez, James Forman Jr., Rachel Barkow, Nicky Dawidoff, Dwayne Betts, Annie Paul, Daniel Markovits, Jessica Sager, MarQuel Horton Woods, Chloe Cockburn, Linc, Jake, Bev, Ilena, my parents, Rick and Eileen, and my husband, Paul, read the manuscript, in whole or in part, and gave me indispensable comments.

I've benefited from the wisdom and work of Angela J. Davis, Issa Kohler-Hausmann, John Pfaff, Nina Morrison, Adam Mansky, Insha Rahman, Nick Turner, Rob Smith, Udi Ofer, Jessica Brand, Josie Duffy Rice, Jessica Pishko, David Menschel, Radley Balko, Shaila Dewan, Rachel Barkow, Erin Murphy, David Sklansky, Ron Wright, Brandon Garrett, Mark Osler, Ellen Yaroshefsky, Bruce Green, Robert Sampson, Pat Sharkey, Nancy Gertner, Jeremy Travis, Bruce Western, Keith Findley, Alexandra Natapoff, Jed Handelsman Shugerman, Franklin Zimring, Paul Heaton, Tom Tyler, Tracey Meares, Jeff Fagan, Jed Rakoff, John Langbein, Carol Steiker, and the late William Stuntz. Thank you to Dan Kobil for the chance to give an early book talk at Capital University Law School and to Douglas Berman and Floyd Weatherspoon for their sharp and helpful responses. I appreciate immensely the talented students who helped me research this project—Nicole Narea, Maya Sweedler,

Kim Jackson, Steve Lance, Chris Haugh, Natalia Nazarewicz Friedlander, Laurel Raymond, David Alpert, Sam Breidbart, and Claire Saint-Amour. Brett Greene also fact-checked the manuscript with great care and dexterity.

While I was working on this book, my dear friend Shaneka Woods died in a sudden accident. She is often in my thoughts, and I'm thankful for the friendship of her giving and accomplished sisters, Alisha and Ashley Woods, and their extended family.

Books like this one are only possible because people tell writers their stories and answer their questions. It's a miracle of nonfiction that never ceases to move me. I'm grateful to every person who took the time to talk to me, and especially to Kevin and Noura for their time and trust. Thank you also to Kiki, Jesus Cortes Rodriguez, Darlene Farah, Cadeem Gibbs, and Octavia Cartwright. My reporting in Brooklyn was possible because of the help of Oren Yaniv, and in Memphis, I relied on the generosity of Ansley Larsson. Thank you to Julie Taylor for a crucial assist with my reporting in Brownsville and to Paige Sutherland for helping me out in New Hampshire.

I'm grateful past measure to my parents, Rick and Eileen, my sisters, Lara, Jill, and Dana, to Joel and Dave, and to my adopted in-law family, Jim, Margery, Michael, and Debbie. I still miss my grandparents: I hope they would feel that their values course through these pages. My husband, Paul, and our two sons, Eli and Simon, are the bedrock I build my life on. I love and depend on you more than I can say. Thank you so much for living through this book with me, and for your curiosity and ideas along the way.

APPENDIX

Twenty-One Principles for Twenty-First-Century Prosecutors

One day while I was working on this book, I had coffee with Miriam Krinsky, the executive director of Fair and Just Prosecution, at a hotel in midtown Manhattan. I think I drank decaf, but by the end of the hour, I couldn't sit still. We'd gotten together to hash out how exactly elected prosecutors could do their jobs differently. Talking to them and listening to them share ideas, what were we learning about what they could aspire to, so that they and their constituents knew they were on the right track? We decided to work together on a list of practical goals the D.A.s could set to transform their offices and, collectively, their profession. Miriam called it "the principles doc."

In the months that followed, we had added two collaborators: L. B. Eisen, a senior fellow at the Brennan Center's Justice Program, and Jake Sussman, managing director of the Justice Collaborative. We also enlisted the aid of a platoon of staff members and law students.

Once we had a draft, we presented it to the elected D.A.s connected with Fair and Just Prosecution, who gave us feedback. We also solicited helpful comments from academics and other experts. This appendix is the result of this collective enterprise. It's organized in two sections. The first is about reducing incarceration, and the second is about increasing fairness. We've included examples of innovative endeavors by prosecutors around the nation, not necessarily as endorsements, but as illustrations of new approaches. We recognize that because prosecution is local, some of these recommendations and examples won't be suited to all jurisdictions. We nonetheless hope that these ideas generate conversation, creative thinking, and change. We have one big hope:

that prosecutors will adopt a new twenty-first-century vision for achieving mercy and justice. They are intertwined.

PART ONE: HOW TO REDUCE INCARCERATION

1. Make Diversion the Rule

Overview: Well-designed programs that divert people from jail or prison—or from the justice system entirely when they precede charging—can conserve resources, reduce re-offending, and diminish the collateral harms of criminal prosecution. These programs keep people in the community instead of locked up.

Recommendations

- Design diversion programs for people facing felony as well as misdemeanor charges. Working with people who commit more serious offenses may offer the greatest payoff in terms of reducing recidivism.
- Make sure people aren't denied the opportunity for diversion because they can't pay. Offer programs free of charge or on a sliding scale (i.e., take income into account in setting fees).
- Wherever possible, don't exclude people because of their criminal history, mental illness, or drug use.
- If a case should be dismissed outright, don't route it to diversion instead.
- Ensure that the program matches the risk and needs of the individual. For example, people who are lower-risk should be placed in a lighter-touch program (or no program at all).
- Carefully consider which program conditions (like abstaining from marijuana use) are necessary to address the underlying causes of misconduct and keep the community safe. Pay attention to whether punitive responses to noncompliance (like ankle bracelets and jail time) serve the purpose of rehabilitation or deterrence.
- Don't require defendants to admit guilt to participate if an admission isn't needed to promote the goals of the program.

Example: In Washington, D.C., a six-month diversion program, Alternatives to the Court Experience (ACE), serves teenagers who commit offenses like vandalism and shoplifting. The program begins with an evaluation of stress, trauma, and behavioral needs. Program coordinators develop plans that can include therapy, tutoring, mentoring, and school support. ACE has also sent participants to academies run by the National Guard and to after-school boxing programs. In the program's first two years of existence, more than 90 percent of ACE participants were not rearrested.

2. Charge with Restraint and Plea-Bargain Fairly

Overview: Prosecutors have nearly unchecked authority to choose the criminal charges they file, with enormous leverage over guilty pleas and the final disposition of cases.

Too often, prosecutors have historically sought sentences that penalize people who exercise their right to trial, and state and federal prosecutors' associations have lobbied state legislatures and Congress for harsher penalties.

Recommendations

- Screen cases rigorously and early to determine if evidence supports all elements of the offense so that weak cases can be declined or dismissed. Screening should be the job of experienced prosecutors who look at the accusation and evidence *before* charges are filed.
- Don't file the maximum possible charge as a matter of course. Adopt office-wide policies making clear that charges should reflect the facts and circumstances of each case and be designed to achieve a just result.
- Absent extenuating circumstances (like the protection of a vulnerable witness), don't withdraw a plea offer if a defendant chooses to wait for the results from the grand jury, a motion requesting relief from a judge, or a pretrial hearing.
- Don't threaten to seek the death penalty, life without parole, habitual offender (three strike) charges, or to transfer a case from juvenile to adult court as a way to leverage a guilty plea.
- Don't make a plea offer if you can't prove the charge beyond a reasonable doubt.
- Consider collateral consequences in plea discussions, such as impacts on immigration status.
- Limit the use (or threatened use) of sentencing enhancements (for example, based on criminal history or the presence of a weapon). Require a supervisor to sign off when a sentencing enhancement is sought.
- In making sentencing recommendations, consider the systemic or socioeconomic factors that may have disadvantaged the defendant and played a part in bringing him or her before the court.
- In general, do not condition plea offers on the waiver of a defendant's right to seek pretrial release or discovery, or to litigate constitutional violations.
- Support legislation to reduce sentence lengths and eliminate mandatory minimum sentences and three-strike laws.

Examples: In 2016, Seattle Prosecuting Attorney Dan Satterberg introduced charging standards designed to ensure that the punishment for an offense is proportionate to the offense (taking into account criminal history) and commensurate with the punishment imposed on others who have committed a similar offense. The standards caution prosecutors against filing every case that can be filed and against overcharging to obtain a guilty plea.

In 2018, Philadelphia District Attorney Larry Krasner instructed the prosecutors in his office to make plea offers below the bottom end of the Pennsylvania sentencing guidelines for most crimes. When a prosecutor thinks that an offer at the bottom end would be too low, he or she must seek a supervisor's approval to go higher. When the sentencing guidelines call for a sentence of two years or less, Krasner instructed prosecutors generally to seek probation, another alternative to incarceration, or house arrest.

3. Move Toward Ending Cash Bail

Overview: Most people in jail in the United States are there because they can't afford bail. This starting point serves no public safety purpose, effectively punishes people for being poor, and pressures them to plead guilty. It costs taxpayers billions of dollars each year, enriching the bail industry.

Recommendations

- In general, recommend release for defendants, including those charged with felonies, unless there is a substantial risk of harm to an individual or the community. Some states, in lieu of money bail, have directed courts to use risk assessment tools in making determinations about public safety. A note of caution: There is a tension in using these tools. While they have helped reduce cash bail, some risk assessment tools have been shown to reinforce patterns of racial disparity. For example, arrest history, a variable used in some assessments, has been associated with racial bias.
- Support pretrial services that help people remember to return to court (for example, notification by phone or text). If a defendant has a record of failing to appear in court, consider weekly calls, check-in appointments, or curfews rather than cash bail or detention.
- Publicly support the elimination of money bail. Educate the public, lawmakers, and local criminal justice leaders about the perverse effects of a system in which detention decisions turn on ability to pay rather than public safety.
- Do not seek pretrial detention because a defendant missed a court date if he or she subsequently reports to court.
- Where there are no alternatives to bail, support alternative methods of payment, like debit and credit card payments or unsecured bonds, and support nonprofit bail funds, which displace the bail industry.

Examples: In June 2017, Cook County State's Attorney Kim Foxx announced that her office would recommend releasing people on their own recognizance when they have no violent criminal history, the current offense is a misdemeanor or low-level felony, and no other risk factors suggest they are a danger to the community or will fail to appear in court. Foxx's policy built on her previous commitment to make a similar recommendation of release for people who were in jail because they couldn't afford to post bail of $1,000 or less.

Kentucky has been at the forefront of pretrial reforms since 1976, when the state banned for-profit bail and established a pretrial services agency to analyze defendants' risk of flight and reoffending. In 2011, Kentucky passed a law requiring judges to release pretrial all individuals considered at low or moderate risk of reoffending or flight. Since then, the number of people arrested while out on release has declined every year: in 2015, the rate was only 10 percent. Following this success, the Kentucky Supreme Court instituted automatic pretrial release for most nonviolent defendants (excluding those accused of sex offenses) below a certain risk threshold.

4. Encourage the Treatment (Not Criminalization) of Mental Illness

Overview: People who struggle with mental illness wind up in the criminal justice system more than they should. As a result, America's largest psychiatric facilities are not hospitals but jails and prisons. People with mental illness are less likely to make bail and more likely to face longer sentences. They make up a large percentage of death row prisoners. Upon release, they are often sent back into the community without a treatment plan or the prospect of good healthcare, and too often find themselves cycling back into the criminal justice system.

Recommendations

- Encourage the use of public health models as a starting point for developing responses to individuals in crisis and promote community-based services to stabilize people who otherwise end up in jail.
- Support crisis-intervention training of law enforcement to deescalate situations involving individuals with mental illness and reduce the likelihood of use of force or arrest as a response.
- When possible, divert individuals who struggle with mental illness to treatment instead of making an arrest that can lead to incarceration rather than help. Screen cases before charging to identify individuals in need of mental health services and support.
- Train line prosecutors and staff on the impact of mental illness and trauma.
- If you have a mental health court, make sure prosecutors don't seek to supervise defendants indefinitely simply to make sure they're continuing to access services.
- Work with correctional and mental health staff to reinstate public benefits, such as Medicaid, at the time of release from custody.
- At various stages of the criminal justice process, employ and listen to individuals who have experienced mental illness as advisors, trainers, and peer support professionals.
- Bring together relevant agencies to collaborate on data-sharing, developing exit ramps from the criminal justice system, and filling gaps in community services and support.

Examples: Miami-Dade County trains police officers in responding to people in crisis so they can better deescalate conflicts. The police have the authority to divert people to treatment instead of jail. When people are booked into jail, they are screened for signs and symptoms of mental illness. Those with a diagnosis who need acute care and are charged with misdemeanors or low-level felonies are transferred to a community-based crisis stabilization unit within forty-eight hours of booking. These individuals are eligible for treatment, support, and housing services. If they complete the treatment, the charges against them may be dismissed or modified.

In 2010, as state attorney in Burlington, Vermont, T. J. Donovan started the Rapid Intervention Community Court to divert into treatment people charged with low-level offenses who suffered from mental illness and addiction. A dedicated staff member in the state attorney's office determines eligibility and conducts a risk and needs assessment. The person's case is dismissed if he or she successfully completes the program's requirements. Preliminary research showed that only 7.4 percent of those who did so were convicted of a new crime.

5. Encourage the Treatment (Not Criminalization) of Drug Addiction

Overview: The "war on drugs" has failed to curb drug use or make communities safer. Instead, it has resulted in destructive policing and prosecution, disproportionately affecting communities of color. It's time to move toward decriminalizing drug addiction.

Recommendations
- Don't prosecute low-level marijuana possession, and don't make exceptions because of someone's criminal record.
- Support legislation that decriminalizes marijuana and reclassifies other simple drug possession as a misdemeanor or civil violation.
- Don't seek mandatory minimum or habitual offender sentences based on underlying charges for drug possession.
- Don't prosecute people who call the police in response to an overdose and don't prosecute users for homicide when they share drugs that cause an overdose when there was no specific intent to cause harm or death.
- Expunge (or seek sentencing reductions for) past convictions that would be treated differently today.
- Offer drug treatment programs with evidence-based solutions, such as medication-assisted treatment, and treat use and relapse as a part of recovery. Support medically assisted drug treatment in jails.
- Support needle exchanges and safe consumption sites.
- Support training and access to naloxone and other overdose-reversal drugs.

Examples: Seattle City Attorney Peter Holmes stopped prosecuting marijuana possession misdemeanors in 2010. Washington State legalized marijuana in 2014, though police can still issue citations for public consumption. In 2018, Holmes moved to vacate the judgments and dismiss all marijuana possession charges brought from 1996 to 2010, citing evidence of racial disparity in arrests.

Seattle also pioneered a widely replicated pre-charge drug diversion program, called LEAD, in 2011. The police can direct low-level drug offenders to community-based treatment and other services instead of prosecution. LEAD participants were 58 percent less likely to be arrested for another offense, compared to others who were criminally charged. In 2018, the Seattle Prosecuting Attorney's Office stopped prosecuting possession of less than a gram of heroin, cocaine, or methamphetamine.

6. Treat Kids Like Kids

Overview: The adolescent brain differs from the adult brain in ways that increase the likelihood of risky and reckless behavior. Neurological development continues until around the age of twenty-five, and most young people who commit crimes don't continue to do so in adulthood. Long-term outcomes for teenagers and young adults are substantially better when they have as little contact with the criminal justice system as possible, or when their cases remain in juvenile court. Prosecutors have enormous power over how teenagers and young adults are treated in the justice system. They influence decisions about whether to bring charges, what charges to bring, whether to transfer a child to the adult system, and whether to ask that a child be incarcerated.

Recommendations

- Do not prosecute kids for typical adolescent behavior such as fistfights, smoking marijuana, disorderly conduct, or infractions at school that don't result in serious physical harm.
- In general, don't seek incarceration for teenagers while their cases are pending. If they can't safely stay home, promote alternatives to detention such as community day supervision and treatment centers.
- After conviction, seek alternatives to incarceration for teenagers whenever possible.
- Advocate for diversion programs and specialized courts that address the needs of young adults.
- Work with law enforcement to prevent the interrogation of kids absent the presence and advice of counsel (and parents, when appropriate).
- Recognize that young people accused of crimes often have experienced trauma, and may lack the ability to express remorse, especially in the days and weeks immediately after an offense. Take that into account in charging, plea bargaining, and sentencing.
- Recognize that implicit racial bias often affects perceptions of adolescent culpability, predictions about reoffending, and recommendations for punishment or treatment, and develop training and policies to reduce the impact of bias when deciding how to proceed at each stage of a case.
- Protect the confidentiality of juvenile records. Expunge juvenile records for cases that are dismissed or when young people don't incur new charges after a few years.
- Don't ask to try children under the age of eighteen in adult court, except in very limited circumstances and based on an evaluation of factors such as the defendant's background and circumstances and the nature of the offense. These decisions should require high-level approval in the office.
- Where a state statute mandates trying a child as an adult for a certain offense, consider charging the child with a lesser included crime if possible.
- When a child must be tried as an adult, consider a sentence at the low end of state guidelines. In general, advocate for incarceration to be close to home and to include educational and vocational programming.
- Don't seek sentences of life without parole (or de facto life without parole) for those who committed their crime of conviction before the age of eighteen.

Examples: The state attorneys in Jacksonville and Tampa, Florida, have put in place a process for issuing citations to many teenagers who would otherwise be arrested.

In San Francisco's Young Adult Court, case managers, who are licensed therapists, evaluate the risks and needs of young people between the ages of eighteen and twenty-five and come up with wellness care plans that can include substance abuse and mental health care as well as educational, vocational, and mentor opportunities. The court accepts teenagers who have committed violent felonies as well as lower-level offenses. The rate of rearrest for participants between 2015 and 2017 was 15 percent, less than half the rate for juveniles statewide.

7. Minimize Misdemeanors

Overview: Misdemeanor charges make up approximately 80 percent of state and local dockets. The majority are for offenses like trespassing, loitering, prostitution, and drug possession. Arrests and prosecutions for misdemeanors and violations can significantly affect people's lives even when they result in short sentences or probation, costing people their employment, housing, student loans, immigration status, and even their children, and contributing to a cycle of incarceration and poverty that is hard to break.

Recommendations
- In general, do not charge misdemeanors, such as trespassing or loitering, which are associated with poverty, mental illness, and homelessness.
- In general, do not charge sex workers or clients when both parties are over eighteen and consent. Don't prosecute underage trafficking victims. Support efforts to decriminalize sex work and instead marshal resources to prosecute trafficking.
- Where it's not possible or doesn't make sense to decline prosecution, develop cite-and-release programs to keep people out of jail.
- Promote procedures or systemic changes that ensure defendants facing misdemeanors have competent lawyers and the cases go before judges.

Examples: In 2018, two district attorneys in Texas stopped charging people with misdemeanors for possessing small amounts of marijuana. In Nueces County, District Attorney Mark Gonzalez began diverting people to drug education classes, also asking them to pay a $250 fine or do twenty-five hours of community service. In Harris County, District Attorney Kim Ogg started sending people to drug education classes without arresting them or giving them a ticket. She also stopped the prosecution of residue amounts of other drugs and ended jail time for small retail thefts.

8. Account for Consequences to Immigrants

Overview: Criminal charges and convictions can trigger detention and deportation proceedings for people who are not U.S. citizens, subjecting them to far greater collateral punishments and taking them away from their families. Being jailed before trial also increases the likelihood of being detained and deported by federal immigration officials. These threats to immigrants discourage the reporting of crimes, making communities less safe.

Recommendations

- Make sure prosecutors and supervisors understand the immigration consequences of plea deals and defendants receive and understand this information.
- In plea discussions and sentencing recommendations, consider the immigration consequences of a conviction. When two similarly weighted charges have different immigration consequences, choose the immigration-neutral charge.
- Support and streamline processes for vacating convictions when an immigrant who pled guilty was unaware of the immigration consequences or when there are other equitable grounds to do so.
- Work with local authorities to protect against ICE enforcement in courthouses and with probation departments to prevent ICE arrests at probation offices. Alert groups that represent immigrants if ICE seeks to question or detain individuals who come to court.
- Protect immigrants who serve as witnesses and report crimes.
- Speak out for protecting the rights of immigrants and oppose policies that entangle local law enforcement in federal immigration enforcement.

Examples: In 2017, Brooklyn District Attorney Eric Gonzalez hired two experienced immigration attorneys to advise prosecutors on tailoring criminal charges and plea offers to avoid placing defendants at risk of deportation. For example, prosecutors initially charged a green card holder who struck a child with endangering the welfare of a child, which carries deportation consequences. Later, however, they amended the charge to fourth-degree criminal mischief, which carries the same weight under criminal law but bears no deportation risk.

In San Francisco, District Attorney George Gascón has worked to end the questioning of witnesses at trial about their immigration status and assigned victim advocates to escort fearful undocumented witnesses or victims through the courthouse. Gascón's policy requires his staff to call the San Francisco Rapid Response Network, a group of nonprofits that can summon immediate legal help, if they learn that federal immigration agents are in the courthouse.

9. Promote Restorative Justice

Overview: Restorative justice is a community-based approach to responding to the harm that crime causes. In a group setting, individuals charged with crimes talk to the people they hurt, sharing stories and working toward accountability, repair, and rehabilitation. Restorative practices can be part of the criminal court process or a substitute for it. Research shows that crime victims often do not feel that prosecution and sentencing serve them well; restorative justice can help address their concerns. These programs have a consistent track record of achieving lower rates of recidivism than traditional penalties, including for serious offenses.

Recommendations

- Learn about and visit best-practice restorative justice programs.
- Establish restorative justice programs, or if they already exist in the community, refer cases to them and treat the outcome as the resolution of the charges.
- Consider restorative justice for adult and juvenile misdemeanor and felony offenses, including cases involving violence and injury.
- Unless necessary for public safety, don't exclude participants because of their criminal records.
- When possible, and with participation by crime victims if they are interested, refer cases to restorative justice programs before arraignment.
- Ensure that statements made during the restorative justice process can't be used against the defendant if the case returns to court.

Examples: District of Columbia Attorney General Karl Racine launched a restorative justice program for young people in 2016. At community conferences, victims meet with those who have done them harm. More than 80 percent of the young people who have successfully completed the program have avoided rearrest. The program has several full-time staff who are not attorneys. Prosecutors are required to observe at least one restorative justice conference to build understanding and acceptance of alternatives to the traditional court system.

10. Shrink Probation and Parole

Overview: The number of people under some form of probation or parole in the United States is about five million. This number is far too high, and periods of supervision are far too long. Supervision increases the likelihood that people who are otherwise at low risk of reoffending will end up incarcerated for technical violations that have little to do with public safety. The majority of violations occur within the first year, suggesting that supervision beyond that point serves little to no rehabilitative purpose. Some states have shortened supervision periods with no increase in crime or recidivism.

Recommendations

- Limit probationary terms after prison to one year, unless there is a compelling reason for a longer term. (For example, if probation is an alternative to incarceration as opposed to an addition to it, a longer term may be appropriate.)
- If longer terms are imposed at the outset, consider supporting requests to terminate parole and probation early for people who have fully complied with the terms of their supervision for one year.
- Limit supervision after local jail sentences to six months.
- Don't treat the use of marijuana or alcohol as a violation of supervision.
- Advocate with parole and probation departments for the use of graduated sanctions for violations. This means starting with mild sanctions (such as community service), and only if necessary moving to moderate sanctions (day reporting centers, intensive supervision) or more serious ones (ankle bracelets and brief jail

stays). Don't advocate sending people back to jail for technical violations of their supervision.

Example: In 2017, the members of the Georgia Council on Criminal Justice Reform, including Houston County District Attorney George Hartwig, unanimously recommended less monitoring for low-risk people on probation after two years of good behavior. The recommendation became law, and within six months affected almost eighteen thousand felony probation cases. In 2018, forty-five prosecutors signed on to a statement that recommended shrinking probation and parole populations, and the district attorneys in Philadelphia and Salt Lake County publicly stressed the importance of these reforms.

PART TWO: HOW TO INCREASE FAIRNESS

11. Change Office Culture and Practice

Overview: Prosecutors are the gatekeepers of America's criminal justice system. The policies and incentives they put into place, and the dynamics inside their offices, have a tremendous effect on the pursuit of justice in their community and the system as a whole. Prosecutors can design (or redesign) key features of the system to make it more accountable, equitable, and just.

Recommendations

- Work with other agencies to gather and share data on charging, plea dispositions, and sentencing (including racial disparity), findings of prosecutorial misconduct, pretrial detention rates resulting from an inability to pay bail, diversion participation and completion, charging children as adults, and other outcomes that will help your office achieve more just results.
- Adopt performance standards that reflect your values. Instead of evaluating performance based on number of convictions, trial wins, or the lengths of sentences, prosecutors should encourage desired outcomes by adopting metrics like reducing incarceration, pretrial detention, and recidivism. You can measure progress by comparing rates from year to year or to other similar jurisdictions. Include these measures in promotion decisions.
- Make data available to the public so you can be held accountable for the performance of the office.
- Conduct mandatory trainings on issues like implicit bias, debunked forensic methods, false confessions, and witness identification.
- Set procedures for defense attorneys to appeal to a supervising prosecutor if they think a charge or plea offer is unfair.
- Consider requiring a supervisor's approval to charge potentially problematic cases, such as those with only one witness, jailhouse informants, or witnesses with credibility issues.
- Hire a diverse staff across all levels of seniority and report on staff diversity. In mid to large offices, hire a director of diversity and inclusion. Research has shown that across disciplines, teams that include people from a variety of racial, ethnic,

and religious backgrounds are more effective and more open to new ideas. Some research shows that increasing the number of minority prosecutors in an office decreases racial sentencing disparities.
- Circulate surveys and seek input from partner agencies to gauge community satisfaction and identify concerns.
- Encourage prosecutors to engage in community outreach, for example by coaching Little League teams, speaking at elementary schools, and mentoring at-risk kids. Consider setting up local storefronts so prosecutors are present in neighborhoods.
- Set up programs and opportunities for prosecutors to meet with formerly incarcerated individuals and their families and with people who have been exonerated (and do so early in prosecutors' careers). Prosecutors should also be expected to visit prisons and jails where the people they prosecute are held.

Examples: Cook County State's Attorney Kim Foxx released a detailed and accessible data-based report on criminal justice in 2017. To exemplify transparency, the report included infographics illustrating the most common types of offenses, the race and ethnicity of people charged, and how cases were resolved in each category of offense. Cook County also created a position for diversity and inclusion director. The Brooklyn D.A.'s office established a policy requiring supervisor approval for cases involving only one witness. The San Francisco D.A.'s office has a Neighborhood Prosecutors Program, in which five A.D.A.s work in the field alongside police and local community groups.

12. Address Racial Disparity

Overview: Extensive evidence shows that racial disparity exists at every stage of the justice system. The causes likely include overpolicing of communities of color and overt and implicit bias. Prosecutors must confront these issues by looking closely at the relevant data and working to promote equity and a healthier, more cooperative relationship with the communities they serve.

Recommendations
- Publicly commit to reducing racial disparities that arise from prosecutorial practices.
- Engage the community and the office in a reflective conversation about the role of prosecutors in racial inequity. Implicit bias training could be part of this process.
- Track and release race and gender data for bail requests, charging children as adults, other charging decisions, plea bargains, sentencing recommendations, and parole board recommendations. Permit an outside source to review the data, evaluate disparities, and make recommendations to reduce them.
- Use risk assessment tools with caution. Educate staff and other stakeholders about the potential to compound bias, and consider tools designed to actively reduce racial disparities.
- Make it part of the office's mission to reduce racial disparities that arise from

police practices. Work with police and other agencies to meaningfully compare and address racial disparity at different points in the system. If you meet resistance, propel changes to police practice by declining to prosecute cases that are clouded by a pattern of racial conduct.

Example: After Milwaukee District Attorney John Chisholm took office in 2007, he opened his office's files to the Vera Institute of Justice for an analysis of racial disparity. Vera showed a higher rate of prosecution of black people arrested for possession of drug paraphernalia. In response, Chisholm stopped prosecuting most paraphernalia cases, instead referring people to treatment programs. The rate of prosecution for the remaining cases equalized for black and white defendants.

13. Create Effective Conviction Review

Overview: Conviction review units (CRUs, also called conviction integrity units) scrutinize old cases to determine whether the outcomes were tainted by unjust practices, faulty evidence, or bias. In addition to righting past wrongs, CRUs provide helpful mechanisms for revisiting cases that an office previously believed to be justly prosecuted but that, in fact, may be materially flawed. Since they were first created in the early 2000s, CRUs have expanded from reviewing claims of actual innocence to reviewing violations of due process and corrupt law enforcement practices. Some offices are considering extending these principles to the review of past excessive sentences.

Recommendations

- Create a CRU (or another conviction review process) if your office does not already have one. Small to midsized offices may consider partnering with a local law school, Innocence Project, or law firm to expand capacity.
- Consider extending the CRU's mandate beyond claims of actual innocence by also scrutinizing cases in which a serious violation of a defendant's rights or other miscarriage of justice may have contributed to his or her conviction.
- Don't exclude convictions from review because they're based on guilty pleas, appeals are pending, or a defendant has served his or her sentence. Include misdemeanors if a systemic failure, for example in a crime lab, led to guilty pleas of innocent people.
- Review convictions that relied on discredited forensic methods like bite marks or questionable diagnoses of shaken baby syndrome.
- Support compensation for the wrongfully convicted and the expungement of wrongful convictions.
- Use the CRU as a tool for identifying and addressing the root causes of flawed prosecutions, such as Brady violations or reliance on discredited science, and incorporate lessons learned into office-wide training and policy changes.
- Create a process for reviewing and supporting clemency and pardon requests, as well as other relief for long sentences that raise concerns about proportional punishment and fairness, or that are being served by individuals who are elderly or ill and no longer pose a danger to the community.

- Structure the unit to demonstrate its independence and importance to the office. The CRU should be led by a respected senior lawyer who reports directly to the D.A. and be staffed with prosecutors and investigators committed to its mission. The CRU should be outside the appellate unit.
- Consider engaging outside expertise and reinforcing confidence in final decisions by creating an external advisory board for the unit.
- Release annual reports of the CRU's work and the outcomes that result, including internal reforms.

Examples: In Brooklyn, the late District Attorney Ken Thompson created a model conviction review unit in 2014 and hosted a summit on wrongful convictions the following year. Brooklyn's CRU has had nine full-time attorneys and three investigators, and had exonerated twenty-four people as of July 2018. It has an external advisory board that reviews case referrals, investigations, and determinations before they are finalized. Its scope is not limited to claims of actual innocence.

In San Francisco, the discovery of racist and homophobic texts by San Francisco police officers led District Attorney George Gascón to convene a task force, including three retired judges, to review more than three thousand cases connected to the police officers implicated in the scandal.

In 2009, Seattle Prosecuting Attorney Dan Satterberg recommended clemency in the case of a man sentenced to life in prison under Washington's three-strikes law. Since then, the office has continued reviewing old cases with life sentences (often involving a minor third-strike charge), recommending clemency for nineteen defendants through fall 2018.

14. Broaden Discovery

Overview: Discovery—the process for sharing evidence with the defense—is essential to the fair administration of justice. Without the information the state gathers through its police powers, defendants cannot make informed decisions and defense attorneys cannot provide effective counsel. Studies have shown that withholding evidence results in disturbingly high levels of the miscarriage of justice. When prosecutors take an expansive approach to discovery by making early and broad disclosures, they enhance the prompt and fair resolution of cases and increase the accountability of law enforcement.

Recommendations

- Establish an open-file policy, disclosing all relevant evidence to the defense, with case-by-case exceptions as necessary to protect witness safety, prevent witness tampering, or shield sensitive private information. Protect witness safety and privacy by redacting materials, as opposed to refusing to turn them over, whenever possible.
- Share the police report and other materials in the government's possession as soon as possible after charges are filed. As more evidence is gathered, it should be disclosed when it becomes available, before plea discussions and in ample time to prepare for trial.

- Form a committee to decide how to collect and disseminate to the defense findings of misconduct in police personnel files. Consider creating a database that prosecutors in the office can easily access and that includes information on police officers who have been found to have lied in the course of their jobs, committed civil rights violations, or used excessive force. Establish clear guidelines about how individual officers are to be included or removed from the list. Flag cases involving officers in the database for the prosecutors handling them.
- Designate an ethics officer to advise staff, provide training, and address allegations of misconduct in the office.
- Explain disclosure obligations to the police and other agencies (like crime labs). Require police to sign a statement in every case charged stating that all relevant documents have been provided to the prosecutor.
- Institute rigorous training and supervision to ensure compliance with the office's open-file policy. Recognize and reward staff who catch and remedy disclosure errors or near misses.
- Ensure appropriate consequences for prosecutors who improperly and intentionally fail to disclose evidence, including discipline, firing, and reporting ethical violations to the state bar.

Examples: In Lowndes County, Mississippi, District Attorney Scott Colom has instituted an open discovery policy: prosecutors are instructed to give all information they receive from law enforcement to the defense. In Kansas City, Kansas, District Attorney Mark Dupree has a similar practice, providing all discovery to the defense immediately upon request.

Seattle Prosecuting Attorney Dan Satterberg negotiated an agreement with law enforcement for facilitating comprehensive disclosure of information on police misconduct. A committee in his office collects and reviews information regarding officer misconduct, including dishonesty or bias, so prosecutors have a systematic way to satisfy their disclosure obligations if they call police officers or crime lab technicians as witnesses.

15. Hold Police Accountable

Overview: Most police officers take great care to protect and respect the communities they serve. But when they do not, their actions can taint their departments and the justice system. When an officer is credibly accused of using excessive force or engaging in misconduct, the allegations must be credibly investigated. The role of prosecutors in conducting such investigations is complicated by the close working relationship they have with local police departments, which can lead to conflicts of interest or the appearance of such conflicts, undermining public confidence. Investigations and prosecutions of police officers should be safeguarded by procedures focused on ensuring independence, impartiality, and transparency.

Recommendations

- If feasible, create an independent internal investigations unit staffed with senior prosecutors and experienced investigators. The unit should report directly to the district attorney or his or her chief deputy. The investigators should have no daily contact with, or reliance on, the local law enforcement agency under investigation.

- Work with local law enforcement on a plan of action in the case of officer-involved shootings and misconduct allegations. The plan should include immediate notification of the D.A.'s office, an opportunity for personnel from the office to go to the scene, timely sharing of information, and investigation of the misconduct by an entity other than the employing agency.

- Work with law enforcement partners on public disclosure of body- and dash-cam videos. Adopt a policy requiring prompt release of the videos in the event of an officer-involved shooting or allegation of excessive force (absent legitimate and specific concerns about witness safety, privacy, compromising the integrity of the investigation, or prejudicing a jury).

- Consider creating an external advisory board to make recommendations before a final charging decision. If permitted, release the record of a grand jury proceeding when there is no indictment. Issue a public report detailing the investigation and explaining the findings.

- Make public all policies and protocols related to investigations of law enforcement misconduct. Report investigations, prosecutions, and dispositions regarding police-involved incidents annually.

- Support a second-look review by the state attorney general's office or an independent prosecutor when your investigation does not result in a decision to file criminal charges.

- Support changes to state law if needed for independent and effective investigations, including reforms that ensure that police are not investigated by the agency that employs them.

Example: In 2016, the San Francisco District Attorney's office created an Independent Investigations Bureau to investigate and review all officer-involved shootings and other cases of excessive use of force. The staff, composed of six attorneys, six investigators, and two paralegals, were hired from outside the D.A.'s office and the San Francisco Police Department. The unit operates independently to address concerns about the close working relationship between prosecutors and the police.

16. End the Poverty Trap of Fines and Fees

Overview: When fines are imposed after a conviction, they're intended as a form of deterrent and punishment. Fees in criminal court play a different role: they shift the costs of the criminal justice system from taxpayers in general to the people who appear in court. While fines have a place as an alternative to incarceration, when they are levied without regard to a person's ability to pay, they can trap poor defendants in a cycle of incarceration and debt. Fixed fines, as well as fees, are also unfair: a $200 fine or fee can be an annoyance for an affluent person and a financial calamity for an indigent one. While debtors' prisons are illegal, they effectively exist when people are sent to jail, or otherwise stuck in the criminal justice system, because they can't afford to pay fines or fees. And pursuing unpaid debt may cost the state more than it brings in.

Recommendations

- Speak out about the problems caused by fines and fees and support efforts to fund courts in a way that reduces reliance on revenue from fines and fees.
- Advocate for assessing fees and fines on a sliding scale based on income and assets, taking into account debts and financial obligations such as child support and health care costs. This model has been successfully implemented in countries around the world.
- Support reasonable payment plans, and oppose requiring people to return to court again and again because of incomplete payments. Advocate against excessive late fees, payment plan fees, collection fees, and interest payments.
- Advocate for the elimination of driver's license revocations and suspensions for nonpayment of fines and fees. Work with courts to reinstate licenses and create diversion programs for people arrested for driving on a suspended license when the suspension is for unpaid fines and fees.
- Advocate for the elimination of all fines and fees in cases involving children and teenagers under the age of eighteen.
- Support defense motions to reduce or waive fines and fees based on indigency. Don't ask to jail people because they can't pay their fines or fees and eliminate the use of arrest warrants for nonpayment.
- Eliminate fees for diversion programs. If there is no way to avoid fees, use a sliding scale and do not restrict access to diversion for people who can't afford to pay. Oppose continuing or extending probation solely because of unpaid fines and fees.

Examples: Sliding-scale fines have worked in the United States. When a Staten Island court replaced fixed fines with sliding-scale fines in 1988, both collection rates and amounts increased. Over the past year, California, Maine, and Mississippi have eliminated driver's license suspension for nonpayment of fines and fees. In Minnesota, prosecutors are lobbying legislators to end driver's license suspensions for nonpayment of fines and fees. Washington State eliminated interest on fines and fees, while California and the cities of Philadelphia and New Orleans have eliminated fees in juvenile cases.

The Cook County State's Attorney's Office charges no fees for its diversion programs, which serve about five thousand defendants a year. The programs are funded through municipal and county budgets, federal grants, and partner organizations.

17. Expunge and Seal Criminal Records

Overview: About seventy million Americans have a criminal record, the same number as have a college education. A criminal record makes it harder to get a job or find housing, accounting for high rates of homelessness among people leaving prison. People may lose access to public benefits and become ineligible to receive federal loans. State laws may bar them from voting or obtaining professional and occupational licenses. Research shows that the stigma of having a record is worse for minority job applicants than for white ones, which means racial disparity in the system continues to affect people long after their sentences are served.

Recommendations

- In general, support petitions for expungement or sealing of records when permitted by statute.
- Support automated expungement for acts that are no longer criminal (for example, marijuana possession after state legalization). Support automated sealing or expungement for arrest records that did not lead to charges or convictions, or after a certain period of time has passed.
- Support clinics and amnesty programs to expunge records and clear old warrants in partnership with the court or the defense bar.
- In general, don't object to reinstating driver's licenses, or to applications for certificates of relief from disability, which inform prospective employers or landlords that an individual has been rehabilitated.
- Host workshops for job trainings, resume programs, and mock interviews. Encourage employers to hire people with criminal records.
- Support efforts to eliminate restrictions on expungement and sealing, such as long waiting periods.
- Support increasing the age for juvenile sealings from eighteen to twenty-one.
- Support efforts to ensure accuracy of criminal records, laws that require private databases to regularly remove expunged or sealed records, and "ban-the-box" legislation that bars employers, housing, and other social service providers from asking early in the application process about criminal records.

Examples: The state attorney in Broward County, Florida, runs one-day workshops to help people fill out paperwork, get fingerprinted, and submit their expungement applications, a process that usually takes several weeks. The San Francisco D.A.'s office is identifying and automatically expunging thousands of old marijuana convictions. The Pennsylvania District Attorneys' Association recently supported a Clean Slate Bill (which became law) to seal some arrests and minor convictions.

The Portsmouth, Virginia, Commonwealth's Attorney's Office offers a monthly seminar to help residents remove crimes from their records and restore their rights. The Albany County District Attorney's Office helps people navigate New York's newly passed sealing statutes to seal their criminal records.

18. Play Fair with Forensic Evidence

Overview: The power of forensic science is unmistakable. Advances in science and technology have helped solve crimes and exonerate people who were wrongfully convicted. The continued use of unreliable and misleading forensic evidence, however, imperils the integrity of the criminal justice system. It's critical for prosecutors to promote efforts that strengthen the reliability of forensic evidence and inform courts and jurors of its limitations.

Recommendations

- Stop using scientifically invalid evidence. Examples include comparison of bullet leads, fire and bloodstain patterns, bite marks, shoe prints, and hair matching.

- Ensure that other types of forensic evidence used are foundationally valid and valid as applied (meaning that the particular method used by the examiner has been validated in contexts like the one at issue in the case).
- Do not offer forensic evidence supported only by an expert's experience, as opposed to validated methods and studies.
- Critically and continually examine emerging scientific literature, which may also call old methods into question, and train staff about these changes.
- Train prosecutors to understand the validity of the proffered evidence and expert testimony. Don't let an expert declare a "match" to a degree of certainty that's not supportable. Juries overvalue such testimony.

Example: In 2016, the Texas Forensic Science Commission conducted a six-month investigation into the use of bite-mark testimony, which had led to wrongful convictions and lacks scientific validation, according to the National Academy of Sciences. The investigation showed that board-certified forensic dentists who analyzed photographs of injuries could not agree on which ones were bite marks. The commission also heard a day of testimony from experts on all sides of the debate. At the conclusion of the investigation, the commission placed a moratorium on the use of bite-mark testimony. It also ordered a review of all past cases in which bite-mark evidence was used, appointing a panel of experts to review trial transcripts.

19. Work to End the Death Penalty

Overview: Countless studies have shown that the death penalty is fraught with error, provides no more public safety benefit than other sentences, and is routinely imposed on people with diminished culpability, including the intellectually disabled and mentally ill, teenagers, and people who have experienced extreme childhood trauma. Studies also show that the death penalty is applied in a racially discriminatory manner. It is expensive and puts victims through decades of litigation and uncertainty. And it has become increasingly concentrated in a small number of jurisdictions: 2 percent of counties are responsible for the majority of death sentences nationwide. This means that whether a killing takes place on one side or the other of a county line often determines whether someone will one day be executed for it.

Recommendations

- Oppose legislation to expand or expedite the death penalty and consider publicly supporting death penalty repeal.
- If state law requires consideration of the death penalty, ensure thorough and uniform review of relevant cases. For example, establish a review committee to make case-by-case determinations. The committee could include members of the bar and the community. It should consider alternative sentences and whether seeking a death sentence is absolutely required to protect public safety. Defense lawyers should have the chance to present to the committee and mitigating evidence should be considered.

- Examine previously imposed death sentences and consider alternative punishments, particularly when there is substantial evidence of reduced culpability.
- Don't threaten to seek the death penalty to coerce a plea.

Examples: After taking office in 2016, Denver District Attorney Beth McCann announced she would no longer seek the death penalty. McCann said she would support a statewide repeal by either voter referendum or legislation. Seattle Prosecuting Attorney Dan Satterberg has publicly supported repealing the death penalty in his state, saying that the system "no longer serves the interests of public safety, criminal justice, or the needs of victims."

20. Calculate Cost

Overview: Reducing spending on prison has bipartisan support. The incentives to cut costs are often misaligned, however. Counties largely fund prosecutors' offices and jails while states largely fund prisons. The result is that prosecutors can send people to prison without incurring a cost for their local jurisdiction, making them less accountable for spending. To change the dynamic, it's important to inform the public about the overall cost of incarceration.

Recommendations

- Calculate the cost-savings of alternatives to incarceration and factor it into plea offers and sentencing recommendations. (The formula will depend on the local per-person cost of prison and jail.)
- Calculate the expected cost of incarceration for a proposed jail or prison sentence and announce it before sentencing, so judges and the public can consider it.
- Report on the annual cost of incarceration and the office's efforts to reduce it.
- Work with legislators to reduce corrections budgets along with declining prison and jail populations. Advocate for the reinvestment of savings in crime prevention, improved law enforcement, recidivism reduction, and improving the lives of people and communities affected by incarceration.

Example: Philadelphia District Attorney Larry Krasner has instructed prosecutors to announce the cost of incarceration at sentencing. In a memo describing the new policy, the D.A. provides the following example: "If you are seeking a sentence of 3 years incarceration, state on the record that the cost to the taxpayer will be $126,000.00 (3 × $42,000.00) if not more and explain why you believe that cost is justified."

21. Employ the Language of Respect

Overview: Commonly used terms like "convict," "ex-convict," and "felon" are dehumanizing. They reduce people to their criminal status and perpetuate the stigma of criminal convictions, promoting negative stereotypes that inhibit reform and impede rehabilitation and reentry.

Language affects perception; it also evolves. Once-established terms are abandoned as offensive (like "coloreds" or "illegals") while terms that once seemed unwieldy ("people of color") become familiar. The words we use also affect policy: mass incarceration has stemmed in part from harsh law-and-order rhetoric.

Recommendations

- When possible, in written materials and in representing the office, use phrases that convey information about criminal status without dehumanizing. Examples include "person convicted of a misdemeanor [or felony]," "incarcerated [or formerly incarcerated] person," "people behind bars," and "person with a criminal record."
- Try to avoid terms like "convict," and "parolee," which reduce a person to his or her criminal status, and terms like "rapist," and "drug dealer," which reduce a person to a particular act. (In an internal report of case outcomes, terms like "parolee" or "inmate" may be appropriate. However, such usage should be the exception.)
- In general, a person charged with a crime should not be called an "offender." The word "defendant" is a good substitute. Try to honor people's wishes about the words used to describe them.
- In cases involving children and teenagers, refer to them and their families by their names and avoid dehumanizing references such as "minor" or "juvenile," which have become synonymous with "criminal offender."
- Help change the narrative of crime and justice. Phrases like "tough on crime," "the wrong element," and "don't do the crime if you can't do the time" reinforced the narrative of mass incarceration. So did calling constitutional protections "technicalities" and "loopholes," or describing alternatives to incarceration as "coddling." To help propel criminal justice reform, prosecutors should talk about "mercy," "justice," "compassion," and "fairness" in ways that resonate with the public.
- Counsel prosecutors to avoid dehumanizing language in court. Words like "animal" and "gangbanger" should be off-limits.

Examples: In 2016, the Justice Department announced that the Office of Justice Programs will no longer use words like "felon" or "convict" to refer to formerly incarcerated people. The new terms are "person who committed a crime" and "individual who was incarcerated." The Department of Corrections in Pennsylvania announced a "people-first" language change for those released from jail or prison: instead of "offender," "felon," or "ex-con," the department adopted the term "reentrant."

NOTES

Introduction

xiv *most disadvantaged communities:* Winnie Hu, "Guardian of a Brooklyn Housing Project," *New York Times*, September 25, 2017.

xiv *measured by health as well as economic insecurity:* Citizens' Committee for Children of New York, *From Strengths to Solutions: An Asset-Based Approach to Meeting Community Needs in Brownsville*, 2017.

xvi *Writing up the results:* Danielle Sered, *Young Men of Color and the Other Side of Harm: Addressing Disparities in Our Responses to Violence*, Vera Institute of Justice, December 2014, citing R. Borum, "Assessing Violence Risk Among Youth," *Journal of Clinical Psychology* (2000) 1263–88; and S. N. Jennifer and R. B. Ruback, "Violent Victimization as a Risk Factor for Violent Offending Among Juveniles," *Juvenile Justice Bulletin* 2002.

xvii *which wasn't the same as self-defense:* Bernard Harcourt, a law and political science professor, puts it like this: "Gun carrying is a *preemptive* measure against victimization." Bernard Harcourt, *Language of the Gun* (Chicago: University of Chicago Press, 2006), 32.

xviii *"although many of the boys":* Victor M. Rios, *Punished: Policing the Lives of Black and Latino Boys* (New York: New York University Press, 2011), 127.

xxii *specialized gun court:* Teitelman decided how to handle gun cases in consultation with the prosecutors who supervised the various parts of Brooklyn, divided into zones, and the assistant D.A.s who shepherded cases through the gun court.

xxiii *It might well increase the chance:* Francis Cullen et al., "Prisons Do Not Reduce

Recidivism: The High Cost of Ignoring Science," *Prison Journal* 91, no. 3 (July 2011).

xxv *poor communities, especially if they are mostly black or brown:* In 2010, the incarceration rate was 450 per 100,000 for white people and 2,306 per 100,000 for black people. Income difference is not the only factor that explains the gap, but it's the primary one. Calculating the probability of ever having been jailed, of being jailed for more than a month, being jailed after arrest, and being jailed for more than a year, Nathaniel Lewis finds that only for the last outcome does being black make a statistically significant difference. "And even in that case, whites in the lowest class group are more likely to have been incarcerated for more than a year than blacks in the second-to-lowest class group." Racial disparity persists when he constructs a counterfactual scenario that eliminates the racial wealth gap, but it's far smaller. Nathaniel Lewis, "Mass Incarceration: New Jim Crow, Class War, or Both?" People's Policy Project, January 30, 2018. See also Cedric Johnson, "The Panthers Can't Save Us Now," *Catalyst*, Spring 2017.

xxv *has* quintupled *since the 1980s, to a total of almost 2.2 million:* Jodi M. Brown et al., *Correctional Populations in the United States, 1994*, Bureau of Justice Statistics, June 1996, 5; Danielle Kaeble and Mary Cowhig, *Correctional Populations in the United States, 2016*, Bureau of Justice Statistics, April 2018, 2.

xxv *five to ten times higher:* Jeremy Travis, Bruce Western, and Steve Redburn, eds., *The Growth of Incarceration in the United States: Exploring Causes and Consequences* (Washington, DC: National Academies Press, 2014), 13.

xxv *a prosecutor's errors (or, less frequently, willful misconduct):* Peter Joy, "The Relationship Between Prosecutorial Misconduct and Wrongful Convictions," *Wisconsin Law Review* 2006, no. 2 (2006): 403.

xxv *the choices of prosecutors are largely to blame:* Sonja B. Starr and M. Marit Rehavi, "Mandatory Sentencing and Racial Disparity: Assessing the Role of Prosecutors and the Effects of *Booker,*" *Yale Law Journal* 123 (October 2013).

xxvi *"The power imbalance blew my mind":* Davis is the author of *Arbitrary Justice: The Power of the American Prosecutor* (Oxford: Oxford University Press, 2009).

xxvii *people tend to uphold:* Tom Tyler, *Why People Obey the Law* (Princeton, NJ: Princeton University Press, 2006). See also Tom Tyler, "Procedural Justice, Legitimacy, and the Effective Rule of Law," *Crime and Justice* 30 (2003): 283–357; and Andrew V. Papachristos, Tracey L. Meares, and Jeffrey Fagan, "Why Do Criminals Obey the Law? The Influence of Legitimacy and Social Networks on Active Gun Offenders," *Journal of Criminal Law and Criminology* 102 (2012).

xxviii *more than 95 percent:* Almost eighteen million defendants were prosecuted for misdemeanors and felonies in state court each year for the past decade or more. Court Statistics Project, "Total Incoming Criminal Caseloads Reported by State Courts, All States, 2007–2016." The share of misdemeanors tends to be about 80 percent and the share of felonies about 20 percent. The number of annual felony filings in federal court is about 140,000. Misdemeanors in federal court are rare. Court Statistics Project, "Statewide Criminal Caseload Composition in 31 States, 2016."

xxviii *close to a fifty-year low:* This remains true despite an uptick in 2015 and 2016, concentrated in several midsized cities. Jeff Asher, "The U.S. Murder Rate Is Up but Still Far Below Its 1980 Peak," *FiveThirtyEight*, September 25, 2017; and Jeff Asher, "U.S. Murder Rate for 2018 Is on Track for a Big Drop," *New York Times*, Dec. 6, 2018.

xxviii *$43 billion a year on prisons and jails, at a cost of $15,000 to $70,000:* Travis Mai and Ram Subramanian, "The Price of Prisons: Examining State Spending Trends, 2010–2015," Vera Institute of Justice, May 2017.

xxviii *sentences for drug offenses have already plummeted:* Jeremy Peters, "Albany Reaches Deal to Repeal '70s Drug Laws," *New York Times*, March 25, 2009.

xxviii *more than half of state prisoners nationwide are now behind bars:* John Pfaff, *Locked In: The True Causes of Mass Incarceration and How to Achieve Real Reform* (New York: Basic Books, 2017), 11.

xxviii *Nationally, cutting the prison population by 50 percent:* One of the first people to make this point was Yale law professor James Forman Jr. In 2011, he wrote that "more prisoners are locked up for violent offenses than for any other type. . . . If every person in prison and jail for a drug offense were released *tomorrow*, the United States would still have the world's largest penal system." James Forman Jr., "Harm's Way: Understanding Race and Punishment," *Boston Review*, January 1, 2011.

xxx *The roles are "obviously unharmonious":* United States v. Bagley, 473 U.S. 667 (1985).

xxx *The prosecutor "is in a peculiar and very definite sense":* Berger v. United States, 295 U.S. 78 (1935).

xxx *"The citizen's safety lies":* Robert Jackson, "The Federal Prosecutor," *Journal of the American Judicature Society* 24 (June 1940): 20.

CHAPTER 1

3 *"Please help me":* Emily Bazelon, "She Was Convicted of Killing Her Mother. Prosecutors Withheld the Evidence That Would Have Freed Her," *New York Times Magazine*, August 1, 2017.

3 *pronounced her dead at 5:18 a.m.: State of Tennessee v. Noura Jackson*, 444 S.W.3d 554 (2014), 5.

12 *extremely rare for daughters to kill their mothers:* Matthew Durose et al., *Family Violence Statistics*, Bureau of Justice Statistics, June 2005, 19.

17 *In 2002, an Illinois commission found:* Illinois Governor's Commission on Capital Punishment, *Report of the Governor's Commission on Capital Punishment*, State of Illinois, April 15, 2002.

17 *a government report in Canada:* FPT Heads of Prosecutions Committee Working Group, *Report on the Prevention of Miscarriages of Justice*, September 2004, 35–41.

18 *2006 article for the* Wisconsin Law Review: Keith A. Findley and Michael S. Scott, "The Multiple Dimensions of Tunnel Vision in Criminal Cases," *Wisconsin Law Review* 2 (June 2006): 327–29.

18 *"must be convinced":* Findley and Scott, "The Multiple Dimensions of Tunnel Vision in Criminal Cases," 329. See also Keith Findley, "Tunnel Vision," in *Conviction of the Innocent: Lessons from Psychological Research*, ed. Brian Cutler

(Washington, DC: American Psychological Association Press, 2011); Alafair Burke, "Improving Prosecutorial Decision Making: Some Lessons of Cognitive Science," *William and Mary Law Review* 47 (March 2006): 1587–633; Bruce Green, "Why Should Prosecutors 'Seek Justice'?," *Fordham Urban Law Journal* 26 (1999): 607–44; and Bennett L. Gershman, "A Moral Standard for the Prosecutor's Exercise of the Charging Discretion," *Fordham Urban Law Journal* 20 (1993): 513–30.

18 *"'The honorable prosecutor'"*: Randolph N. Jonakait, "The Ethical Prosecutor's Misconduct," *Criminal Law Bulletin* 23 (1987): 550–67, quoted in Findley and Scott, "The Multiple Dimensions of Tunnel Vision in Criminal Cases," 329.

18 *"unindicted co-ejaculator"*: Findley and Scott, "The Multiple Dimensions of Tunnel Vision in Criminal Cases," 316.

18 *"conviction psychology"*: George Felkenes, "The Prosecutor: A Look at Reality," *Southwestern University Law Review* 7 (1975): 110.

19 *"I want to give the death penalty"*: Ronald Wright and Kay Levine, "The Cure for Young Prosecutors' Syndrome," *Arizona Law Review* 56 (2014): 1065–128.

19 *prosecutorial culture*: Deborah Rhode, *Character* (Oxford: Oxford University Press, 2019).

19 *"everyone is guilty all the time"*: The former prosecutors I quote here asked me not to use their names because they still work as lawyers in Memphis.

20 *"devil's advocate"*: Findley and Scott, "The Multiple Dimensions of Tunnel Vision in Criminal Cases," 389.

CHAPTER 2

26 *"the criminal is to go free"*: People v. Defore, 150 N.E. 585 (1926).

26 *"'There is another consideration'"*: Mapp v. Ohio, 367 U.S. 643 (1961).

26 *In* Miranda v. Arizona: *Miranda v. Arizona*, 384 U.S. 436 (1966).

27 *carving out significant exceptions*: It's fair to say the framers didn't have this in mind when they wrote the Constitution. "Supporters of the exclusionary rule cannot point to a single major statement from the Founding—or even the Antebellum or Reconstruction eras," Akhil Reed Amar wrote in "Fourth Amendment First Principles," *Harvard Law Review* 107 (February 1994): 757–819.

27 *the state gets a pass*: United States v. Leon, 468 U.S. 897 (1984).

27 *"isolated negligence"*: Herring v. United States, 555 U.S. 135 (2009).

27 *Courts increasingly do a cost-benefit test*: Richard Re, "The Exclusionary Rule on the Brink," *Washington Post*, March 3, 2014.

27 *As the exceptions swallow the rule*: Other countries have also rejected the automatic exclusion of evidence, favoring a balancing test that weighs the gravity of police misconduct against the gravity of losing the evidence, but they have a different law enforcement culture from the United States. Adam Liptak, "U.S. Exceptionalism Extends to Evidence Rule," *New York Times*, July 18, 2008.

28 *"the warnings have become"*: Dickerson v. United States, 530 U.S. 428 (2000).

28 *The Court has since*: Berghuis v. Thompkins, 560 U.S. 370 (2010).

28 *William Stuntz*: William Stuntz, *The Collapse of American Criminal Justice* (Cambridge, MA: Harvard University Press, 2011).

30 *large-scale study in the Bronx:* James Anderson, Maya Buenaventura, and Paul Heaton, "The Effect of Holistic Defense on Criminal Justice Outcomes," *Harvard Law Review* (forthcoming).

30 *rejected more than half:* J. David Goodman and Al Baker, "Prison Diversion Programs in New York Face New Scrutiny After Police Officer's Killing," *New York Times*, December 15, 2015.

31 *The* New York Post *blamed:* Rebecca Rosenberg and Laura Italiano, "How Accused Cop Killer Dodged Prison for Freedom Before Fatal Shooting," *New York Post*, October 25, 2015.

32 *less than 10 percent:* Citizens' Committee for Children of New York, *From Strengths to Solutions.*

CHAPTER 3

38 *90 percent of state judges:* Jed Handelsman Shugerman, *The People's Courts* (Cambridge, MA: Harvard University Press, 2012).

38 *owed the city $2 million:* John Eligon, "New York City Is Owed More than $2 Million in Delinquent Forfeitures," *New York Times*, January 9, 2011.

38 *credit card:* Independent Commission on New York City Criminal Justice and Incarceration Reform, *A More Just New York City*, April 2, 2017, 44.

39 *"was the only important factor":* Mary Phillips, *Research Brief No. 9: Prosecutors' Bail Request and the CJA Release Recommendation: What Do They Tell the Judge?*, New York City Criminal Justice Agency, August 2005, 2, 7; Independent Commission on New York City Criminal Justice and Incarceration Reform, *A More Just New York City*, 43.

39 *Bill of Rights of 1689:* The English prohibition against "excessive bail" challenged the customary practice of automatically detaining the accused. Bail represented the chance to go free before trial by guaranteeing one's return to court, and early on, that guarantee could take a form other than cash. People could pledge property as their bond, to be forfeited only if they fled, or ask someone to pledge money on their behalf. Sometimes the accused simply gave his word that he would return to court—what's called a personal or signature bond.

39 *"reasonably calculated":* Stack v. Boyle, 342 U.S. 1 (1951).

39 *thousands of people remained:* Sam Ervin, "The Legislative Role in Bail Reform," *George Washington Law Review* 35 (March 1967): 434.

40 *"problem, simply stated":* "Testimony by Attorney General Robert Kennedy on Bail Legislation," Subcommittees on Constitutional Rights and Improvements in Judicial Machinery, Senate Judiciary Committee, August 4, 1964.

40 *passed the Bail Reform Act:* Bail Reform Act of 1966, Pub. L. 89-465, 80 Stat. 214-17, June 22, 1966.

40 *by one-third:* Some cities went even further. In Minneapolis, for example, the rate of pretrial detention fell from more than 50 percent to less than 15 percent. Bail agents went out of business. Wayne H. Thomas, *Bail Reform in America* (Berkeley: University of California Press, 1976); Cassie Miller, "The Two-Tiered Justice System: Money Bail in Historical Perspective," Southern Poverty Law Center, June 6, 2017.

40 *Congress amended the Bail Reform Act:* Bail Reform Act of 1984, Pub. L. 98–473, 98 Stat. 1976–87, October 12, 1984. The precursor to the 1984 law was an amendment to allow for pretrial detention proposed by Richard Nixon, who called for no bail for "dangerous hardcore recidivists" who he claimed were "being arrested two, three, seven times for new offenses while awaiting trials." Samuel Wiseman, "Discrimination, Coercion, and the Bail Reform Act of 1984: The Loss of the Core Constitutional Protections of the Excessive Bail Clause," *Fordham Urban Law Journal* 36 (January 2009): n. 67. See also John Mitchell, "Bail Reform and the Constitutionality of Pretrial Detention," *Virginia Law Review* 55 (November 1969): 1223.

40 *For crimes of violence:* The presumption of confinement also applies to *any* felony if the offender has been convicted of two or more crimes of violence or certain drug crimes.

40 *"the norm":* United States v. Salerno, 481 U.S. 739 (1987).

40 *the reverse has become true:* In the 1970s and 1980s, in response to rising crime, most states passed laws that directed judges to consider whether the accused posed a threat to public safety. See Paul Heaton, Sandra Mayson, and Megan Stevenson, *The Downstream Consequences of Misdemeanor Pretrial Detention,* University of Pennsylvania Institute for Law and Economics Research Paper No. 16–18 (2016), 5; John Goldkamp, "Danger and Detention: A Second Generation of Bail Reform," *Journal of Criminal Law and Criminology* 76, no. 1 (1985): 2. New York is a notable exception. See N.Y. Criminal Procedure Law Sec. 510.30 for New York's bail-setting criteria. Eric Washington, "Brennan Lecture: State Courts and the Promise of Pretrial Justice in Criminal Cases," *New York University Law Review* 91, no. 5 (2016): 1091.

40 *nearly 60 percent:* Amaryllis Austin, "The Presumption for Detention Statute's Relationship to Release," *Federal Probation,* September 2017, 53, 60.

40 *740,000 held on any given day, about two-thirds:* Zhen Zeng, *Jail Inmates in 2016,* Bureau of Justice Statistics, February 2018, 1, 4.

40 *because they can't afford to post bail:* Brian A. Reaves, *Felony Defendants in Large Urban Counties, 2009—Statistical Tables,* Bureau of Justice Statistics, December 2013, 17.

40 *all of the growth:* Zeng, *Jail Inmates in 2016,* 9.

41 *The annual total is $9 billion:* Eric Holder, speech at National Symposium on Pretrial Justice, Pretrial Justice Institute, June 1, 2011, Washington, D.C., in *National Symposium on Pretrial Justice: Summary Report of Proceedings,* 30.

41 *Eighty-eight percent of those:* Clifford Keenan, "We Need More Bail Reform," Pretrial Services Agency for the District of Columbia, September 2013.

41 *the rate of return to court:* Matthew DeMichele et al., "The Public Safety Assessment: A Re-Validation and Assessment of Predictive Utility and Differential Prediction by Race and Gender in Kentucky," Laura and John Arnold Foundation, April 25, 2018, 21.

41 *Colorado:* Michael Jones, *Unsecured Bonds: The As Effective and Most Efficient Pretrial Release Option,* Pretrial Justice Institute, October 2013, 11.

41 *Bronx Freedom Fund and the Brooklyn Community Bail Fund:* Sarah Phillips, *National Survey of Community Bail Funds: Report to the Community*, Smart Decarceration Initiative, Washington University in St. Louis, 3. By law, the Brooklyn and Bronx bail funds are not permitted to pay bail for people accused of felonies.

41 *95 percent:* Plaintiffs' Summary of Other Jurisdictions, *O'Donnell v. Harris County*, No. H-16-1414, 2017 WL 1542457 (S.D.T.X. April 28, 2018), 2. Multnomah County in Oregon started using automated reminders for court appearances and reported a drop in no-shows of more than 30 percent and savings of more than $1.5 million in fiscal year 2007. Matt O'Keefe, "Court Appearance Notification System: 2007 Analysis Highlights," Multnomah County Local Public Safety Coordinating Council, June 2007.

41 *only 1 percent are arrested:* Criminal Justice Policy Program, Harvard Law School, "Moving Beyond Money: A Primer on Bail Reform," October 2016, 15; Nicole Hong and Shibani Mahtani, "Cash Bail, a Cornerstone of the Criminal-Justice System, Is Under Threat," *Wall Street Journal*, May 22, 2017.

41 *about the same for Kentucky:* DeMichele et al., "The Public Safety Assessment," 21.

42 *biggest-ever bail study:* Heaton et al., *The Downstream Consequences of Misdemeanor Pretrial Detention*, 4.

42 *"government intrusion":* Marc Levin, "Bail Reform: Smart Choice for Taxpayers and Public Safety," *TribTalk*, May 19, 2017.

42 *The Charles Koch Foundation:* "Penn Law's Quattrone Center Launches New Research on Reforming, Improving Criminal Justice System with $2.2 Million from Charles Koch Foundation," University of Pennsylvania Law School, March 7, 2017. The Kochs are also spending $26 million to study criminal justice and education reform at a consortium of historically black colleges and $4.5 million on the Drug Enforcement and Policy Center at Ohio State University. Molly Hensley-Clancy, "The Koch Foundation Is Flooding Colleges with Money," *BuzzFeed News*, February 6, 2018.

42 *the state could have prevented four thousand new crimes:* Heaton et al., *The Downstream Consequences of Misdemeanor Pretrial Detention*, 45.

43 *25 percent more likely:* Heaton et al., *The Downstream Consequences of Misdemeanor Pretrial Detention*, 22.

43 *twice as great for first-time defendants:* Heaton et al., *The Downstream Consequences of Misdemeanor Pretrial Detention*, 23–24.

43 *plea mills:* Kevin Pantazi quoting Paul Heaton, one of the authors of the Penn Law study, in "Lawsuit Says Jacksonville Can't Jail Defendants for Being Too Poor to Pay Bail," *Florida Times-Union*, August 31, 2017.

43 *they often take the deal:* Issa Kohler-Hausmann, *Misdemeanorland: Criminal Courts and Social Control in an Age of Broken Windows Policing* (Princeton, NJ: Princeton University Press, 2018).

43 *a quarter of criminal cases end in dismissal:* Reaves, *Felony Defendants in Large Urban Counties, 2009—Statistical Tables*, 24.

43 *$30,000 in earnings:* David Arnold, Will Dobbie, and Crystal S. Yang, "Racial Bias in Bail Decisions," *Quarterly Journal of Economics* (forthcoming), 2. In Baltimore, a father who couldn't make bail of about $2,000 emerged from jail without a job or savings. He and his wife wound up living in a minivan with their young children. Shaila Dewan, "When Bail Is Out of Defendant's Reach, Other Costs Mount," *New York Times*, June 10, 2015.

44 *"relying on inaccurate stereotypes":* Arnold et al., "Racial Bias in Bail Decisions," 3. See also Color of Change, ACLU Campaign for Smart Justice, *Selling Off Our Freedom: How Insurance Corporations Have Taken Over Our Bail System*, May 2017, 18: "There is enormous and arbitrary variation as well as demonstrated racial disparity in the bail amounts and conditions set for people."

45 *evidence doesn't bear that out:* The bail industry often cites a 2007 Bureau of Justice Statistics report on failure-to-appear rates from 1990 to 2004. The failure-to-appear rate for defendants released on surety bonds (processed through a bail agent) was 18 percent, compared to 22 percent for defendants released on deposit bonds (not through a bail agent) and on conditional release, and 26 percent for defendants released on their own recognizance. When the BJS controlled for other factors, however, such as the likelihood that bail agents were less likely to post bond for defendants with criminal histories, the new rates were 20 percent for surety bonds, 24 percent for conditional release, 20 percent for deposit bonds, and 24 percent for release on their own recognizance. So surety bonds processed through bail agents actually *aren't* any more effective than deposit bonds after controlling for variables that influence bail agents' decisions. Thomas Cohen and Brian Reaves, *Pretrial Release of Felony Defendants in State Courts*, Bureau of Justice Statistics, November 2007, 9–10.

45 **New York Times** *published a story:* Jessica Silver-Greenberg and Shaila Dewan, "When Bail Feels Less Like Freedom, More Like Extortion," *New York Times*, March 31, 2018.

45 *"In England, Canada and other countries":* Adam Liptak, "Illegal Globally, Bail for Profit Remains in U.S.," *New York Times*, January 29, 2008. The second part of the quote paraphrases F. E. Devine, who wrote a book surveying the international bail scene; F. E. Devine, *Commercial Bail Bonding* (New York: Praeger, 1991).

46 *$2 billion a year:* Gillian White, "Who Really Makes Money Off of Bail Bonds?", *Atlantic*, May 12, 2017. Here's how bail companies make money: If your bail is set at $10,000 and you have the money on hand, you can get out of jail *and* get your money back from the courts when your case is over. But if you don't have $10,000 in cash, you go to a bail agent who guarantees your bond, usually for a 10 percent fee. You don't get that $1,000 back, and if you can't pay it up front, you'll pay on an installment plan with interest, sometimes at sky-high, payday-lending rates. As long as you don't flee, the agent gets the money back at the end of your case and pockets your fee and interest payments, too.

46 *Tokio Marine:* Color of Change, ACLU Campaign for Smart Justice, *Selling Off Our Freedom*, 22; Tokio Marine, *Integrated Annual Report 2017*, 23.

46 *Courts there take bail payments:* Heaton et al., *The Downstream Consequences*

of Misdemeanor Pretrial Detention, 4. Three other states—Illinois, Kentucky, and Oregon—have banned for-profit bail.

46 *tried to push:* Brendan Fischer, "Wisconsin GOP Sneaks ALEC-Supported For-Profit Bail Bonding into Budget Bill," PRWatch, Center for Media and Democracy, June 10, 2013; Michael Phillis, "Wisconsin Judges Say Bail Bonds System Would Shortchange Crime Victims," *Milwaukee Journal Sentinel*, June 15, 2013.

46 *the American Legislative Exchange Council:* The group has circulated a dozen or more bills to cement the role of for-profit bail. An ABC newsletter praised ALEC for being a "life preserver." "The American Bail Coalition's Iliad," *American Bail Coalition Newsletter*, October 2010, 3.

46 *Governor Scott Walker vetoed it:* Jason Stein and Karen Herzog, "Scott Walker Issues 57 Vetoes, Signs $68 Billion Wisconsin Budget," *Milwaukee Journal Sentinel*, June 30, 2013.

46 *in a sweep the previous year:* California Department of Insurance, "South Bay Bail Agents Targeted in Law Enforcement Sweep," September 9, 2015; Dave Jones, "Recommendations for California's Bail System," California Department of Insurance, February 2018.

47 *Mama's Bail Out Day:* Charlotte Alter, "Black Lives Matter Groups Are Bailing Black Women Out of Jail for Mother's Day," *Time*, May 12, 2017.

47 *support from Jay-Z and John Legend:* Shawn Carter, "Jay-Z: For Father's Day, I'm Taking On the Exploitative Bail Industry," *Time*, June 16, 2017; and John Legend (@johnlegend), "On Father's Day and every day, let's make sure these kids feel supported and stay connected to their dads," Twitter, June 16, 2017.

47 *"Declaration of War":* Alan Feuer, "New Jersey Is Front Line in a National Battle over Bail," *New York Times*, August 21, 2017.

47 *a well-connected California lobbying group:* Charles Davis, "For Now, California Bails on Bail Reform," *American Prospect*, August 30, 2017.

47 *lobbying arm for prosecutors:* Jessica Pishko, "Prosecutors Are Banding Together to Prevent Criminal-Justice Reform," *Nation*, October 18, 2017.

47 *"negative impact on public safety":* California District Attorneys Association, "Re: AB 42—Oppose," Letter to Rob Bonta, April 11, 2017.

48 *California appeals court heard: In re Humphrey*, 228 Cal. Rptr. 3d 513 (Ct. App. 2018).

48 *reversed the presumption:* Max Rivlin-Nader, "California Could Soon End Money Bail, But at What Cost?" *The Appeal*, August 22, 2018; Jeff Adachi, "This Is Not the Bail Reform California Needs," *Sacramento Bee*, August 13, 2018.

49 *Stuart Rabner:* Kate Zernike, "Panel Proposes Changes to New Jersey Bail System," *New York Times*, March 20, 2014.

49 *more than fifteen hundred people:* Marie VanNostrand, *New Jersey Jail Population Analysis: Identifying Opportunities to Safely and Responsibly Reduce the Jail Population*, Drug Policy Alliance, March 2013, 13.

49 *a risk assessment tool:* Developed by the Laura and John Arnold Foundation, the assessment tool isn't perfect. Including prior convictions means it reflects racial bias in the system from charging on. But the tool tries to avoid penalizing people

for living alone or in poor neighborhoods, asking no questions about where a defendant lives or about his family and community ties. The Drug Policy Alliance and the state ACLU backed it, monitoring the effects.

49 *population dropped: Criminal Justice Reform Statistics: Jan. 01, 2017–Dec. 31, 2017,* New Jersey Judiciary, January 8, 2018.

49 *crime, including violent offenses, also fell:* New Jersey State Police, *Uniform Crime Reporting 2017 Current Crime Data,* May 4, 2018; Pretrial Justice Institute, *State of Pretrial Justice in America,* November 2017, 4.

49 *putting bond agents out of business:* Michaelangelo Conte, "Bail Reform Is Killing Our Business, Bail Bondsmen Say," *Jersey Journal,* January 16, 2017. In New Jersey, police and prosecutors decide whether to charge a given arrestee with a complaint-summons or a complaint-warrant, taking into account a preliminary public safety assessment and the nature of the offense. Defendants issued complaint-summonses are automatically released; those with complaint-warrants are subject to release at a judge's discretion. In 2017, 69 percent of defendants were released on complaint-summonses shortly after arrest. Of the people issued complaint-warrants, 18.1 percent were ultimately detained. That's about 5.6 percent of the total number of defendants. Glenn Grant, *Criminal Justice Reform Report to the Governor and the Legislature for Calendar Year 2017,* New Jersey Judiciary, February 2018, 4.

CHAPTER 4

54 *Barry Goldwater and Richard Nixon:* Goldwater appealed to white voters in his 1964 run for president with calls for law and order that linked crime and civil rights protests. Nixon ran four years later on the promise to "restore order and respect for law in this country." Elizabeth Hinton, *From the War on Poverty to the War on Crime: The Making of Mass Incarceration in America* (Cambridge, MA: Harvard University Press, 2016), 137–40; Beverly Gage, "America Is Safer than It Used to Be. So Why Do We Still Have Calls for 'Law and Order'?," *New York Times Magazine,* August 30, 2016.

54 *disturbing pattern:* Hynes also faced criticism for a 2011 case in Crown Heights in which, it was revealed, prosecutors did not disclose that a young Orthodox Jewish woman who accused four black men of rape had later partly recanted. Charges were dropped against all four.

55 *"offering young, gun-toting people":* Goodman and Baker, "Prison Diversion Programs."

55 *stage of development:* Neuroscience research, which has shown that young adults, into their mid-twenties, haven't fully developed the capacity for impulse control or withstanding peer pressure. Laurence Steinberg, "Should the Science of Adolescent Brain Development Inform Public Policy?," *Issues in Science and Technology* 28, no. 3 (Spring 2012): 67–78; Laurence Steinberg, "A Social Neuroscience Perspective on Adolescent Risk-Taking," *Developmental Review* 28, no. 1 (March 2008): 78–106; Beatriz Luna and Catherine Wright, "Adolescent Brain Development: Implications for the Juvenile Criminal Justice System," in Kirk Heilbrun et

al., *APA Handbook of Psychology and Juvenile Justice*, 91–116 (Washington, D.C.: APA, 2016).

56 *Brooklyn had a track record:* Jim Parsons et al., *End of an Era? The Impact of Drug Law Reform in New York City*, Vera Institute of Justice, January 2015, 14.

56 *Red Hook Community Justice Center:* Cynthia G. Lee et al., *A Community Court Grows in Brooklyn: A Comprehensive Evaluation of the Red Hook Community Justice Center*, National Center for State Courts, November 2013.

59 *Twelve states:* "Concealed Carry," Giffords Law Center to Prevent Gun Violence, https://lawcenter.giffords.org/gun-laws/policy-areas/guns-in-public/concealed-carry. Because most states outlaw only unpermitted carry, sometimes only under certain circumstances, New York's CPW laws differ from their statutes. Those in Massachusetts and Washington, D.C., are comparable to New York's. In Massachusetts, which requires owner's licenses, simple possession is punishable by up to two years and/or a $500 fine. Possession outside the home is punishable by eighteen months to five years.

In D.C., anyone who possesses an unregistered gun is subject to a fine of up to $2,500 and/or prison for up to one year. Anyone who carries a gun without a permit to carry is subject to up to five years in prison and/or a fine of up to $12,500.

59 *Bloomberg wanted Congress to ban assault rifles:* Michael Bloomberg, "6 Ways to Stop Gun Madness," *USA Today*, December 18, 2012.

59 *approval from the NYPD:* "A license to carry or possess a pistol or revolver, not otherwise limited as to place or time of possession, shall be effective throughout the state, except that the same shall not be valid within the city of New York unless a special permit granting validity is issued by the police commissioner of that city." NY Penal L § 400.00 (2017).

59 *prosecutors could charge CPW2:* 6A N.Y. Prac., "*Criminal possession of weapon— Criminal possession of weapon in second degree*," Criminal Law § 33:13 (4th ed.) Another subdivision of CPW2 requires prosecutors to prove intent. State courts have inferred intent "from the defendant's actions and surrounding circumstances," including the presence of drugs. Technically, the most severe gun possession charge in New York is criminal possession of a weapon in the first degree (CPW1), which includes possession of explosives with intent to use and possession of ten or more firearms. But it's rarely used. In New York City, only one person was charged with CPW1 between 2014 and 2016. Data from the New York State Division of Criminal Justice Services. In 2013, New York again made its gun laws more punitive by turning another offense, criminal possession of a firearm, which applies to unloaded weapons in the home, into either a felony or a misdemeanor.

60 *"I would say to every colored soldier":* Quoted in Adam Winkler, "The Secret History of Guns," *Atlantic*, September 2011.

60 *"Remember there are 80,000":* James Forman Jr., *Locking Up Our Own: Crime and Punishment in Black America* (New York: Farrar, Straus and Giroux, 2017), 67.

61 *"by whatever means necessary":* Winkler, "Secret History"; Forman, *Locking Up Our Own*, 69.

61 *bought some of their first guns:* Winkler, "Secret History."

60 *In 1967, thirty members:* Thad Morgan, "How the Black Panthers Inspired California's Strict Gun Laws," History.com. Backlash followed. Governor Ronald Reagan told reporters that day that he saw "no reason why on the street today a citizen should be carrying loaded weapons" and got behind a bill to prohibit the open carrying of loaded weapons.

60 *"Black people know":* Forman, *Locking Up Our Own*, 70.

61 *the young men of their communities:* Forman, *Locking Up Our Own*, 72–75.

61 *"The people who will be stopped":* Forman, *Locking Up Our Own*, 196–203.

62 *"Did Martin Luther King":* Forman, *Locking Up Our Own*, 195.

62 *Project Exile:* Steven Raphael and Jens Ludwig, "Prison Sentence Enhancements: The Case of Project Exile," in *Evaluating Gun Policy: Effects on Crime and Violence*, ed. Jens Ludwig and Philip J. Cook (Washington, D.C.: Brookings Institution Press, 2003).

62 *"greatly exaggerated":* Steven Levitt, Comment on Raphael and Ludwig, "Prison Sentence Enhancements," in *Evaluating Gun Policy*, 277–78.

62 *other studies:* Bluhm Legal Clinic, Northwestern School of Law, *Combating Gun Violence in Illinois: Evidence-Based Solutions*, October 17, 2013, 3.

62 *more than in any other U.S. city:* "Chicago Was Nation's Murder Capital in 2012: FBI," *Ward Room*, September 19, 2013.

62 *Mayor Rahm Emanuel proposed:* Cheryl Corley, "Proposed Minimum Sentencing Law in Illinois Faces Scrutiny," NPR, October 24, 2013.

63 *"There is no credible evidence":* Bluhm Legal Clinic, *Combating Gun Violence in Illinois*, 2. See also Mike Riggs, "Could Stiffer Penalties for Illegally Carrying a Gun Reduce Violence in Chicago?," *CityLab*, October 17, 2013.

63 *Jens Ludwig:* Jens Ludwig, "Analysis of Potential Costs and Benefits of Illinois HB2265/SB2267: Sentence Enhancements for Unlawful Use of a Weapon (UUW) Offenses," University of Chicago Crime Lab, October 7, 2013.

63 *an op-ed in the* Chicago Sun-Times: Franklin Zimring, "False Premise of Gun Sentences," *Chicago Sun-Times*, October 16, 2013.

63 *Black legislators:* Ray Long, "Black Lawmakers Block Emanuel's Gun Bill," *Chicago Tribune*, November 8, 2013.

63 *an uncomfortable parallel:* Ben Levin does an excellent job of laying out this argument in his article "Guns and Drugs," *Fordham Law Review* 84 (2016): 2173–226.

64 *arrests and incarceration for drugs skyrocketed:* Travis, Western, and Redburn, eds., *The Growth of Incarceration*, 48–50; Howard Snyder, Alexia Cooper, and Joseph Mulako-Wangota, "Arrest Rates of All Persons for Drug Abuse Violations," Arrest Data Analysis Tool, Bureau of Justice Statistics.

64 *arrested for it four times as often:* Howard Snyder, Alexia Cooper, and Joseph Mulako-Wangota, "Arrest Rates of Whites and Blacks for Weapons Offenses," Arrest Data Analysis Tool, Bureau of Justice Statistics. Black people are arrested for weapon possession at a rate of 129 per 100,000 compared with 32 arrests per 100,000 for white people.

64 *24 percent compared with 36 percent:* Kim Parker, Juliana Horowitz, Ruth Igielnik, Baxter Oliphant, and Anna Brown, *America's Complex Relationship with Guns*, Pew Research Center, June 2017, 7.

64 *The crisis is real:* For an invaluable discussion of the problem, see Paul Butler's chapter "Black Male Violence" in *Chokehold: Policing Black Men* (New York: New Press, 2017), 117–148.

64 *leading cause of death:* Marty Langley and Josh Sugarmann, *Black Homicide Victimization in the United States*, Violence Policy Center, April 2018; "Leading Causes of Death (LCOD) by Age Group, Black Males—United States, 2015," *Leading Causes of Death in Males, 2015*, Centers for Disease Control and Prevention, April 16, 2018.

64 *half of murder victims:* Black men and women accounted for about 52 percent of murder victims in 2016 and about 50 percent of offenders from 1980 to 2008. FBI, *Crime in the United States, 2016*; Alexia Cooper and Erica Smith, *Homicide Trends in the United States, 1980–2008*, Bureau of Justice Statistics, November 2011. One study, cited by Paul Butler, showed that if black men graduated from college and earned the same incomes as white men, the homicide disparity would fall by more than half; Julie A. Phillips, "White, Black, and Latino Homicide Rates: Why the Difference," *Social Problems* 49, no. 3 (2002).

64 *70 percent of gunshot victims:* Andrew V. Papachristos, Christopher Wildeman, and Elizabeth Roberto, "Tragic, but Not Random: The Social Contagion of Nonfatal Gunshot Injuries," *Social Science and Medicine* 125 (2015): 142. Another analysis showed that being the victim of a shooting or an assault in Chicago was far *more* predictive of committing gun violence than being arrested on charges of gun possession. Jeff Asher and Rob Arthur, "Inside the Algorithm That Tries to Predict Gun Violence in Chicago," *New York Times*, June 13, 2017.

64 *"a different kind of violence":* Maya Schenwar, "Reduce Gun Penalties," *New York Times*, March 14, 2014.

64 *"Guns—and gun violence":* Forman, *Locking Up Our Own*, 77.

65 *National Rifle Association:* The NRA said of the proposed mandatory minimums in Illinois that the law "incorrectly targets otherwise law-abiding citizens, rather than deterring *violent* criminals with harsher penalties." "Illinois: Bill to Create Mandatory Jail Time for Victimless Crimes to Be Heard as Early as October 22," NRA Institute for Legislative Action, October 10, 2013. The NRA has been criticized for failing to defend people killed by the police, like Philando Castile, an African American licensed gun owner who was shot to death by an officer after being pulled over in a Minnesota suburb.

65 *the number of police stops plummeted:* Azi Paybarah, Brendan Cheney, and Colby Hamilton, "De Blasio on Stop-and-Frisk: 'We Changed It Intensely,'" *Politico*, December 8, 2016. Broken-windows policing didn't end entirely and continued to provoke tragedy. Eric Garner's death at the hands of police in Staten Island occurred after he was stopped for the quintessentially minor offense of selling loose cigarettes.

65 *murder rate fell:* U.S. Department of Justice, Federal Bureau of Investigation, *Crime in the United States, 2016*. "Crime in New York City Plunges to a Level Not Seen Since the 1950s" read the headline of Ashley Southall's article in the *New York Times* on December 27, 2017.

66 *did not depend:* Kyle Smith, "We Were Wrong About Stop-and-Frisk," *National Review*, January 1, 2018.

66 *incarceration rate had been falling:* Judith A. Greene and Vincent Schiraldi, "Better by Half: The New York City Story of Winning Large-Scale Decarceration While Increasing Public Safety," *Federal Sentencing Reporter* 29 (October 2016): 22–38.

66 *stuck where it was in the mid-1980s:*

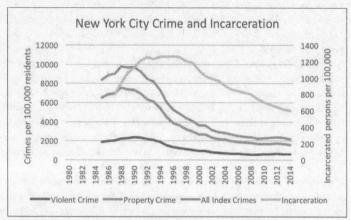

Permission of Brett Greene and Natalia Friedlander

(Data from the Vera Institute of Justice Incarceration Trends Project, and from the FBI.)

66 *seriously difficult question:* Matt Ford, "What Caused the Great Crime Decline in the U.S.?," *Atlantic*, April 15, 2016.

66 *increased access to abortion:* Steven Levitt, "Understanding Why Crime Fell in the 1990s: Four Factors That Explain the Decline and Six That Do Not," *Journal of Economic Perspectives* 18 (Winter 2004): 163–90; John Donohue III and Steven Levitt, "The Impact of Legalized Abortion on Crime," *Quarterly Journal of Economics* 116 (May 2001): 379–420.

66 *exposure to lead:* Kevin Drum, "Lead: America's Real Criminal Element," *Mother Jones*, February 11, 2016. See also Kevin Drum, "An Updated Lead-Crime Roundup for 2018," *Mother Jones*, February 1, 2018.

66 *increasing access to treatment:* Samuel Bondurant, Jason Lindo, and Isaac Swensen, "Substance Abuse Treatment Centers and Local Crime," National Bureau of Economic Research, Working Paper No. 22610, September 2016.

67 *change in the racial composition:* Franklin Zimring, *The City That Became Safe*, (New York: Oxford University Press, 2011), 59–60. In 2017, Heather Mac Donald claimed in the *National Review* that crime in New York fell because some city neighborhoods became more white because of gentrification. The economist Noah Smith made mincemeat of Mac Donald's argument. Posting the graph below on Twitter, Smith wrote: "Since murder peaked around 1990, the black population % has fallen by around 3 percentage points, while the white population % has fallen by over 8 percentage points. Inescapable conclusion: NYC's epic crime

drop was NOT due to the population of the city shifting from black to white. Don't let racial stereotypes eat your brain, folks! Always look at the data." Noah Smith (@Noahpinion), Twitter, December 28, 2017, https://twitter.com/Noahpinion/status/946630526210678786.

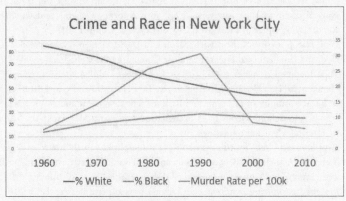

Permission of Brett Greene and Natalia Friedlander

67 *single parents . . . dropping out of high school:* Zimring, *The City That Became Safe*, 71–72.

67 *levels of wealth and social isolation:* Zimring, *The City That Became Safe*, 78–79, 45.

67 *by incapacitating them:* Levitt, "Understanding Why Crime Fell," 177–78.

67 *"modest at best":* Travis, Western, and Redburn, eds., *The Growth of Incarceration*, 131. See also Aaron Chalfin and Justice McCrary, "Criminal Deterrence: A Review of the Literature," *Journal of Economic Literature* 55, no. 1 (2017): 26. The authors call the incapacitation effect "inefficient" because it has diminished over time as prison populations grow.

67 *strong evidence for:* David Roodman, "Impact of Incarceration on Crime," Open Philanthropy Project, September 25, 2017.

67 *never turned to draconian prison sentences:* Alex Kozinski, "Criminal Law 2.0," *Georgetown Law Journal Annual Review of Criminal Procedure* 44 (2015): xvii; "The Curious Case of the Fall in Crime," *Economist*, July 20, 2013.

67 *California has reduced:* Magnus Lofstrom and Steven Raphael, "Incarceration and Crime: Evidence from California's Public Safety Realignment Reform," *Annals of the American Academy of Political and Social Science* 664.1 (2016): 196–220.

67 *Nationally, the population of teenagers:* Violent crime arrests of youth dropped by 68 percent between 1994 and 2014, while from 2001 to 2013, youth incarceration declined 53 percent. Patrick McCarthy, Vincent Schiraldi, and Miriam Shark, "The Future of Youth Justice," *National Institute of Justice* (October 2016).

68 *In New York, law enforcement:* Levitt, "Understanding Why Crime Fell," 173.

68 *CompStat:* Zimring, *The City That Became Safe,* 141–44.

68 *most rigorous licensing processes:* Jonathan Wolfe, "New York Today: What Are New York's Gun Laws?," *New York Times,* October 4, 2017.

68 *police recovered firearms:* Tracing Analytics Platform, "Target on Trafficking: New York Gun Crime Analysis," New York Attorney General, and *Gun Trace Report 2017,* Office of the Mayor, City of Chicago, October 2017.

68 *Civil-law gun control:* Erin Richardson and David Hemenway, "Homicide, Suicide, and Unintentional Firearm Fatality: Comparing the United States with Other High-Income Countries, 2003," *Journal of Trauma and Acute Care Surgery* 70 (January 2011): 238–43; Kevin Anglemyer, Tara Horvath, and George Rutherford, "The Accessibility of Firearms and Risk for Suicide and Homicide Victimization Among Household Members: A Systematic Review and Meta-analysis," *Annals of Internal Medicine* 160 (2014): 101–10.

68 *Gun homicides fell (by 40 percent):* Kara Rudolph, Elizabeth Stuart, and Daniel Webster, "Association Between Connecticut's Permit-to-Purchase Handgun Law and Homicides," *American Journal of Public Health* 105, no. 8 (August 2015).

68 *loosened permitting requirements:* Arizona passed permitless carry in 2010. By 2016, aggravated assaults with a firearm had increased by 44 percent. In 2017, the year Missouri's permitless carry law took effect, the city of St. Louis saw a 23 percent increase in aggravated assaults with a firearm. Ray Hardman, "Connecticut and Missouri: A Contrast in Gun Policy and Gun Suicide Rates," Connecticut Public Radio, September 3, 2015; "Permitless Carry: Concealed Carry in Public with No Permit and No Training," Everytown for Gun Safety Support Fund, March 13, 2018.

68 *Eighty percent:* U.S. Department of Justice, Federal Bureau of Investigation, Uniform Crime Reporting Data Tool, http://www.ucrdatatool.gov.

69 *Guns = Prison never became the reality:* Sam Roberts, "Prison Isn't as Mandatory as State's Gun Laws Say," *New York Times,* January 20, 2013. Back in 2003, when Joe Hynes was the Brooklyn D.A., he came under the same pressure Ken Thompson later felt to move gun cases faster and impose harsher punishments. Hynes also agreed to open a gun court. For a brief time, more gun offenders in Brooklyn went to jail. Then the docket swelled, as a result of the increased arrests from stop-and-frisk, and the 2007 sentencing hikes kicked in. Cases slowed to a crawl. In 2009, the first gun court shut its doors, and Brooklyn returned to the norm of relatively light sentences—until the gun court opened once more in 2016. Robin Noble, "Gun Courts," *Swift and Certain* [National District Attorneys Association newsletter] 4, nos. 3–4 (2008).

69 *the power of prosecutors could surpass:* There's historical precedent for prosecutors mitigating the effects of a harsh law in New York, as John Pfaff points out in his book *Locked In.* In 1973, the state passed the Rockefeller drug laws to increase penalties for small-time dealing to fifteen years to life. But imprisonment for drug charges didn't shoot up until the mid-1980s, more than a decade *after* the laws passed. That's when the number of drug arrests and resulting felony cases, initi-

ated by prosecutors, also climbed. After another decade, when the Rockefeller laws were deemed harmful and felony filings fell, the number of prison sentences fell, too, long before the law changed.

69 *"Laws don't":* Issa Kohler-Hausmann, "Jumping Bunnies and Legal Rules," in *The New Criminal Justice Thinking,* ed. Sharon Dolovich and Alexandra Natapoff (New York: New York University Press, 2017), 257. See also Pfaff, *Locked In,* 29–31.

69 *The odds of being killed there:* Ford Fessenden and Haeyoun Park, "Chicago's Murder Problem," *New York Times,* May 27, 2016.

70 *quarterly reports:* Mayor's Office on Criminal Justice, Project Fast Track, June 30, 2016, 8.

CHAPTER 5

77 *founded in the wake of Hurricane Katrina:* Gideon Lewis-Kraus, "How to Build a Civil Rights Movement for the Digital Age," *Wired,* October 25, 2016.

77 *GLAAD:* Formerly called the Gay and Lesbian Alliance Against Defamation.

77 *ran for reelection unopposed:* Ronald F. Wright, "Beyond Prosecutor Elections," *Southern Methodist University Law Review* 67 (2014); Ronald F. Wright, "How Prosecutor Elections Fail Us," *Ohio State Journal of Criminal Law* 6 (2009): 581, 592–95.

78 *"more power":* A year later, Obama published an article in which he detailed "the approaches that Presidents can take to promote change at the state and local level, recognizing that the state and local justice systems tend to have a far broader and more pervasive impact on the lives of most Americans than does the federal justice system." Barack Obama, "The President's Role in Advancing Criminal Justice Reform," *Harvard Law Review* 130 (January 2017): 815–16.

78 *sixteen hundred likely voters:* ACLU Campaign for Smart Justice, "Prosecutorial Reform Nationwide Survey," internal analysis provided to author, October 2017, 6. Twenty percent of respondents said prosecutors were elected by the governor or another office. Twenty-seven percent didn't know.

79 *sought execution frequently:* Emily Bazelon, "Where the Death Penalty Still Lives," *New York Times,* August 23, 2016.

79 *Soros funded:* Rather than donations to the candidates, the Soros spending in 2015 took the form of independent expenditures for activities including TV, radio, mail, digital, and field operations. That was also true in most of the 2016 races because of state campaign finance laws.

79 *Caddo Parish:* Rachel Aviv, "Revenge Killing," *New Yorker,* July 6 and 13, 2015.

79 *incumbents known for overzealousness:* In 2004, Soros funded David Soares, a candidate for D.A. in Albany, New York. Soares won, but the election didn't lead to a national effort to elect progressive prosecutors. Instead, the goal was to put pressure on New York legislators to repeal the Rockefeller drug laws.

79 *in the Revolutionary era:* At first the prosecutor didn't really exist. The American colonies adopted the model of England in the sixteenth and seventeenth centuries, which relied on victims or complaining witnesses to enforce the criminal law by

pressing charges themselves. English trials were lawyer-free, with victims gathering and presenting evidence, and people suspected of crimes required to answer for themselves. John Langbein, *The Origins of Adversary Criminal Trial* (Oxford: Oxford University Press, 2003); John Langbein, "Understanding the Short History of Plea Bargaining," *Law and Society* 13 (Winter 1979): 261–72; John Langbein, "The Historical Origins of the Privilege Against Self-Incrimination at Common Law," *Michigan Law Review* 92 (1994): 1047–85. The first Congress provided for the president to appoint federal prosecutors to pursue federal crimes Judiciary Act of 1789, 1 Stat. 73, Sec. 35, September 24, 1789.

79 *half the salary of the cabinet:* Michael J. Ellis, "The Origins of the Elected Prosecutor," *Yale Law Journal* 121 (2012): 1539.

79 *prosecutors are still appointed:* Matt Ford, "The Problem with Electing Prosecutors," *Atlantic*, October 16, 2017.

79 *the only country in which voters:* Ellis, "Origins of the Elected Prosecutor," 1528. Electing prosecutors hardly ended corruption. In some cases, it was more like the opposite. Between 1853 and 1869, for example, the district attorney for New York County won four terms with the support of the Tammany Hall machine. To reap the votes of Irish and German immigrants who drank in taverns, he "pigeonholed"— tucked away—indictments for liquor-law violations. In the 1880s, New York newspapers accused district attorneys of failing to try cases "when the offenders happen to be politicians with a 'pull.' " Ellis, "Origins of the Elected Prosecutor," 1565.

79 *rubber stamps:* John Langbein, "Controlling Prosecutorial Discretion in Germany," *University of Chicago Law Review* 41 (1974): 439, 445. The adage is that a grand jury would indict a ham sandwich.

80 *"White suburbanites' power":* Stuntz, *The Collapse of American Criminal Justice*, 192.

80 *reentry and diversion programs:* Emily Bazelon, "Kamala Harris, a 'Top Cop' in the Era of Black Lives Matter," *New York Times Magazine*, May 25, 2016. The Senate includes about a dozen former prosecutors, and in the last decade, twenty states have picked a prosecutor to be governor. Wendy Sawyer and Alex Clark, "New Data: The Rise of the 'Prosecutor Politician,' " Prison Policy Initiative, July 13, 2017.

81 *springboard to higher office:* Jed Handelsman Shugerman, " 'The Rise of the Prosecutor Politicians': Database of Prosecutorial Experience for Justices, Circuit Judges, Governors, AGs, and Senators, 1880–2017," *ShugerBlog*, July 7, 2017.

81 *Local groups like SOUL:* The groups included People's Action, Center for Racial and Gender Equity, National Nurses United, Chicago Votes Action Fund, and United Working Families.

81 *pinned his tie:* Nicole Gonzalez Van Cleve, *Crook County: Racism and Injustice in America's Largest Criminal Court* (Stanford, CA: Stanford University Press, 2016), 70–71.

82 *changing how prosecutors measure success:* Shawn Jones, "State's Attorney Race: An Interview with Candidate Kim Foxx," *Evanston Round Table*, January 13, 2016.

83 *Civic Participation Action Fund:* The fund was created with a $50 million grant from the Atlantic Philanthropies. Illinois Safety and Justice, the PAC, reported expenditures to Berlin Rosen and a polling institute.

83 *"It was an amazing moment":* Paul Engler, Sophie Lasoff, and Carlos Saavedra, *Funding Social Movements: How Mass Protest Makes an Impact*, Ayni Institute, May 2018. Cockburn noted the work of Assata's Daughters, SOUL (Southsiders Organized for Unity and Liberation) in Chicago, and BYP100.

83 *Open Society Foundations:* American Civil Liberties Union, "ACLU Awarded $50 Million by Open Society Foundations to End Mass Incarceration," press release, November 7, 2014. In October 2017, Soros disclosed gifts of $18 billion total to the Open Society Foundations, making it the second-largest charitable foundation behind the Bill and Melinda Gates Foundation. Over the last thirty-six years, the Open Society Foundations have spent $14 billion, mostly abroad.

84 *Open Philanthropy Project:* The Open Philanthropy Project publishes grant information on its website.

84 *Alec Karakatsanis:* Karakatsanis and the groups he helped found (Equal Justice Under Law and the Civil Rights Corps) launched additional suits in smaller cities. The litigation resurrected an argument from the 1960s to claim that counties violated the Constitution's guarantee of due process and equal protection when they detained poor people for want of money while letting richer people in like circumstances go free. The Obama Justice Department filed a brief agreeing that bail practices were unconstitutional when they didn't account for poverty. The suits succeeded in changing bail practices in parts of Alabama, Kansas, Louisiana, Mississippi, and Missouri.

84 *setting bail:* Eli Rosenberg, "Judge in Houston Strikes Down Harris County's Bail System," *New York Times*, March 9, 2017. Lawyers from the Texas Fair Defense Project and the law firm Susman Godfrey also worked on the Harris County suit.

84 *recommend the pretrial release:* Casey Tolan, "Making Freedom Free," *Slate*, March 29, 2017.

84 *"We do not want to be complicit":* Brief for Harris County District Attorney Kim Ogg as Amicus Curiae, 2, *O'Donnell v. Harris County*, No. H-16-1414 (S.D.T.X. March 3, 2017).

85 *landmark opinion: O'Donnell v. Harris County*, No. H-16-1414, 2017 WL 1735456 (S.D.T.X. April 28, 2017), 178.

85 *95 percent were white:* Nicholas Fandos, "A Study Documents the Paucity of Black Elected Prosecutors: Zero in Most States," *New York Times*, July 7, 2015.

86 *Trump falsely insisted:* Jeremy Diamond, "Trump Falsely Claims US Murder Rate Is 'Highest' in 47 Years," CNN, February 7, 2017.

86 *Richard Nixon campaigned in 1968:* Travis, Western, and Redburn, eds., *The Growth of Incarceration*, 115–16.

86 *restore law and order:* Even George H. W. Bush had his race-baiting Willie Horton ad, which blamed his opponent, Massachusetts governor Michael Dukakis, for a crime spree committed by a black man convicted of murder while on furlough from prison.

86 *states mostly spend their own money:* Pfaff, *Locked In*, 101–2.

86 *Americans exaggerate the level of crime:* Gallup Crime Polling, https://news.gallup.com/poll/1603/Crime.aspx.

87 *important to reduce the prison population:* American Civil Liberties Union, "91 Percent of Americans Support Criminal Justice Reform, ACLU Polling Finds," press release, November 16, 2017.

87 *think about the price of incarceration:* Fully 75 percent of the respondents in another poll said they didn't want prosecutors to lock up as many criminals as possible, no matter the cost. ACLU Campaign for Smart Justice, "Prosecutorial Reform Nationwide Survey," 16.

87 *"Prosecutors Gone Wild":* "In Texas, we've succeeded in reserving prison beds for those we are afraid of, and treated those in the community with mental health and drug addiction," Pat Nolan, director of the Center for Criminal Justice Reform at the American Conservative Union Foundation, said at the 2017 panel. "It's cut $3 billion from the budget and the crime rate is the lowest it's been since 1968." David Keene, a former president of the National Rifle Association, praised other Republican governors for taking similar steps.

87 *"the conservative movement's most important":* Grover Norquist, "Conservatives for Criminal Justice Reform," *Wall Street Journal*, September 26, 2017.

87 *Charles and David Koch:* Molly Ball, "Do the Koch Brothers Really Care About Criminal Justice Reform?," *Atlantic*, March 3, 2015.

87 *RAND study:* Lois M. Davis et al., "How Effective Is Correctional Education and Where Do We Go from Here?," RAND Corporation, 2014.

88 *a bogeyman to the right:* The Open Society Foundations spend $150 million a year in the United States for a variety of programs and topics. Soros said he planned to spend $15 million on the 2018 elections. The Koch network said it plans to spend $400 million related to the elections. Michael Kranish, "'I Must Be Doing Something Right': Billionaire George Soros Faces Renewed Attacks with Defiance," *Washington Post*, June 9, 2018; John McCormick, "Koch Network Plans to Spend $400 Million in U.S. Midterm Cycle," *Bloomberg*, January 27, 2018.

88 *"staggering" campaign:* Josh Siegel, "The 'Staggering' Campaign of Liberal Billionaire George Soros to Swing Local Prosecutor Elections," *Daily Signal*, December 19, 2016.

89 *dropped by more than half:* Independent Commission on New York City Criminal Justice and Incarceration Reform, *A More Just New York City*, 22.

89 *to five thousand:* Independent Commission on New York City Criminal Justice and Incarceration Reform, *A More Just New York City*, 30.

90 *report by Human Rights Watch:* "New York City: Bail Penalizes the Poor," Human Rights Watch, December 2, 2010.

92 *ask for bail:* Eric Gonzalez, "Policy Regarding Requests for Bail on Misdemeanor Cases," interoffice memo in the Brooklyn D.A.'s office, April 13, 2017.

92 *could fight the Trump administration:* Alan Feuer, "Brooklyn Moves to Protect Immigrants from Deportation over Petty Crimes," *New York Times*, April 24, 2017.

96 *"becoming completely unelectable":* Maura Ewing, "A 'Completely Unelectable'

Progressive Will Probably Win Philadelphia's DA Race," *Atlantic*, November 6, 2017.

96 *seventy-five times:* Alan Feuer, "He Sued Police 75 Times. Democrats Want Him as Philadelphia's Top Prosecutor," *New York Times*, June 17, 2017.

96 *a city with the highest rate of imprisonment:* Maura Ewing, "A Reckoning in Philadelphia," *Atlantic*, March 3, 2016.

96 *bias and shootings:* George Fachner and Steven Carter, *An Assessment of Deadly Force in the Philadelphia Police Department*, Collaborative Reform Initiative, Community Oriented Policing Services, Department of Justice, March 23, 2015, 71.

97 *several New York advocacy groups:* The New York cosponsors were Communities United for Police Reform, Faith in New York, Make the Road Action, National Action Network, VOCAL-NY Action Fund, and MomsRising.

97 *probation and community service:* Liang's lenient penalty in February 2016 contrasted with the nineteen-year prison sentence the Brooklyn D.A.'s office demanded and won for a sixteen-year-old who set fire to a mattress in a high-rise hallway, accidentally leading to the death of a police officer who responded to the blaze. Christina Carrega-Woodby, "Brooklyn Teen Who Set Mattress Fire That Ended Up Killing NYPD Officer Gets 19 Years to Life," New York *Daily News*, June 15, 2016.

100 *raising $2 million:* The donations included around $70,000 from the police union and other law enforcement groups and nothing from Soros.

100 *contributions from bail companies:* Erin Durkin, "Advocates Urge City's District Attorneys to Reject Political Gifts from Bail Bond Industry," New York *Daily News*, August 8, 2017.

101 *the biggest promise of the Thompson-Gonzalez tenure:* Beth Fertig and Jenny Ye, "Brooklyn DA's Pledge to Reduce Marijuana Prosecutions Makes Little Difference," WNYC, September 7, 2017.

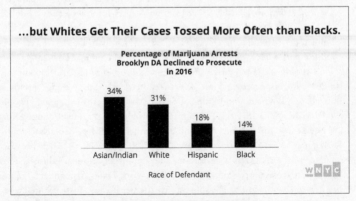

Permission of Beth Fertig, Jenny Ye, Clarisa Diaz/WNYC DataNews

101 *still being prosecuted:* The number of *arrests* had fallen, but that was true citywide, and it was still above four thousand in Brooklyn. For much of the broken-windows era, arrests for marijuana possession (often made when the police asked

people to empty their pockets) were the city's largest category for arrests. The numbers began to fall in 2011. Kohler-Hausmann, *Misdemeanorland*, 44–45.

CHAPTER 6

103 *those of early modern Britain:* Sheldon Krantz, "Pretrial Discovery in Criminal Cases: A Necessity for Fair and Impartial Justice," *Nebraska Law Review* 42 (1963): 127–54; Roger Traynor, "Ground Lost and Found in Criminal Discovery in England," *New York University Law Review* 39 (1964): 749–70; Langbein, *Origins of Adversary Criminal Trial*, 86–97.

103 *element of surprise:* In 1792, the Lord Chief Justice in Britain rejected a defendant's request to see the evidence against him in advance of trial, saying that such disclosure would "subvert the whole system of criminal law."

103 *In 1957, the Supreme Court ruled:* The case is *Jencks v. United States*, 353 U.S. 657 (1957). After the Court's ruling, Congress enacted the Jencks Act, which set rules for producing the statements of witnesses for the prosecution in federal criminal trials. See 18 U.S.C. § 3500.

103 *speech at Washington University's law school:* William J. Brennan Jr., "The Criminal Prosecution: Sporting Event or Quest for Truth?" *Washington University Law Quarterly* 1963 (June 1963): 279–95.

104 *the Warren Court decreed:* In a strange twist, John Brady was not released from prison after the Warren Court's ruling in his favor. The majority opinion misinterpreted Maryland law to say that the missing confession from Brady's codefendant mattered only for determining his punishment, not his guilt. Afraid that a new sentencing would merely reinstate the death penalty, Brady's lawyers told him to stay in prison—even though, in effect, he no longer had a sentence. Ten years later, in 1973, the governor granted Brady clemency. He got married and became a truck driver. Paul Shechtman, "How a Man Named Brady Made History 50 Years Ago," *New York Law Journal*, May 13, 2013. Brady's story is the subject of a book, *Between Life and Death*, which quotes extensively from letters he wrote. Richard Hammer, *Between Life and Death* (New York: Macmillan, 1969).

104 *"because police have unparalleled":* Alex Kozinski, "Criminal Law 2.0," *Georgetown Law Journal Annual Review of Criminal Procedure* 44 (2015): xxxiii.

104 *(In 2017, Kozinski retired:* Matt Zapotosky, "Federal Appeals Judge Announces Immediate Retirement amid Probe of Sexual Misconduct Allegations," *Washington Post*, December 18, 2017. I recognize the problematic nature of quoting Kozinski. See Leah Litman, Emily Murphy, and Katherine H. Ku, "Comeback but No Reckoning," *New York Times*, August 2, 2018. I've relied on his article because of its place in the record as a devastating and important critique. Editorial Board, "Dishonest Prosecutors, Lots of Them," *New York Times*, September 30, 2015.

105 *In a five-to-three decision:* The vote was five to three because Justice Powell recused himself. *United States v. Bagley*, 473 U.S. 667 (1985).

105 *"reasonable probability":* Ibid. at 682. See also *Kyles v. Whitley*, 514 U.S. 419, 433 (1995).

105 *"perform the impossible task":* *United States v. Bagley*, 473 U.S. 667 (1985), at 701.

105 *707 cases of prosecutorial misconduct:* Kathleen Ridolfi and Maurice Possley, *Pre-*

ventable Error: A Report on Prosecutorial Misconduct in California 1997–2009, Northern California Innocence Project, October 4, 2010.

105 *In a national study:* Center for Public Integrity, *Harmful Error: Investigating America's Local Prosecutors,* June 2003.

106 *Weirich's obligation:* Tennessee Rules of Criminal Procedure 16(a)(1)(F–G).

112 *"repeating the conclusion":* Keith Findley, "Tunnel Vision," 312. The *New Yorker* writer David Grann devastatingly described witnesses hardening over time against Cameron Todd Willingham, who was almost certainly wrongfully convicted—and executed—after his house burned down with his children in it. After the fire, a neighbor and a police chaplain described Willingham, sympathetically, as hysterical. But over time, as Willingham came under suspicion for arson, their characterizations shifted. The chaplain started to characterize Willingham as *overly* emotional; upon reflection, he had a "gut feeling" that Willingham set the fire. The neighbor said Willingham only tried to go back into his house after the fire trucks arrived, "as if he were putting on a show," Grann wrote. David Grann, "Trial by Fire," *New Yorker,* September 7, 2009.

113 *Tennessee law would prevent her:* The exceptions to the rule against inheriting are killings that are accidental or in self-defense. Tenn. Code Ann. § 31-1-106 (Lexis 2018).

115 *television interview:* "My Mother's Murder," *48 Hours,* produced by Jay Young and Sara Ely Hulse, CBS, July 28, 2012.

116 *the defense rested:* After the trial, Corder interviewed an alternate juror who heard all the testimony but didn't participate in rendering a verdict. "I think you did a pretty good job," he told her. "The only thing is, I couldn't believe you just rested when they were done."

118 *"comment by the prosecutor on the accused's silence":* Griffin v. California, 380 U.S. 609 (1965).

CHAPTER 7

122 *hearings about suppressing evidence:* "Data provided by the Manhattan district attorney's office indicates that only about 2.4 percent of felony cases that do not end in a guilty plea at the initial arraignment wind up having suppression hearings in Manhattan." Joseph Goldstein, "Police 'Testilying' Remains a Problem. Here Is How the Criminal Justice System Could Reduce It," *New York Times,* March 22, 2018.

124 *more likely to have:* Jennifer A. Tallon, Dana Kralstein, Erin J. Farley, and Michael Rempel, "The Intelligence-Driven Prosecution Model: A Case Study in the New York County District Attorney's Office," Center for Court Innovation, September 2016, 55–57.

124 *refused to cooperate as witnesses:* John Eligon, "Top Prosecutor Creates a Unit on Crime Trends," *New York Times,* May 24, 2010; Chip Brown, "Cyrus Vance Jr.'s 'Moneyball' Approach to Crime," *New York Times,* December 3, 2014.

124 *only 25 percent:* Tallon et al., "The Intelligence-Driven Prosecution Model," vi.

125 *Project Redirect:* Testimony of Brooklyn Defender Services Social Worker Rebecca Kinsella Before the New York City Council Committee on Public Safety, June 13, 2018.

125 *near-total control over who gets diversion:* "Because prosecutors have wide lati-

tude to design the programs, different jurisdictions have different rules, resulting in substantial inequities for defendants," the *New York Times* reporters Shaila Dewan and Andrew Lehren found in 2016 after investigating 225 programs in thirty-seven states. They also concluded that "the prosecutors who grant diversion often benefit directly from the fees." (This was not the case in Brooklyn.) Shaila Dewan and Andrew W. Lehren, "After a Crime, the Price of a Second Chance," *New York Times*, December 12, 2016.

130 *had a cold:* Psychologists warn of the mounting toll of trauma, especially as adverse experiences collect during childhood and youth, and of living in a neighborhood "where multiple risks concentrate," as the report on Brownsville by the Citizens' Committee for Children puts it. The negative effects could be measured in educational achievement, or mental health, or even life expectancy, which was a full seven years shorter in Brownsville than in the rest of the city. Citizens' Committee for Children of New York, *From Strengths to Solutions*, 7, 20; Paul Tough, "The Poverty Clinic," *New Yorker*, March 21, 2011.

131 *"a shield against tyranny":* Jed Rakoff, "Why Innocent People Plead Guilty," *New York Review of Books*, November 20, 2014.

131 *"the only anchor":* Thomas Jefferson, "To Thomas Paine," July 11, 1789, Founders Online, National Archives.

131 *"they were unwilling":* Blakely v. Washington, 542 U.S. 296 (2004).

131 *"Juries were, in a sense":* Akhil Reed Amar, *America's Constitution* (New York: Random House, 2005), 234.

131 *There was no right to counsel:* The right to counsel in regular state cases comes from the Supreme Court's ruling in the 1963 case of *Gideon v. Wainwright*.

132 *"vanishing jury":* Raymond Moley, "The Vanishing Jury," *Southern California Law Review* 2 (December 1928): 97–127.

132 *plea rate for felonies:* William Stuntz, "*Bordenkircher v. Hayes*: The Rise of Plea Bargaining and the Decline of the Rule of Law," Harvard Law School, Public Law Research Paper No. 120, November 22, 2005, 31.

132 *added new offenses:* Edwin Meese III, "Big Brother on the Beat: The Expanding Federalization of Crime," *Texas Review of Law and Politics* 1 (Spring 1997): 1–23.

132 *"truth-in-sentencing":* Travis, Western, and Redburn, eds., *The Growth of Incarceration*, 82–83.

132 *"In the span":* Stuntz, *The Collapse of American Criminal Justice*, 34.

133 *trigger a mandatory minimum:* More than a decade ago, Angela J. Davis described the dynamic in her book *Arbitrary Justice: The Power of the American Prosecutor* (New York: Oxford University Press, 2007). Other academics writing about prosecutors include Stephanos Bibas, "The Need for Prosecutorial Discretion," *Temple Political and Civil Rights Law Review* 19 (Spring 2010): 369–75; Daniel Medwed, *Prosecution Complex* (New York: New York University Press, 2012); Burke, "Improving Prosecutorial Decision Making"; Green, "Why Should Prosecutors 'Seek Justice'?"; Ellen Yaroshefsky, "Duty of Outrage," *Hofstra Law Review* 44 (Summer 2016): 1207–26; Bruce Green and Ellen Yaroshefsky, "Prosecutorial Accountability 2.0," *Notre Dame Law Review* 92 (2016): 51–116; Rachel Barkow, "Prosecutorial Administration: Prosecutor Bias and the Department of Justice,"

Virginia Law Review 99 (2013): 271–342; Lara Bazelon, "The Good Prosecutor," *Politico Magazine*, March 24, 2015; David Sklansky, "The Changing Political Landscape for Elected Prosecutors," *Ohio State Journal of Criminal Law* 14 (2017): 647–74; David Sklansky, "The Progressive Prosecutor's Handbook," *UC Davis Law Review Online* 50 (2017): 25–42; Katherine Moy, Dennis Martin, and David Sklansky, *Rate My District Attorney: Toward a Scorecard for Prosecutors' Offices*, Stanford Criminal Justice Center, January 2018; David Sklansky, "The Problems with Prosecutors," *Annual Review of Criminology* 2018: 451–69; Gerard Lynch, "Our Administrative System of Criminal Justice," *Fordham Law Review* 83 (March 2015): 2117–51.

133 *the number of prosecutors across the country:* Pfaff, *Locked In*, 131. The rate of growth from 1990 to 2007 is more than three times the rate in the decades from 1970 to 1990, when the number of prosecutors increased from seventeen thousand to twenty thousand.

133 *the total number of felony filings:* Pfaff, *Locked In*, 72. Pfaff used data from the Court Statistics Project of the National Center on State Courts, between 1994 and 2008.

133 *another data set:* The data set showing a modest increase in felony filings in the seventy-five largest urban counties in the country in the 1990s and 2000s is the State Court Processing Statistics Series from the Bureau of Justice Statistics. See John Pfaff, "The Causes of Growth in Prison Admissions and Populations," January 24, 2012. For a critique of Pfaff, see Jeffrey Bellin, "Reassessing Prosecutorial Power Through the Lens of Mass Incarceration," *Michigan Law Review* 116 (2018): 835–57. Pfaff further explores the data in "Response: Reassessing Prosecutorial Power Through the Lens of Mass Incarceration," *Michigan Law Review* (forthcoming).

133 *Conviction rates per arrest:* My graph below shows a slight rise in felony convictions per arrest, using data from the National Judicial Reporting Program, Bureau of Justice Statistics, and the FBI's Uniform Crime Reporting Program.

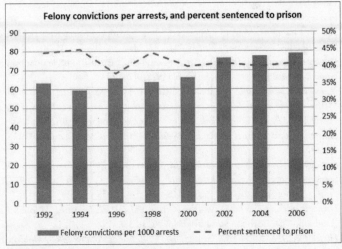

Permission of Brett Greene and Natalia Friedlander

133 *so did prison admissions:* Pfaff, *Locked In*, 130. Between 1978 and 2005, the number of prison admissions rose about 3.5-fold. E. Ann Carson and Joseph Mulako-Wangota, "Count of Total Admissions," Generated Using the Corrections Statistical Analysis Tool, Bureau of Justice Statistics, https://www.bjs.gov/index.cfm?ty=nps. We hear a lot about long sentences in the United States, and of course they affect people's lives and the size of the prison population. But the number of people who are admitted to prison or jail for any length of time is an even greater cause of the American incarceration explosion.

133 *towering court dockets:* See George Fisher, *Plea Bargaining's Triumph: A History of Plea Bargaining in America* (Stanford, CA: Stanford University Press, 2003), 111–36, 175–80; Milton Heumann, *Plea Bargaining: The Experiences of Prosecutors, Judges, and Defense Attorneys* (Chicago: University of Chicago Press, 1978) 144–48.

133 *small fraction of the many hours:* Albert Alschuler, "Plea Bargaining and Its History," *Columbia Law Review* 79 (1979): 1–43; Malcolm Feeley, "Plea Bargaining and the Structure of the Criminal Process," *Justice System Journal* 7 (1982): 338–54.

133 *Replacing trials with deals:* Albert W. Alschuler, "The Trial Judge's Role in Plea Bargaining," *Columbia Law Review* 76 (1976): 1063–7; Alschuler, "The Defense Counsel's Role in Plea Bargaining," *Yale Law Journal* 84 (1975): 1179; Alschuler, "The Prosecutor's Role in Plea Bargaining," *University of Chicago Law Review* 36 (1968): 50.

134 *"In 2012, the average sentence":* Rakoff, "Why Innocent People Plead Guilty."

134 *upward of 95 percent:* Gary Fields and John R. Emshwiller, "Federal Guilty Pleas Soar as Bargains Trump Trials," *Wall Street Journal*, September 23, 2012; Mark Motivans, *Federal Justice Statistics, 2014—Statistical Tables*, Bureau of Justice Statistics, March 2017, 17; Reaves, *Felony Defendants in Large Urban Counties, 2009—Statistical Tables*, 24.

134 *"If the menu is long enough":* William Stuntz, "Plea Bargaining and Criminal Law's Disappearing Shadow," *Harvard Law Review* 117 (2004): 2548.

135 *hurting his job prospects:* Kohler-Haussman, *Misdemeanorland*, 9.

135 *250 plea bargains:* Mayor's Office of Criminal Justice, Project Fast Track Quarterly Meeting Presentation, June 6, 2017, 27–28.

136 *"There is of course a difference":* John Langbein, "Torture and Plea Bargaining," *University of Chicago Law Review* 46 (1978): 12–13.

136 *repeat their admissions:* Langbein, "Torture and Plea Bargaining," 7.

136 *"'Has anyone coerced'":* Nancy Gertner, Letter in Response to "Why Innocent People Plead Guilty," *New York Review of Books*, January 8, 2015.

136 *Supreme Court banned coerced confessions:* Brown v. Mississippi, 297 U.S. 278 (1936).

136 *analogy between a coerced confession:* Loftus Becker, "Plea Bargaining and the Supreme Court," *Loyola of Los Angeles Law Review* 21 (April 1988): 769, 776.

137 *"evil":* United States v. Jackson, 390 U.S. 570 (1968).

137 *Hayes lived:* Carolyn Boyes-Watson, *Crime and Justice: Learning Through Cases* (Lanham, MD: Rowman and Littlefield, 2018), 386.

137 *Hayes took the case to trial:* Stuntz, *The Collapse of American Criminal Justice*, 257–58.

137 *"'vindictive exercise'"*: Bordenkircher v. Hayes, 434 U.S. 357 (1978).

138 *convictions dwarf appeals:* Brandon L. Garrett, "Patterns of Error," *Harvard Law Review Forum* 130 (May 2017).

138 *More than a million:* Sean Rosenmerkel, Matthew Durose, and Donald Farole Jr., *Felony Sentences in State Courts, 2006—Statistical Tables*, Bureau of Justice Statistics, December 2009.

138 *"'is not some adjunct'"*: Missouri v. Frye, 566 U.S. 134 (2012), quoting Robert E. Scott and William Stuntz, "Plea Bargaining as Contract," *Yale Law Journal* 101, no. 8 (June 1992): 1912.

138 *"Once you get used":* Amy Bach, *Ordinary Injustice* (New York: Henry Holt, 2009), 115.

138 *lobbying for stiffer sentencing laws:* Rachel Barkow, "Administering Crime," *UCLA Law Review* 52 (February 2005): 728 and n. 25. See also Rachel Barkow, "Institutional Design and the Policing of Prosecutors: Lessons from Administrative Law," *Stanford Law Review* 61 (April 2010): 869–922.

139 *"cornerstone":* Robert Gay Guthrie, President of the National Association of Assistant United States Attorneys, Letter to Senators Patrick Leahy and Charles Grassley, "Re: Mandatory Minimum Sentencing," January 31, 2014. See also Rachel Barkow and Mark Osler, "Designed to Fail," *William and Mary Law Review* 59 (2017): 402–3, 414–15.

139 *ultimately didn't take:* In 1983, in the case *Solem v. Helm*, another defendant sentenced to life for passing a bad check, this time for a hundred dollars, actually won at the Supreme Court when his lawyers argued he was being disproportionately punished. But eight years later, the Court shut the door his victory opened, for all intents and purposes extinguishing claims of disproportionate punishment. *Solem v. Helm*, 463 U.S. 277 (1983); *Harmelin v. Michigan*, 501 U.S. 957 (1991).

139 *"If the threatened sentence":* Stuntz, "*Bordenkircher v. Hayes*," 26. Also Gerard E. Lynch, "Our Administrative System of Criminal Justice." Look at Lynch's idea of a common law across cases that plea dispositions would arise from.

140 *"Prosecutors rarely":* Angela J. Davis, "Prosecutors, Democracy and Race," in *Prosecutors and Democracy*, ed. Máximo Langer and David Sklansky (New York: Cambridge University Press, 2017), 205.

140 *black defendants in various settings:* For an exhaustive collection of studies on racial bias in criminal justice (with links), see Radley Balko, "There's overwhelming evidence that the criminal-justice system is racist. Here's the proof," *Washington Post*, Sept. 18, 2018. For one of the many studies Balko mentions, see Carlos Berdejo, "Criminalizing Race," *Boston College Law Review* 59, no. 4 (2018).

140 *one of many examples:* Sonja B. Starr and M. Marit Rehavi, "Mandatory Sentencing and Racial Disparity: Assessing the Role of Prosecutors and the Effects of Booker," *Yale Law Journal* 123 (2013): 5.

140 *What would happen to plea bargaining:* Another response is to involve judges in plea negotiations, as Connecticut and Florida do.

140 *refrain from piling on charges:* Ronald Wright and Marc Miller also suggest that prosecutors could start with "appropriate" charges rather than piling on a trial penalty and take cases to the judge without an explicit bargain. They think many

defendants would still plead guilty in hopes of getting a discount from the judge. Ronald Wright and Marc Miller, "The Screening/Bargaining Tradeoff," *Stanford Law Review* 55 (October 2002): 29–118.

140 *A judge in Ohio:* Kozinski, "Criminal Law 2.0," xvii.

141 *inquisitorial:* Erik Luna and Marianne Wade, "Prosecutors as Judges," *Washington and Lee Law Review* 67 (2010): 1468–69. See also Langbein, "Controlling Prosecutorial Discretion in Germany," 443–66.

141 *In Germany:* John Langbein, "The Turn to Confession Bargaining in German Criminal Procedure" (unpublished paper on file with author). Langbein is concerned about the rise in Germany of a practice he calls an "eerie parallel" to plea bargaining, in which judges offer reduced sanctions, in serious cases, in exchange for a confession. But tracing its development, he shows that it's not a transplant from the U.S.

141 *choose to appeal:* Langer and Sklansky, "Epilogue," in *Prosecutors and Democracy*, 315; Shawn Boyne, "German Prosecutors and the Rechtsstaat," in *Prosecutors and Democracy*, ed. Langer and Sklansky, 141.

141 *The British system is adversarial:* Luna and Wade, "Prosecutors as Judges," n. 313; Jacqueline Hodgson, "The Democratic Accountability of Prosecutors in England and Wales and France: Independence, Discretion and Managerialism," 102, in Langer and Sklansky, *Prosecutors and Democracy*.

141 *"Most European professionals":* Luna and Wade, "Prosecutors as Judges," 1494.

141 *European prosecutors were shocked:* Luna and Wade, "Prosecutors as Judges," 1498.

141 *Weldon Angelos: United States v. Angelos*, 345 F. Supp. 2d 1227 (2004).

142 *Judge Paul Cassell:* Eva S. Nilsen, "Indecent Standards: The Case of U.S. Versus Weldon Angelos," *Roger Williams University Law Review* 11 (2006): 543.

142 *five other countries:* Luna and Wade, "Prosecutors as Judges," 1498–501.

142 *Obama, who took no action:* The Obama administration had a project to streamline the clemency process, and Angelos satisfied all the criteria, but Obama took no action. (Presidents turn down the vast majority of clemency petitions without explanation.)

143 *less harmful than alcohol:* L. M. Squeglia, J. Jacobus, and S. F. Tapert, "The Influence of Substance Use on Adolescent Brain Development," *Clinical EEG and Neuroscience* 40 (2009): 31–38; Barbara J. Weiland et al., "Daily Marijuana Use Is Not Associated with Brain Morphometric Measures in Adolescents or Adults," *Journal of Neuroscience* 35, no. 4 (January 2015): 1505–12.

145 *"soft judge":* Kirstan Conley, Kevin Sheehan, and Bruce Golding, "Biker Thug Caught Prison Break from Soft Judge," *New York Post*, October 6, 2013. "She's notorious for having a blanket policy of never taking a plea to a program EVEN if the DA's office is on board," a court staff member wrote of Judge Mondo on The Robing Room, a website where lawyers and court personnel posted comments about judges.

CHAPTER 8

150 *tracking her work:* Reclaim Chicago, The People's Lobby, and Chicago Appleseed Fund for Justice, *In Pursuit of Justice for All: An Evaluation of Kim Foxx's First Year in Office*, December 2017.

150 *Court Watch NYC:* The three groups were VOCAL-NY, the Brooklyn Community Bail Fund, and 5 Boro Defenders. Beth Schwartzapfel, "The Prosecutors," Marshall Project, February 26, 2018.

150 *$1,500 bail request:* @CourtWatchNYC, "Last night in Brooklyn: DA asked for $1500 bail on someone accused of stealing 4 bars of SOAP, knowing that bail would likely mean he'd miss the first day of a back to work program that started today. The person supports 5 kids btwn ages 1-10. Thankfully judge agreed to release," Twitter, January 29, 2018, 7:50 a.m. https://twitter.com/courtwatchnyc /status/958004401230229507?.

150 *Gonzalez had to answer for it:* Eric Gonzalez, Interview with Brian Lehrer, *The Brian Lehrer Show*, WNYC, January 30, 2018.

151 *"If there was ever a case for the death penalty":* Frances Robles and Alan Blinder, "Florida Prosecutor Takes a Bold Stand Against Death Penalty," *New York Times*, March 16, 2017.

151 *fury against Ayala:* Ayala ruled out the death penalty just as the Republican-led legislature redoubled the state's commitment to it. A few days before Ayala's announcement, lawmakers enacted a new death penalty statute after months of turmoil following a state supreme court ruling that struck down the state's earlier version of the law for failing to require juries to vote unanimously for execution.

151 *issued orders:* Fla. Exec. Order No. 17-66 (March 16, 2007).

151 *"good and sufficient reason":* Fla. Stat. § 27.14(1).

151 *Florida Supreme Court ruled against her: Ayala v. Scott*, No. SC17-653 (Fla. 2017).

151 *"Unfortunately, a lot of people":* Ayala was speaking by invitation at a meeting of the National Association of Hispanic Journalists. Scott Powers, "Aramis Ayala Moving On After Losing Death Penalty Battle," *Florida Politics*, October 12, 2017.

152 *Fair and Just Prosecution:* The group had the backing of the Open Philanthropy Project (which spent $8 million between 2015 and 2017 on nonpolitical work, including assistance for new prosecutors), the Ford Foundation, and the Chan Zuckerberg Initiative.

152 *not to trigger mandatory minimum penalties:* Attorney General Eric Holder, Memorandum to United States Attorneys and Assistant Attorney General for the Criminal Division, U.S. Department of Justice, Washington, D.C., August 12, 2013.

153 *"unnecessary and unfortunate":* "Open Letter from State and Local Prosecutors," Fair and Just Prosecution, May 18, 2017.

153 *brief circulated by Fair and Just Prosecution:* The brief was filed in support of a suit California brought to block the Justice Department from withholding federal funds.

153 *Kalief Browder's case:* Barack Obama, "Why We Must Rethink Solitary Confinement," *Washington Post*, January 25, 2016.

154 *Obama's stated commitments:* Barkow and Osler, "Designed to Fail," 392–93.

154 *pushed states to change:* Eric Holder, National Symposium on Pretrial Justice, June 1, 2011; Loretta Lynch, speech at White House Convening on Incarceration and Poverty, U.S. Department of Justice, December 3, 2015, Washington, D.C. In 2016, the Justice Department took the position that misdemeanor bail could be unconstitutional, submitting a brief in the suit *Walker v. City of Calhoun*, part of the litigation effort by Alec Karakatsanis, who brought the suit against misdemeanor bail practices in Harris County. Brief for the United States as Amicus Curiae Supporting Plaintiff-Appellee and Urging Affirmance on the Issue Addressed Herein, *Walker v. City of Calhoun*, No. 16-10521, 682 Fed. Appx. 721 (11th Cir. August 18, 2016). On the separate topic of fines and fees, which also disproportionately affect the poor, Barkow and Osler say that the Obama Justice Department "was at the forefront in addressing excessive fines and fees in the state and local systems" but "did nothing to threaten federal practice." Barkow and Osler, "Designed to Fail," 455.

154 *tried to fix:* "Certainly, many in the Obama Administration worked hard on clemency, but in part that was because of the inefficiency of the process—you have to pedal hard to get a rusty bicycle to move." Barkow and Osler, "Designed to Fail," 435.

154 *overall rate:* Barkow and Osler, "Designed to Fail," 437–38.

154 *balked at applying:* Barkow and Osler, "Designed to Fail," 411–18.

154 *too difficult to obtain guilty pleas:* Barkow and Osler, "Designed to Fail," 421–22.

154 *strengthen forensic science:* Barkow and Osler, "Designed to Fail," 453.

154 *"maintaining a status quo":* Barkow and Osler, "Designed to Fail," 392.

156 *"it's about to be twenty-four":* Mark Denny, the twenty-fourth exoneree, had been in prison for thirty years, ever since he was misidentified as a culprit in a rape and robbery at the age of seventeen. There was no bombshell proof of Denny's innocence, no DNA to retest, and no long-hidden evidence to reveal. But when the Innocence Project brought the case to the attention of the D.A.'s office, the conviction review unit reinvestigated and decided he was innocent. "This exoneration would not have happened in almost any other place," Denny's lawyer, Nina Morrison, told me. See "Brooklyn Man Exonerated After Nearly Three Decades in Prison; Declared 'Actually Innocent' by Brooklyn D.A. Conviction Review Unit," Innocence Project, December 20, 2017.

156 *first conviction review units:* Conviction Integrity Units: Vanguard of Criminal Justice Reform, Center for Prosecutor Integrity White Paper, 2014, 2–3.

156 *thirty-three offices:* National Registry of Exonerations, *Exonerations in 2017*, March 14, 2018, 2. In 2000, a deputy district attorney in San Diego sent letters to hundreds of inmates offering to retest the DNA evidence that had been used to convict them. Santa Clara County and Dallas launched official Conviction Review Units (also called Conviction Integrity Units) several years later. Inger H. Chandler, "Conviction Integrity Review Units," *Criminal Justice*, Summer 2016.

156 *preventing future wrongful convictions:* Chandler, "Conviction Integrity Review Units," 7.

156 *raise the threshold for felony theft:* Foxx said her office would also continue to charge shoplifting as a felony if the accused thief had at least ten prior felony convictions. Steve Schmadeke, "Top Cook County Prosecutor Raising Bar for Charging Shoplifters with Felony," *Chicago Tribune*, December 15, 2016.

156 *in Knoxville, Tennessee:* Jessica Pishko, "How Walmart Is Helping Prosecutors Pursue 10-Year Sentences for Shoplifting," *The Appeal*, May 8, 2018.

157 *prosecutors get the political benefit:* Pfaff, *Locked In*, 142–43; Juleyka Lantigua-Williams, "Are Prosecutors the Key to Justice Reform?" *Atlantic*, May 18, 2016. Following a 2011 state ballot initiative to realign criminal sentencing, California reassigned people convicted of certain crimes from state prison to county jail. The prison population fell much more than the jail population rose, suggesting prosecutors were protecting local budgets. Magnus Loftstrum and Steven Raphael, *Impact of Realignment on County Jail Populations*, Public Policy Institute of California, June 2013; Mike Males, *Eight Months into Realignment: Dramatic Reductions in California's Prisoners*, Center on Juvenile and Criminal Justice, June 2012. In one study, prosecutors reported charging up to get prison time for some serious crimes and offering a combination of jail and probation for less severe offenses. With local money on the line, it seemed as if they had more reason to triage. W. David Ball and Robert Weisberg, "The New Normal? Prosecutorial Charging in California After Public Safety Realignment," Stanford Criminal Justice Center, January 2014.

159 *article in 2001:* Abbe Smith, "Can You Be a Good Person and a Good Prosecutor?," *Georgetown Journal of Legal Ethics* 14 (Winter 2001): 355–400.

159 *"wear the white hats":* Smith, "Can You Be a Good Person," 355. See also Kay L. Levine and Ronald F. Wright, "Images and Allusions in Prosecutors' Morality Tales," *Virginia Journal of Criminal Law* 5 (2017): 38.

159 *band together:* Would the criminal justice system be better and fairer if prosecutors and defense lawyers routinely switched places? In Britain, this used to be seen as important for "the development of criminal advocates' skills" and for encouraging "a balanced approach to the presentation of evidence." See the Lord Chancellor's Advisory Committee on Legal Education and Conduct, *Rights of Audience of Employed Barristers: Advice to the Lord Chancellor on the Question Raised by the Director of Public Prosecutions and the Head of the Government Legal Service*, April 3, 1992, 94. But it's less common now because the Crown Prosecution Service mostly relies on in-house advocates. Electoral Reform Research, *General Council of the Bar Exit Survey 2011*, General Council of the Bar, December 2011, 40.

    In the mid-1970s, a D.C.-based nonprofit was given federal funding to conduct a switch-hitting experiment in Philadelphia, Minneapolis, and Yuma, Arizona. The study sought to determine whether switch-hitting would make participants more objective and better at their jobs. In each city, a handful of prosecutors and defense attorneys spent a few months working for the other side. When I interviewed Charles Cunningham, a judge who participated in the program as a young prosecutor in Philadelphia, he told me that his experience working as a public defender influenced how he responded to motions by defense lawyers to prevent the jury from learning about the defendants' criminal histories. He'd learned it could be prejudicial, because innocent people who took the stand could "come off looking bad at cross-examination."

159 *TED talk:* Adam Foss, "A Prosecutor's Vision for a Better Justice System," TED, February 2016.

161 *"When the pirates":* In Houston, Kim Ogg similarly let go three dozen lawyers promoted by the previous D.A. when she took office in 2016.

162 *"the most radical DA":* Daniel Denvir, "Philadelphia Just Elected the Most Radical DA in the Country—Now What?," *Nation*, November 10, 2017.

163 *pair of rulings: Miller v. Alabama,* 567 U.S. 460 (2012); *Montgomery v. Louisiana,* 136 S. Ct. 718 (2016).

165 *top-down memo:* District Attorney Larry Krasner, "New Policies Announced February 15, 2018," Memorandum to Assistant District Attorneys, District Attorney's Office, Philadelphia, March 13, 2018.

166 *people on parole of any state:* Pennsylvania's incarceration rate increased by 16 percent in the decade leading up to 2014 even as the incarceration rate fell in New Jersey and New York. Vincent Schiraldi, "The Pennsylvania Community Corrections Story," Columbia University Justice Lab, April 25, 2018, 1.

168 *major felony charges:* Krasner's policy didn't apply to homicides, violent crimes, sexual assault, and economic crimes of $50,000 or more.

168 *Krasner's rationale:* If Krasner's memo thrilled liberal advocates—"I've never seen anything like this document," wrote Shaun King, a writer and activist who helped start the PAC Real Justice—his intervention in the case of Meek Mill elated people who'd elected him. Mill was a rapper whose case had come to stand for the excessive punishment of a violation of probation. Convicted of drug charges and gun possession at nineteen, he was still on probation ten years later when he was arrested on minor charges (for fighting in an airport and popping a wheelie on his dirt bike in a music video). Though one charge was dropped and the other was dismissed, the judge cited two other minor violations (a failed drug test and unauthorized travel), revoked Mill's probation, and sentenced him to two to four years in prison. A few months later, a problem with Mill's original conviction came to light. It was based on the testimony of a police officer who'd been accused, by another cop, of lying on the stand at Mill's trial. When prosecutors have good reason to think a police officer has lied, they have three choices: they can look the other way, they can quietly decline to prosecute, or, in theory, they can declare the cop to be unreliable. Option three is practically unheard of. But in Meek Mill's case, Krasner didn't try to defend the conviction. He said he couldn't stand by it. When the judge refused to release Mill, his lawyers appealed, with Krasner's office, in effect, on their side. The Pennsylvania Supreme Court ordered Mill to be released on bail in April. Krasner signaled there would be more releases like Mill's to come.

168 *basic contours:* For more on restorative justice, I very much recommend a recent book by my sister Lara Bazelon, *Rectify: The Power of Restorative Justice After Wrongful Conviction* (Boston: Beacon Press, 2018).

169 *ancient and in a sense familiar:* Eliezer Segal, "Jewish Perspectives on Restorative Justice," in *The Spiritual Roots of Restorative Justice*, ed. Michael Hadley (Albany: State University of New York Press, 2001), 181–97; Richard Delgado, "Goodbye to Hammurabi: Analyzing the Atavistic Appeal of Restorative Justice," *Stanford Law Review* 52 (April 2000): 751–75; Jon'a F. Meyer, "History Repeats Itself: Restorative Justice in Native American Communities," *Journal of Contemporary Criminal Justice* 14 (February 1998): 42–57; John Pratt, "Colonization, Power and Silence: A History of Indigenous Justice in New Zealand Society," 137–56, in *Restorative Justice: International Perspectives*, ed. Burt Galaway and Joe Hudson (Monsey, NY: Criminal Justice Press, 1996); Bruce R. O'Brien, "From Morðr to Murdrum: The Preconquest Origin and Norman Revival of the Murder Fine," *Speculum* 71 (April 1996): 321–57.

169 *restorative justice in the United States:* Mark Obbie, "'They Knew It Was the Right Thing to Do,'" *Slate*, December 29, 2015.

169 *teenage shoplifting and vandalism:* Dana Greene, "Repeat Performance: Is Restorative Justice Another Good Reform Gone Bad?" *Contemporary Justice Review* 16 (September 2013): 359–90.

169 *victims' rights movement:* For example, the movement has worked on ensuring that victims can give testimony, called victim impact statements, at the sentencing phrase of trial. Paul Cassell, "In Defense of Victim Impact Statements," *Ohio State Journal of Criminal Law* 6 (Spring 2009): 612–16.

169 *Research backs up:* Lawrence Sherman and Heather Strang, *Restorative Justice: The Evidence*, Smith Institute, 2007.

169 *a metastudy:* Heather Strang et. al., "Restorative Justice Conferencing (RJC) Using Face-to-Face Meetings of Offenders and Victims," *Campbell Systematic Reviews* 2013:12.

169 *James Rhodes:* Bazelon, "Where the Death Penalty Still Lives."

170 *Angela Corey:* She had a record of seeking the death penalty more than any other prosecutor in Florida and punishing black teenagers more harshly than white ones for similar crimes. Bazelon, "Where the Death Penalty Still Lives"; Human Rights Watch, *Branded for Life: Florida's Prosecution of Children as Adults Under Its "Direct File" Statute*, April 2014. In 2012, Governor Rick Scott tapped Corey to oversee the prosecution of George Zimmerman for killing Trayvon Martin. She was criticized for overcharging Zimmerman, and he was acquitted. In 2010, Corey charged Marissa Alexander, a thirty-one-year-old black woman who had been abused on multiple occasions by her husband, with three counts of aggravated assault for firing a warning shot at the wall near him while his two children were in the room. Alexander, who had no criminal history, said she acted out of fear that her husband would hurt her. Each of the charges Corey brought carried a twenty-year mandatory minimum sentence. Alexander was convicted and spent nearly three years in prison before an appeals court threw out the verdict against her.

171 *Johnie Miller:* Ramon Antonio Vargas, "'Grateful': Released Despite Guilty Plea in Florida Murder, 'Uncle Louie' Returns to New Orleans," *New Orleans Advocate*, May 17, 2018.

172 *"He came clean"*: Robert Farah was talking to the *Florida Times-Union*. Eileen Kelley, "Popular Street Performer Pleads Guilty to Decades-Old Jacksonville Killing and Is Now Free," *Florida Times-Union*, April 25, 2018.

CHAPTER 9

181 *the best trial lawyer in town:* Lindsay Jones, "The General," *Memphis*, October 1, 2011.

181 *many large metropolitan areas:* Pew Research Center, "Party Affiliation by Metro Area (2014)," *Religious Landscape Study*, November 2015.

181 *Founded on the backs:* Preston Lauterbach, "Memphis Burning," *Places*, March 2016.

182 *Memphis ranked first:* Elena Delavega, "2015 Memphis Poverty Fact Sheet," Department of Social Work, School of Urban Affairs and Public Policy, University of Memphis, September 2015.

182 *barred the submission:* Tennessee Supreme Court Rules 30(I).

185 *"implicitly encouraged the jury":* Noting the rule that did not allow them to admit video footage of a trial proceeding as evidence, the Tennessee justices said they "have not considered as evidence" the clip Corder played for them. *Tennessee v. Noura Jackson*, n. 47.

186 *suing Noura for her mother's estate:* The exceptions to the bar against inheriting are killings that are accidental or in self-defense. Tenn. Code Ann. § 31-1-106 (Lexis 2018).

187 *affirmed the man's:* Cone v. Bell, 492 F.3d 743 (2007).

188 *"covered up the love letters":* Owens v. Guida, 549 F.3d 399, 425 (2008).

188 *most skilled trial lawyer:* Shelby County District Attorney's Office, "After 40 Years, This Prosecutor Rests," press release, August 1, 2016.

188 *discredited 1857 opinion:* Scott v. Sandford, 60 U.S. 393, 407 (1856).

190 *"human error":* Toby Sells, "The Prosecution Rests," *Memphis Flyer*, January 30, 2014.

191 *"It was hard enough":* I tried to reach Henderson through the D.A.'s office and at the home number listed for him. He didn't return my calls.

191 *"If the civil plaintiff":* Miriam H. Baer, "Timing *Brady*," *Columbia Law Review* 115 (January 2015): 25.

191 *"When I entered law":* Walter Dellinger, "What to Do About the Problem of Overzealous Prosecutors," *Slate*, June 22, 2017.

192 *study of wrongful convictions:* Ridolfi and Possley, *Preventable Error*.

192 *forced federal judges:* AEDPA said a state court's adjudication of a federal claim would bind the federal courts unless it "resulted in a decision that was contrary to, or involved an unreasonable application of, clearly established Federal law, as determined by the Supreme Court of the United States." Antiterrorism and Death Penalty Prevention Act of 1996, Pub. L. 104–132, 110 Stat. 1214–319, April 24, 1996.

192 *"The collapse of habeas corpus":* Stephen Reinhardt, "The Demise of Habeas Corpus and the Rise of Qualified Immunity," *Michigan Law Review* 113 (May

2015): 1219. Reinhardt explained how the Supreme Court's interpretation of AEDPA further tied the hands of federal judges like him.

192 *singled out Weirich:* Fair Punishment Project, "The Recidivists," July 13, 2017.

193 *found in the files a manila envelope: Braswell v. Tennessee,* Court of Crim. App. of Tennessee, No. W2016-00912-CCA-R3-PC (2017).

CHAPTER 10

198 *murder capital:* "Brownsville," DNAinfo.com Crime and Safety Report, 2011.

198 *historical low:* CompStat data is available by precinct online from the NYPD. "Historical New York City Crime Data," New York City Police Department. The number for the Upper West Side is for the 24th Precinct, a residential area. In 2008, Brownsville's thirty-one homicides gave it the highest murder rate in the city. Suvi Hynynen, *Community Perceptions of Brownsville,* Center for Court Innovation, December 2014, 1.

199 *violent as any crime-ridden city:* Patrick Sharkey, "Two Lessons of the Urban Crime Decline," *New York Times,* January 13, 2018.

199 *safer than the wealthy parts:* Patrick Sharkey, *Uneasy Peace* (New York: W. W. Norton, 2018), 111–12.

199 *its decline improved:* Sharkey, "Two Lessons."

199 *gap in academic achievement:* Sharkey, *Uneasy Peace,* 93, and interview with author. Now he can show this with district-by-district data.

199 *reason to be wary:* The Center for Court Innovation's *Community Perceptions of Brownsville* report surveyed more than eight hundred Brownsville residents and found that more than half viewed the community's relationship with the police as negative. At the same time, the strong police presence was identified as one of the community's top strengths. Hynynen, *Community Perceptions,* 8–9.

199 *Morgue Boys:* Exposing the ring, a city commission blamed "willfully blind supervisors." Three officers in the 73rd pled guilty. Three others were tried in federal court and acquitted of extortion and conspiracy. In those cases, the jury hung on charges of civil rights violations. Joseph Fried, "In the Trial of 'Morgue Boys,' Former Police Officer Tells of His Tour as Predator in Blue," *New York Times,* March 19, 1995; "Pockets of Corruption," *New York Times,* April 9, 1995.

199 *Omnipresence:* John Surico, "Omnipresence Is the Newest NYPD Tactic You've Never Heard Of," *Vice,* October 20, 2014; Joseph Goldstein, "'Stop-and-Frisk' Ebbs, but Still Hangs over Brooklyn Lives," *New York Times,* September 19, 2014.

199 *lit up the neighborhood:* Stephen Farrell, "Omnipresence: New Stop-and-Frisk?" *New York Times,* September 20, 2014.

200 *study of almost nine thousand residents:* Robert Sampson, Stephen Raudenbush, and Felton Earls, "Neighborhoods and Violent Crime: A Multilevel Study of Collective Efficacy," *Science* 277 (August 1997): 918–24.

200 *So does health:* Eric Klinenberg, *Heat Wave* (Chicago: University of Chicago Press, 2002).

200 *Chicago's 2016 homicide spike:* Fessenden and Park, "Chicago's Murder Prob-

lem." About one in two hundred young black men in Chicago is a victim of a nonfatal shooting. Papachristos et al., Tragic, but Not Random.

200 *outbreak of murders:* Chicago's increase in homicides in 2015 and 2016 also correlates with a decrease in police stops that followed an agreement between the department and the American Civil Liberties Union, according to research in March 2018. See Paul Cassell and Richard Fowles, "What Caused the 2016 Chicago Homicide Spike? An Empirical Examination of the 'ACLU Effect' and the Role of Stop and Frisks in Preventing Gun Violence," *University of Illinois Law Review* (forthcoming). But another analysis of the same potential causal link pointed out that other cities like New York have experienced a decline in stops without a rise in violence, saying that while it is possible effects could differ across cities, this isn't "well understood." University of Chicago Crime Lab, "Gun Violence in Chicago, 2016," January 2017. John Pfaff criticized Cassell and Fowles for not using enough variables and failing to consider the effect of other changes, like the defunding of the city's Cure Violence program, on the homicide rate. John Pfaff (@JohnFPfaff), "So, some thoughts on this Cassell and Fowles report on Chicago's 2016 homicide spike and the city's agreement with the ACLU," Twitter, March 26, 2018, https://twitter.com/johnfpfaff/status/978269848810803205?.

200 *just 17 percent in 2017:* Elizabeth Van Brocklin and Francesca Mirabile, "Chicago Police Aren't Solving Enough Murders," *The Trace*, September 26, 2016.

The FBI and Chicago Police Department data count a crime as "cleared" when someone is arrested, charged, and/or turned over to the court for prosecution, or if there is a circumstance outside an agency's control that keeps them from apprehending a suspect but they've identified one.

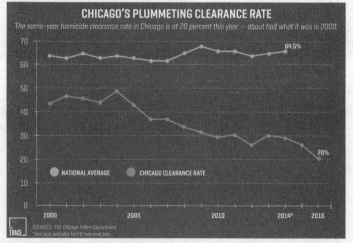

Permission of Akoto Ofori-Atta/The Trace

200 *fell to 5 percent:* Max Kapustin et al., *Gun Violence in Chicago, 2016*, University of Chicago Crime Lab, January 2017, 23, http://urbanlabs.uchicago.edu/projects/

gun-violence-in-chicago-2016. No national comparison is available because many cities don't track nonfatal shootings. The FBI compiles solve rates for homicides and violent crime.

200 *the national rate:* In big cities where violent crime has significantly declined, the solve rate for homicides in 2016 ranged from 45 percent in Philadelphia to the mid-50s in Houston and to around 70 percent in Los Angeles and New York. Murder Accountability Project, Clearance Rate Data, MurderData.org. See also Steven Rich, Ted Mellnik, Kimbriell Kelly, and Wesley Lowery, "Murder with Impunity," *Washington Post*, June 6, 2018. (Many cities don't track the solve rate for nonfatal shootings.)

200 *solve rate for homicides in 2016 ranged:* Murder Accountability Project, Clearance Rate Data, MurderData.org. See also Steven Rich, Ted Mellnik, Kimbriell Kelly, and Wesley Lowery, "Murder with Impunity," *Washington Post*, June 6, 2018.

201 *Impunity for shooters:* This is the story of Jill Leovy's excellent book *Ghettoside* (New York: Random House, 2015).

201 *presence of nonprofit organizations:* Robert Sampson, Doug McAdam, Heather MacIndoe, and Simón Weffer-Elizondo, "Civil Society Reconsidered: The Durable Nature and Community Structure of Collective Civic Action," *American Journal of Sociology* 111 (November 2005): 673–714. Sampson has also been gathering evidence for a link between an influx of immigrants and falling crime in a neighborhood. He thinks that for starters, the newcomers may revitalize the area by filling up vacant housing. Robert J. Sampson, "Immigration and America's Urban Revival," *American Prospect*, Summer 2015. See also Graham Ousey and Charis Kubrin, "Immigration and Crime: Assessing a Contentious Issue," *Annual Review of Criminology* 1 (January 2018): 63–84.

201 *data from 264 cities:* The study found a causal effect: "We find that every 10 additional nonprofits per 100,000 residents leads to a 9 percent decline in the murder rate, a 6 percent decline in the violent crime rate, and a 4 percent decline in the property crime rate." Patrick Sharkey, Gerard Torrats-Espinosa, and Delaram Takyar, "Community and the Crime Decline: The Causal Effect of Local Nonprofits on Violent Crime," *American Sociological Review* 82 (December 2017): 1215.

201 *"Considering that this segment":* Sharkey, "Two Lessons."

201 *Brownsville had few resources:* Citizens' Committee for Children of New York, *From Strengths to Solutions*.

201 *low number of arrests per homicide:* Rich et al., "Murder with Impunity."

202 *Shea testified:* Statement of NYPD chief Dermot Shea, chief of detectives, Before the New York City Council Committee on Public Safety, June 13, 2018.

202 *city documents showed:* The information was released in response to a Freedom of Information Law request from CUNY law professor Babe Howell. See also K. Babe Howell, "Gang Policing: The Post Stop and Frisk Justification for Profile-Based Policing," University of Denver Criminal Law Review 5 (2015).

203 *Ceasefire:* Ceasefire was launched in New York in 2014 in collaboration with David Kennedy a professor at John Jay College of Criminal Justice. In the 1990s, Kennedy helped conduct a study in Boston showing that 1 percent of the young adult

population was responsible for at least 60 percent of youth killings with a gun or knife. He developed a set of interventions that focused "on one problem, on the core offenders," as he put it in his 2011 book, *Don't Shoot*. The idea was to find those people, sit them down with other people they knew and would listen to, and stop the violence by mobilizing people's capacity to influence each other. The suspected gang members were supposed to receive offers of social services; if they continued to commit crimes, they'd feel the iron fist of a coordinated crackdown by law enforcement. Kennedy's approach has gotten credit in some cities for dramatically reducing gun violence. It has also been criticized for stressing heavy-handed tactics. David Kennedy, Anthony Braga, and Anne Piehl, "The (Un)Known Universe: Mapping Gangs and Gang Violence in Boston," in *Crime Mapping and Crime Prevention*, ed. David L. Weisburd and J. Thomas McEwen (Monsey, NY: Criminal Justice Press, 1997), 219–62; Anthony Braga, David Hureau, and Christopher Winship, *Losing Faith? Police, Black Churches, and the Resurgence of Youth Violence in Boston*, Rappaport Institute for Greater Boston, Kennedy School of Government, Harvard University, October 2008, 3. David Kennedy, *Don't Shoot: One Man, a Street Fellowship, and the End of Violence in Inner-City America* (New York: Bloomsbury, 2011), 54. Kevin Braga and David Weisburd, "The Effects of Focused Deterrence Strategies on Crime," *Journal of Research in Crime and Delinquency* 49 (August 2012): 323–58.

203 *according to Shea:* At the public hearing in June 2018, Shea said, "Knowing criminal group membership helps guide our efforts to New York City Ceasefire."

203 *you got a letter:* The Brooklyn D.A.'s Office released the letter in response to a freedom of information request by Anthony Posada at Legal Aid.

204 *successes of Cure Violence:* Sheyla Delgado, Laila Alsabahi, Kevin Wolff, Nicole Alexander, Patricia Cobar, and Jeffrey Butts, *Denormalizing Violence: The Effects of Cure Violence in the South Bronx and East New York, Brooklyn,* John Jay College Evaluation of Cure Violence Programs in New York City.

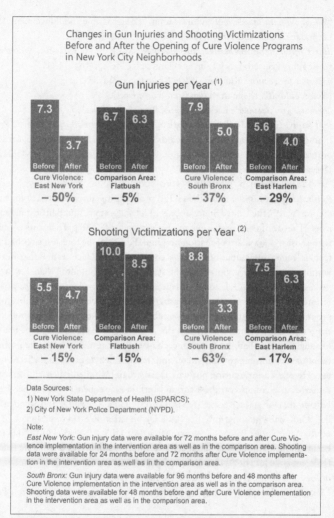

Changes in Gun Injuries and Shooting Victimizations Before and After the Opening of Cure Violence Programs in New York City Neighborhoods

Gun Injuries per Year [1]

7.3	6.7	6.3	7.9	5.0	5.6	4.0
3.7						
Before	After	Before	After	Before	After	Before	After
Cure Violence: East New York	Comparison Area: Flatbush	Cure Violence: South Bronx	Comparison Area: East Harlem
− 50%	− 5%	− 37%	− 29%

Shooting Victimizations per Year [2]

5.5	4.7	10.0	8.5	8.8	3.3	7.5	6.3
Before	After	Before	After	Before	After	Before	After
Cure Violence: East New York	Comparison Area: Flatbush	Cure Violence: South Bronx	Comparison Area: East Harlem
− 15%	− 15%	− 63%	− 17%

Data Sources:
1) New York State Department of Health (SPARCS);
2) City of New York Police Department (NYPD).

Note:
East New York: Gun injury data were available for 72 months before and after Cure Violence implementation in the intervention area as well as in the comparison area. Shooting data were available for 24 months before and 72 months after Cure Violence implementation in the intervention area as well as in the comparison area.

South Bronx: Gun injury data were available for 96 months before and 48 months after Cure Violence implementation in the intervention area as well as in the comparison area. Shooting data were available for 48 months before and after Cure Violence implementation in the intervention area as well as in the comparison area.

Permission of Jeffrey Butts/John Jay College of Criminal Justice

204 *more than a year passed:* Jim Dwyer, "Six Blocks, 96 Buildings, Zero Shootings: New Recipe at the Queensbridge Houses," *New York Times,* Jan. 19, 2017. Four shootings took place in Queensbridge later in 2017.

209 *their community's top problems:* Hynynen, *Community Perceptions of Brownsville,* 2010.

210 *"deterrent" first appeared:* Emily Bazelon, "The Soft Evidence Behind the Hard Rhetoric of 'Deterrence,' " *New York Times,* October 20, 2015.

211 *"When a potential criminal":* Phil Gramm, "Drugs, Crime and Punishment; Don't Let Judges Set Crooks Free," *New York Times*, July 8, 1993.

212 *didn't impose the threatened consequences:* Mark A. R. Kleiman, *When Brute Force Fails* (Princeton, NJ: Princeton University Press, 2009), 34–41.

212 *a former prosecutor:* Kleiman, *When Brute Force Fails*, 35.

212 *"You wouldn't":* Kleiman, *When Brute Force Fails*, 35.

212 *"because you decided":* Kleiman, *When Brute Force Fails*, 39.

212 *that study:* Angela Hawken and Mark Kleiman, *Managing Drug Involved Probationers with Swift and Certain Sanctions: Evaluating Hawaii's HOPE*, Final Report to the National Institute of Justice, Grant No. 2007-IJ-CX-0033, NCJ229023, December 2009.

212 *"as if they":* Kleiman, *When Brute Force Fails*, 40.

213 *Replicating the results:* After the HOPE program was implemented in four jurisdictions across the United States as part of a trial, a study found little difference in rates of revocation of probation and recidivism for HOPE participants compared with those in a standard probation program. However, the four test sites had some trouble replicating some of HOPE's core provisions, such as holding hearings within three days of a violation. The study authors also noted that they weren't necessarily testing HOPE against a true control. The standard probation program in one test jurisdiction was fairly progressive and effective, and features of the programs in the other three may have influenced the results as well. Responding to these findings, Kleiman pointed out that the study failed to measure the tendency of judges and probation officers in each of the four test sites to revoke probation (how "revocation-happy" they were) and the HOPE-style programs' effect on drug use. He argued for figuring out why these programs failed when HOPE worked rather than giving up on the swift-and-certain-consequences model. See Pamela Lattimore, Doris MacKenzie, Debbie Dawes, Elaine Arsenault, and Stephen Tueller, "Outcome Findings from the HOPE Demonstration Field Experiment," *Criminology and Public Policy* 15 (November 2016): 1103–41; Daniel O'Connell, John Brent, and Christy Visher, "Decide Your Time," *Criminology and Public Policy* 15 (November 2016): 1073–102; and Mark Kleiman, "Swift—Certain—Fair," *Criminology and Public Policy* 15 (November 2016): 1185–93.

213 *"Severity is the enemy":* Hawken and Kleiman, *Managing Drug Involved Probationers*, 30.

213 *40 percent of its 851 cases:* Fifty of those cases began in 2016. Mayor's Office of Criminal Justice, Project Fast Track Quarterly Meeting Presentation, March 20, 2017.

213 *cases inched along more slowly:* Mayor's Office of Criminal Justice, Project Fast Track Quarterly Meeting Presentation, February 28, 2017.

213 *testing every gun:* Ann Givens and Robert Lewis, "Gun Cases Are Notoriously Hard to Make Stick. New York Thinks It Has the Answer," *The Trace*, July 24, 2017.

213 *testing took months:* In the spring of 2018, the median time was shorter than it had been, but still sixty days. Mayor's Office of Criminal Justice, Project Fast Track Quarterly Meeting Presentation, June 12, 2018.

214 *close to half the gun arrests:* Mayor's Office of Criminal Justice, Project Fast Track Quarter 3 Report, December 12, 2017, 11.

214 *felony convictions rose in Brooklyn:* Mayor's Office of Criminal Justice, Project Fast Track Quarter 3 Report, December 12, 2017, 32.

214 *higher percentage:* Mayor's Office of Criminal Justice, Project Fast Track Quarterly Meeting Presentation, February 28, 2017, and data from the New York State Unified Court System.

215 *process itself was the punishment:* The phrase comes from the classic 1979 book of the same name by Malcolm Feeley, *The Process Is the Punishment* (New York: Russell Sage Foundation, 1979).

CHAPTER 11

224 *"Better to let ten":* William Blackstone, *Commentaries on the Laws of England* (Oxford: Clarendon Press, 1768), 2:352.

224 *"unreal dream":* Jeffrey Rosen, "The Wrongful Conviction as Way of Life," *New York Times*, May 26, 2011.

224 *"Our society has":* Herrera v. Collins, 506 U.S. 390, 420 (1993).

225 *roughly eighteen hundred exonerations:* The numbers come from the National Registry of Exonerations, which also tries to unravel the cause of each wrongful conviction. The group has found that about half involved misconduct by police, prosecutors, or both. The figure was 60 percent for the 143 exonerations counted in 2017, and the most common form of misconduct was the concealment of exculpatory evidence. National Registry of Exonerations, *Exonerations in 2017*, 6. The registry is a joint project of Michigan Law School and Northwestern Law School.

225 *expose bad police work:* When my sister Lara, a former federal public defender, led the Loyola Project for the Innocent, she and her students convinced a judge to free a man imprisoned for murder by showing that prosecutors had relied on false eyewitness testimony. "It took enormous human effort to undo human error," she wrote. Lara Bazelon, " 'A Mistake Has Been Made Here, and No One Wants to Correct It,' " *Slate*, December 17, 2013.

225 *five thousand death sentence appeals:* James Liebman, Jeffrey Fagan, Andrew Gelman, Valerie West, Garth Davies, and Alexander Kiss, *A Broken System, Part II: Why There Is So Much Error in Capital Cases, and What Can Be Done About It*, Columbia Law School (2002).

225 *351 convictions:* Liebman et al., *A Broken System, Part II*, n. 167.

225 *"Our analyses reveal":* Liebman et al., *A Broken System, Part II*, 411–12.

225 *defendants who pleaded guilty:* National Registry of Exonerations.

226 *"prosecutor-dictated":* Rakoff, "Why Innocent People Plead Guilty."

226 *Joseph Buffey:* Emily Bazelon, "Who Should Have Access to DNA Evidence?," *New York Times Magazine*, September 28, 2015.

228 *"The adversary system assumes":* David Bazelon, "The Defective Assistance of Counsel," *University of Cincinnati Law Review* 42 (Winter 1973).

228 *"foisted upon the poor":* Stephen Bright, "Counsel for the Poor: The Death Sentence Not for the Worst Crime but for the Worst Lawyer," *Yale Law Journal* 103 (1994): 1835–83.

229 *Adam Bowers:* Ethan Bronner, "Lawyers, Saying DNA Cleared Inmate, Pursue Access to Data," *New York Times*, January 3, 2013.

230 *"There is no basis":* Herrera v. Collins, 427–28.

231 *Supreme Court has never held:* Michael Nasser Petegorsky, "Plea Bargaining in the Dark: The Duty to Disclose Exculpatory *Brady* Evidence During Plea Bargaining," *Fordham Law Review* 81 (May 2013): 3599–650; Kevin McMunigal, "Guilty Pleas, *Brady* Disclosure, and Wrongful Convictions," *Case Western Reserve Law Review* 57 (Spring 2007): 651–70.

231 *"that the Constitution":* In re Davis, 557 U.S. 952, 955 (2009).

231 *the Supreme Court has never said this:* In 2002, the Supreme Court ruled that the Constitution does not require the government to disclose evidence that's material to impeaching a witness before a defendant enters a plea agreement. *United States v. Ruiz,* 536 U.S. 622 (2002). The Court has not decided whether the same rule applies to evidence that directly relates to factual innocence.

231 *repeatedly ruled:* U.S. v. Conroy, 567 F.3d 174 (5th Cir. 2009); U.S. v. McLean, 419 Fed. Appx. 473 (5th Cir. 2011); U.S. v. Hooper, 621 Fed. Appx. 770 (5th Cir. 2015); and Alvarez v. City of Brownsville, 860 F.3d 799 (5th Cir. 2017).

231 *The reasoning was simple:* The Fifth Circuit said that defendants waive their right to see Brady evidence when they plead guilty. It's a bad argument but not a crazy one, based on Supreme Court precedent. In 2002, the Supreme Court held that before plea bargaining, defendants don't have a right to see information that could impeach a critical witness. The ruling didn't address other kinds of exculpatory evidence. *United States v. Ruiz,* 536 U.S. 622 (2002).

232 *"intelligent choice":* Brief for the United States as Amicus Curiae in Support of Appellant City of Brownsville and Reversal, *Alvarez v. City of Brownsville,* 2017 WL 6453751 (5th Cir. December 13, 2017).

232 *"neither reason":* Brief of Amici Curiae Former State and Federal Prosecutors in Support of Affirmance, 18, *Alvarez v. City of Brownsville,* No. 16-40772 (5th Cir. January 12, 2018).

232 *"There's no question":* Jeni Diprizio, "Judge in Noura Jackson Trial Speaks About the Case for First Time," *Local Memphis,* February 16, 2017.

234 *harder to prove with the passage of time:* Megan Rose, "Innocent but Still Guilty," *New York Times,* January 17, 2018.

237 *charges against Weirich and Jones:* Katie Fretland, "Tennessee Supreme Court Board Files Disciplinary Charges Against DA Amy Weirich, Prosecutor Jones," *Commercial Appeal,* January 29, 2016.

CHAPTER 12

242 *More than 4.6 million people:* Danielle Kaeble and Lauren Glaze, *Correctional Populations in the United States, 2015,* Bureau of Justice Statistics, December 2016, 2. See also Michelle Phelps, "Mass Probation: Toward a More Robust Theory of State Variation in Punishment," *Punishment and Society* 19 (2017): 53–73; Columbia Justice Lab, *Too Big to Succeed,* Columbia University, January 29, 2018.

242 *number of conditions:* Columbia Justice Lab, *Too Big to Succeed,* 5; and Jenni-

fer L. Doleac, "Study After Study Shows Ex-prisoners Would Be Better off Without Intense Supervision," Brookings Institution, July 2, 2018.

242 *majority have tried:* Public Safety Performance Project, "35 States Reform Criminal Justice Policies Through Justice Reinvestment," Fact Sheet, Pew Charitable Trusts, July 11, 2018. Adam Gelb and Connie Utada, "For Better Results, Cut Correctional Populations," Public Safety Performance Project, Pew Charitable Trusts, August 25, 2017.

242 *studied probation violations:* Jesse Jannetta, Justin Breaux, Helen Ho, and Jeremy Porter, *Examining Racial and Ethnic Disparities in Probation Revocation*, Urban Institute, April 2014, 4.

244 *user fees for probation:* Emma Anderson, Alyson Hurt, and Joseph Shapiro, "State-by-State Court Fees," NPR, May 19, 2014.

244 *fees as high as $5,000:* Dewan and Lehren, "After a Crime, the Price of a Second Chance." The supervision-related payments are one part of the increasing reliance by states and cities on fines and fees following an arrest. Obama's Justice Department warned states against some forms of the practice, but after Trump took office, the department withdrew that guidance. Matt Zapotosky, "Justice Department Warns Local Courts About Unlawful Fines and Fees," *Washington Post*, March 14, 2016; Matt Zapotosky, "Sessions Rescinds Justice Dept. Letter Asking Courts to Be Wary of Stiff Fines and Fees for Poor Defendants," *Washington Post*, December 21, 2017.

244 *"a great deal of responsibility":* Human Rights Watch, *Profiting from Probation: America's "Offender-Funded" Probation Industry*, February 2014, 1.

244 *banned debtors' prisons:* Eli Hager, "Debtors' Prisons, Then and Now: FAQ," Marshall Project, February 24, 2015.

244 *declared it unconstitutional: Bearden v. Georgia*, 461 U.S. 660 (1983).

244 *to this day:* Human Rights Watch, *Profiting from Probation*, 1.

244 *Court has never set limits:* Joseph Shapiro, "Supreme Court Ruling Not Enough to Prevent Debtors Prisons," NPR, May 21, 2014.

245 *job market was tightening:* People without a high school degree were finally in demand in New York City, including those with criminal records. Ben Casselman, "As Labor Pool Shrinks, Prison Time Is Less of a Hurdle," *New York Times*, January 13, 2018. In his classic books *The Truly Disadvantaged* (Chicago: University of Chicago Press, 1987) and *When Work Disappears* (New York: Knopf, 1996), William Julius Wilson linked the loss of manufacturing jobs in cities to the increasing danger and deprivation in the urban core, which he argued both conservatives and liberals were missing. In recent decades, the case that adding jobs to the local labor market helps reduce crime has only grown stronger. See also Chalfin and McCrary, "Criminal Deterrence: A Review of the Literature," 32–38.

CHAPTER 13

253 *set of model rules:* David Keenan, Deborah Jane Cooper, David Lebowitz, and Tamar Lerer, "The Myth of Prosecutorial Accountability after *Connick v. Thompson*," *Yale Law Journal Online* 121 (October 2011): 229.

253 **has urged judges:** National District Attorneys Association, "Resolution Urging Courts to Use 'Error' Instead of 'Prosecutorial Misconduct,'" April 10, 2010. In 2010, the NDAA enlisted the American Bar Association in the effort. American Bar Association, Resolution 100B, August 9–10, 2010.

255 **have repeatedly held:** See for example *Hartman v. State*, 896 S.W.2d 94, 101 (Tenn. 1995); *Johnson v. State*, 38 S.W.3d 52, 55–56 (Tenn. 2001); and *Berry v. State*, 366 S.W.3d 160, 175 (Tenn. Crim. App. 2011). The U.S. Court of Appeals for the Sixth Circuit, for its part, has made it clear that the "ethical obligations imposed on a prosecutor" are *more* demanding than the *Brady* standard for materiality.

256 **"Who exactly":** Kozinski, "Criminal Law 2.0," xxxix.

256 **Paul Imbler:** *Imbler v. Craven*, 298 F. Supp. 795 (C.D. Cal. 1969).

256 **whether prosecutors could be sued:** *Imbler v. Pachtman*, 424 U.S. 409 (1976).

256 **preparing or trying:** In a later case, *Buckley v. Fitzsimmons*, 509 U.S. 259 (1993), the Supreme Court found that a prosecutor who fabricated evidence only had qualified immunity because he fabricated it in order to manufacture probable cause for an arrest, which meant that he was acting as an investigator, not as an advocate preparing for trial. Since the obligation to disclose exculpatory evidence arises once a trial is under way, concealment of evidence is covered by absolute immunity. See Douglas J. McNamara, "*Buckley, Imbler,* and Stare Decisis: The Present Predicament of Prosecutorial Immunity and an End to Its Absolute Means," *Albany Law Review* 59 (1996): 1135–96.

257 **"vigorous and fearless":** *Imbler v. Pachtman* at 427.

257 **"can be as reckless":** Kozinski, "Criminal Law 2.0," xl.

257 **subverting the system:** Judge Frederic Block, a federal district court judge in Brooklyn for twenty-three years, called for ending absolute immunity for prosecutors in 2018. "We all hold dear to the time-honored notion that 'no one is above the law,'" he wrote. "Truly horrendous prosecutors who have put innocent people in jail should not be an exception." Frederic Block, "Let's Put an End to Prosecutorial Immunity," Marshall Project, March 13, 2018.

257 **"a prosecutor stands":** *Imbler v. Pachtman*, 429.

257 **"Despite numerous cases":** Kozinski, "Criminal Law 2.0," xxxix.

258 **Connick v. Thompson:** 563 U.S. 51 (2011).

258 **she unearthed a microfiche copy:** John Hollway, "Innocent on Death Row," *Slate*, October 5, 2010.

258 **institutional failure:** The Supreme Court case is *Kyles v. Whitley*, 514 U.S. 419 (1995). The NOLA Innocence Project put total *Brady* violations at nine in death penalty cases during Connick's tenure and at least nineteen in noncapital cases. The National Registry of Exonerations listed fifteen complete exonerations, twelve of which involved withholding exculpatory evidence.

258 **In the ten years before:** Brief for the Orleans Public Defenders Office as Amicus Curiae Supporting Petitioner, *Smith v. Cain*, 565 U.S. 73 (2012) (No. 10-8145).

259 **cases showed a pattern:** At the trial in Thompson's civil suit, Connick and supervisors in his office appeared ill-informed. They misstated the requirements of *Brady*, at once exposing and playing down mistakes they'd made or overseen. When the Supreme Court overturns a death sentence because prosecutors have messed up, it

generally expects D.A.s to get their house in order. Connick, however, testified that in the wake of the 1995 decision, he saw no need to make any changes, not in supervision and not in training about the Brady rule. An outside special prosecutor, assigned to investigate Connick's office, testified, "We should have indicted these guys. Instead, the investigation was called off." John Thompson, "The Prosecution Rests, but I Can't," *New York Times*, April 9, 2011.

259 *pattern of previous Brady violations: Connick v. Thompson*, 62–63.

259 *"to do the same thing":* Thompson, "The Prosecution Rests."

259 *none resulted:* "APR Panelists Examine Why Prosecutors Are Largely Ignored by Disciplinary Offices," *ABA/BNA Lawyers Manual on Professional Conduct* (2006), 90. For more studies, see Deborah L. Rhode, David Luban, Scott L. Cummings, and Nora Freeman Engstrom, *Legal Ethics*, 7th ed. (New York: Foundation Press, 2017), 448.

259 *Only six:* Ridolfi and Possley, *Preventable Error*. In 2010, the Illinois disciplinary commission—the only one in the country to release such data—docketed ninety-nine misconduct charges. Only one even reached a formal hearing. Keenan et al., "The Myth of Prosecutorial Accountability," 239.

260 *"those who are":* Keenan et al., "The Myth of Prosecutorial Accountability," 221.

263 *Michael Morton:* Pamela Colloff wrote an amazing two-part series on the Morton case. Colloff, "The Innocent Man, Part One" and "The Innocent Man, Part Two," *Texas Monthly*, November and December 2012.

263 *never done before:* M. Alex Johnson, "Ex-Texas Prosecutor First in History to Be Jailed for Withholding Evidence," NBC News, November 2, 2015.

264 *"as soon as practicable":* Texas Appleseed and Texas Defender Service, *Towards More Transparent Justice: The Michael Morton Act's First Year*, April 8, 2015.

264 *"need only be negligent":* Schultz v. Commission for Lawyer Discipline of the State Bar of Texas, Board of Disciplinary Appeals, December 17, 2015.

264 *"Don't get burned":* Melissa Hervey, "Just Disclose It," *Texas Prosecutor* 46 (March–April 2016).

264 *more exonerations:* Harris County contributed most of them, with more than 138 between 2010 and 2017, primarily in drug cases. National Registry of Exonerations, *Exonerations in 2017*, March 14, 2018, Appendix Table A.

264 *five exonerations from death row:* The Justice Project, "Expanded Discovery in Criminal Cases," 2007, 8.

264 *Michael Nifong:* Associated Press, "Day in Jail for Ex-Duke Prosecutor," *New York Times*, September 1, 2007.

265 *altered or withheld test results:* Mandy Locke, Joseph Neff, and J. Andrew Curliss, "Scathing SBI Audit Says 230 Cases Tainted by Shoddy Investigations," *News and Observer*, August 11, 2010.

265 *strengthening the open-file law:* Forensic Sciences Act of 2011, §9, S.L. 2011–19, N.C. Gen. Stat. 15A-903, March 31, 2011.

265 *open-file law worked well:* Jenia I. Turner and Allison D. Redlich, "Two Models of Pre-Plea Discovery in Criminal Cases: An Empirical Comparison," *Washington and Lee Law Review* 73 (January 2016): 354–55. Open-file can be reciprocal, with defense lawyers required to share witness lists.

265 *"We get so convinced":* Open-file laws, on their own, don't ensure that criminal justice will be fair. Ben Grunwald, a law professor at Duke who has studied the impact of these laws, has called their promise "fragile." The police can still home in on one suspect while ignoring other evidence, Grunwald pointed out, and over-loaded defense lawyers may not take advantage of the leads the state makes available. But if open-file isn't sufficient, it is better than any other alternative. Ben Grunwald, "The Fragile Promise of Open-File Discovery," *Connecticut Law Review* 49 (February 2017): 776.

265 *exception of Brooklyn:* Beth Schwartzapfel, "Defendants Kept in the Dark About Evidence, Until It's Too Late," *New York Times*, August 7, 2017; Jake Offenhartz, "Movement to Reform New York's Discovery Statute Faces a Familiar Foe: Prosecutors," *The Appeal*, March 6, 2018.

265 *district attorneys have opposed:* Alan Feuer and James C. McKinley Jr., "Rule Would Push Prosecutors to Release Evidence Favorable to Defense," *New York Times*, November 8, 2017.

265 *Asked why he saw:* Offenhartz, "Movement to Reform."

265 *in only six states:* Darryl Brown, "Discovery in State Criminal Justice," in *Reforming Criminal Justice*, ed. Erik Luna (Phoenix: Arizona State University Press, 2017), 3:155. Darryl Brown found broad discovery laws in Alaska, Florida, Minnesota, New Jersey, and North Carolina. In Indiana, discovery, defined by local court rules, is similarly broad.

266 *Federal prosecutors are bound:* Department of Justice, "Issues Related to Discovery, Trials, and Other Proceedings," *U.S. Attorneys' Manual*, 9-5.000–9-5.110.

266 *the Justice Department found:* Investigation of the Shelby County Juvenile Court, U.S. Department of Justice, Civil Rights Division, April 26, 2012, 1.

267 *troubling report:* Sandra Simkins, *Compliance Report #9—April 2017*, U.S. Department of Justice, June 13, 2017.

268 *"Any competent prosecutor":* Thomas v. Westbrooks, 849 F.3d 659 (6th Cir. 2017).

269 *The panel refused: In re Jones*, No. 2016-2534-9-KH, Tennessee Board of Professional Responsibility (Disciplinary District IX March 2, 2011).

CHAPTER 14

273 *felonies accounted for tens of thousands:* Kohler-Hausmann, *Misdemeanorland*, 25. Of the total arrests in the city, more than 80 percent were for misdemeanors in the last several years. See also Preeti Chauhan et al., *Trends in Admissions to the New York City Department of Correction, 1995–2015*, The Misdemeanor Justice Project, John Jay College of Criminal Justice, December 13, 2016, 18.

273 *as stop-and-frisk ebbed:* Kohler-Hausmann, *Misdemeanorland*, 25, 41.

273 *ended in dismissals:* Michael Rempel et al., *Jail in New York City: Evidence-Based Opportunities for Reform*, Center for Court Innovation and the Vera Institute of Justice, January 2017, 75, and data from the New York State Unified Court System.

273 *people in Brooklyn:* The borough's rates were roughly in line with the Bronx and Queens, and mostly Staten Island, while Manhattan's were far higher. Rempel et al., *Jail in New York City*, 75–76, and data from the New York State Unified Court System.

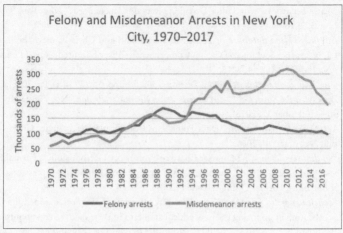

Felony and Misdemeanor Arrests in New York City, 1970–2017

Permission of Brett Greene and Natalia Friedlander

274 *way too entangled:* Alexandra Natapoff, *Punishment Without Crime* (New York, NY: Basic Books, 2018) and Kohler-Hausmann, *Misdemeanorland*.

280 *the cop who'd made the arrest:* Graham Rayman and Rocco Parascandola, "NYPD Cop Known for Bursting into Homes Sued 23 Times Costing City $280G," New York *Daily News*, March 17, 2018.

280 *better offers:* The percentage of defendants in the gun court who pled guilty and went to jail or prison fell slightly from 66 percent in the gun court's first year to 62 percent in the beginning of 2018. The backlog was also shrinking. Mayor's Office of Criminal Justice, Project Fast Track Quarterly Meeting Presentation, June 12, 2018, 15.

282 *"can mean the difference":* Jonathan Abel, "*Brady*'s Blind Spot: Impeachment Evidence in Police Personnel Files and the Battle Splitting the Prosecution Team," *Stanford Law Review* 67 (April 2015): 746.

282 *laws that sealed them:* Abel, "*Brady*'s Blind Spot," 762–79.

282 *strictest secrecy laws:* Robert Lewis, Xander Landen, and Noah Veltman, "New York Leads in Shielding Police Misconduct," WNYC, October 15, 2015.

283 *disciplinary records:* Kendall Taggart, Mike Hayes, and Scott Pham, "Here Are the Secret Records on Thousands of New York Police Misconduct Cases," *BuzzFeed News*, April 16, 2018. That same spring, a *New York Times* investigation found that New York cops were being promoted after judges reprimanded them for giving false testimony. Joseph Goldstein, "Promotions, Not Punishments, for Officers Accused of Lying," *New York Times*, March 19, 2018; Joseph Goldstein, " 'Testilying' by Police: A Stubborn Problem," *New York Times*, March 18, 2018.

283 *committing "offenses":* Kendall Taggart and Mike Hayes, "Secret NYPD Files: Officers Who Lie and Brutally Beat People Can Keep Their Jobs," *BuzzFeed News*, March 5, 2018.

283 *Talk of changing the secrecy law:* Ashley Southall, "4 Years After Eric Garner's

Death, Secrecy Law on Police Discipline Remains Unchanged," *New York Times*, June 3, 2018.

283 *carefully vetted database of cops:* Mark Fazlollah and Chris Palmer, "Philly DA Larry Krasner Seeking to Develop Comprehensive List of Tainted Cops," *Philadelphia Inquirer*, June 4, 2018.

284 *gave ICE access: Philadelphia v. Sessions*, 309 F. Supp. 3d 289 (E.D. Pa. 2018).

285 *Pennsylvania Supreme Court sided: Pennsylvania v. Brown*, No. 728 CAP, —A 3d— (October 17, 2018).

287 *Yet Memphis continued:* "Data Points: Incarceration Rates," Smart City Memphis, February 10, 2015.

288 *"so that the defense":* Tennessee Board of Professional Responsibility, Formal Ethics Opinion 2017-F-163, quoting ABA Committee on Ethics and Professional Responsibility, Formal Opinion 09-454 (2009).

288 *"sensitiveness to fair play":* The three U.S. attorneys in Tennessee joined the state prosecutors in opposing the new ethical standard in their own letter, submitted to the board in June 2018. Donald Cochran, J. Douglas Overbey, and Michael Dunavant, Letter to Sandra Garrett, Chief Disciplinary Counsel of the Tennessee Board of Professional Responsibility, "Re: Tennessee Formal Ethics Opinion 2017-F-163," June 4, 2018; Bert, "TN: Prosecutors Resist State Bar's Ethical Ruling," *Prosecutorial Accountability*, August 2, 2018; Eli Hager, "Why Tennessee Is Challenging the DOJ's Ethics," Marshall Project, August 13, 2018.

288 *The Tennessee D.A.s:* The Tennessee board adopted the new ethical rule anyway, but then agreed to hear the prosecutors' arguments in favor of repealing it.

289 *evidence that a commission was needed:* Joaquin Sapien and Sergio Hernandez, "Who Polices Prosecutors Who Abuse Their Authority? Usually Nobody," ProPublica, April 3, 2013.

290 *jail population was still rising:* Jacob Kang-Brown and Ram Subramanian, *Out of Sight: The Growth of Jails in Rural America*, Vera Institute of Justice, June 2017; Michael Haugen, "In Rural Areas, Jail Populations Are Skyrocketing—Including Pretrial Detainees," *National Review*, July 3, 2018.

290 *mostly white areas:* Some red states were trying to reverse the trend. Since Texas took a whack at its ballooning prison population a decade ago, criminal justice reform bills have passed in Georgia, Mississippi, Alabama, Louisiana, and Oklahoma. In general, state D.A. associations in these southern states have vehemently opposed reform. Groups like Right on Crime, the American Conservative Union, and the Koch Network have gone up against the prosecutors but haven't persuaded them. Larry Hannan, "Is the 'Incarceration Capital of the World' Finally Ready to Lose Its Title?," *Slate*, April 6, 2017; Julia Craven, "This Letter from Louisiana Prosecutors Perfectly Explains Why Criminal Justice Reform Is So Hard," *Huffington Post*, September 14, 2016.

293 *With their intensive demands:* "Drug Courts Are Not the Answer," Drug Policy Alliance (March 2011).

294 *Justice Sonia Sotomayor:* Rachel E. Barkow, "Justice Sotomayor and Criminal Justice in the Real World," *Yale Law Journal Forum*, March 2014.

295 *The officer's discovery: Utah v. Strieff*, 136 S. Ct. 2056 (2016). The Court had eight rather than nine members in the period between the death of Justice Antonin Scalia and the confirmation of Justice Neil Gorsuch.

296 *E-ZPass:* This graphic from the Community Service Society illustrates how penalties are skewed:

Permission of Jeff Jones/Community Service Society

Jeff Jones and Harold Stolper, "No Easy Pass for Transit Riders," Community Service Society, March 1, 2018.

297 *operate as a black box:* David Alan Sklansky, "The Nature and Function of Prosecutorial Power," Journal of Criminal Law & Criminology 106 (2016): 475–77.

EPILOGUE

305 *uptick in violence:* Police Department City of New York, CompStat report through August 19, 2018.

APPENDIX

315 *enlisted the aid:* Some of our principles draw from previous recommendations by the Brennan Center (found in "Criminal Justice: An Election Agenda for Candidates, Activists, and Legislators"), Fair and Just Prosecution (including from issues briefs on the Fair and Just Prosecution website, https://fairandjustprosecution.org/resources/issues-at-a-glance-briefs/), and The Justice Collaboratory. For their great work on this project, our thanks to FJP staff Buki Baruwa, Emily Bloomenthal, John Butler, Hannah Raskin-Gross, Courtney Khademi, Liz Komar, Julius Lang, Marie Lively, Meghan Nayak, Scarlet Neath, Rosemary Nidiry, Taylor Phares, Andy Schwarm, and Greg Srolestar; Justice Collaborative staff Jessica Brand, Sarah Lustbader, Jevhon Rivers, and Rob Smith; Bryan Furst, Katz Fellow at the Brennan Center; Columbia law student David Alpert; Yale law students Katya Botchkina, Sam Breidbart, and Laurel Raymond; and Yale College student Brett Greene.

315 *collective enterprise:* We thank Roy Austin, Dana Bazelon, Rose Cahn, Lisa Foster, Karen Friedman-Agnifilo, Seema Gajwani, Mac Heavener, Kristin Henning, Brook Hopkins, Venus Johnson, Beth McCann, Mitali Nagrecha, Melissa W. Nelson, Courtney M. Oliva, Dan Satterberg, David Alan Sklansky, and Joanna Weiss.

316 *more than 90 percent:* Armando Tull, "How a D.C. Diversion Program Helps Get Young Lives off the Ropes," WAMU, June 30, 2016.

318 *associated with racial bias:* See Lauren-Brooke Eisen and Inimai Chettiar, *Criminal Justice: An Election Agenda for Candidates, Activists, and Legislators*, Brennan Center for Justice, March 22, 2018. They point out that risk assessment tools "can negatively affect African American and Latino defendants due to structural societal inequities" if the tools consider social factors, such as education level, family structure, or employment history. In a recent study, the risk assessment tool created by the John and Laura Arnold Foundation has been found to be fairly race neutral and to select risk factors carefully to minimize risk of bias. See DeMichele et al., "The Public Safety Assessment."

318 *by phone or text:* Notification systems that use phone calls and texts have achieved high success rates for court appearances. See Plaintiffs' Summary of Other Jurisdictions, *O'Donnell v. Harris County*, No. H-16-1414, 2017 WL 1542457 (S.D.T.X. April 28, 2018), 2. Multnomah County in Oregon started using automated reminders for court appearances and reported a drop in no-shows of more than 30 percent and savings of more than $1.5 million in fiscal year 2007. Matt O'Keefe, "Court Appearance Notification System: 2007 Analysis Highlights," Multnomah County Local Public Safety Coordinating Council, June 2007.

318 *the rate was only 10 percent:* Kentucky Justice and Public Safety Cabinet Criminal Justice Council, *2015 HB463 Implementation Report*, October 2015, 3.

319 *face longer sentences:* Improving Outcomes for People with Mental Illnesses Involved with New York City's Criminal Court and Correction Systems, the Council of State Governments, Justice Center, December 2012.

319 *they are often sent back:* Fair and Just Prosecution, "Bail Reform," issue brief, September 25, 2017; John K. Iglehart, "Decriminalizing Mental Illness—The Miami Model," *New England Journal of Medicine* 374 (May 2016): 1701–3.

320 *Preliminary research:* Peter Wicklund, Patricia Breneman, and Tim Halvorsen, *Chittenden County Rapid Intervention Community Court Outcome Evaluation Final Report*, Vermont Center for Justice Research, February 2013.

320 *The "war on drugs":* Brian Stauffer, *Every 25 Seconds: The Human Toll of Criminalizing Drug Use in the United States*, Human Rights Watch, October 12, 2016.

320 *LEAD:* Susan E. Collins, Heather S. Lonczak, and Seema L. Clifasefi, "Seattle's Law Enforcement Assisted Diversion (LEAD): Program Effects on Recidivism Outcomes," *Evaluation and Program Planning* 64 (2017): 49–56.

321 *young people accused:* Fair and Just Prosecution, "Juvenile Justice and Young Adult Issues: Promoting Trauma-Informed Practices," issue brief, September 25, 2017.

322 *The rate of rearrest:* Jennifer Henderson-Frakes, Sengsouvanh Leshnick, and Hannah Diaz, *An Evaluation of San Francisco's Young Adult Court: Findings on Planning and Early Implementation*, Social Policy Research Associates, May 2017.

322 *cycle of incarceration:* Alexandra Natapoff, "Misdemeanors," in *Reforming Criminal Justice*, ed. Erik Luna (Phoenix: Arizona State University Press, 2017), 1:71.

322 *In Harris County:* Ronald Brownstein, "Will Texas Follow Houston's Lead on Drug-Policy Reform?," *Atlantic*, May 24, 2018.

323 *immigration attorneys:* Hillary Blout, Rose Cahn, and Miriam Aroni Krinsky, "The Prosecutor's Role in the Current Immigration Landscape," *Criminal Justice Magazine*, Winter 2018; Fair and Just Prosecution, "Addressing Immigration Issues," issue brief, September 25, 2017; Immigrant Defense Project, "Immigration Consequences of Crimes Summary Checklist," 2017.

323 *Research shows that crime victims:* Alliance for Safety and Justice, "Crime Survivors Speak" (April 2016).

324 *five million:* See Danielle Kaeble and Thomas P. Bonczar, *Probation and Parole in the United States, 2015*, Bureau of Justice Statistics, April 2018, 1.

324 *shortened supervision periods:* In 2012, for example, Missouri passed a law that decreases supervision time by creating "earned compliance credits." People can shorten their time on probation or parole by thirty days for every full calendar month that they comply with the conditions of their sentences. The Pew Charitable Trusts found that in the first three years of implementation, more than thirty-six thousand probationers and parolees reduced their supervision terms by an average of fourteen months without changing recidivism rates. Pew Charitable Trusts, "Missouri Policy Shortens Probation and Parole Terms, Protects Public Safety," August 2016.

325 *almost eighteen thousand felony probation cases:* Council of State Governments, "Changes to Georgia's Probation System Yield Positive Early Results," April 18, 2018.

325 *In 2018, forty-five prosecutors:* Larry Krasner and Miriam Krinsky, "Time to Rethink Probation and Parole," *Philadelphia Inquirer*, May 25, 2018.

325 *comparing rates:* These metrics may be used in performance evaluations, or tied to promotions or other recognition. Research shows that merely keeping track of the metrics, with no further incentives, encourages performance. See Lauren-Brooke

Eisen, Nicole Fortier, and Inimai Chettiar, *Federal Prosecution for the 21st Century,* Brennan Center for Justice, September 23, 2014, 44.

325 *Hire a diverse staff:* Steps for diversifying office staff include developing targeted recruitment to diverse groups (like bar association affinity groups); reassessing hiring criteria to address barriers to hiring people of color; and ensuring that underrepresented groups on staff are appropriately supported, considered for promotion, and involved in office hiring decisions.

326 *Encourage prosecutors:* Fair and Just Prosecution, "Building Community Trust: Restorative Justice Strategies, Principles and Promising Practices," issue brief, December 2017.

326 *data-based report:* David Sklansky, "The Progressive Prosecutor's Handbook," *UC Davis Law Review Online* 50 (2017): 25–42; American Bar Association, *Criminal Justice Standards for the Prosecution Function* (February 2015); Fair and Just Prosecution, "Building Community Trust: A Compendium of Community Prosecution Models from Across the Nation," issue brief, April 2018.

326 *Extensive evidence:* Frank R. Baumgartner, Derek A. Epp, and Kelsey Shoub, *Suspect Citizens: What 20 Million Traffic Stops Tell Us About Policing and Race* (New York: Cambridge University Press, 2018); Stephen Demuth, "Racial and Ethnic Differences in Pretrial Release Decisions and Outcomes: A Comparison of Hispanic, Black, and White Felony Arrestees," *Criminology* 41 (August 2003): 898; Arnold et al., "Racial Bias in Bail Decisions," 3; Marvin D. Free Jr., "Racial Bias and the American Criminal Justice System: Race and Presentencing Revisited," *Critical Criminology* 10 (October 2001): 195–223; L. Song Richardson and Philip Atiba Goff, "Implicit Racial Bias in Public Defender Triage," *Yale Law Journal* 122 (June 2013): 2626–49; Cassia Spohn, "Race, Sex, and Pretrial Detention in Federal Court: Indirect Effects and Cumulative Disadvantage," *University of Kansas Law Review* 57 (2009): 898–99.

326 *The causes:* Michelle Alexander, *The New Jim Crow: Mass Incarceration in the Age of Colorblindness* (New York: New Press, 2012), 16; Anthony G. Greenwald and Linda Hamilton Krieger, "Implicit Bias: Scientific Foundations," *California Law Review* 94 (July 2006): 966; L. Song Richardson, "Police Efficiency and the Fourth Amendment," *Indiana Law Journal* 87 (Summer 2012): 1145.

327 *The rate of prosecution:* Jeffrey Toobin, "The Milwaukee Experiment," *New Yorker,* May 11, 2015.

327 *Conviction review units:* Fair and Just Prosecution, "Conviction Integrity Units and Internal Accountability Mechanisms," issue brief, September 25, 2017.

328 *Studies have shown:* Ridolfi and Possley, *Preventable Error.*

329 *providing all discovery:* A recent study comparing discovery practices in Manhattan and Brooklyn demonstrated that open-file discovery, in addition to being fairer, is cost effective. In Manhattan, where prosecutors keep their files relatively closed, defendants use pretrial suppression hearings to learn about the evidence the government possesses. In Brooklyn, where the D.A.'s office has had an open-file policy since the 1990s (though prosecutors can make exceptions for cases involving gangs, sex crimes, and homicides), defendants request far fewer suppression hearings,

saving the state time and money. Dan Svirsky, "The Cost of Strict Discovery," *New York University Review of Law and Social Change* 38, no. 3 (2014): 523–50.

329 *Investigations and prosecutions:* Amari L. Hammonds, Katherine Kaiser Moy, Rachel R. Suhr, and Cameron Vanderwall, *At Arm's Length: Improving Criminal Investigations of Police Shootings*, Stanford Criminal Justice Center, October 2016. Further resources: *Final Report of the President's Task Force on 21st Century Policing*, May 2015.

330 *Support changes:* Hammonds et al., *At Arm's Length*.

330 *pursuing unpaid debt:* For instance, a study in New Orleans found that the cost of jailing people who could not pay criminal debt was $2 million *greater* than the revenue obtained from that debt. Mathilde Laisne, Jon Wool, and Christian Henrichson, *Past Due: Examining the Causes and Consequences of Charging for Justice in New Orleans*, Vera Institute of Justice, January 2017, 22.

331 *countries around the world:* When the sliding-scale fine system was introduced in West Germany in the 1970s as a replacement for incarceration, the number of short-term prison sentences dropped by 90 percent. Germany still uses day fines as the only sanction imposed for three-quarters of all property crimes, and two-thirds of all assaults. "How to Use Structured Fines (Day Fines) as an Intermediate Sanction," Bureau of Justice Assistance, U.S. Department of Justice, November 1996.

331 *Sliding-scale fines:* Putting a sliding-scale system in place is typically possible with about three months of planning. Justice Management Institute and Vera Institute of Justice, "How to Use Structured Fines (Day Fines) as an Intermediate Sanction," Bureau of Justice Assistance, U.S. Department of Justice, November 1996, 7.

331 *The programs are funded:* See Bannon et al., *Criminal Justice Debt*; Lauren-Brooke Eisen, "Paying for Your Time: How Charging Inmates Fees Behind Bars May Violate the Excessive Fines Clause," *Loyola Journal of Public Interest Law* 15 (Spring 2014): 319–42; Justice Management Institute and Vera Institute of Justice, "How to Use Structured Fines (Day Fines) as an Intermediate Sanction."

331 *seventy million Americans:* Matthew Friedman, "Just Facts: As Many Americans Have Criminal Records as College Diplomas," Brennan Center for Justice, November 17, 2015.

331 *sentences are served:* Devah Pager et al., "Sequencing Disadvantage: Barriers to Employment Facing Young Black and White Men with Criminal Records," 623 *Annals of the American Academy of Politics and Science* 623 (2009): 195, 199 (concluding that the negative impact of criminal records for black ex-offenders is "substantially larger" than for white ex-offenders); Scott H. Decker et al., Criminal Stigma, Race, Gender, and Employment: An Expanded Assessment of the Consequences of Imprisonment for Employment 13 (2014).

332 *seal their criminal records: Disrupting the Cycle: Reimagining the Prosecutor's Role in Reentry*, NYU Center on the Administration of Criminal Law, 2017; Lauren-Brooke Eisen, "Curbing Cash Register Style Justice," American Constitution Society, October 26, 2015.

332 *It's critical for prosecutors:* In 2009, the National Research Council issued a report critical of the state of forensic science. In 2015, President Obama tasked the Presi-

dent's Council of Advisors on Science and Technology (PCAST), made up of leading scientists, engineers, lawyers, and policy makers, to advise him on improvements. Most of the principles and recommendations above come from PCAST's report, *Forensic Science in Criminal Courts: Ensuring Scientific Validity of Feature-Comparison Methods*, September 2016.

333 *Ensure that other types:* Determine whether the type or method of collecting evidence has credibility in the scientific community by consulting well-designed, peer-reviewed studies and organizations such as the National Institute of Standards and Technology.

333 *Countless studies:* As of fall 2018, there have been 163 exonerations of people who were convicted and sentenced to death. On average, those individuals spent over a decade on death row before their exoneration. Death Penalty Information Center, "Innocence: List of Those Freed from Death Row" (2018).

333 *provides no more public safety:* Dozens of studies have found no proof that the death penalty deters crime. See Max Ehrenfreund, "There's Still No Evidence That Executions Deter Criminals," *Washington Post*, April 30, 2014. An analysis of thirty years of empirical studies of the death penalty concluded that there was insufficient evidence of any deterrent effect. *Glossip v. Gross*, 135 S. Ct. 2726, 2768 (2015), citing Daniel Nagin and John Pepper, eds., *Deterrence and the Death Penalty* (Washington, DC: National Academies Press, 2012).

333 *imposed on people with diminished culpability:* See Frank R. Baumgartner and Betsy Neill, "Does the Death Penalty Target People Who Are Mentally Ill? We Checked," *Washington Post*, April 3, 2017. Analyses of the death penalty in Oregon, Florida, Arkansas, and Ohio have all reached the same conclusion—the death penalty targets our most vulnerable.

333 *Studies also show:* Numerous studies have found that African American defendants are more likely to face a possible death sentence than white defendants. Matt Ford, "Racism and the Execution Chamber," *Atlantic*, June 23, 2014. For example, one study of Harris County, Texas, found that black defendants were three times more likely to face the death penalty. Ed Pilkington, "Research Exposes Racial Discrimination in America's Death Penalty Capital," *Guardian*, March 13, 2013. Juries are also much more likely to sentence someone to death when the victim is white than when the victim is black. Frank R. Baumgartner, "Capital Punishment and the Invisible Black Male: Race-of-Victim Effects in US Executions, 1977–2013," University of North Carolina Chapel Hill, August 8, 2014.

333 *It is expensive:* Carol Williams, "Death Penalty Costs California $184 Million a Year, Study Says," *Los Angeles Times*, June 20, 2011.

333 *increasingly concentrated:* Richard Dieter, "The 2% Death Penalty: How a Minority of Counties Produce Most Death Cases at Enormous Costs to All," Death Penalty Information Center, October 2013.

334 *"no longer serves": Capital Punishment in Pennsylvania: The Report of the Task Force and Advisory Committee*, Joint State Government Commission, Pennsylvania General Assembly, June 2018; Brandon L. Garrett, Alexander Jakubow, and Ankur Desai, "The American Death Penalty Decline," *Journal of Criminal Law and Criminology* 107 (Fall 2017): 561–642; Robert J. Smith, "The Geography of

the Death Penalty and Its Ramifications," *Boston University Law Review* 92 (January 2012): 227–90; American Bar Association, "Guidelines for the Appointment and Performance of Defense Counsel in Death Penalty Cases," 2003.

334 *announce the cost of incarceration:* Further resources: Saneta deVuono-Powell, Chris Schweidler, Alicia Walters, and Azadeh Zohrabi, *Who Pays? The True Cost of Incarceration on Families*, Ella Baker Center for Human Rights, Forward Together, and Research Action Design, September 2015; Peter Wagner and Bernadette Rabuy, *Following the Money of Mass Incarceration*, Prison Policy Initiative, January 25, 2017; Chris Mai and Ram Subramanian, *The Price of Prisons: Examining State Spending Trends, 2010–2015*, Vera Institute of Justice, May 2017.

335 *"reentrant":* In 2016, former attorney general Loretta Lynch delivered the closing remarks at National Reentry Week without once referring to "criminals," "convicts," or "felons." Instead, she referred to formerly incarcerated people as "returning citizens," a term that affirms their dignity and potential for successful reintegration. Further resources: Bill Keller, "The Other F-Word: What We Call the Imprisoned Matters," Marshall Project, April 27, 2016; Nancy La Vigne, "People First: Changing the Way We Talk About Those Touched by the Criminal Justice System," *Urban Wire*, April 5, 2016; "Labels Like 'Felon' Are an Unfair Life Sentence," *New York Times*, May 7, 2016.

INDEX

PHOTO: © NINA SUBIN

EMILY BAZELON is a staff writer for *The New York Times Magazine* and the Truman Capote Fellow for Creative Writing and Law at Yale Law School. She is the bestselling author of *Sticks and Stones: Defeating the Culture of Bullying and Rediscovering the Power of Character and Empathy* and a cohost of the weekly *Slate* podcast Political Gabfest. Before joining the *Times Magazine,* Bazelon was a writer and editor for nine years at *Slate,* where she cofounded the women's section, "DoubleX." She is a graduate of Yale College and Yale Law School. She lives in New Haven with her husband and her younger son.

emilybazelon.com
Twitter: @emilybazelon